JULIEN, Claude. America's empire, tr. by R. Bruce. Pantheon, 1971. 442p tab bibl 75-113719. 7.95. ISBN 0-394-41481-0

CHOICE   JAN. '72

History, Geography & Travel

North America

Julien, French journalist and foreign editor of *Le monde*, seeks to cover too much ground, most of which is highly controversial. He endeavors to describe the nature of the "empire" without ever really providing a clearcut definition of either "empire" or "imperialism." He attempts to identify the economic, the military, and the cultural aspects of the empire and throws some barbs at the C.I.A. and the U.S.I.A. for good measure. The book, which betrays a strong anti-American bias, is often weakly supported by documentary sources. While attempting to cover much of the field of American diplomatic history, the author relies on such elementary books as the Beards' *New basic history of the United States* (rev. ed., 1960) and other general texts. American specialists in the field are generally ignored. For an alleged sober piece of research, this book falls far short of objectivity. It is a polemic which bears some resemblance to Ronald Steel's *Pax Americana* (CHOICE, Jan. 1968). It might also be compared with Merlo Pusey's *The U.S.A. astride the globe* (see Political Science). As a presentation of European points of view, many of them well argued, this volume probably belongs in collections dealing with American foreign relations.

AMERICA'S EMPIRE

Claude Julien is the foreign editor of *Le Monde*. Born in France in 1925, he has studied in France and the United States. Before joining *Le Monde*'s foreign news department in 1951, he was editor-in-chief of the Tangiers daily *La Depêche Marocaine*. His books include *Le nouveau Nouveau Monde*, *La Révolution cubaine*, *God's Trombones*, and *Canada: Europe's Last Chance*.

AMERICA'S EMPIRE

Claude Julien

TRANSLATED FROM THE FRENCH

BY RENAUD BRUCE

Pantheon Books

NEW YORK

A Division of Random House

Copyright © 1971 by Random House, Inc.

All rights reserved under International and Pan-American Copyright Conventions. Published in the United States by Pantheon Books, a division of Random House, Inc., New York, and simultaneously in Canada by Random House of Canada Limited, Toronto.

Originally published in France as *L'Empire Americain* by Éditions Bernard Grasset, Paris. Copyright © 1968 by Claude Julien.

ISBN: 0-394-41481-0

Library of Congress Catalog Card Number: 75-113719

Manufactured in the United States of America
by H. Wolff, New York.

FIRST AMERICAN EDITION

Contents

AMERICA'S
EMPIRE

Ambiguities of the Empire

Throughout the world, the American empire possesses, along with its more or less resolute opponents, its more or less reticent partisans. If vigorous propaganda attacks are unleashed against it they rarely describe the mechanics of its interventions and, more rarely yet, analyze its motivations. On their part the avowed defenders of the empire often draw a prudish veil over the works of that impressive machine, unless they prefer to find cautious justifications for it. Those are not lacking. For the power of the United States is certainly not guilty of all the disasters afflicting humanity, and its very presence has prevented even worse calamities from striking the earth.

A day may come when it will be possible to measure and to compare the good works and the misdeeds of this empire which so strongly affects contemporary events. But, such is not in any case the ambition of this book, which proposes, more modestly, to take apart, piece by piece, with concrete examples, the means of action at the disposal of the empire, and to retrace the stages of its prodigious growth. Facts must speak for themselves: here they are gathered in a dossier—which is probably incomplete but which will not have been useless if it opens the way to more probing research and analysis.

A first examination throws light on the extraordinary complexity of the multiple wheels of an empire which exercises its influence over every continent and over all areas of human activity. It does not neglect any country, any race, any area of economic production or intellectual creativity.

Above all, the study of the American empire today brings out the contrast between the simplicity of its objectives and the ambivalence of its actions. For the behavior of the powerful ultimately obeys rather elementary laws; power calls for more power; wealth for more wealth; and to the extent that the national framework is not sufficient to satisfy those needs of increased wealth, there is no other solution but to take control of banana plantations in Central America, rich mineral deposits in South America, oil fields in the Middle East, etc. Thus are born empires with their outposts and lines of communications, their resources and means of defense, their diplomats and soldiers, their missionaries and police force, their physicians and bankers. The empire nourishes and enriches the mainland by putting at its disposal new means of expansion. But the genius of the American empire is to have set no limits to its influence. No map can show its frontiers. It so little resembles classic colonial empires that it sometimes becomes almost imperceptible and seems itself to doubt its own existence.

For it does not escape the ambiguities of human nature and, more precisely, of the men who serve it. Those have no need to be guided by an irresistible thirst for power. Is it not sufficient for them eagerly to seek liberty, justice, progress, and peace? It is in the defense of freedom that they encircle the globe with a network of pacts and military bases, which rest quite often on the most dictatorial regimes. It is in the name of justice and progress that they cultivate the friendship of reactionary governments, in the name of peace that they crush Dresden, Hiroshima, or the villages of Vietnam under the fire of their military arsenal. The dream and the ideal coexist fairly well with the reality which denies them. Naturally, tensions arise at times which shake to the depths the stability of the empire. But until now it has known how to dominate and master them. One day, however, these tensions will become too strong. For the dramas of the empire are not only those of the colonized; no less seriously appear the dramas of the colonizer. When the conflict erupts it not only opposes the colonized to the colonizers but the latter are divided and tear themselves apart, very often dragging down in their fall the values that they pretended to serve.

American idealism is not, however, incompatible with the American empire. On the contrary, it serves it, supplies it with justifications, makes it more acceptable in the eyes of some, intensifies its glow, promotes its expansion—until the day when idealism, gangrened by the unspeakable methods of imperialism, runs the risk of dying under the ruins of the empire.

For the American empire has been nourished by American idealism. The phenomenon is not new: every colonial power has exalted under one form or another its "civilizing mission," which consisted in bringing to other peoples Western culture, the progress of hygiene, the wonders of modern technology, and peace between hostile peoples. Hospitals and schools are always surety for mopping up operations and reprisal raids, the landings of Marines and napalm bombardments.

If, in the last century, the pioneers of the empire spoke a fairly tough and often ridiculous language, more sophisticated and distinguished minds learned very quickly to make more elegant speeches. The baptism of respectability was received by American imperialism from a leading figure whose idealism obscured warlike actions, and whose internationalism is still considered, although wrongly, as the clearest denial of any nationalist ambition. It was in fact President Woodrow Wilson who stated: "I have sometimes heard gentlemen discussing the questions that are now before us with a distinction between nationalism and internationalism in these matters. It is very difficult for me to follow their distinction. The greatest nationalist is the man who wants his nation to be the greatest nation, and the greatest nation is the nation which penetrates to the heart of its duty and mission among the nations of the world. . . . the nation that has that vision is elevated to a place of influence and power which it cannot get by arms, which it cannot get by commercial rivalry, which it can get by no other way than by that of spiritual leadership which comes from a profound understanding of humanity." [1]

Thus the moral law of American imperialism spans fundamental ambiguities. On the one hand, it bases national power which neither arms nor the profits of business could produce on "spiritual leadership"—but Woodrow Wilson, the great figure of American idealism, himself strengthened the American empire in the Caribbean through numerous military interventions and financial operations related in this book. And, as will be seen, his successors referred to the same principles of idealism and internationalism while extending the same methods to the most distant regions of the globe.

On the other hand and above all, the moral law defined by Wilson tore down the barrier which, for many Americans, irrevocably separated nationalism and internationalism. Indeed, his immediate successors believed that they served the national interests of the United States by withdrawing into a haughty isolationism. But that retreat was to be ephemeral, and very quickly *internationalism*—intervention in world affairs—became again the prime rule of a *nationalism* which henceforth manifested itself vigorously in all the trouble spots of the globe.

The distinction that Wilson denied between nationalism and internationalism no longer troubles an empire which today asserts its influence throughout the world. But the ambiguity is more marked than ever. For most Americans, when the United States intervenes in world affairs it is not to defend their interests or their national ambitions but to serve selflessly an international order. And woe to its allies who do not intend to submit to the will of the empire; they are immediately denounced as narrow-minded nationalists exclusively preoccupied with the interests of their own countries. It is thus that an internationalist mystique becomes the alibi of strictly nationalist politics. It is not therefore surprising that an American university professor could write: "For Wilson, . . . American national values were identified with progressive liberal values, and an exceptionalist America had a mission to lead mankind toward the orderly international society of the future." The same author remarks that "for Wilson, . . . the national interest became merged with liberal ideology in such a way that he could act simultaneously as the champion of American nationalism and as the spokesman for internationalism and anti-imperialism." [2] In fact, it is one of the historic roles of American liberalism that compared to conservative and isolationist Republicans such as Harding, Coolidge, and Hoover, liberal Democrats like Wilson, Franklin D. Roosevelt, Truman, Kennedy, and Johnson will be internationalists. American liberalism, which translates on the domestic scene into a certain opposition to trusts and to racism, into encouragement of trade unions and farmers, etc., finds expression in foreign policy in an internationalism which the two Democratic Presidents who drew the United States into the two world wars and their successors exemplified. The identification goes so far that N. Gordon Levin could several times use the formula: "to liberalize or to Americanize international politics." In the American vocabulary the two terms tend to become synonymous. And their kinship will become closer as "liberal" America will be confronted with "totalitarian" Communism.

Thus idealistic America, convinced that it is invested with a "spiritual leadership"—which after Woodrow Wilson would be claimed by Robert Kennedy a few months before his assassination—could organize in the name of its liberalism a new international order, of which it will assume the direction while pretending that such an order could be independent from American nationalistic aims. Its liberalism incites America to expand its empire over the world. It is not the fallacious moral justification of imperialism, but one of its principal sources.

Does an examination of the facts sustain this analysis? In order to limit as much as possible the field of controversy, the documents quoted in this book are all from American government sources. If need be they are clarified by the work of American historians and of various authors who are considered authorities in their own country, and, more rarely, by texts from Western authors considered free of partiality.

Many aspects of the American empire may have been forgotten or left in the shade. Others remain protected by the secrets of archives which are, for the time being, inaccessible. But the elements assembled and organized in this book will seek to give a general view of a problem which undoubtedly calls for more thorough study.

July 1968   Claude Julien

I

An Empire without Frontiers

The American empire is not only the most powerful that history has known, it is in many ways unique.

Never have such a small number of men succeeded in extending their influence so far, in putting their stamp on the daily life of such a great number of people. With 200 million inhabitants, the United States in fact represents only an infinitesimal portion—hardly 6 per cent—of the world's population. But it alone produces more than all the Communist countries put together and accounts for 43 per cent of the production of the non-Communist world. No point of the globe is outside the reach of its weapons and it possesses the potentiality of annihilating all life on the planet several times over. Americans produce 14 per cent of the wheat, 45 per cent of the corn, 20 per cent of the meat sold on world markets.* They have recently decided to reduce their agricultural production and liquidate their cereal stockpiles, but if they wanted to they could alone feed almost all humanity. At the same time, without using their most fearsome military power, they have demonstrated, in

* Statistics in this chapter are taken from the *Statistical Abstract of The United States* (Washington, D.C.: U.S. Bureau of the Census, 1967).

Vietnam as in Korea and during two world wars, the effectiveness of their formidable destructive apparatus. They can decide the life or death of the human species and, more than any other people, they contribute to its scientific and technological progress.

But this unprecedented empire, which holds within its hands the destiny of humanity, is extraordinarily voracious. A fabulous producer, it is also an avid consumer. The United States alone consumes almost as much as the rest of the world, although it is 17 times less populous. An American uses 3 times more electric power than a European, 8 times more than a Japanese, 160 times more than any inhabitant of any other Asian country. In the whole world, with 3½ billion human beings, the production of electricity totaled 3,339.7 million kilowatt hours but the United States —with only 200 million inhabitants—produced more than a third of it, or 1,157.3 million, and still must import some from Canada. Figured in millions of tons of coal, the volume of power consumed each year in the world represents 5,767 million of which a third—1,973.5 million tons—is used by the United States. Per capita, no people in the world consume more meat, more paper, more timber, more oil, more steel, more uranium than the people of the United States. That crushing superiority inspires fear or envy, admiration or jealousy. Those are superficial reactions, which derive only from a cursory examination of the prosperity and power of the United States: they can generate emotional attitudes—not inspire a realistic political choice. "If the British Empire, as Macaulay once said, was acquired in a fit of absent-mindedness, the American Empire came into being without the intention or the knowledge of the American people," [1] wrote Ronald Steel. But empires are not founded either through absent-mindedness or by accident. Neither are they, necessarily, the fruit of a consistent will, pursuing from one generation to the other the realization of a vast design or of a great ambition. Throughout the history of the United States, there has certainly not been a dearth of men who have loudly proclaimed their desire for power, their conviction that the United States has been invested with a mission which would not be limited by any geographic barriers. But the dynamism and the authority of those strong personalities would not have been sufficient to build an empire. One of the most deeply rooted American traditions is probably that of withdrawal, of isolationism, and yet America has built an empire on a world scale. It was not necessary for America to want it, to deliberately tend toward it. It was sufficient for America to be faithful to itself.

Indeed Max Lerner has written: "The thrust of expansionism has been a continuous impulse in American history. Land hunger, power hunger, newness hunger, and bigness hunger, have proved wants that feed themselves." And he adds: "It would be rash to think that an energy forceful enough to push the frontiers to their continental limits would stop at the ocean's edge." [2]

For that force not only existed in the will of a few thinkers, statesmen, businessmen, and military leaders carrying within them a grandiose vision of the destiny of their people. It sank its roots into the most basic needs of daily life. The need for land to settle millions of immigrants—and to achieve that, it would be necessary to break the resistance of the Indians, to buy Louisiana from France, Alaska from Russia, and through conquest to amputate a good part of Mexico's territory. The need to sell and to buy —which gave birth to a Merchant Marine—to barter furs for the spices and silk of the Orient, to import bananas from Central America and coffee from Brazil, to transport oil from the Middle East which was cheaper than that from Texas. The need to intervene in two world wars, which neither Woodrow Wilson nor Franklin Roosevelt wanted.

The need to build an unequaled military force to oppose any expansion of Communism. The need to export capital, less to ensure commercial outlets than to have access to raw materials almost everywhere on the surface of the globe: copper from Chile, oil from Saudi Arabia, jute from India, rubber from Indonesia, etc.

This is how, in answer to America's needs, was born the empire which resembles no other, the empire without frontiers. Old geography maps assigned one color to the regions of the four continents belonging to the French empire, another color to the countries incorporated in the British empire. That little game is hardly possible on the American globe, and the Stars and Stripes flying over Puerto Rico, the Virgin Islands, Guam, Samoa, the Panama Canal Zone do not represent the vastness of the American empire. In order to give a graphic representation of it, it would be necessary to add up the immense regions it holds under a tight dependency by the combined interplay of its oil and mining concessions, the deployment of its ground, naval, and air forces, its private investments as well as its governmental credits, its financial or political influence, the strength deriving from its position of big buyer, sincere or self-seeking friendships, the fear of numerous countries of being exposed to eventual reprisals from such a powerful partner. And Max Lerner does not hesitate to say: "Hostile critics called this American imperialism; certainly it was, in the sense of an American imperium—a vast structure of military, economic, and administrative power that could be used to override competing structures and achieve its power purposes." [3]

For Americans who reflect on the place of their country in the world do not think of denying the reality of United States "imperialism." What they dispute is that national egoism brought them to such a road. "This is not imperial ambition, but it has led us to use imperial methods: establishment of military garrisons around the globe, granting of subsidies to client governments and politicians, application of economic sanctions and even military force against recalcitrant states, and employment of a veritable army of colonial administrators working through such organizations as the State Department, the Agency for International Development, the United States Information Agency, and the Central Intelligence Agency," [4] writes Ronald Steel.

Whether or not there has been a deliberate imperialist goal, the empire has not ceased to expand and get stronger, extending its ramifications further, consolidating its hold. No American author disputes that fact. Their arguments deal solely with the motivations of the builders of that empire. And, with slight variations, they agree on insisting that generosity inspired expansionism. "The pattern of Big Empire as practiced by Americans has actually been an empire unknown in the history of imperialism. For where imperial powers in the past have aimed at exploiting the colonial and economically backward areas for their own economic advantage, taking out whatever resources they could and exploiting native labor, American imperialism is the first on record to pour its resources into undeveloped areas and weak economies, exporting capital, technicians, and technical skills to them," [5] wrote Max Lerner, for example. Ronald Steel also believes that the United States attitude is "heavily tinged with altruism." [6]

But what conquest has not invoked noble and generous motives in order to justify itself? Senator Fulbright rightly remarks that "the policy of power is practiced under different names." And he adds: "The British called it the 'white man's burden.' The French called it their 'civilizing mission.' Nineteenth-century Americans called it 'manifest destiny.' It is now being called the 'responsibilities of power.' What all these terms have in common is the assumption of involuntariness . . . . something outside of rational choice." [7]

And so, allegedly, America did not want to build an empire. It was obliged to do so by its fidelity to an ideal of liberty and happiness which it was privileged to incarnate. The American empire was thus the unavoidable consequence of a "deep-rooted instinct in our national character —an instinct to help those less fortunate and permit them to emulate and perhaps one day achieve the virtues of our own society," [8] again writes Ronald Steel.

Since Rome, all empires have nourished the ambition of bringing civilization to the barbarians. It is at least with that excuse that, in modern times, they have tried to obtain indispensable popular support. When he asks himself what the real American intentions are, Max Lerner arrives at a less emotional answer: "The motive is not altruistic. Partly there is a fear of the growth of Communist world power if such countermeasures are not taken. Partly also there is a fear, on the part of strong business and even labor groups, that the American economic machine will slow down if defense production is not kept going at full blast and if there is no way to dispose of surplus products and investment through programs of international aid. But while the motive is self-interested, the consequences are unlike those of the colonial or ideological empires of the past." [9]

Behold, here is an empire which has succeeded in reconciling the "selfish" interests of a great power and the generosity of a benefactor. The adventure of the American empire-builders, again writes Ronald Steel, rests "upon the belief that it was America's role to make the world a happier, more orderly place, one more nearly reflecting our own image." [10] Like God creating man in his image, America dreams of remodeling the face of humanity. In the last century, Herman Melville wrote: "We Americans are the peculiar, chosen people—the Israel of our time; we bear the ark of liberties of the world." [11] This is an old dream. In 1765 John Adams was already writing: "I always consider the settlement of America with reverence and wonder, as the opening of a grand scheme and design in Providence for the illumination and emancipation of the slavish part of mankind all over the earth." [12]

A seductive dream but lacking in originality. The builders of the British and French empires also found their bards lyrically to celebrate an exalted messianic role. The American empire would be devoid of any individual trait if that were all. Its only distinctive characteristic would come from the particular type of "slavery" that it was called upon to combat: "the Communist slavery."

The originality of the American empire is found elsewhere. A few days after the first bombing of North Vietnam, in February 1965, Mr. George Ball, Under Secretary of State, stated that the United States was engaged in "something new and unique in world history—a role of world responsibility divorced from territorial or narrow national interests." [13] Those interests are not "narrow[ly] national" to the extent that America identifies its interests with those of the "free world" and with those of peoples only waiting for their liberation. And America does not pursue "territorial interests," as it ended its geographic expansion in the last century. It no longer feels the need of pushing back its national frontiers. When it was tempted to do so, in 1898, through the conquest of the Philippines, it soon discovered the handicaps of a classic-style empire. While England and France were specifically pursuing the building of a territorial empire, America was discovering that military conquest was not the surest means of establishing a sphere of influence. The classic empires have collapsed, while on the contrary the American empire has not stopped expanding. And it has grown through necessity, in answer to its internal needs, of which the most pressing is the procurement of raw materials.

For the days have ended when the United States could find in its own subsoil the resources to feed its industries.

Thoughtless exploitation and enormous waste have appreciably reduced its known reserves. But, above all, constantly increasing consumption has compelled the United States to seek beyond its borders raw materials which it does not possess at home in sufficient quantities or of which it is even practically deprived. Furthermore, foreseeing the time when it might be cut off from distant sources of supplies, it quite often gives priority to the exploitation of foreign deposits in order to spare its national reserves. In any case, and in often unsuspected proportions, American industrial production and American consumption depend on the procurement of minerals which it is obliged to seek in South America, in Africa, or in Asia. And, naturally, it must also import the tropical produce of which it is a great consumer. The fact remains that the United States cannot maintain its high standard of living if it loses its freedom of access to the raw materials of the Third World. At this point, a few documented examples are indispensable to show how Americans consume an impressive proportion of the raw materials available in the whole world.

The great United States steel centers, like Pittsburgh, Cleveland, Gary, and Detroit, were born because the Great Lakes offered a cheap means of transportation between the ore deposits of Minnesota and the coal of Pennsylvania. For a long time, its iron and coal mines created the industrial wealth of the United States. But anthracite production in Pennsylvania fell from 44 million tons in 1950 to 14.8 million tons in 1965. Similarly, the production of American iron mines declined from 103 million tons in 1955 to 90 million in 1966. In order to compensate for that decrease while satisfying an increased demand, the quantity of imported iron ore doubled—rising from 23.4 to 46.2 million tons during the same period. In terms of consumption, the proportion of imported iron ore, therefore, went from 18 per cent to 34 per cent in some ten years. The American steel industry could not function if the empire were deprived of the possibility of buying cheap ore from foreign mines, notably from Labrador, other parts of Canada, and Venezuela.

Another example is still more striking. The most powerful aluminum industry in the world is located in the United States. Here is, in thousands of tons, the aluminum production of the United States and of the whole world:

	1950	1955	1960	1964	1965
U.S. Production	962	1,902	2,344	3,105	3,395
World Production	1,640	3,460	4,950	6,720	7,415

Thus, in 1965, the United States accounted for 45 per cent of the world's aluminum production. Practically all was consumed domestically, and only 313,000 tons were exported, or barely 9 per cent. But the United States is very poor in bauxite. Here are, in thousands of tons, the quantities of bauxite extracted in the United States and imported for domestic consumption:

	1950	1955	1960	1964	1965	1966
Extracted in the U.S.	1,335	1,788	1,998	1,601	1,654	1,796
Imported	2,516	4,882	8,739	10,180	11,199	11,529

The world production of bauxite is actually 36 million tons. These figures mean that the United States, with 6 per cent of the world population, consumes more than 33 per cent of the bauxite produced in the entire world. This is possible thanks to a massive program of imports: while in 1950 the United States imported only twice the quantity of bauxite extracted in the country, in 1966 its imports were seven times greater than its domestic production. In fact, the United States depends on 88 per cent imported bauxite for its aluminum consumption.

Since the bauxite deposits in the United States are estimated at only 33 million tons, it is understandable that the

empire closely watches the political evolution of the min-
eral-rich countries where they get their supplies: British
Guiana (reserves: 65 million tons), where the CIA engi-
neered the fall of Cheddy Jagan's progressive government;
also Jamaica (reserves: 320 million tons); Surinam (50 million); Brazil (200 million); Guinea, where Sekou Touré's
politics did not fail to cause the masters of the empire some
anxiety; Ghana and Indonesia, where they welcomed with
satisfaction the fall of Kwame Nkrumah and Sukarno; Yugoslavia with its reserves of 105 million tons of bauxite;
Greece; Malaysia; etc.

During the Second World War, because of the difficulties of transportation by sea, the United States accelerated
the exploitation of its rather poor-grade Arkansas deposits.
But in peacetime, it is more advantageous for the United
States to buy bauxite abroad. "The Americans," wrote Jean
Gottman, "prefer to keep the somewhat limited reserves of
Arkansas for possible emergency situations. In normal
times, imported bauxite comes cheaper to United States
mills, which transform it into aluminum oxide." [14] Let dras-
tic political upheavals take place in bauxite-producing
countries, and the American aluminum industry, the most
powerful in the world, would be cut off from its sources of
supply. And, most important, the known deposits are in
countries of the Third World, which have unstable regimes
and may be susceptible to popular uprisings, which could
make them pass into the Communist camp.

That is exactly what happened when Fidel Castro's revolution deprived the United States not so much of Cuban
sugar but of nickel. The whole world suffers from a general
scarcity of nickel, of which the United States is also the
largest consumer (figures below are in tons).

	1955	1960	1966
U.S. Production	4,411	14,079	15,036
U.S. Consumption	110,100	108,159	187,640
World Production	263,000	353,000	475,000

Thus the United States consumes 40 per cent of the nickel produced in the entire world, while it produces only 3 per cent. For a long time, the United States bought its nickel from Canada, a country in which it controls 60 per cent of the industrial investments and foreign trade. The principal world producer, Canada, supplied, for example, 145,000 tons of nickel out of the 185,000 tons the world produced in 1954. But if Canadian reserves are estimated at more than 4 million tons, Cuba's exceed 24 million and are, by far, the most important in the world. Before the Castro revolution, the American government—and not a private corporation—had built a refinery for the treatment of that mineral. But not foreseeing that a revolution might break out in Cuba, it operated it at a low level (13,200 tons in 1954) and Cuban nickel was kept as a "strategic reserve." After the break between Havana and Washington, the U.S.S.R. undertook the operation of those installations. In this way, the American empire lost access to the richest nickel deposits in the world, while the steel industry uses constantly increasing quantities of it. In 1965 Fidel Castro's government obtained the revision of the nickel agreement with the U.S.S.R. in order to be able to sell a large part of the island's production to France; this permitted Havana to finance the purchase of new industrial equipment in France. Washington immediately reacted by threatening French exports to the U.S. (see Chap. VI), a move which seems rather far from the efforts of a "benevolent" empire concerned only with bringing freedom to enslaved peoples and happiness to backward countries. Ideology, in the form of militant anti-Communism, is certainly not absent from the struggle which takes very concrete shape when there is a question of guarantee of access to a raw material of which the American empire is the largest consumer.

What is true for iron ore, bauxite, and nickel is also true for most of the raw materials indispensable to American industry. In fact, the United States is really self-sufficient in only two metals—molybdenum and magnesium, which it produces in quantities large enough to allow for substantial exports. In 1966, for example, with molybdenum production in the non-Communist world reaching 126.2 million pounds, the United States produced 90.5 million of it and was able to export 29.7 million tons. That same year, with 79,794 tons, it accounted for more than half of the world production of magnesium and could export 15,448 tons. Molybdenum and magnesium are both strategic materials which play a very important role in the arms industries. Their production in the United States increased considerably during the Second World War, then dipped after 1945, to rise again during the Korean and Vietnam wars. But they represent the only notable exception to a rule valid for all important minerals: with the exception of molybdenum and magnesium, American industry must effect massive imports from countries of the Third World. The prosperity of the richest country in the world is dependent on its ability to get to raw materials contained in the subsoil of countries that are among the poorest on the earth.

Manganese, for example, is indispensable to the metallurgical industry, and of course, American steel mills are large consumers of it. In 1966, the United States produced only 35,000 tons of manganese ore, with the result that it imported almost all its supply, or 2,365,000 tons. The principal manganese producers are India, Brazil, Morocco, Cuba, the Congo (Kinshasa), Egypt, Mexico, etc.

It is the same with the only used chrome ore—chromium. The United States is entirely dependent on imports: 1,864,000 tons in 1966, or 36 per cent of the world production. And, outside the U.S.S.R. which is amply supplied with it, the important chromium producers are Turkey (a NATO member), South Africa, Rhodesia, and the Philippines.

Tungsten also plays a key role in the manufacture of special steels. The United States saw its tungsten production fall from 15,883,000 to 6,669,000 pounds from 1955 to 1960. In 1966 the United States, which consumes almost one-fourth of the world production, imported about 25 per cent of the 17,710,000 pounds of tungsten used by its industry. In spite of the fact that it finds an important part of the tungsten it needs at home, it must import some from South Korea, Portugal, Bolivia, Burma, etc.

The United States is among the major producers of copper, but while it was, before 1930, its largest exporter, it is now its largest importer. In 1966, its refineries produced 1,711,000 tons of copper, of which 368,000—or 21 per cent of the total—was produced from imported ore. The Americans consume, therefore, more than one-fourth (6,020,000 tons) of the world's copper. To those figures ought to be added reclaimed copper, which plays an increasing role. But the United States closely watches the big producers like Chile, where the Christian Democratic government of Eduardo Frei and now the Socialist government of Salvador Allende have been attempting—not without difficulties—to give priority in the exploitation of Chilean copper to the benefit of the Chilean economy rather than to the American companies Anaconda and Kennecott, which exert a dominant influence on the world copper market.

In 1965 the United States imported 44 per cent of the zinc it consumed, or 443,000 tons out of 994,000 tons. It imports 28 per cent of the lead it uses, or 125,349 tons out of 443,995 tons. The United States absorbs 41 per cent of the world production of tin, or 85,000 tons out of 208,000, but it produces only 29,271 tons itself, that is to say, it imports 60 per cent of its consumption. And the three great tin producers in the world are Malaysia, Indonesia (where American investments have multiplied since the fall of Sukarno and the massacre of several hundred thousand Communists), and finally Bolivia (where the CIA and the special forces Green Berets lent armed help to the Bolivian authorities to crush the underground led by Ernesto "Che" Guevara in 1967).

In 1965 the United States accounted for 26 per cent of world oil production, but nevertheless it imported sizable quantities. On the one hand, the cost of American oil is higher than the cost of Middle Eastern oil; on the other hand, official policy endeavors to spare domestic deposits in order to preserve strategic reserves. Be that as it may, in 1966 the United States produced 3,039 million barrels of crude oil and imported 496 million (or 14 per cent of the total) plus 449 million barrels of refined oil.

Americans consume a quarter of the world production of asbestos (3,570,000 tons). But in order to do so, although producing 118,000 tons in 1965, they had to import four times more, or 684,000 tons. And their imports increased, reaching 720,000 tons in 1966.

Therefore, in most areas, a dual disproportion is obvious: the United States consumes much larger quantities of raw materials than anyone in the world, and much more than it produces itself. It consumes 28 per cent of the world production of potash, and imports 1,108,000 tons of it. It consumes 27 per cent of the world production of gypsum, but it produces only 9,635,000 tons and imports 5,479,000.

Obviously, the disproportion is still greater with tropical products. Although 87 per cent of the rubber used in the United States is of synthetic origin, America nevertheless imported 436,000 tons of natural rubber in 1966, or 17 per cent of world production. And naturally, the United States imports 100 per cent of its consumption of bananas, cocoa, raw silk, coffee, etc. By itself it consumes half the world's coffee production, or, taking 1964 as an example, 1,527,000 tons out of 3,400,000. The United States produces annually some 6 million tons of sugar and imports more than

4 million, for a total consumption of 15 per cent of world production.

Therefore, the internal prosperity of the United States depends in very large part on its freedom of access to the natural resources of the entire world, and more especially of the poor countries. In its very complex reality, the American economic empire is organized to protect and extend that freedom of access to the minerals and to the agricultural products of the Third World—an essential condition for the maintenance of its domestic prosperity. Treasures of ingenuity, of energy, of courage have been spent in order to ensure to the United States, through the branches of its empire, that position of privileged consumer. And, every day, considerable efforts are expended in maintaining and reinforcing the positions already acquired.

"The business spirit has informed American foreign policy as it has informed every other aspect of American power —the political machines, the legal system, the course of constitutional interpretation, the churches, the press, even the labor movement," in the words of Max Lerner.[15] Motivated by the same spirit, the principal forces of the nation have thus converged and given top priority to this objective: to ensure the economic power of the empire. Disregarding any "dogmatism" or strict legalism, some laws have received varied interpretations in the interests of the empire. During the same period that the antitrust legislation was "suspended" to permit American corporations to participate in the exploitation of Iranian oil, it was used to compel the United Fruit Company to relax its grip on the countries of Central America. But in both cases the objective was the same: to more solidly establish the foundations of the empire. According to the circumstances, sacrosant laws of economic liberalism were in turn invoked and violated to support the expansion of the empire. In the same spirit, American authorities have wisely given priority at one time or another to either public or private investments to guarantee access to strategic regions of the world under the most favorable conditions. The political, diplomatic, and military apparatus of the United States, the large American corporations as well as trade unions and, if need be, religious organizations all lend support to the same cause. "The amassing of American imperial power has scarcely followed the classic pattern. It has operated by the techniques of trade, investment, and profitable sales in foreign markets; it has not been adverse toward using 'dollar diplomacy' to remove the obstructions in the path of business profits, to start convenient revolutions or quell inconvenient ones, and it has more recently operated by economic and technical aid to underdeveloped areas." [16]

These methods and many others have served to increase the power of the empire. This book proposes to analyze them by showing how American pragmatism has made effective and flexible use of the different weapons at its disposal.

Thanks to the power of this empire without frontiers, the per-capita steel consumption is twice as high in the United States as in a country like France, which nonetheless belongs to the "club" of privileged nations. In effect, it reaches 1,446 pounds in the United States, 730 in France, 86 in Brazil, and only 35 in India. Similar proportions are found also in the consumption of chrome, nickel, manganese, copper, textiles, paper, coffee, meat, etc. It is not by accident that Paragraph 4 of the Atlantic Charter, signed by Roosevelt and Churchill on August 14, 1941, declares that the Allied powers ". . . shall endeavor, with due respect for their existing obligations, to further the employment of all States, great or small, victor or vanquished, of access, on equal terms, to the trade and to the raw materials of the world which are needed for their economic prosperity." [17]

No country can live in autarchy, but the United States,

being the world's largest consumer, needs, more than any other, to have access to the raw materials "needed for their economic prosperity." And, naturally, it does not guarantee to all countries that freedom of access "on equal terms." For armed conflict has been succeeded by another conflict. In the great world confrontation, the United States refuses to export strategic materials destined for Communist countries with whom it competes for the raw-material deposits of the Third World. If vast portions of South America, of Africa, or of Southeast Asia were to pass under Communist control, the United States would be deprived of minerals and agricultural products which it cannot afford to lose without risking the collapse of its standard of living. So large a stake justifies on its part a military effort superior to that of the U.S.S.R. and of Western Europe combined. In 1966 for example it devoted to its national defense $54,200 million; the six countries of the Common Market, $12,077 million; and the U.S.S.R., around $35 billion, according to American estimates. Such a considerable effort is possible since its gross national product is more than twice as great as that of the Six: $681,200 million in the United States, against $298,700 million for the Common Market—or $3,501 per capita in the United States and $1,645 in the Six.

The United States is not satisfied merely to compete with Communist countries for the natural resources of which the advanced countries are major consumers. It also endeavors to get them at the best price. In 1955 the production cost of a barrel of oil was $2.77 in the United States and $2.47 in Venezuela, and still cheaper in the Middle East; through devices of the "cartel," American corporations have knowingly maintained world prices at levels that suit them. In 1965 the United States bought Venezuelan iron ore at $7.97 a ton, whereas the ore extracted in the United States cost $9.53. By launching synthetic fibers—of which it is a major producer—on the world market, it has contributed more than any other country to the decline of the price of wool, which it imported in 1965 at 99 cents per pound instead of $1.28, as fifteen years earlier. Similarly, in 1965, it bought wood at $63.15, instead of the $79.27 in 1950, rubber at 17 cents per pound instead of 24 cents. For fifteen years it has maintained the price of manganese at about the same level (from 2.3 to 2.8 cents per pound), while the price of coffee fell from 45 to 39 cents per pound, of cocoa from 23 to 15 cents per pound and of Ceylon tea from 48 to 46 cents. Only the prices of the rarest minerals increased, whereas industrial and agricultural equipment so greatly needed by the exporters of raw materials underwent a general rise. If the balance of payments of the United States shows a deficit which is due primarily to the export of capital and enormous military expenses, its balance of trade is mostly favorable. In 1966, for example, American exports of merchandise came to $29,899 million, and imports to $25,550 million, showing an excess of $4,349 million.

As a result the gulf continues to widen between the poor countries and the rich countries, headed by the United States. As far back as 1957, in a report requested by President Eisenhower, Nelson Rockefeller noted that economic progress in underdeveloped areas hardly kept pace with the population growth. A decade later, the problem was still expressed in the same terms. However, President Kennedy had well understood that poor countries would not be able to provide for their economic development as long as they were not guaranteed sufficient resources, and he had envisaged a plan for the stabilization of raw-materials prices supplied by the Third World to rich nations. But that declaration of intent was hardly implemented (see Chap. VI). Speculation on the prices of raw materials continues to deprive the backward continents of the resources they need to industrialize. Rather than exhaust that source of profits, the empire prefers to operate through loans and direct investments, which bring the beneficiary countries under tighter subjugation. This highly profitable system offers the empire the double advantage of not attacking the roots of the problem and of maintaining its reputation for generosity. In this regard Ronald Steel remarked: ". . . many will ask, have we not been generous with our clients and allies, sending them vast amounts of money, and even sacrificing the lives of our own soldiers on their behalf? Of course we have. But this is the role of an imperial power. If it is to enjoy influence and command obedience, it must be prepared to distribute some of its riches throughout its empire and, when necessary, to fight rival powers for the loyalty of vulnerable client states. Empires . . . can be held together only by cash, power, and even blood. We learned this in Korea, in Berlin, and in Cuba; and we are learning it again in Vietnam." [18]

Sure of its power, strong in its prosperity, proud of its historic role, the American empire thirsts for moral justification. When it widens its economic and political sphere of influence, it is never to conquer new markets, to secure profitable outlets, or to guarantee the security of its supplies. In any area where it ventures, America, to repeat Melville's statement, "bears the ark of world liberties." As American forces were destroying Vietnam's towns and villages which the soldiers of the National Liberation Front had infiltrated, President Johnson was stating: "What America has done, and what America is doing now around the world draws from deep and flowing springs of moral duty, and let us not underestimate the depth of flow of those wellsprings of American purpose." [19] The war is not intended to protect material advantages. It aims at a much more lofty ideal. John F. Kennedy said that Americans are: "by destiny rather than choice—watchmen on the walls of world freedom." [20] Henry Luce—publisher of *Time* and

Life—saw in America at one and the same time "the dynamic leader of the business world" and "the Good Samaritan who knows there is more joy in giving than in receiving."

The Good Samaritan has spent, in some twenty years, more than 120 billion dollars in foreign aid, and at the same time his dynamism has permitted him to increase his national wealth while developing an unequaled military potential. But he does not dream only of bringing to the world material happiness; he also wants, above all, to offer it that most precious good: liberty. He did not choose his mission of liberator. It was imposed upon him. Refuge of those who have been fleeing every kind of despotism, America cannot hide the torch of liberty under a bushel. Abraham Lincoln said that America "cannot endure permanently half slave and half free." [21] Since the Second World War, the Presidents of the United States consider the world incapable of surviving half slave and half free.

Nevertheless, the Communist menace has tempered America's messianic zeal. With more or less success, Washington has encouraged everywhere a decolonization policy, without, however, giving in to the pressure of extremist elements which advocated a systematic policy of "liberation" of peoples subjected to Communist regimes. Powerless to intervene in favor of the Budapest insurgents in 1956, it had decided to help peoples whose freedom was threatened. "It must be the policy of the United States to support free peoples who are resisting attempted subjugation by armed minorities or by outside pressure," [22] President Truman declared when he announced the granting of aid to Turkey and Greece in 1947. But, twenty years later, the Greece of the colonels seems to show that in United States eyes Communism remains the only real enemy of freedom. It was to resist Communism that the United States first supported Diem's dictatorship in Saigon, and even ventured, through dubious elections, to organize a parody of democracy with generals Thieu and Ky. In spite of its devotion to freedom, it was nothing but complacent in regard to the Batista dictatorship, but cannot find terms harsh enough to condemn Fidel Castro's regime which, under the guise of a vague Marxism, achieves in Cuba what the United States has vainly preached to the other countries of South America: agrarian reform, a great increase in education, development of health services, etc.

In order to contain Communism within its borders, the United States consorts, throughout the world, with regimes which are in themselves the negation of freedom. Anti-Communism perverts the American messianic ideal and persuades the United States sometimes to lean on dictatorial regimes in its great crusade for freedom. Nevertheless, the United States does not doubt that it is devoted to the defense of democratic freedoms.

Senator Beveridge expressed the same conviction more crudely when he asserted, at the end of the last century, that "of all our race, He has marked the American people as His chosen nation to finally lead in the regeneration of the world." [23] As a "chosen" people, Americans are daily confronted with the difficulty of giving to the entire planet the freedom that they know at home. If the freedom they enjoy cannot more widely spread over the surface of the globe, it is because Americans really represent a "species apart." And so in order to fight more effectively the only serious menace, they are condemned to consort with the enemies of freedom, to ally themselves with the least dangerous—as long as they are not Communists. And to the extent that the U.S.S.R. of peaceful coexistence is less frightening than the China of Mao, that rule itself is capable of many accommodations. When the confrontation of the great powers is involved, absolute principles show themselves to have an unsuspected flexibility. It is not true that liberty is indivisible: such is the harsh lesson learned by the leader of the free world. President Truman did not suspect that somber reality when, in 1952, he congratulated himself that America had finally accepted the role for which Almighty God had destined her.

For God himself plays a prime role in this great struggle for freedom. Cardinal Spellman chose Christmas Day 1966 to identify the Vietnam War with a crusade for the defense of Christian civilization. His intemperate remarks provoked a strong backlash. But President Johnson did not express a different conviction when, saluting soldiers leaving for Saigon, in February 1968 he affirmed that the hopes of countless nations accompanied them and invoked the blessing of the Almighty. Divine protection appears all the more necessary, since the enemy adheres to an atheistic philosophy. Although Americans have abandoned their continental isolation, religion is still necessary for the fulfillment of their world mission. That is the reason President Johnson was so irritated by the Vatican's attempts to intervene for a negotiated settlement in the Vietnamese tragedy. That is also why the CIA found it natural to grant subsidies to certain religious orders, clearly stating there were no political conditions attached to the money: in order to be useful to the empire, all that the beneficiaries had to do was to be faithful to their own mission.

When, in the worst moments of the "witch hunts," Cardinal Spellman publicly gave his support to Senator Joseph McCarthy, he specified that good Americanism is the best answer to Communism and its best foundation is religion. All the American Presidents have remained attached to that conviction. On June 14, 1954, Eisenhower signed the new text of the pledge of allegiance in which Congress had just added an explicit reference to God, and he added that in such manner did America reaffirm its basic religious heritage.

Thus, an old tradition is continued down to the most immediate conflicts. Benjamin Franklin solicited divine help for the success of the American Revolution. Abraham Lincoln saw in the Civil War "a punishment inflicted upon us for our presumptuous sins." McKinley looked to the conquest of the Philippines to "uplift and civilize and Christianize them." [24] According to the prediction made by Woodrow Wilson in 1919, "the vengeful Providence of God" triggered the Second World War because the United States had not ratified the League of Nations agreement. Franklin Roosevelt stated that a democracy cannot live without a viable religion. Harry Truman saw in the Bible the fundamental basis of the American Constitution. Eisenhower declared that only a people strong in the love of God can be free and make others free. His defeated opponent, Adlai Stevenson, was no less convinced of America's divine mission: "God has entrusted us with a terrifying mission," he said, "nothing less than the leadership of the free world." On November 22, 1963, the eve of his assassination, John F. Kennedy corrected the speech he was to make in Dallas the following day, in which, quoting the Psalms, he declared: "Except the Lord keep the city, the watchman waketh but in vain." Champion of liberty and democracy in the world, the empire does not count solely on its economic and military power. Like many other nations before, it must put God on its side. And it was quite natural that, announcing on March 17, 1968, that he was entering the race for the Presidency, Senator Robert Kennedy spoke of "our right to the spiritual direction of the planet."

Tocqueville observed that "some profess the doctrines of Christianity from a sincere belief in them, and others do the same because they fear to be suspected of unbelief." [25]

And recalling that the law of the majority is supreme, he added: "In the United States the sovereign authority is religious, and consequently hypocrisy must be common." [26] There was, therefore, great indignation when Arthur Sylvester, assistant to Robert McNamara at the Pentagon, asserted that the government has "the right, if necessary, to lie to save itself." [27] Such statements undermine the morale of the empire which needs, in order to fulfill its world mission, to keep its good conscience intact, its faith in the purity and generosity of its intentions. The Puritan tradition considers wealth and material power a sign of divine blessing. The empire is strong, because it is generous and disinterested. The moral foundations of the enterprise would be undermined, the empire would lose its self-confidence were it suddenly to discover that all its energy, all its talents, all its power are tending, not toward an ideal of liberty and progress but toward the more tangible objectives of preserving America's access to the raw materials it needs, and protecting the vast regions of every continent where it needs to export its capital. Some theoreticians want to see this second objective as the only vital one for the American economy. But, obviously, it is not a one-way process, and the export of capital quite often brings access to raw materials. After Sukarno's fall and the massacre of Communists, American dollars flowed into Indonesia where the soil is rich in lead, in oil, in coal, in bauxite, in manganese, in copper, in nickel, besides rubber, gold, and silver. On the other hand, the Cuban revolution has deprived the American economy not only of the billion dollars invested in the island, but also of the possibility of access to the sugar cane plantations and to the richest nickel deposits in the world.

But, if there is no proof that the "Domino Theory," which is invoked as justification for American intervention in Vietnam, corresponds to a military reality, it undoubtedly represents an economic reality. Washington maintains that the military loss of a country like Vietnam would bring about the fall of its neighbors. No facts substantiate this postulate. However, the "Domino Theory" is of enormous efficaciousness on the economic level. Let the United States lack firmness in its relations with Cuba, and private capital will hesitate to go to the other countries of the hemisphere, all more or less exposed to revolutionary contagion. On the other hand, the frank hostility of Washington toward Havana reassures private enterprise and protects the flow of capital to South America, repatriating at the same time substantial profits. In the same way, the military engagement of the United States in Vietnam prompted the Bank of America and the Chase Manhattan Bank to open branches in Saigon in 1965, and the First National City Bank and American Express soon thought of following them. And Henry M. Sperry, a Vice-President of the First National City Bank, stated "We believe we're going to win this war. . . . Afterwards, you'll have a major job of reconstruction on your hands. That will take financing, and financing means banks." [28]

The American government, with a military budget greater now than during the Second World War (more than $75 billion), has shown that it does not quibble over the means. Therefore the flow of dollars (direct private investments) going abroad keeps growing:

	1960	1963	1965
		(in millions of dollars)	
Canada	11,198	13,044	15,172
Latin America	8,387	8,662	9,371
Europe	6,681	10,340	13,894
Africa	925	1,426	1,904
Asia	2,291	2,793	3,611
Oceania	994	1,460	1,811
Total	30,476	37,725	45,763

The sums devoted to the defense budget are thus, each year, much greater than the total of all investments abroad. Yet those investments have to be protected so that private enterprise will retain the confidence to export its capital. Those investments prefer to go to places like Canada and Europe which are not exposed to the threat of subversion, but the empire cannot deliberately confine itself to a narrow geographic sphere, it cannot abandon countries which, with their enormous, largely undeveloped natural resources run the risk of passing into the other camp. The empire must prove, even at the price of the destruction of a country, its ability to prevent militarily any progress of Communism, in order to dissuade the enemy from carrying the revolution any further. Thus private capital ventures into the most exposed regions of the world and—in five years—grew by 58 per cent in Asia. And it is not paying too high a price to devote about half of the federal budget to defense, for three-fifths of military monies, or about $30 billion, are earmarked for contracts signed with private industry. All sectors of production (mining, the steel industry, electrical and electronic equipment, chemical and textile industries, etc.) benefit from the manna scattered by the Pentagon, which contributes to general prosperity—not only in maintaining 3 million men in uniform but also in creating many jobs in industry and in research.

Undoubtedly, such major expenses hardly permit the simultaneous pursuit of the ambitious objectives of the Great Society promised by President Johnson, but the empire did not want a situation which burdened it with such heavy military expenditures. It dreams only of liberty, peace, and prosperity. Therefore, it is necessary to pay a high price to take care of a situation which has been imposed from the outside. Better days will come when the entire world will have recognized the purity of America's intentions. And that waiting period is all the more tolerable when the military expenses stimulate production and maintain domestic prosperity at a level that could not be attained if the defense budget were substantially cut. Besides, it is not for itself alone that America carries such a burden. God and history have condemned it to be the "Sentinel of Liberty," a role that it would willingly relinquish if it could withdraw to its frontiers and turn over to another power the mission which had fallen to it. America would have self-doubts if it considered its interventions in the world simply as means of ensuring sources of supplies and raw materials and outlets for its capital. Providentially, such efforts coincide with a great crusade for the liberty of peoples oppressed by their poverty and exposed to Communist domination.

An economist like John Kenneth Galbraith—John F. Kennedy's former consultant and former Ambassador to India—had envisaged other means for the United States to utilize its surplus capital. In brief it consisted of turning the United States progressively away from productive investments and toward other tasks which met the Johnsonian objectives of a Great Society: education, public health, leisure and culture, natural-resource conservation, and the fight against pollution of water and air.

But the characteristic of private capital is to invest in sectors which guarantee tangible profits. Only state intervention, through taxes and public investments, can furnish the necessary resources for works of public welfare, but, of course, devoid of any business benefits. Therefore, private capital continues to move toward the vast opportunities opened up by the outside world. It is thus that, in 1965, American investments abroad were represented by $3.7 billion in mining and refining of minerals, $15.3 billion in oil, $30 billion in manufacturing industries, earning a total profit of $3,961 million, which, in turn, must be in large part reinvested.

Thus unfolds the infernal cycle whereby private American capital is forced to unceasingly find new possibilities for investment abroad over which the military power of the Pentagon keeps watch. The empire develops and spreads thanks to its momentum, convinced that no force in the world will be able to check its march. On the contrary, the world has right before its eyes proof of the power and vitality of the empire, of its capacity to produce and to destroy, of its generosity toward its friends and its resolution in facing its enemies. There is no question of knowing *how* to resist it; more simply, *why* should anyone resist it? President Johnson told the people of the earth that his only ambition was to devote all his energies "to build a great world society—a place where every man can find a life free from hunger and disease, a life offering the chance to seek spiritual fulfillment unhampered by the degradations of bodily misery." He was more precise when he said, "The world cannot remain divided between rich nations and poor nations, or white nations and colored nations. In such division are the seeds of terrible discord and danger in decades to come. For the wall between rich and poor is a wall of glass through which all can see." [29] John F. Kennedy did not express any other ideal when he declared, "Never before has man had such capacity to control his own environment: to end thirst and hunger, to conquer poverty and disease, to banish illiteracy and massive human misery. We have the power to make this the best generation of mankind in the history of the world—or to make it the last." [30] (September 20, 1963.) Thus, two months before his death, we meet the themes that he developed on the very day he entered the White House. "I have sworn before you and Almighty God the same solemn oath our forebears prescribed nearly a century and three quarters ago. . . . Man holds in his mortal hands the power to abolish all forms of human poverty and all forms of human life. And yet the same revolutionary beliefs for which our forebears fought are still at issue around the globe—the belief that the rights of man come not from the generosity of the State but from the hand of God. . . . To those old allies whose cultural and spiritual origins we share, we pledge the loyalty of faithful friends. . . . To those peoples in the huts and villages of half the globe struggling to break the bonds of mass misery, we pledge our best efforts to help them help themselves, for whatever period is required—not because the Communists may be doing it, not because we seek their votes, but because it is right. . . . Whether you are citizens of America or citizens of the world, ask of us here the same high standards of strength and sacrifice which we ask of you. With a good conscience our only sure reward, with history the final judge of our deeds, let us go forth to lead the land we love, asking His blessing and His help, but knowing that here on earth God's work must truly be our own." [31] (January 20, 1961.)

Many men would be afraid to have to accomplish the work of God on earth. Fortunately, American democracy is better prepared to fulfill that task than any other political system. "Our form of government has no sense unless it is founded in a deeply felt religious faith." [32] However, the ambiguity remains, and the dilemma is everlasting. America dreams of universal happiness and world brotherhood, but the empire if it has friends also has clients, and must confront enemies, calm jealousies, appease rivalries and hatreds. America dreams of liberty and democracy, but over all continents the empire cultivates the good will of strong regimes and, if need be, establishes dictatorships over the ruins of democratic systems whose fall has been provoked by American agents. America proclaims very loudly irreproachable principles that its acts often contradict. At American instigation, Article 15 was introduced into the Bogotá Charter, which solemnly affirms: "No state or group of states has the right to intervene, directly or indirectly, for any reason whatever, in the internal or external affairs of any other state." But six years later, the CIA, with the agreement of the White House, the State Department, and the Pentagon, organized the overthrow of Guatemala's legitimate government and then, in 1961, an invasion of Cuba. At the request of Washington, Article 17 of the same Bogotá Charter asserts: "The territory of a state is inviolable; it may not be the object, even temporarily, of military occupation or of other measures of force taken by another state, directly or indirectly, on any grounds whatever." But in 1965 some 20,000 American soldiers occupied the Dominican Republic. Conscious of its power, America emerges as the defender of weaker nations. All small nations, Dean Rusk once pointed out, have the right to be left in peace by their neighbors. But in the mind of the Secretary of State that statement of universal scope applies to Vietnam threatened by China, but does not apply either to Cuba or to the Dominican Republic although these two countries are close neighbors of a great power. America wishes that international relations be founded on respect of truth, but Eisenhower declared that Gary Powers' spy-plane, brought down above the U.S.S.R., was carrying out a weather mission, and Adlai Stevenson from the rostrum of the United Nations, maintained that the fighting in the Bay of Pigs concerned only Cubans. In his election campaign against Senator Barry Goldwater, President Johnson made categorical commitments: "Some . . . are eager to enlarge the conflict. They call upon us to supply American boys to do the job that Asian boys should do [August 12, 1964]. . . . There are those that say you ought to go north and drop bombs [September 25, 1964]. . . . We are not going north and we are not going south [September 28, 1964]. . . . We are not going to send American boys nine or ten thousand miles away from home to do what Asian boys ought to be doing for themselves [October 21, 1964]." And eighteen months later America was bombing North Vietnam and then sending soldiers to South Vietnam, who soon came to total 500,000.

Did not Machiavelli write: "How laudable it is for a prince to keep good faith and live with integrity, and not with astuteness, every one knows. Still the experience of our times shows those princes to have done great things who have had little regard for good faith, and have been able by astuteness to confuse men's brains, and who have made loyalty their foundation. . . . A certain prince of the present time, whom it is well not to name, never does anything but preach peace and good faith, but he is really a great enemy to both, and either of them, had he observed them, would have lost him state or reputation on many occasions." [33]

But the American tradition is, rather, found in what John Adams wrote in 1778: "This is the established order of things, when a Nation has grown to such an height of Power as to become dangerous to Mankind, she never fails to loose her Wisdom, her Justice and her Moderation and with these she never fails to loose her Power, which however returns again if these Virtues return." [34]

Has America reached that stage of power where it might be tempted to lose the qualities which allowed it to expand its world empire? Should we believe, as Max Lerner writes in concluding his voluminous study on American civilization, that "the temptation of a successful people is to make a cult of the artifacts of its success, rather than celebrate the daring and large outlook that made the achievements possible." [35] America is confounded because the tremendous instruments of its economic and military power, in which it has placed all its hopes, are held in check in the rice paddies and jungles of Vietnam by a small country seven times less populous than America, a country whose economy is essentially agricultural and which, at the same time, relies for its resistance on fewer men and arms. But most Americans may not properly gauge the importance of the game that is played in Vietnam and in all the countries watching the progress of that tragedy. In the bottom of their hearts, they probably share the conviction expressed by Emerson, a century ago: "We think our civilization is near its meridian, but we are yet only at the cockcrowing and the morning star." [36]

The destiny of empires is at once fragile and unpredictable. America possesses in itself sufficient resources to achieve many recoveries and to surprise the world in many ways. It is therefore less important to ponder the future of the American empire than to examine its structure and its methods.

Faced with such a vast task the present work can only represent a modest introduction to the study of an infinitely complex problem. The door remains open for more thorough research calling on a vast array of competences. It is hoped that specialized teams in different areas will pursue in depth the work outlined in these pages. In order to give a global picture of the American empire, it seemed necessary to envisage two very distinct parts. Naturally, this empire was not built in a day. Chapters II, III, IV, and V retrace its historical evolution from the end of the last century to the Second World War, bringing out the forces which have molded it and which are still at work today: the role of some theoreticians who have defined the objectives of the empire and worked out its political justifications, the importance of public opinion shaped by mass media, the reactions of different sociological groups (business circles, trade unions, religious organizations, intellectuals, etc.), the attitude of military and political leaders, and the influence of economic and business considerations. The second part is devoted to the period which, from the Second World War to the present, marks the triumphant stage of the American empire. Three chapters examine the methods of the empire in three essential areas—the economic empire, the military empire, the cultural empire—while another chapter deals with the techniques and activities of one of the principal weapons in the service of the empire: the CIA. Finally, another chapter is devoted to the government of the empire, the men in power, their recruitment, the relationship between political personnel, businessmen, and military leaders.

Several aspects thus remain in the shade, or are hardly mentioned. But, however incomplete, this book should give a better knowledge of the techniques utilized by the United States to build not only the most powerful empire that history has known, but one that is unique.

Part One

THE HISTORY
OF THE EMPIRE

II

The Birth of Imperialism

The building of the empire began quite naturally at the very doorstep of the United States. South America and, especially, the small countries of Central America were natural prey. This first stage of the imperialist adventure deserves to be studied in detail because it reveals the principal mechanisms which will later be used when the empire branches out toward Asia, Europe, and Africa.

This period highlights the desire to limit—and then to exclude—any outside influence on the American continent. The Monroe Doctrine, which defines that policy, was designed to protect American democracies against any interference from the autocratic regimes ruling Europe. In one way it presages the "containment" doctrine, the damming up of Communism, which will guide American diplomacy after the Second World War. But then there will no longer be any question of protecting a single continent from European colonialist powers; the aim will be to protect the whole of the free world from the aggressive or subversive actions of international Communism. Under the cover of containment, the empire will extend its economic interests throughout the whole of the free world as it has already done in Latin America under cover of the Monroe Doctrine.

In many respects, this first imperialist stage foreshadowed policies that will be characteristic of the American empire at its zenith. In the first place, a strong messianic urge should be mentioned: The nineteenth-century United States of America represented an ideal of democracy and progress, to which the United States will still be subscribing in the middle of the twentieth century in its great confrontation with Communism. In both periods, this messianism seduced large segments of the population who were not necessarily aware of the material interests that were at stake.

The idealism is well matched by strategic considerations which naturally become more important as the United States assumes world responsibilities. In this respect, the great project was the building of the Panama Canal at the turn of the century, a project cherished for several decades, and the installation of means for its defense. Later, a network of air and naval bases will be built around the world, fulfilling the wishes expressed a century earlier by the harbingers of imperialism.

The role that the press will be called upon to play in the great crusade against Communism was already evident before 1898 in the vicious campaign that the Hearst newspapers launched against Spain's policy in Cuba. One finds in it the same mixture of true and false, the same exaggerations, and also the same dualism and astonishing simplifications.

In addition, the most incredible aspect of American penetration in the Caribbean was the appearance of forerunners of James Bond. Its most picturesque actors were authentic adventurers who will later be replaced by agents of the CIA and their confederates. But by then the tasks will no longer be performed by amateurs, and they will be transformed into an industry having at its disposal all the modern techniques and resources of corruption. The old buccaneers will become "agents" whose field of action, starting with Central America, expands to the four corners of the world. Besides, their adventures reveal a consistent pattern: officially disavowed when they fail, they receive support as long as the government sees in their actions a means of extending its empire.

Finally, historical research is necessary to reveal the finer points of hard-dying legends. In 1898 the most powerful business circles were opposed to the colonial conquests desired by large segments of the population. Their attitude was naturally dictated strictly by economic considerations, and the interests of big business are not necessarily served by every kind of imperialist operation. Their self-interest sometimes even forces them to oppose adventurism: such was the case at the end of the last century for certain industrial tycoons like Carnegie, such is the case seventy years later when Wall Street advocates negotiations in Vietnam.

Only the abandonment of sketchy simplification permits the discovery of this major phenomenon: while France and Great Britain were still striving to build classic colonial empires, the United States, tentatively, and propelled by often-contradictory influences, pragmatically invented this neocolonialism whose complexity the Third World did not begin to perceive until after the Second World War.

The historical research outlined in the pages that follow has no other *raison d'être*. It shows how methods were born and perfected which are still in use throughout the world. A swift playback thus plunges us into the heart of the most immediate problems.

It was through "a splendid little war"—the expression came from John Hay, Secretary of State—that the United States in 1898 took its first step on the road of imperialism.[1] In the adventure it lost 2,446 men—most of them victims of disease, only 289 were killed or fatally wounded in combat. Although not very bloody the campaign was nonetheless profitable, as it permitted the United States to harvest the last bountiful fruits of the Spanish empire: Cuba, Puerto Rico, and the Philippines. In the past, in order to extend their territory, Americans had only had recourse to arms to "pacify" Indian tribes and to wrest from Mexico the vast western territories: Texas, New Mexico, Arizona, and California. They had remained faithful to the tradition expressed in George Washington's Farewell Address, the Jefferson messages, and the Monroe Doctrine: the fundamental interests of the American people could not go beyond their continental possessions. The Spanish-American War of 1898, by taking the Star-Spangled Banner overseas, marked the *de facto* break with an isolationism which, however, would survive or be reborn, following the disappointments which resulted from a policy of intervention.

Paradoxically, President McKinley, who declared war on Spain, was not in any way an imperialist. He was carried along, pushed on by a set of circumstances and by a handful of very active, influential men he could not resist. As if against his own judgment, he inaugurated a new phase in the history of the United States. The conquest of the west had ended: In 1889 the last government lands—in Oklahoma, taken from the Indians—had been parceled out and put on sale. Their energies now called Americans toward "new frontiers" located outside the continent. By the same stroke, the United States became a world power with all the obligations and temptations that this title implies. In any case, the adventure carried out the wishes of the harbingers of American imperialism.

During the two-and-a-half centuries which followed the settlement of Jamestown, Americans had been absorbed by the colonization of the vast territory whose western frontier, on the shores of the Pacific, seemed so far away. However, since the beginning of the nineteenth century, their merchant ships had traveled the oceans, sometimes under the protection of warships, seeking markets. Under instructions from President Fillmore, Commander Perry had opened the ports of Japan to the United States in 1853–1854. But many other naval officers had, before him, dreamed of seizing remote islands; at home no one was interested then in projects that seemed so illusory. The first base would only be set up in Samoa in 1889. Until the Civil War, southern planters had toyed with the idea of finding land in Cuba and Mexico that their slaves could profitably work. Besides, the southerners were not the only ones to search for means of territorial expansion: Antislavery men like William Seward, Lincoln's Secretary of State, did not doubt that the country's frontiers ought to coincide with the geographic limits of North America. In 1867 he bought Alaska from Russia for $7,200,000, but that decision was hardly popular and Seward had to take recourse to questionable procedures to obtain Congressional approval. He also tried to buy the Danish possessions in the Antilles, but this time the Senate refused to go along with him, and the United States had to wait till 1917 to acquire the Virgin Islands. Seward did not hesitate to look further: he advocated a war against Russia in Manchuria to assure the hegemony of the United States in the Far East. President Grant tried to annex the Dominican Republic, but the Senate prevented him from doing it because public interest was limited to the continent proper.

Only exporters and sailors could nourish ambitious imperialist projects. The wars of 1840–1842 and of 1856–1860 between Great Britain and China transferred part of the Chinese trade to American hands. The American fleets could see new markets opening to them because of the revolutions of 1848 which dislocated European commerce, and because of the Crimean War during which European ships were assigned to the transportation of troops and military material. At the same time, the production of the United States was growing, bringing about a rapid increase in exports which had gone from $19 million in 1791 to $33.5 million in 1860. During the same period, imports climbed from $29 to $353 million. This commercial expansion called for a powerful Merchant Marine. But American ship-yards were lagging behind their European competitors in the launching of steamships and the replacement of wood by iron in ship construction. Then the Civil War dealt a heavy blow to the Merchant Marine of the United States. The government was not interested in the problem, private capital preferred to invest in more profitable activities which absorbed the attention of the country and trans-formed it: development of the railroads, of mines, of major industries. American tonnage fell from 2,496,894 tons in 1860 to 826,694 tons in 1900. During the same period, the share of imports and exports carried under the American flag fell from 66.5 per cent in 1860 to 7.1 per cent in 1900.[2]

That rapid decline called for a reaction. It was not long in coming. The first cry of alarm was sounded by Admiral Alfred Mahan, the real theoretician of American imperialism. In 1890 he published *The Influence of Sea Power upon History*, then a study on the role of naval power during the French Revolution and the empire, and finally a biography of Nelson, all the while spreading, through hundreds of lectures, articles, and brochures, his master thesis: naval power and maritime commerce are inseparable, both are indispensable to the strength and prosperity of the country. Denouncing the myth of traditional isolationism, he predicted that Americans, whether they wanted it or not, could not remain out of world affairs; it is illusory, he said, not to want to be drawn into international whirlpools. Such speeches went counter to accepted opinion and, to his critics, Admiral Mahan had to reiterate that there was "no aggressive action in our pious souls."[3]

Besides, certain "pious souls" were heading in the same direction. A Protestant missionary, Josiah Strong, published in 1886 *Our Country*, several times republished, in which he proclaimed that the Anglo-Saxon race had been selected by God to civilize the world. However, Kipling, who lived a few years in Vermont following his marriage to an American in 1892, had not yet invented the "white man's burden." We can see Josiah Strong, as the missionary preceding the soldier and the merchant, staking out the lands which they will only have to take over.

But the ideas of an Admiral and a Protestant minister alone can not change prevalent opinion. Very concrete and powerful interests must be involved to pull the United States away from its congenital isolationism. In thirty years —from 1870 to 1900—the population had almost doubled, going from 38.5 to 75.9 million, but there still remained vast spaces to occupy and the United States was not at all looking for colonies to settle. At the time of the Spanish-American War, it was preoccupied with finding foreign outlets for its capital and for its burgeoning production. In 1898, in spite of the fact that they represented only one-tenth of national production, American exports reached more than a billion dollars. From that time on, the United States financed its own economy and began to export capital: its investments abroad, which reached only $684 million in 1897 were to surpass $2,500 million in 1914. The country possessed enormous natural wealth, which then seemed inexhaustible. In order to exploit it the country had at its disposal growing manpower: more than 8 million immigrants had arrived between 1830 and 1870, but 10½ million landed during the following three decades and 12½ million between 1900 and 1920. The accumulation of capital gave birth to gigantic enterprises whose power inspired the passing of the Sherman Antitrust Law (1890), which, however, remained ineffective except when, paradoxically, the power structure used it against trade unions. Thus the United States met all conditions for a rapid economic expansion: its national wealth, estimated at $7 billion in 1850, had quadrupled twenty years later, then it reached $80 billion at the turn of the century before doubling again between 1900 and 1912 to climb to $186 billion. From that time on, it left far behind the national wealth of Great Britain ($80 billion), of Germany ($77 billion), and of France ($57 billion). At the time of its war with Spain, the United States was already the leading economic power in the world, but its political role on the international scene remained insignificant. During the last thirty years of the nineteenth century, England had added to its colonial possessions 12,900,000 square kilometers peopled by 88 million inhabitants, and France more than 9 million square kilometers with 37 million inhabitants. Was the United States immunized against colonial fever?

In fact, in the best isolationist tradition it was mostly preoccupied with its own wealth. The Dingley Tariff of 1897 protected its production behind the highest custom barriers that had yet existed. Indeed this played a role in an incident which gave the United States a foretaste of imperialism by inducing it to take over Hawaii. There again the missionaries who had been on the islands since the beginning of the nineteenth century had opened the way; they had encouraged the development of the sugar cane industry on which, thanks to sales to the United States, the prosperity of the population came to rest. Under different pretexts, the Americans kept the islands in a state of feverish agitation, which in 1893 reached the proportions of a real revolt. They obliged the Queen to abdicate and proclaimed a republic. Pursuing an old dream, they immediately negotiated a treaty of annexation to the United States. But President Cleveland, having discovered that the revolution had taken place with the direct complicity of the United States Ambassador and under the threatening protection of American warships, refused to submit the treaty to the Senate.

Nevertheless, four years later, the situation in the islands became alarming. The Dingley Tariff struck a heavy blow to the archipelago's economy, especially since it granted important subsidies to American sugar producers. Another annexation treaty was immediately negotiated by President McKinley: Hawaiians were to have free access to the American market in which they would be able to sell what sugar they produced. In saving them from economic ruin, the annexation took on the appearance of a philanthropic deed. It crowned besides the 1875 treaty, in which the autonomous government had promised not to give to a third power any place in the islands—through sale or lease—and it guaranteed the agreement of 1887 by which the United States had obtained the exclusive right to build a naval base at Pearl Harbor.

President McKinley then sent the annexation treaty to the Senate for ratification. It was being debated when the war against Spain broke out. The White House which, under such circumstances, feared interminable delays, replaced the treaty, whose ratification demanded a two-thirds vote of the Senate, with a simple resolution which could be adopted by a simple majority. That subterfuge was fully successful and the annexation of Hawaii was approved August 12, 1898. Its inhabitants would receive American citizenship in 1900 and the archipelago would become the fiftieth state of the Union in 1960.

Those were only modest preliminaries to the imperialist phase which according to American historians begins in 1898 when the United States declares war on Spain. The imperialist adventure had found its theoretician in Alfred Mahan and its preacher and moral vindicator in Josiah Strong. The need to export a growing number of goods and capital justified the venture in the eyes of the realists. But it also needed organizers and politicians.

The most famous, Theodore Roosevelt, will one day,

after entering the White House, receive the Nobel Peace Prize for offering his mediation in the Russo-Japanese War (1904), using his good offices at the Algeciras Conference (1906), and advocating systematic recourse to the Court of International Justice in the Hague. Before the Spanish-American War, Theodore Roosevelt had played a part in the political life of New York—without great success—then retired to his ranch in Dakota. From it, he brought back the highly colorful manners of the westerner, which had turned into a distinctive trait of his personality. Called back to New York as the Republican candidate for Mayor of New York City, he acquired some fame when President Harrison appointed him as a member of the Civil Service Commission. Then, for two years as head of the police force in New York City, he instituted a program of reforms which brought him into direct conflict with the most corrupt and the most reactionary elements of the political machine. He climbed another step when President McKinley named him Assistant Secretary of the Navy (1897). In that post, he began to put into practice the theories of Admiral Mahan: The United States needs naval bases for its protection and "whether they will or no, Americans must now begin to look outward." [4] But young Theodore Roosevelt only stayed a few months in Washington. He was forty years old when the United States declared war on Spain. He resigned immediately to head a cavalry regiment which became famous as The Rough Riders and embarked for Cuba, whence he easily returned a hero.

Full of ambition for himself and his country, Theodore Roosevelt thought that, thirty years after the Civil War, the United States was growing dangerously "soft" in a climate of peace. In 1895 he had warmly approved the firmness shown by President Cleveland toward England at the time of its dispute with Venezuela over the borders of British Guiana. Accusing London of having violated the Monroe Doctrine, Cleveland stated: "Today the United States is practically sovereign on this continent." [5] The British reply being judged unsatisfactory, Cleveland decided to send a commission of inquiry to the scene, while he specified that the United States "must resist by every means in its power" [6] any attempt by England to ignore the findings of the commission. On both sides of the Atlantic fever mounted, although Cleveland's abrupt style was vigorously criticized by most of the American newspapers. It is then that Theodore Roosevelt wrote to Senator Henry Cabot Lodge: "Personally, I rather hope the fight will come soon. The clamor of the peace faction has convinced me that the country needs a war." [7] But peace was preserved, and Theodore Roosevelt was indignant. Finally, three years later in Cuba, he realized his dream. "Americanizing of the world," he said, "is our destiny." Later, clarifying his thought, he delivered the famous slogan which illustrates his politics: "Speak softly and carry a big stick. You will go far."

Such concepts found favorable echoes in Congress with men like Senator Henry Cabot Lodge, who later would use all his energy to prevent the United States from joining the League of Nations. Won over to the ideas of Admiral Mahan, he fought in the Senate for a more powerful Army and Navy. Son of a Boston merchant who had made his fortune in trade with China, he was convinced that the United States, because of its power, had to play a leading role on the world scene, even at the expense of small states which he bluntly said "are of the past and have no future." [8]

One of his colleagues, Albert Beveridge, Senator from Indiana, hoped that the United States would secure new markets and take over colonies where it could unload the surplus of agricultural and industrial production. In a ringing speech, he clearly stated the profound conviction held by imperialists: "God has not been preparing the English-speaking and Teutonic peoples for a thousand years for nothing but vain and idle self-contemplation and self-admiration. He has made us the master organizers of the world to establish system where chaos reigns. . . . He has made us adept in government that we may administer government among savage and senile peoples. Were it not for such a force this world would relapse into barbarism and night. And of all our race He has marked the American people as His chosen nation to finally lead in the regeneration of the world."

The messianic spirit which marked this speech by Senator Beveridge was not in itself a novelty in the history of the United States: the Puritan tradition made America a Promised Land where Providence would ensure, according to George Washington in his inaugural address, "the preservation of the sacred fire of liberty." Jefferson had proposed that the United States seal represent not an eagle, but "the children of Israel, led by a cloud by day and a pillar of fire by night." America was a new Promised Land for the good of its inhabitants and for the benefit of the rest of the world in whose eyes it would soon appear as an example to imitate. But, until then, it had not envisaged imposing on "savage and senile peoples" its concepts and its institutions. It was a torch and did not want any other role. Imperialists have turned its idealism and its messianic spirit away from their true significance. The American theologian Reinhold Niebuhr wisely noted, "Except in moments of aberration we do not think of ourselves as the potential masters, but as tutors of mankind in its pilgrimage to perfection." [9] The turn taken in United States history at the instigation of the imperialists corresponds in fact to a moment of aberration, but one heavily fraught with consequences.

Men like Theodore Roosevelt, Henry Cabot Lodge, and Albert Beveridge were led not only by the desire to launch the United States in the game of world politics. Their actions were also a reflection of the preoccupations on the domestic scene. The economic crisis of 1893–1898 had incited many disorders, with riots, hunger marches, explosions of violence which, for some people, foreshadowed a revolution. Actual armies of the unemployed in the cities sustained a climate of anxiety and bitterness which was no less great in the country where the malcontents organized the Greenback Party and the Populist Party. Small farmers and small landowners were alarmed by the concentration of agricultural and industrial property. In the spring of 1894, during the great Pullman strike in Chicago, the new American Federation of Labor confronted the violence of the army that President Cleveland had sent against the workers. Thus, "a diversion of the people's thought from domestic discontent over plutocracy and poverty, such as embroiled the land in the campaign of 1896, to world politics and wars would damp if not extinguish radicalism at home. It would smother, they trusted, those other agitators: Bryan, Debs, John P. Altgeld, and all such 'incendiaries' as they were described in conservative circles." [10] For, less powerful but more dynamic than the American Federation of Labor, the Industrial Workers of the World Union, asserted that they were "founded on the class struggle." [11] When, in 1895, a conflict seemed imminent with England over the dispute between Venezuela and British Guiana, a Texas Democrat, Thomas Pascal, stated that a war would drain the "anarchistic, socialistic, and populistic boil" in such a radical way that it would not "corrupt our people for the next two centuries." [12]

Thus a tangle of schemes, ambitions, and interests pushed the United States toward a colonial war from which the imperialists expected new markets, increased prosperity, and a decisive position in world affairs. At the same time, social conflicts will be relegated to second place and the wounds of the Civil War will fade away in a great surge of national unity: the former Confederate Generals Joe

Wheeler and Fitzhugh Lee were going back in the service, but this time in the Army of the United States against Spain. The Republican president, McKinley, put his old Democratic opponent, William Jennings Bryan, at the head of a National Guard regiment. Americans were throwing themselves enthusiastically into a conflict which will be "their own little war for liberty and democracy against all that was tyrannical, treacherous, and fetid in the Old World." [13]

Cuba must be "liberated" from Spanish colonialism. Forty years earlier Senator Stephen Douglas, famous for his debates with Lincoln, had said: "It is our destiny to have Cuba and it is folly to debate the question. It naturally belongs to the American continent." [14] Jefferson Davis, the Secretary of War under President Pierce, had demanded in 1854 the annexation of Cuba. That same year, on February 28, an American merchant ship, the *Black Warrior*, had been seized by Spanish authorities in Havana for violating port regulations. The south, which eight years later during the Civil War was to elect the same Jefferson Davis to the Presidency of the Confederation, was then unanimously ready to wage war against Spain—in principle to avenge the affront to the *Black Warrior*, in fact to take over new plantations; negotiations were opened with Madrid to settle the incident, but Pierre Soulé, United States Ambassador to Spain, adopted such a harsh attitude that Washington ordered him to confer immediately with James Buchanan, United States Ambassador to London and soon to be President of the United States (1857–1861), and with John Y. Mason, former Secretary of the Navy and then Ambassador to Paris. These three diplomats wrote the "Ostend Manifesto," which proclaimed that the United States had to buy Cuba. If Spain refused to sell the island, they continued, the United States had to take it by force. The American government immediately disavowed that document: the northern states feared that the annexation of Cuba by introducing another slave-holding state into the Union might break the delicate equilibrium that the nation strove to maintain.

After the Civil War, the former Commander in Chief of the northern armies strangely came around to the southern point of view. A combination of revolts and repression kept Cuba in an almost permanent state of insecurity to the point that, on December 7, 1875, in a message to Congress, President Grant could speak of events which would take place two decades later: "Each party seems quite capable of working great injury and damage to the other, as well as to all the relations and interests dependent on the existence of peace in the island; but they seem incapable of reaching any adjustment, and both have thus failed of achieving any success whereby one party shall possess and control the island to the exclusion of the other. Under these circumstances, the agency of others, either by mediation or intervention, seems to be the only alternative which must sooner or later be invoked for the termination of the strife." [15]

Cuba has tempted the covetousness of the United States for a long time. But the aspirations which inspired some Americans had first to be shared by a large number of their countrymen. The press would serve as the instrument of that conversion.

The politicians who wanted to launch the United States on an imperialist venture had no chance of securing the adherence of the people by expounding Admiral Mahan's thesis. To reach the masses they had to have recourse to more emotional arguments. They would have to reach people's feelings by inviting them to join in a great crusade on behalf of the most certain values of American idealism. Two gifted men took over the delicate mission; the newspapermen Joseph Pulitzer and William Randolph Hearst.

In 1887, when he was twenty-four, Hearst had received as

a gift from his father the *San Francisco Examiner*, which then had a circulation of 24,000. In a short time, through the most questionable sensationalism, he doubled its circulation. In 1895 Hearst started the conquest of New York City by buying the *Morning Journal*. His objective was to dethrone the powerful old Pulitzer group whose presses daily printed 500,000 copies. Hearst lowered the price of the *Morning Journal*, added a number of pages, took the best writers away from his competitors, increased the number of scandal stories, organized bicycle races—all at a cost of $100,000 a year. The situation worsened when Hearst lost many advertising accounts because of his endorsement in the elections of 1896 of William Jennings Bryan who polled only 6,509,000 votes against 7,111,000 votes for the Republican McKinley. During the month preceding the election, Hearst showed a deficit of $158,000. But he was determined to let nothing prevent him from winning the battle which would make him king of the daily press.

Providentially, Spain was obstinately intent upon repressing the insurrection which had broken out in Cuba a year before. Two correspondents sent to the island by the *Morning Journal* were arrested by the Spanish authorities. Hearst protested: "No surer road is open for popularity of the new president than the abandonment of the cold-blooded indifference to Cuba to which Cleveland has committed our government." He organized soup kitchens for the unemployed, he turned the sad subjects of scabrous news items into heroes, organized excessively sumptuous galas for the benefit of the poor, and invented every day a new idea to seduce the public. He was thirty-four years old, bursting with energy, and dispatched his reporters on the trail of criminals that the police could not find. This was not to the liking of the young New York City Police Commissioner, Theodore Roosevelt, five years older than Hearst. The

Morning Journal ridiculed the pink shirts and the wide, fringed silk sash sported by Roosevelt and reproached him for being too aristocratic and for despising the people: "He has a very poor opinion of the majority, but there is one compensation: the majority has a very poor opinion of Mr. Roosevelt," wrote Hearst. The two men were nonetheless similar in their ambition and their taste for action.

All that virulence was not sufficient, however, to guarantee the success of the Hearst press. The master stroke would be made possible by the Cuban revolution, which in New York was fought essentially between Hearst's *Morning Journal* and Pulitzer's *World*. A great affair in Madison Square Garden honored the Cuban insurgents' leader, General Maximo Gomez, as the greatest soldier of the day. Hearst made a personal contribution of $2,000 to offer him a ceremonial sword which he kept in his office and on which he had the following inscription engraved: TO MAXIMO GOMEZ, COMMANDER IN CHIEF OF THE ARMY OF THE CUBAN REPUBLIC. VIVA CUBA LIBRE! He entrusted a young journalist to deliver it to its famous recipient right under the nose of the Spaniards. But the Spaniards jailed Sylvester Scovel, the *World*'s Cuban correspondent, which gave Pulitzer an opportunity to launch a huge campaign to "Free Scovel." As a countermove, Hearst sent a reporter and the famous illustrator Frederic Remington to Cuba. Remington sent the following telegram from Havana:

. . . EVERYTHING IS QUIET. THERE IS NO TROUBLE HERE. THERE WILL BE NO WAR. I WISH TO RETURN.

Which earned Hearst's famous reply:

PLEASE REMAIN. YOU FURNISH THE PICTURES AND I'LL FURNISH THE WAR.

The *Morning Journal* was unceasing in its praise of the insurgents, "animated by the same fearless spirit that inspired the Council of the patriot fathers who sat in Philadelphia on the 4th of July 1776." The columns of the competing newspapers were filled with stories where the imaginary transcended the real and where the savagery of the Spaniards put in relief the heroism of the Cubans. If the Hearst papers were to be believed, Havana had been occupied several times—even before the patriots had been able to get near it, and the leaders of the insurrection, Maximo Gomez and Antonio Maceo, had died gloriously several times. In spite of the bloody repression which gripped the island, the insurgents won some territory. Madrid recalled General Martínez de Campos and replaced him with a hard-fisted man, Valeriano Weyler, whom the *Morning Journal* described in these terms: "Weyler the brute, the devastator of haciendas, the destroyer of families, and the outrager of women. . . . Pitiless, cold, an exterminator of men. . . . There is nothing to prevent his carnal, animal brain from running riot with itself in inventing tortures and infamies of bloody debauchery."

The Spanish Ambassador to Washington put the responsibility for the campaign in the American press on the rebels who, he said, "hope in some way to create bad blood, and, ultimately, war between Spain and the United States, with the idea of having their fighting done by American troops." Indeed, the Cubans had organized a committee to mobilize public opinion in New York. But Hearst did not really need it to spur his quest for sensational news. It was his own correspondents in Havana who created the story according to which three Cuban girls had been undressed and searched as they were embarking on an American boat, which produced the screaming headline; "Does our flag protect women?" Joseph Pulitzer, furious at having lost out, had the *World* interview the girls on their arrival in New York. They denied the whole affair, and the storm raised in Congress quieted down.

Something else had to be found. A few days later, a Cuban with American citizenship committed suicide in the cell where the Spaniards had thrown him. According to Hearst, it was an assassination, and to avenge it he asked that the United States declare war on Cuba. He interviewed Senator John Sherman, who had given his name to the 1890 antitrust law and who became Secretary of State in 1897–1898 after having been chairman of the Foreign Affairs Committee of the Senate. The *Morning Journal* attributed to him the following statements: "If the facts are true, as reported, and American citizens are being murdered in Cuba in cold blood, the only way to put an end to the atrocities is to declare war on Spain." Senator Sherman denied this declaration: "It is a lie from beginning to end." But, William A. Swanberg noted: "Yet it had to be admitted that Sherman was not too reliable himself. One of the oddities of the time was that the seventy-four-year-old senator had been selected for the most important Cabinet post under McKinley although he was failing mentally. Sherman often forgot what he said, what he did, and on at least one occasion forgot where he was."

Hearst was not so easily discouraged. While taking rhetorical precautions ("If it is true that—"), he asked Washington to declare war on Spain. "War is a dreadful thing, but there are things more dreadful even than war, and one of them is dishonor."

But President McKinley was not to be swayed. In his inaugural address, March 1897, he did not make any allusion to Cuba and, on the contrary, declared: "We want no wars of conquest. We must avoid the temptation of territorial aggression." The *Morning Journal* then deplored: "McKinley is listening with eager ear to the threats of Big Business Interests." [16]

In fact, the banking and industrial interests were hostile to a conflict which they feared risked provoking an avalanche of selling in Wall Street. The stake represented by the Cuban sugar plantations was important enough to incite some Americans to wish for a military intervention which would re-establish order and normal conditions of production in the island. But such a preoccupation was important only to a minority. American investments in Cuba hardly came to $50 million, and Cuban-American trade represented $100 million a year, out of a total trade volume of $2 billion. The hold of the United States on the Cuban economy would develop on a grand scale only after the elimination of Spain. Mark Hanna, who had been instrumental in McKinley's choice as a Republican candidate and who reigned over a vast economic empire (iron and coal mines, foundries, shipyards, marine transport, banks, etc.), symbolized the close union between the Republican Party and big business; he made enough money in the United States, feared to lose some in colonial adventures, and therefore was opposed to the war. Among businessmen he was not alone. Because Andrew Carnegie violently condemned the spirit of conquest, the Secretary of State, John Hay, asserted that the "steel king" had lost his mind. These very powerful men represented the attitude of big business and of Wall Street. For their own motives they found themselves in the same camp with Mark Twain, who ridiculed the politicians who, like Senator Beveridge, were "for giving civilization to the man who waits in darkness." [17] The "capitalists" did not want war. Only a few activist politicians wanted it, but thanks to the campaign led by Hearst and Pulitzer, an increasing sector of public opinion soon carried along with it a majority of the members of Congress. Pulitzer had waited before having his newspapers come out in favor of the conflict: he gave up preaching the cause of nonintervention when he realized that war was popular and that the bellicose campaign had increased circulation. Hearst's and Pulitzer's newspapers directly reached 1½ million readers, and through the news agencies their articles fed most of the other papers in the country. Against them, the pacifist press only had 200,000 readers—and it remained faithful to a tradition of sobriety and moderation not calculated to excite the public.

For Hearst, to the contrary, demagoguery remained a favorite weapon. And he struck a master stroke when his correspondents in Havana reported to him in August 1897 the case of a Cuban girl, Evangelina Cosio y Cisneros, jailed by the Spaniards. In the *Morning Journal*, she became the Cuban Joan of Arc, "the Flower of Cuba." And two hundred Hearst correspondents in the United States received an order to elicit the support of American women for the heroine. Very quickly, a petition gathered thousands of signatures which filled twelve columns of the *Journal*. Among the best-known names were those of President McKinley's mother; Mrs. Sherman, wife of the Secretary of State; Mrs. Mark Hanna; the widows of former President Grant and of Jefferson Davis. Irresistibly, the campaign crossed the Atlantic and spread throughout England where a committee, in which Lady Rothschild participated, gathered 200,000 signatures. An appeal was made to Pope Leo XIII, and hundreds of meetings provided a forum for public indignation. The United States Consul in Havana tried to restore the whole affair to its proper proportions, but his voice was not heard. Besides, the exaggerated publicity was reaching its climax: his pockets filled with Hearst dollars, a certain Karl Decker landed in Havana and arranged what complicity was needed for the escape from Cuba of "the Cuban Joan of Arc," who landed in New York on October 13, 1897. Her arrival provoked mass hysteria. After the thundering campaign which had mobilized the women of America, the sensational liberation of "the Flower of Cuba" overheated public opinion to the point where the most peaceful minds were also swept away by the current. Secretary of State Sherman proclaimed that "everyone would sympathize with the *Journal*'s enterprise" and President McKinley himself approved that statement which "correctly voiced the unofficial sentiment of the administration."

The most detestable kind of sensational journalism had succeeded in molding public opinion at the whim of an unscrupulous man who was used to eliminating all obstacles in his path. If he does not conceal a certain admiration for that unique personality, Swanberg rightly notes in the excellent biography that he devoted to him, that Hearst had set a fashion and that he justly "deserves some dubious recognition as a pioneer." [18]

Henceforth, the course of events accelerated. Not anxious to distinguish true from false, transforming the Cuban events into fiction, Hearst had overwhelmed the American public. Without him, Admiral Mahan's theories, Josiah Strong's dangerous missionary dreams, the messianic delirium of Senator Beveridge, the imperialist ambitions of Theodore Roosevelt and of Henry Cabot Lodge would not have triumphed over President McKinley's peaceful intentions. But the President was finally unable to resist the pressure of public opinion stirred up by the Hearst press. In the future, in more or less comparable situations, the popular press would still be called upon, through its creation of a climate of hysteria, heavily to influence Washington's decisions. At the end of the nineteenth century, Cuba was only the first experience of that kind.

The conditions maintained by Spain in Cuba were, however, dramatic enough to exempt Hearst from resorting to demagoguery. For a long time, the colonial regime had proved itself to be "corrupt, tyrannical, and cruel," and each year drained away two-fifths of the island's income. Taxes were too great a burden on both agriculture and the mining industry. Neither life nor property was secure "Any Cuban might be summarily arrested and 'shot while trying to escape,'" an American historian observed, and added: "The Church, which was in the hands of Spanish prelates, was corrupt, inefficient, and out of sympathy with the plain people. Its reactionary hierarchy kept such a strangulating grip upon education that illiteracy was general. A heavy standing army had to be supported by the people. Revolt lay always just underneath the surface; and when a heavy depression, accentuated by an American tariff upon sugar, fell upon the island, the suffering masses could no longer be restrained. The patriot José Martí raised his flag in 1895, and soon the whole country was aflame." [19]

But neither American historians nor Hearst at the time mentioned the real feelings of the Cubans toward the United States. Of course, a whole segment of the Cuban bourgeoisie wished to see the island join the Union. But the "patriots" who rallied around José Martí, "the apostle of Cuba" who landed on April 11, 1895, with five companions to liberate their country, looked upon the United States with profound distrust. "The greatest danger for our America [i.e. Latin America]," wrote José Martí in 1891, "is our formidable neighbor who scorns and does not understand us." A few months later, knowing well that the domination of a distant and weakened Spain was in danger of being replaced by the domination of a young and powerful country very close to Cuba, José Martí felt the need to be specific about Cuba's hopes. "We are not engaging in a search for purity or simplicity that will entail new sacrifices nor do we want to perpetuate in our lives the colonial spirit in the new dress of a Yankee uniform." On the eve of his death, a few months after the insurrection, José Martí clearly envisioned with his soldier's and poet's faith the destiny of his country. He had spent a few years of exile in the United States; he knew the covetousness with which some Americans looked at Cuba, and in a letter which remains his political testament he offered his countrymen the famous warning: "I've lived inside the monster, and know its guts; my weapon is David's." [20]

However, the war continued after Martí's death, rallying an increasing number of Cubans. In the fall of 1896, Spanish General Valeriano Weyler transformed entire cities into concentration camps, and put the technique of "population resettlement" into practice under such conditions that mortality rose shockingly. At the end of 1897 more than half of the 101,000 inhabitants of Havana Province placed in "concentration zones" had died. The Consul General of the United States pointed out at the same time that in the whole of the island some 400,000 women and children were reduced to such poverty that they died daily by the hundreds from hunger and fever. At the beginning of 1898 Spain had 200,000 soldiers in Cuba and did not succeed in stemming the revolutionary tide. The Cuban patriots well knew that victory was within their reach. For American historians, the United States military intervention put an end to Spain's domination. For Cuban patriots that same intervention was only a means of depriving them of a victory which by right belonged to them. The subsequent events show that the United States, while helping to shorten the fighting, prevented the Cubans from obtaining the complete freedom for which they had taken up arms.

President McKinley was still striving not to be drawn into the war. He had some hope in the autumn of 1897, when a more moderate government took power in Madrid. In his message to Congress, in December 1897, McKinley affirmed his intention not to oppose the actions of that government whose "sincerity," he said, "I shall not impugn." And he added, ". . . nor should impatience be suffered to embarrass it in the task it has undertaken."

If American opinion was outraged by the stories—some true, others imaginary—which reached it from Cuba, other motives than the wish to liberate the Cuban people from

Spanish colonialism were going to determine United States entrance into the war. In the struggle which bathed the island in blood, American citizens had to suffer in regard to their persons and their property; some of them lost their freedom, others their lives. As a precautionary measure, the *Maine*, a 24-gun battleship, was sent on a "courtesy visit" to Havana where it cast anchor on January 25, 1898. The Commander and his officers were treated with courtesy by the Spanish authorities, although Madrid had decided to reply to that warning by sending the cruiser *Vizcaya* on a "friendly visit" to New York City. In the meantime, there occurred an incident which greatly irritated McKinley. The Spanish Ambassador to Washington, Dupuy de Lome, wrote a letter to a friend in which he called McKinley a "would-be" politician anxious above all to flatter the feelings of the crowd.[21] That letter fell into Hearst's hands, who hastened to publish it in his newspaper, thus provoking the indignation of the vast majority of Americans. To make amends for that affront to the President of the United States, Madrid immediately repudiated Dupuy de Lome and recalled him.

However, the excitement had not died down when there occurred the catastrophe which was to sweep away any remaining hesitation. On the evening of February 15, 1898, a little after 9 o'clock, a powerful explosion shook the port of Havana: the *Maine* had blown up. In the coded dispatch that he immediately sent to Washington, the battleship Commander recommended calming public opinion "until further report." And he added: "Many Spanish officers now with me to express sympathy." [22] Of 350 men on board, 260 had died. Foreseeing the political consequences of the tragedy, the Spanish General, Blanco, did not hide his anxiety, while his men were striving to save the ninety survivors, in spite of the danger that repeated explosions aboard the *Maine* created. Kennan recalls that "Spanish authorities, as

well as our own consul-general in Havana, had begged us
not to send the vessel there at that time for the very reason
that they were afraid this might lead to trouble. The Spanish government did everything in its power to mitigate the
effects of the catastrophe, welcomed investigation, and
eventually offered to submit the whole question of responsibility to international arbitration—an offer we never accepted." [23]

Thanks to that catastrophe, the circulation of the different editions of the *Journal* passed for the first time the million mark. And Hearst, naturally, had the Commander of
the *Maine* stating that the ship was blown up by a mine. He
even published on a half-page a sketch purporting to show
the position of the mine and the wires which connected it
to the engine room. Theodore Roosevelt, against whom the
Journal had launched fierce attacks when he headed the
New York police, was then Assistant Secretary of the Navy.
He confirmed to anyone who listened that beyond the
shadow of a doubt the battleship had been blown up by a
mine. He and his friends heaped sarcasm on McKinley, saying that the President refused to go to war because he had
"no more backbone than a chocolate éclair." In a highly
publicized interview he said, "It is cheering to find a newspaper of the great influence and circulation of the *Journal*
tell the facts as they exist." [24] In an exchange of courtesies
the *Journal* praised him, contrasting the fiery Roosevelt
with President McKinley, who was shown as a weakling, in
the pay of Wall Street and the great capitalists hostile to
imperialist conquests.

In the meantime, the *Vizcaya* was approaching New
York for its "friendly visit" and Pulitzer's *World*, in order
not to be left behind his competitor, cautioned New York-
ers against the Spanish cruiser which, he wrote, was going to
open fire on their city.

For two months, President McKinley resisted public

clamor which took up the slogan "Remember the Maine." The report submitted to Congress on March 28, 1898, completely absolved Spain of any responsibility whatever in the sinking of the battleship—but the results of the inquiry could not in any way change the attitude of the newspapers determined to obtain a declaration of war. Hearst offered to organize a regiment of the best American sportsmen. The brother of the famous bandit Jesse James was to lead a troop of cowboys. The well-known Buffalo Bill, at the head of a few thousand Indians, would crush the Spaniards. Hearst proposed to equip a cavalry regiment for half-a-million dollars. President McKinley declined the offer but the respectable *Times*, while reiterating its scorn for Hearst's journalistic methods, felt it had to acknowledge that patriotic and generous gesture. And the Navy accepted the use of the Hearst yacht.

However, on March 29, twenty-four hours after sending Congress the report of the inquiry on the *Maine* catastrophe, President McKinley sent Madrid a note requesting an immediate armistice, the liberation of prisoners, and the acceptance of mediation between Spain and Cuba. Madrid's reply did not of course subscribe to these three conditions, but it revealed a major concern: to avoid at all cost a war with the United States. A few days later, on April 9, Cuba's Governor-General proposed an armistice to the insurgents. The same day the United States Ambassador to Madrid, Woodford, sent a dispatch to Washington: if nothing intervened which might humiliate Spain, he was on the point of obtaining Cuba's independence or even the transfer of the island to the United States. On April 10 the Queen of Spain ordered a total armistice on the island. These concessions were so important that they should have been amply sufficient to disarm the warmongers. But President McKinley, desiring not to antagonize an overexcited public and to protect his popularity, was already resigned to giving in.

And so, the next day, April 11, 1898, he sent Congress a message which concealed the Spanish concessions in verbiage about general considerations. In conclusion he stated: "I have exhausted every effort to relieve the intolerable condition of affairs which is at our doors. . . . I await your action." [25] At the end of a week of debate, the Senate by a slim majority of forty to thirty-five voted in favor of the war. McKinley was surprised to discover that the peace partisans were so many. Could he not, by adopting a firmer attitude, have reinforced their camp? But the House's attitude dispelled any illusions: the representatives ratified the Senate vote by 310 to 6 votes. By going with the tide, McKinley had protected his popularity. The United States entered the war. "It was an unnecessary war," writes Hearst's biographer, Swanberg.[26]

It is true that the concessions from Madrid may have come too late, and that the Cuban insurgents were not disposed to accept them. But, according to George F. Kennan, the decision to declare war on Spain must apparently be attributed "to the state of American opinion, to the fact that it was a year of congressional elections, to the unabashed and really fantastic warmongering of a section of the American press, and to the political pressures which were freely and bluntly exerted on the President from various political quarters. It is an interesting fact, incidentally, that financial and business circles, allegedly the instigators of wars, had no part in this and generally frowned on the idea of our involvement in the hostilities." [27]

Indeed, McKinley himself confessed in 1899: "But for the inflamed state of public opinion, and the fact that Congress could no longer be held in check, a peaceful solution might have been had." [28] Most historians confirm that point of view: "The war with Spain could have been avoided. American diplomats handled their affairs with great skill, and Spain for its part went to unusual lengths to avoid hostilities. But the nation looked at its progress since Appomattox, felt a deep pride in its accomplishments, and hoped to prove itself a great international power, able to smash an arrogant, decadent European monarchy. The decisive factor in precipitating the Spanish War was neither political manoeuvering nor diplomatic failure, but popular mood. 'It wasn't much of a war,' said Roosevelt, 'but it was the best we had.' At the same time it marked a definite turning point in United States foreign policy. For the first time America deliberately extended its sovereignty beyond the North American continent. For the first time America accepted control of territories to which it had no intention of granting eventual statehood. And for the first time the United States, in establishing a colonial system, assumed the full responsibility for the future welfare of an alien people." [29]

The slaveowners had coveted the vast lands of South America. Others considered it the "Manifest Destiny" of the United States to occupy the whole of the continent. But in 1898 the anti-imperialist camp remained strong. Fearful of competition, the tobacco and sugar cane producers were opposed to the conquest. They were supported by some trade union leaders, like Samuel Gompers, founder of the American Federation of Labor, who foresaw that annexation of territories would lead to an influx of cheap labor, harmful to the interests of American workers. On the other hand, that possibility was not displeasing to some captains of industry, who saw in it a brake to rising wages and were beginning to be won over to the idea of extending their sphere of activity overseas. The war partisans made Congress adopt a resolution on April 20, 1898, which proclaimed: "It is the duty of the United States to demand, and the Government of the United States does hereby demand, that the Government of Spain at once relinquish its authority and government in the Island of Cuba and withdraw its land and naval forces from Cuba and Cuban waters." To that end, Congress gave the President power "to use the entire land and naval forces of the United States . . . to such extent as may be necessary." An ultimatum was sent to Spain, which had three days to comply with that resolution. "We knew they would not, and could not, accept it," notes George Kennan. Effectively, Madrid on April 21 replied that the Congressional resolution was "the equivalent of a declaration of war" and broke off relations with Washington. Thus, George Kennan adds, "our government, to the accompaniment of great congressional and popular acclaim, inaugurated hostilities against another country in a situation of which it can only be said that the possibilities of settlement by measures short of war had by no means been exhausted." [30]

The anti-imperialists, however, had succeeded in having the following amendment, proposed by Senator Henry Teller, inserted in the resolution: "The United States hereby disclaims any disposition or intention to exercise sovereignty, jurisdiction, or control over said island except for the pacification thereof, and asserts its determination, when that is accomplished, to leave the government and control of the island to its people."

Another resolution, voted on April 25, 1898, declared a state of war. The Army had only 18,000 men: its size was increased to 60,000, and recruitment of 125,000 volunteers was authorized. Transportation facilities were so insufficient that the first American infantrymen landed in Cuba only at the end of June.

The debates in Congress had made no mention of the Philippines: this was "a war for the liberation of Cuba from Spanish dominion—an altruistic, moral war." [31] However, on May 1, one week after the declaration of war, the Pacific fleet, under the orders of Admiral Dewey, arrived in Manila Bay, and, without losing a single man, destroyed the Spanish fleet. A few days later, McKinley authorized the sending of an army of occupation, which in August took over the capital. In order to wrest Cuba from Madrid's control, it may have been necessary to destroy the Spanish Philippine fleet, but not to conquer the country. How and why should the President then go beyond the mission entrusted to him by Congress? George Kennan points out that the elements that could give a fully satisfactory answer to that question are not known. Of course, Theodore Roosevelt, Assistant Secretary of the Navy, had thought of taking over the Philippines for a long time, and had by devious means obtained Admiral Dewey's appointment as head of the Pacific fleet— which makes one think that there existed between them a secret agreement according to which Dewey would enter Manila "regardless of the circumstances of the origin or the purpose of the war." Eventually, President McKinley was to declare that at the time of the battle of Manila he had not at all envisaged the conquest of the Philippines. But then why did he send ground troops? Kennan concluded that "we can only say that it looks very much as though, in this case, the action of the United States government had been determined primarily on the basis of a very able and quiet intrigue by a few strategically placed persons in Washington, an intrigue which received absolution, forgiveness, and a sort of public blessing by virtue of war hysteria." [32]

American troops landed in in Cuba between the 20th and the 25th of June without encountering any resistance. The fighting was far from reaching the scope that the presence of more than 200,000 Spanish soldiers might suggest. In the battles of El Caney and of San Juan, only 1,700 Spaniards confronted 15,000 Americans. On July 3 Admiral Cervera's fleet went to its doom upon leaving its anchorage at Santiago; the Atlantic squadron, under the command of

Admiral Sampson, completely destroyed it. On July 15 the city of Santiago surrendered. Things were even easier on the island of Puerto Rico, which American troops occupied without a fight.

As Spain had asked for peace, President McKinley dictated his conditions on July 30: immediate evacuation and final abandonment of Cuba, surrender of Puerto Rico, as well as the island of Guam in the Pacific, and finally the occupation of the city and port of Manila. A preliminary agreement was signed to that effect on August 12.

"That war," wrote one historian, "was nothing but a military and naval parade due to the large disproportion of forces." [33] And another commented: "It seemed an ideal war. Its casualty lists were short, it cost no great debt, it raised American prestige abroad, and the nation emerged with its pockets full of booty." [34]

Naturally, the campaign gave rise to some historic words, reported by the Hearst and Pulitzer correspondents, which quickly became part of legend before being consecrated in the history books. Accordingly Admiral Dewey is said to have sent the following message before sinking the Manila fleet, "You may fire when ready, Gridley." A grateful nation subsequently offered the Admiral a house in Washington. Captain Philip, on board the *Texas*, while watching a Spanish vessel sink, told his men: "Don't cheer, boys, the poor fellows are dying." During the battle of Santiago, Joe Wheeler, who had been a southern general during the Civil War, exclaimed that a single battle under the Union's Stars and Stripes was worth fifteen years of his life. Of all those who brought back a hero's halo, the greatest prestige attached to Theodore Roosevelt, whose political career was duly served by it.

But, above all, the Spanish-American War taught a lesson to the United States. It had taken two months to transport 18,000 men to Cuba, and that "caused more confusion than conveying two million [men] to France twenty years later." After that experience, the Army and the Navy were strengthened and a permanent General Staff was created for the first time.

Negotiations for the peace treaty opened in Paris on October 1, 1898. Spain was resigned to losing the Philippines, Puerto Rico, and Cuba. The real problem was to determine the fate of the former colonies.

In the Philippines, an insurrection had broken out several years before the Spanish-American War, and José Rizal, the most widely known leader of the revolt, had been executed by the Spaniards in 1896. His successor, Emilio Aguinaldo, who had had to seek exile in Hong Kong, was encouraged by Admiral Dewey, after the destruction of the Spanish fleet and the conquest of Manila, to go back to his country to proclaim a republic. "The obvious thing to do was to turn the Philippines over to the Filipinos." But Admiral Dewey informed Washington that the republic did not have real authority over the whole of the archipelago. It was not possible to give the islands back to the Spaniards. Moreover, the Emperor Wilhelm II had in August sent to Manila a squadron more powerful than Dewey's and even troops, some of which had landed on the Bataan peninsula. The United States, therefore, decided to remain, and in return for a payment of $20 million to Spain, the transfer of the Philippines to the United States was included on December 10, 1898, in the Treaty of Paris. President McKinley hesitated for a long time, but finally, as he told a group of Methodists, he had decided "to take them all and to educate the Filipinos, and uplift and civilize and Christianize them." That last point, at least, had been taken care of by Spain for three centuries. The Americans, for a beginning, only occupied the capital, and Dewey encouraged Emilio

Aguinaldo to organize the fight of Filipinos against Spaniards still present in the archipelago. The Philippine patriots won great military victories, without too many casualties, a situation which encouraged them to protest against
the transfer of their country to the United States. They did
not want to change masters, they were demanding their independence. Not having been able to prevail in his talks
with Dewey, Aguinaldo, on February 4, 1899, triggered another insurrection, this time against the United States. But
the following year he had to find refuge in the mountains,
where he was finally captured in March 1901. One month
later he pledged his allegiance to the United States. In
Washington only a minority opposed annexation. President
McKinley strove to appease his opponents by repeating to
them: "No imperial designs lurk in the American mind.
They are alien to American sentiment, thought and purpose. If we can benefit those remote peoples, who will object? If in the years of the future they are established in
government under law and liberty, who will regret our perils
and sacrifices?" General Arthur MacArthur, Douglas Mac-
Arthur's father, when he was Governor of the Philippines
(1900–1901), also asserted: "The idea of personal liberty
. . . we are planting in the Orient. Wherever the American flag goes, that idea goes. . . . The planting of liberty—
not money—is what we seek." [35] McKinley's anti-imperialist proclamations corresponded to a real conviction: the
United States did not at all want to carve out for itself a
colonial empire in the classic sense, comparable to those of
England or of France, and in fact the Philippines would
become independent at the end of the Second World War.
But from the beginning of the twentieth century, new
means of control were effected. A future President of the
United States, William Howard Taft, from 1901 to 1904
Governor-General of the Philippines, summarized policy in
a slogan which was to have many future adaptations: "The

Philippines for the Filipinos." American investments remained limited, but the archipelago represented an important market for American exporters, and the Philippines became almost entirely dependent on the United States for the sale of sugar, coconut, and hemp. The 1909 treaty, renewed in 1913, created a system of free exchange between the Philippines and the United States, further accentuating their economic dependence. A new orientation emerged when the Democrats, who wanted independence for the Philippines in short order, came back to power with Wilson in 1912. The Filipinos were then in large numbers active in local government and two legislative assemblies were established. Through the Jones Law, the Congress of the United States promised independence in general terms, but rejected the two-year and four-year delays which were then proposed. The first coherent efforts of economic development were then undertaken (creation of the National Bank, railroads, reorganization of agriculture, etc.).

But in Washington the Republican Warren G. Harding succeeded Woodrow Wilson in 1920 and named General Leonard Wood, who had been his unhappy opponent in the race for the Republican nomination, Governor-General of the Philippines in 1921. At the beginning of the Spanish-American War, Wood had joined Theodore Roosevelt's Rough Riders in Cuba; he had become Governor of Santiago and of Oriente Province before becoming Military Governor of Cuba from 1899 to 1902. He then served in the Philippines from 1903 to 1908. As Governor-General of the archipelago, he completely reversed the policy followed by his predecessor and in such a way that he became as unpopular there as he had been in Cuba. Considering the system of self-government inefficient, he terminated most of the experiments that had been recently undertaken, suppressed the State Council of indigenous leaders and imposed—in practice—a direct administration through strict military rule. The conflict which placed him in opposition to responsible local Filipinos became so acute that in 1923 the Philippines cabinet resigned, and in 1925 the Senate of Manila, irritated by Wood's methods, unanimously voted a resolution advocating organization of a referendum on independence. In 1926 an inquiry commission sent there by President Coolidge wrote a report which was a vigorous criticism of Wood's administration. Wood died a year later and was replaced by Henry L. Stimson (1927–1929), former President Taft's Secretary of War (1911–1913). Stimson, who subsequently would become Secretary of State (1929–1933) in the Hoover Cabinet, and Secretary of War (1940–1945), had just performed a delicate mission in Nicaragua, which the Marines had occupied for the second time in several years. Although he pursued General Wood's policies without concessions to Philippine nationalist aspirations and opposed independence, he nevertheless showed more skill than his predecessor and was able to calm the storm somewhat.

However, in the United States the opposition to the colonization of the Philippines grew, essentially for economic reasons. On the one hand, trade unions protested against the free entry granted to Filipino workers into the United States. On the other hand, diverse economic interests, in particular American sugar producers and planters who had invested in Cuba, were complaining of the competition of Philippines products which were entering the domestic market tax free. The pressure exerted in Washington by both sides led Congress to vote a law in 1932 setting Philippines independence for 1945. President Hoover vetoed the document, which was nevertheless adopted by the required majority the following year. But the law, worked out with the cooperation of some important Filipinos, did not win the support of Manuel Quezon, a former comrade of Aguinaldo and head of the Nationalist Party, who voiced two major complaints: First of all, the United States intended to keep naval bases in the Philippines, and second, by becoming independent the archipelago lost free access to the American market. Therefore the Legislative Assembly of Manila rejected the draft, and a new basis for accord had to be found. Under Franklin D. Roosevelt's Presidency, an amended draft was accepted in 1934 without enthusiasm either in Washington or in Manila. The following year, a constitution approved by Roosevelt was ratified by the Philippines in a referendum, and Manuel Quezon became President, twenty-five years after he had submitted the first petition for independence to the Assembly. In principle, the country was to be liberated from American tutelage at the end of ten years on July 4, 1946. In order to prevent too great an economic shock, the Manila government obtained that preferential tariffs only be progressively abolished between that date and 1960.

In Cuba, the hold of the United States manifested itself in a completely different way. The 1898 Teller Resolution asserted the will of Congress "to leave the government and control of the island to its people." [36] After the Spanish surrender the country was first placed under a military occupation regime from 1898 to 1902. General Leonard Wood, who twenty years later was going to abolish self-government in the Philippines, exercised practically absolute power for three years although he had only 6,000 soldiers under his command. Most of the American historians emphasize the beneficent role of that occupation: "The conquest of yellow fever as a result of experiments in Cuba by Dr. Walter Reed and others of the army medical staff was a triumph alone worth the whole cost of the war." [37] Thanks to the initiative of General Wood, "a highly competent and sympathetic military governor," four military surgeons worked under Dr. Walter Reed: "The outstanding features of [this] regime were medical." [38] There are a few authors who, like Samuel Eliot Morison, point out that the victory over disease gained by the Americans crowned the research of a Cuban, Dr. Carlos Finlay. Meanwhile, the United States secured from Cuba the transfer of the Guantanamo base, destined to play a major role in American Caribbean strategy.

Meanwhile, in accord with the Teller Resolution, the United States had to prepare Cuba progressively for independence. A Constituent Assembly met in Havana and adopted in 1901 the constitution of the new republic. But rather phenomenally it was compelled to include in the document an amendment voted by the American Senate. That text, proposed by Senator Orville Hitchcock Platt, stipulated in one of its eight articles that the government of Cuba accords the United States "the right to intervene for the preservation of Cuban independence and the maintenance of a government adequate for the protection of life, property, and individual liberty." This procedure—at the very least unusual—part of an amendment to the Army Appropriation Bill of 1901—raised strong protests not only in Cuba but also among American liberals.

The following year the occupation troops left the country and Tomas Estrada Palma was elected first President of the Cuban republic, although he first had to abandon his American citizenship, adopted during his exile in the Spanish colonial period. In 1906 when the President was trying to have himself re-elected by the conservatives, the liberals revolted and Tomas Estrada Palma invoked the Platt Amendment to request intervention from the United States, whose troops then occupied the country from 1906 to 1909. Thus from the beginning of General Wood's reign to the end of the second military occupation, the United States had a good ten years to settle down firmly in the country. Most American historians believe that the Platt Amendment made of Cuba a "veritable American protectorate." In 1903, under conditions where freedom of choice in Cuba seemed very doubtful, the first reciprocal treaty was signed between Cuba and the United States, granting the United States preferential tariffs with bonuses of from 20 to 40 per cent, with the result that American exports on the Cuban market jumped from 45 to 75 per cent. In return, Cuba enjoyed preferential tariffs for sugar, which the United States bought at the domestic price.

Thus the dreams of American imperialists were realized: according to the wish of Admiral Mahan a powerful naval base was built at Guantanamo, while the island's economy passed under the control of the United States which, besides, had the right of military intervention. American planters cunningly used that period to take over the best land. In 1958, at the time when Fidel Castro's revolutionaries overthrew Batista's dictatorship, eleven American companies controlled 1,181,088 hectares, representing 47.4 per cent of the acreage devoted to sugar cane, the principal Cuban resource. They had all assumed their position during the privileged period at the beginning of the century.

In Puerto Rico the problem was even easier, as the Treaty of Paris determined its pure and simple annexation by the United States. The island was first placed under a regime of military occupation until 1900, when Washington named an American governor. A 1900 law prohibiting a farmer from owning more than two hundred hectares was never put into effect. On the contrary, the lands were sold off to facilitate the cultivation of sugar cane and small farmers were reduced to the status of day laborers. Thirty years later, owners residing in the United States controlled at least 60 per cent of the island's resources. In 1917 Puerto

Ricans gained American citizenship, which permitted them to leave a country where they could no longer earn a living and to emigrate to New York where they constitute a sub-proletariat accepting the least remunerative work.

Guam Island, the most important of the Marianas, became an important base, being directly administered by the Navy Department.

When the Treaty of Paris was submitted to the Senate for ratification, the anti-imperialist Senators started a vigorous campaign as they feared that the principles they had defended in 1898, and which had been translated in particular in the Teller Resolution, would not be respected. Of course this opposition only represented a minority but the treaty had to get a two-thirds vote to be ratified. The move was especially delicate, since the 1900 Presidential election was approaching with McKinley and Theodore Roosevelt as candidates for the Presidency and Vice-Presidency, opposing the Democrats William Jennings Bryan and Adlai E. Stevenson, who had already been Vice-President under Cleveland in 1893–1897. President McKinley emphasized that the treaty's rejection by the Senate would deal a harsh blow to the prestige of the United States. Republicans were going down to certain defeat without Democratic and Populist support. Hence McKinley welcomed Bryan when he, in the name of national honor, asked his supporters to ratify the treaty. The annexation of territories conquered from Spain, McKinley repeated, is "a purely altruistic decision." The President further declared: "The Philippines like Cuba and Puerto Rico were intrusted to our hands by the war, and to that great trust, under the Providence of God and in the name of human progress and civilization, we are committed. . . . We could not discharge the responsibilities upon us until these colonies became ours,

either by conquest or treaty. Our concern was not for territory or trade or empire, but for the people whose interests
and destiny, without our willing it, had been put in our
hands." The draft of the treaty was finally approved by a
majority vote of one on February 6, 1899, with a clause
holding in abeyance the future status of the Philippines
whose annexation the imperialists still hoped to obtain.
And so a year later, January 9, 1900, Senator Beveridge declared before the Senate: "The Philippines are ours forever.
. . . and just beyond the Philippines are China's illimi-
table markets. We will not retreat from either. We will not
renounce our part in the mission of our race, trustee, under
God, of the civilization of the world." [39]

In the Presidential campaign which ensued, apparently
forgetting the very conciliatory proposals made by Spain
two years before, McKinley repeated that "the war with
Spain had been unsought and patiently resisted." The victory over Spain brought to Americans "a new and noble responsibility," while "to ten millions of the human race
there was given a new birth of freedom." Naturally, the
Philippines, under the leadership of Aguinaldo, fought
American troops as they had fought Spanish troops. But the
revolt would be suppressed, promised McKinley, and the
Philippines once pacified would not be long in benefiting
from "the blessings of liberty and civilization."

Although Bryan had favored ratification of the Treaty of
Paris, the Democrats made anti-imperialism one of the
principal planks in their electoral campaign. On that point
they were supported by men as diverse as Thomas B. Reed,
former Republican Speaker of the House, Andrew Carnegie, Mark Twain, the philosopher William James, and
former President Cleveland. The Democratic electorate, as
a whole, was quite proud of the recent victory over Spain.
But Bryan and his friends campaigned for the independence of the Philippines, whose conquest was not envisioned

by the Congressional resolution, and they denounced the "criminal aggression" launched against Aguinaldo's partisans. Only "the greedy commercialism" had been able to inspire this war, a startling manifestation of a dangerous "militarism" which pushed the Republicans to practice a policy of "conquest abroad and intimidation and oppression at home." The Democrats indiscriminately used all sorts of arguments: either the Filipinos would get American citizenship, they said, and that Asiatic contribution would undermine the foundation of United States civilization, or they would become colonized subjects, which was incompatible with the very principles of the Republic. But the Democrats did not want either "to surrender our civilization or to convert the Republic into an empire." [40] At the same time they exploited the scandals of the military administration: uniforms unsuitable to the tropical climate during the Cuban campaign, epidemics which claimed more casualties than Spanish arms, rotten meat supplied to the troops resulting in numerous cases of poisoning, etc.

On their part, the Republicans were carried along by the prestige of military victory and by the euphoria of economic prosperity. Theodore Roosevelt met with great personal success when he stumped the country wearing his wide-brimmed Rough Rider hat. McKinley got 7,219,530 votes against 6,358,071 for his Democratic opponent. The Republicans wanted to interpret that victory as an approval of imperialist policy. In fact, the Democrats remained powerful but they had lost votes in the west where the rise in farm prices had brought a good number of farmers to the Republican side.

President McKinley's second mandate was tragically cut short on September 6, 1901, by two bullets from Leon Czologosz's revolver. The flamboyant Theodore Roosevelt whom Senator Platt had nominated for the Vice-Presidency in the hope of neutralizing him was the new President.

Mark Hanna, whose vast industrial empire and strong personality enabled him to dominate the Republican Party, told Senator Platt: "Now look! That damned cowboy is President of the United States!" [41] At the same time, William Randolph Hearst, the man who had done the most to create a public opinion favorable to the war against Spain, set out on a political career. In 1900 he became chairman of the Democratic National Committee; four years later he was elected to the House of Representatives. But his sights were higher: he aimed at the White House. A multimillionaire, a newspaper tycoon who campaigned against the trusts, he denounced the collusion between the Republican Party and big business. The virulence of the criticism that Hearst had aimed at McKinley led Theodore Roosevelt in his first message to Congress to attack "the reckless utterances of those who, on the stump and in the public press, appealed to the dark and evil spirits of malice and greed, envy and sullen hatred. The wind is sowed by the men who preach such doctrines, and they cannot escape their share of responsibility for the whirlwind that is reaped." These two men who symbolized imperialist policy would subsequently clash on more than one occasion.

"It shall be my aim to continue absolutely unbroken the policy of President McKinley" said the "damned cowboy" on entering the White House.[42] He was 43 years old and a personality who would strongly influence the policies of the United States.

III

―――

From "The Big Stick" to "Dollar Diplomacy"

The young Theodore Roosevelt was made of different stuff from McKinley. He took a starring role in the partisan chorus of expansionism, which uninhibitedly used the most diverse arguments: the economic and strategic advantages of conquest, the civilizing role of the United States, the achievement of the "Manifest Destiny" of a country called upon to play a major role in the history of the world. The dream of grandeur and power found supplementary and probably decisive justification in another consideration: if the United States did not take over the remnants of the Spanish empire, other powers would promptly do so.

During the debate on the ratification of the Treaty of Paris, Roosevelt became the target of a violent diatribe by Senator George F. Hoar of Massachusetts. This Republican, who had broken with his own party and with the government, maintained that the war against Spain violated the principles of the Declaration of Independence and undermined the foundations of the Constitution. He said that the Founding Fathers had never foreseen that their descendants "would be excited by the smell of gun powder and the sound of the guns of a single victory as a small boy by a firecracker on some Fourth of July morning." [1]

Roosevelt was particularly responsive to this form of intoxication to which McKinley, on the contrary, seemed immune. In that respect, Theodore Roosevelt symbolized the feelings of his contemporaries—for none of the arguments of the imperialists sufficed in themselves to explain the hunger for territorial expansion. And, in the perspective of history, George Kennan agreed with Senator Hoar's interpretation when he wrote: "at the bottom of it all lay something deeper, something less easy to express, probably the fact that the American people of that day, or at least many of their more influential spokesman, simply liked the smell of empire and felt an urge to range themselves among the colonial powers of the time, to see our flag flying on distant tropical isles, to feel the thrill of foreign adventure and authority, to bask in the sunshine of recognition as one of the great imperial powers of the world." [2]

However, Theodore Roosevelt was one of the first to regret the annexation of the Philippines. In 1902 he was instrumental in the passage of a law that promised the Philippines progressive autonomy. Although he had the ambition to play a major role in world affairs for himself and for his country, he discovered very quickly that territorial conquests were not necessarily the best instrument for attaining prestige and power.

The big stick that Roosevelt was able to use was, first, the Army, whose strength had been reenforced for the war against Spain; then the Navy, increased by a few ships captured from Spain and which Roosevelt, to show his power, sent on a great cruise around the world in 1908-1909. It was, lastly, an economy whose rapid expansion was shown in the foreign trade figures which had tripled between 1860 and 1900. The industrialization of the country was mirrored in exports which went from $1,370 million to $1,710 million between 1900 and 1910. During the same period, exports of foodstuffs showed a decline (in percentages of the total) of 39.80 per cent to 21.58 per cent—while exports of raw materials rose from 24.81 per cent to 33.57 per cent, semifinished products from 11.18 per cent to 15.66 per cent, and finished products from 24.20 per cent to 29.19 per cent.

But Roosevelt's trump cards were not only economic. While pursuing a progressive domestic policy, which notably included a campaign against trusts and some encouragement of trade unionism, he enjoyed a strong popular support, without which his foreign policy could not have been carried out.

It was in Panama that Theodore Roosevelt made first use of the big stick. During the war against Spain the cruiser *Oregon*, based in San Francisco, took sixty-eight days to reach Cuban waters by way of Cape Horn. Such a long delay was an argument in favor of the construction of a canal through Central America. As the United States was assuming responsibilities in the Caribbean and the Pacific, its fleet had to be able to go rapidly from one ocean to the other. But such a project went contrary to an agreement concluded with Great Britain half a century earlier. In fact, the 1850 Clayton-Bulwer Treaty stipulated that neither of the two countries could "obtain or maintain for itself any exclusive control over the said ship canal." Neither England nor the United States could "occupy, or fortify, or colonize" the Canal Zone. At the time, the treaty represented a clear victory for the United States as it put a brake to British expansion in Central America, especially in Nicaragua. But by the turn of the century, as United States power emerged more clearly, the treaty appeared—on the contrary—as an obstacle to American interests and as a violation of the Monroe Doctrine. Three Secretaries of State vainly tried to have it modified. First, William E. Everts, President Hayes's Secretary of State from 1877 to 1881, forcefully proclaimed that a canal had to be under the exclusive control of the United States. This, at a time when the French project, under the direction of Ferdinand DeLesseps, was

already under way. Then, the same position was taken by
James G. Blaine, President Garfield's Secretary of State in
1881, and by F. T. Frelinghuysen, President Chester A. Arthur's Secretary of State (1881–1886). The latter even succeeded in signing a treaty with Nicaragua authorizing the
United States to build a canal across its territory. It was
clear that the canal would be of great strategic importance
to the United States, which therefore intended to assume
sole control of it and fortify it to ensure its defense—all of
which was prohibited by the Clayton-Bulwer Treaty.

Negotiations were then opened with Great Britain and a
new proposal, signed February 5, 1900, by Secretary of State
John Hay and Lord Julian Pauncefote, Great Britain's Ambassador to Washington, satisfied the American point of
view: it authorized the United States to build and administer the projected canal as long as it was considered neutral
and subject to the same regulations as the Suez Canal by
virtue of the 1888 Convention of Constantinople. The Senate of the United States ratified that draft after insertion of
three amendments according to which (a) the Treaty of
1850 was abolished; (b) the principles of neutrality stated
by the Treaty of Constantinople would not prevent the
United States from adopting measures which it might judge
necessary to ensure its own defense and to maintain order in
the vicinity of the canal; (c) an article allowing other countries to join in the treaty was annulled.

London refused to ratify the amended treaty, and another draft had to be negotiated, the Hay-Pauncefote
Treaty of November 18, 1901, which (a) declared void the
agreement of 1850; (b) authorized the United States to
build the canal and have full control of it; (c) affirmed the
principle of neutrality of the canal under the sole warranty
of the United States, which would assume police powers;
(d) authorized works of fortification; (e) envisioned equal
treatment of ships of all nations.

That agreement came two months after McKinley's

death and Theodore Roosevelt's accession to the Presidency. A private American company had already tried its luck in the interior of Nicaragua but had gone bankrupt. The Hay-Pauncefote Treaty came at the right time, for after nine years of effort, expenditures of $260 million, and the loss of hundreds of lives, Ferdinand DeLesseps also had to give up in 1889. Another American company with a strong lobby in Washington had bought a concession in Nicaragua and wrangled about it with Ferdinand DeLesseps' representatives.

After a close fight and the report from an inquiry commission whose conclusions were supported by Roosevelt, Congress authorized the President to buy the French concession for $40 million on June 28, 1902. The area was territorially part of Colombia, whose representative in Washington signed a treaty on January 22, 1903, granting to the United States, for a period of one hundred years, a zone sixteen kilometers wide in return for $10 million and a yearly payment of $250,000.

In spite of a rather threatening warning from Secretary of State John Hay, Colombia rejected the treaty on August 12, 1903. It objected at the same time to its loss of sovereignty over the Canal Zone and to the agreement concluded between Washington and the French company without its consent. Theodore Roosevelt chose to consider the vote of the Bogotá Parliament an affront; its members, he said, were "greedy and corrupt." In fact Roosevelt seemed very eager to settle the affair before the convening of Congress in December. The French company representatives had to fight for their $40 million. The Panamanians were fearful that the canal might be constructed in Nicaragua, which would deprive them of the profits they hoped to get from it. A coalition of interests was thus activated to force the hand of the Bogotá government. The *Review of Reviews*, published by a friend of Roosevelt's, carried a sensational article

entitled: "What If Panama Should Revolt?" [3] Insurrection
rumors were circulating in Washington. October 19 three
American ships left port and moved toward Panama. On
November 2, their commanders were ordered to seize the
Panama railroad if a revolution broke out and to prevent
any landing of Colombian troops within a radius of thirty-
five kilometers. On November 3, immediately after the
arrival of the cruiser *Nashville* in Colon, the State Department sent the following telegram to the United States
Consul in Panama:

UPRISING ON ISTHMUS REPORTED. KEEP DEPARTMENT
PROMPTLY AND FULLY INFORMED.

The Consul immediately replied:

NO UPRISING YET. REPORTED WILL BE IN NIGHT.

A few hours later the same Consul finally sent the telegram that Washington expected with visible impatience
but without any astonishment:

UPRISING OCCURRED TONIGHT; NO BLOODSHED. GOVERN-
MENT WILL BE ORGANIZED TONIGHT.[4]

As a matter of fact, there was only one casualty, a Chinese killed by an exploding shell. The *Nashville* landed its
Marines. The fire brigade of Panama was transformed into
an "army." A government, created during the night, proclaimed the independence of Panama on November 4. Two
days later, on instructions from Theodore Roosevelt, Secretary of State John Hay recognized the new republic; Bunau-
Varilla, who represented the DeLesseps Company, was
named its Ambassador to Washington, where he was received by Theodore Roosevelt on November 13. The Hay–
Bunau–Varilla Treaty of November 18 took up again the
financial clauses proposed to Colombia a few months earlier. But the concession was made in perpetuity rather than

for one hundred years. The text specified that the United States would exercise its complete sovereignty over the Canal Zone, "To the entire exclusion of the exercise by Panama of any . . . sovereign rights, power and authority." [5]

A few years later, in 1911, Theodore Roosevelt thus commented on his initiative: "If I had followed traditional conservative methods I should have submitted a dignified state paper of probably two hundred pages to Congress and the debate would be going on yet. But I took the Canal Zone and let Congress debate, and while the debate goes on the canal does also." [6]

Roosevelt was reproached by Congress for the "arbitrary procedures" that he had used to remove Panama from Colombian sovereignty. William Howard Taft, who had succeeded John Hay at the head of the State Department, gave this astonishing reply: "I agree that to the Anglo-Saxon mind a titular sovereignty is . . . a 'barren ideality,' but to the Spanish or Latin mind—poetic and sentimental, enjoying the intellectual refinements, and dwelling much on names and forms—it is by no means unimportant." [7]

In order to justify an intervention which wrested Panama from Colombia, the American government invoked the treaty signed by President Polk in 1846, which authorized the United States, in case of any trouble, to send to the Isthmus armed forces which would ensure the functioning of the Panama railroad. The railroad, finished in 1855, had been entirely financed with American capital. At the time it was the fastest and the surest means of transportation from the eastern United States to California, where the gold rush of 1848 was still attracting tens of thousands of pioneers and adventurers who hesitated to run the risk of attacks from Indian tribes in the interior of the country. In New York or New Orleans boats loaded their passengers, who disembarked in Panama, used the railroad to cross the Isthmus, and embarked for the Pacific on another ship which sailed to San Francisco. This railroad which had cost $7 million—and the lives of 12,000 workmen—charged the highest rates for fifteen years, until the first transcontinental railroad was finished in the United States in 1868. Year in and year out it transported more than thirty thousand passengers and all sorts of merchandise, including the mail sent from New York to California. That is to say, it represented a vital interest of the United States. And the private company which ran it, entirely with American capital, was powerful enough to prevent, for almost a century, the construction of a road across the Isthmus which would have been in competition with it. It took the Second World War and the fear, after the attack on Pearl Harbor, that Japan might bomb the canal, for the United States to build a road.

Before escaping, with Washington aid, from Colombian domination, the Panamanians had attempted a good fifty revolutions—approximately one a year. At different times, to protect the railroad the United States landed a few troops by virtue of the treaty signed by Polk, which promptly re-established order and security. But invoking the same treaty to wrest Panama from Colombia in 1903 "flew in the face of international law and morality." [8]

Theodore Roosevelt's attitude was a mass of contradictions. He in turn invoked the treaty signed by Polk to justify his intervention, confessed that he had acted deliberately on his own while Congress was debating the issue, and denied any participation in the affair. It is interesting to note that ever since arguments quite as contradictory have been advanced, including in our own day in relation to crises in Latin America or elsewhere.

Colombia did not easily forget that Theodore Roosevelt's big stick had wrenched Panama from it, and strove to obtain reparations. Finally, in 1914 under Wilson's Presidency, at the time the canal opened for traffic, the United States offered it an indemnity of $25 million. That was a little balm for a wound that would not so easily heal, either in Colombia or in the other countries of South America. But the treaty would only be ratified seven years later, in 1921, and Colombia would then recognize the independence of Panama.

Meanwhile another difficulty arose with Great Britain. In 1912 the United States passed the Panama Canal Act, which exempted from the toll all American ships that passed through the canal while traveling between the eastern and western United States. London protested, because the law violated both the Hay-Pauncefote Treaty and the Convention of Constantinople, both of which guaranteed equality of treatment to ships of all countries. The settlement of that dispute also had to wait for Wilson who, in 1914, would persuade Congress to abrogate the exemption clause.

"I believe in power," Theodore Roosevelt had stated. He was always very careful, in his own words, not to "take a step in foreign policy unless I am assured that I shall be able eventually to carry out my will by force." [9] That is to say, on occasion, using the big stick.

Having resulted in the construction of an American railroad in Panama to facilitate access to California in the middle of the century, the gold rush exacerbated the problem of Alaska's boundaries which, not defined clearly by the 1825 Anglo-Russian agreement, had been contested since the purchase of Alaska by the United States in 1867. The discovery of gold deposits in the Yukon (1897–1900), in Alaska, and then in British Columbia gave rise to a sharp controversy concerning the frontier between the last two territories. During the preceding decade, two disputes— about fishing rights in the Bering Straits and in Newfoundland—had been settled through arbitration and to the satisfaction of the British in Canada. But this time the stakes were higher and in spite of the recourse to arbitration the conclusion was to be different. The United States wanted to move the borders some fifty kilometers toward the east; Great Britain refused. Theodore Roosevelt decided in 1903 to submit the dispute to an arbitration tribunal made up of six "impartial jurists—three American and three British." The Senate accepted the arbitration proceeding only after having received assurances from the White House that the three American judges would show great firmness. Their selection quieted all fears as it included Elihu Root, the former Secretary of War under McKinley and future successor of Hay as head of the State Department (1905–1909), who would receive the Nobel Peace Prize in 1912 but always sided with the most conservative Republicans and those most closely tied to big business; Senator Henry Cabot Lodge, one of the prophets of imperialism; and George Turner, former Senator from Washington. On the other side were two Canadians and an Englishman, Lord Chief Justice Alverstone. The vote of the latter was therefore to decide the majority. Then, as Henry Steele Commager writes, "Roosevelt, intent upon winning, waved the big stick." [10] With Supreme Court Justice Holmes, as intermediary, Roosevelt informed the British government of his unshakable determination that the United States would have to prevail "by armed force" if the arbitration tribunal did not rule for the American position. Lord Alverstone received instructions from his government to vote with the Americans in order to spare Anglo-American friendship, at all costs, especially since Germany's naval power was growing. And the American viewpoint won, four votes to two.

Another vigorous intervention permitted Roosevelt to prevail over London, this time with regard to Venezuela's debts to several European powers. In 1895 Roosevelt had warmly approved President Cleveland's firmness toward England in its dispute with Venezuela over the boundaries of British Guiana. On this occasion, in a letter to Senator Henry Cabot Lodge, he had expressed the wish for a war against Great Britain, in order to drown the clamors of the pacifist clique. The Secretary of State was then Richard Olney, former counsel for the railroad companies, providentially named Attorney General (1893–1895) at the time of the Chicago railroad strike, which he broke by bringing in troops and sending the union leader, Eugene V. Debs, to jail. Leaving that post for the State Department, Richard Olney was the author of a threatening letter sent to London apropos the border dispute between Venezuela and British Guiana. In that message, taking the form of an ultimatum, Richard Olney asserted: "Today the United States is practically sovereign on this continent, and its fiat is law upon the subjects to which it confines its interposition." A compromise was eventually reached, but to this day, Venezuela has not ceased to contest the 1899 agreement and claims a very sizable portion of British Guiana.

Passions raised by this affair were hardly beginning to cool off when in 1902 Great Britain, Germany, and Italy decided to organize a joint naval expedition to compel Venezuela to pay its debts to their respective nationals. In his own words, Theodore Roosevelt was quite willing "to let the European nations give a trouncing" to Latin American countries which deserved it, but intervention from British, German, and Italian ships violated the Monroe Doctrine. That, Roosevelt could not accept, although his relations with the Venezuelan President had been very poor. He therefore brought pressure upon London, which agreed without difficulty to withdraw its ships, then on Germany which finally resigned itself to do the same. Theodore Roosevelt refused to act as mediator, but he succeeded in having the matter submitted to the International Court of Justice at The Hague, which reduced the European powers' claims from $40 million to $8 million.

The incident is of interest, both legally and politically. The "Calvo Doctrine," named after the Argentine jurist-diplomat, stated the principle that a foreigner must submit his claims to the judiciary of the country in which he operates, rather than try to obtain reparations through a diplomatic intervention. In 1902 the Argentine Minister of Foreign Affairs, Luis Maria Drago, protested the action taken by the European powers, asserting that no country should have recourse to armed force to compel an American country to pay its debts. The "Drago Doctrine" was not accepted either by the 1906 Pan-American Congress, or by the 1907 Conference of The Hague, which agreed with the proposal made by the American diplomat Horace Porter: no nation was to forcibly oblige a weaker nation to pay its debts prior to the submission of the dispute to arbitration, and until this procedure has failed through the fault of the debtor. But it is in the political field that the consequences of the Venezuelan affair were to be singularly meaningful. At first, Theodore Roosevelt had expressed satisfaction at England's and Germany's acceptance of the decision of The Hague tribunal, which cut their financial claims by four-fifths. These two countries, he said, "kept with an honorable good faith" their intention not to violate the Monroe Doctrine.[11] But in his 1904 annual message, Roosevelt extended the Monroe Doctrine a final step by formulating the following "corollary": "If a nation shows that it knows how to act with reasonable efficiency and decency in social and political matters, if it keeps order and pays its obligations, it need fear no interference from the United States. Chronic wrongdoing, or an impotence which results in a general loosening of the ties of civilized society, may in America, as elsewhere, ultimately require intervention by some civilized nation, and in the Western Hemisphere the adherence of the United States to the Monroe Doctrine may force the United States, however reluctantly, in flagrant cases of such wrongdoing or impotence, to the exercise of an international police power." [12]

The South American countries had hoped that the Drago Doctrine would be a "corollary" of the Monroe Doctrine, which would have protected them from armed interventions of foreign powers. In fact, following the very logic of the Monroe Doctrine and in its name, the United States proclaimed the "Roosevelt Corollary," which justified United States armed intervention under the pretext of re-establishing order and justice. With the Spanish-American War and the military occupation of Cuba, the United States asserted its right, under the Platt Amendment, to intervene in Cuba. Without any war, and occasioned by a minor crisis provoked by some Venezuelan debts, the right of intervention was solemnly extended to all of Latin America. Or, more precisely, through a simple unilateral declaration, the United States arrogated that right to itself. But it is true that through Richard Olney's pen nine years earlier, President Cleveland had let Great Britain and the whole world know that the United States was now "practically sovereign" on the continent and that its will was law. To prevent the European powers from finding cause to intervene in Latin America, the United States would itself intervene—invoking a need to safeguard law and order. It set itself up as judge of the Latin American countries' conduct and as policeman of the continent, which in the event would permit it to protect and extend its interests in the hemisphere. As a logical progression of that action, it would half a century later become the policeman of the world.

With the "Roosevelt Corollary," the United States assumed the rights and undertook the mission which would permit it to intervene at will on the whole of the American continent. In this manner it completed to its advantage the doctrine proclaimed by President Monroe December 2,

1823, and invoked by President Kennedy in 1962 during the international crises triggered by the installation of Soviet missiles in Cuba. Rarely quoted, this declaration, 140 years old, had never ceased to be applied by Washington. According to Nikita Khrushchev in 1960, "now the remains of this Doctrine should best be buried, as every dead body is, so that it does not poison the air by its decay." But his appeal had no chance of being heard in Washington, where only a few people like Mrs. Eleanor Roosevelt considered the Monroe Doctrine "out of date." On the contrary, Senator Kenneth Keating declared that it is the "cornerstone of American foreign policy." A Democratic Congressman from Texas, O. C. Fisher, wrote to President Kennedy requesting him to order a naval blockade of Cuba in the name of the Monroe Doctrine. Senator Dodd, Democrat from Connecticut, intervened in the same vein, while Spruille Braden, former Under Secretary of State for Latin America, advocated a military invasion of Cuba by reason of the same document. Former President Truman did not miss the chance to accuse his Republican successor in the White House: "The reason we're in trouble in Cuba is that Ike didn't have the guts to enforce the Monroe Doctrine." Senator Prescott Bush of Connecticut proposed an amendment which would clearly let Moscow know "that the Monroe Doctrine is not dead, but remains an integral part of American foreign policy." Innumerable declarations of the same kind echoed in the Senate, in the House of Representatives, and on television. And *Time* magazine commented: "In the flux of history, the most earnest pronouncements tend to be ephemeral. The archives of nations are stuffed with decrees, declarations, edicts, enunciations, protocols and pronouncements that were meant to resound for decades but lasted only for weeks or months. Yet the Monroe Doctrine lives on in the hearts and minds of Americans." [13]

In truth, a good many Americans have completely forgotten the Monroe Doctrine, or the interpretation that they give it is not correct. But it flourishes to the extent that it has remained a useful tool in the interest of the United States for a century and a half.

As the legal basis for the American reaction to the installation of Soviet missiles in Cuba, the Monroe Doctrine is a good illustration of the methods of the empire. Remarkably enough, from the beginning of the nineteenth century, even before embarking on its imperialist venture, the United States had shown the scope of its ambition and the extent of its interests by proclaiming a "doctrine." Enlargement of the empire and confrontation with Communism would give birth to other "doctrines" concerning other parts of the world. Indeed, Monroe's gesture would be imitated 124 years later when the "Truman Doctrine" would assert the will of the United States to protect Greece and Turkey against Communism, then again when the "Eisenhower Doctrine" would play the same role in the Middle East. That astonishing continuity justifies an examination in depth of the conditions under which the Monroe Doctrine was born.

A Captain when nineteen years old, Lieutenant Colonel when twenty-one, young Monroe was recognized by George Washington as "a brave, active and sensible officer." He was elected to the Senate when he was thirty-two years old, then was sent to Paris by Washington as United States Ambassador, but he fell into disgrace because he advocated a Franco-American alliance when the United States had intended to remain neutral between France and England. Monroe was next elected governor of Virginia and then in 1803 Thomas Jefferson sent him to Paris to negotiate navigation rights on the Mississippi and he arrived in France in time to participate in the negotiations which led to the Louisiana Purchase. His career continued brilliantly, he became Secretary of State at the same time that he headed the War Department and then was elected President in

1816, and re-elected in 1820 by 231 electoral votes against a single one for John Quincy Adams, who became his Secretary of State. In 1822 the United States was the first power to recognize the new Latin American nations which had just freed themselves from Spanish colonialism.

That same year, the United States was disturbed by two European moves. Czar Alexander I proclaimed Russia's right to part of the Pacific coast, from Alaska, which then belonged to Russia, and neighboring waters to the 51st parallel at the northern tip of Vancouver Island. On instructions from Monroe, John Quincy Adams informed the Russian Ambassador to Washington that the United States: "should contest the right of Russia to any territorial establishment on this continent, and that we should assume distinctly the principle that the American continents are no longer subjects for any new European colonial establishments." The Secretary of State wrote to the United States Ambassador to Russia: "There can, perhaps, be no better time for saying, frankly and explicitly, to the Russian government, that the future peace of the world, and the interest of Russia herself, cannot be promoted by Russian settlements upon any part of the American continent."

In the fall of 1822 at the Verona Congress, France and the powers of the Holy Alliance (Russia, Austria, and Prussia) decided to intervene in Spain where a revolution had forced Ferdinand VII, called Ferdinand the Undesired, to accept a liberal constitution. In 1823 Louis XVIII sent an army across the Pyrenees to help Ferdinand restore absolute power. The United States feared that the Verona powers might next attack the former Spanish colonies in America. London proposed to Washington a joint Anglo-American declaration warning the European powers against any attempt to reconquer Spanish America. The United States made one condition: that England first recognize the independence of the former Spanish colonies. Faced with that firmness, London withdrew. President Monroe, his Secretary of State noted, was "alarmed" when the French forces took Cadiz, last stronghold of the revolutionaries, and the Secretary of War, Calhoun, was "perfectly moonstruck." Monroe then realized that it was high time for the United States to ask Europe to leave the whole of the American continent alone. His Secretary of State, Adams, rejoiced in that decision, for he believed that it was "more candid as well as more dignified to avow our principles explicitly to Russia and France" rather than intervene in the wake of the British who, in any case, seemed hesitant. Thus came into being the famous Monroe Doctrine.

By what means? Adams urged that a message be transmitted by normal diplomatic channels to France and Russia. But President Monroe preferred a solemn declaration integrated into his State of the Union message. The first part was aimed at Russia's claims on the Pacific coast: "The occasion has been judged proper for asserting, as a principle in which the rights and interests of the United States are involved, that the American continents, by the free and independent condition which they have assumed and maintain, are henceforth not to be considered as subjects for future colonization by any European powers."

The second part of the State of the Union message was concerned more specially with the designs that the European powers could have on Latin America. Pointing to the difference between American democracy and the monarchic structure of the countries of the Holy Alliance, Monroe remarked that "the political system of the allied powers" was "essentially different" from that of America, and that the United States was dedicated to defend its own system. Then he continued: "We owe it, therefore, to candor and to the amicable relations existing between the United States and those powers to declare that we should consider any attempt on their part to extend their system to any portion of this hemisphere as dangerous to our peace and safety. . . . It is impossible that the allied powers should extend their political system to any portion of either continent without endangering our peace and happiness; nor can anyone believe that our southern brethren, if left to themselves, would adopt it of their own accord. It is equally impossible, therefore, that we should behold such interposition in any form with indifference." [14]

President Monroe then firmly asked the European powers not to intervene in America, but in the same message, as a balance to his ultimatum, he reaffirmed the neutrality policy inaugurated by George Washington and pledged not to intervene in European affairs. He declared in particular: "In the wars of the European powers in matters relating to themselves we have never taken any part, nor does it comport with our policy to do so. It is only when our rights are invaded or seriously menaced that we resent injuries or make preparations for our defense." [15]

The Monroe Doctrine thus consists of inseparable components: no European intervention in America and no American intervention in Europe. It has never been ratified by any vote of the United States Congress. Even more importantly it has never been submitted for approval to the Latin American countries. By a unilateral act the United States established a doctrine that served its national interest and which it intended to apply to the whole of the continent. When he compared the European monarchies with American democracy, Monroe forgot that in 1823 Mexico and Brazil were monarchies, not republics. In the same way the United States will, henceforth, forget that the regimes it protects in Latin America are not necessarily democracies. But dictatorships at least as tyrannical as the monarchies of Louis XVIII and Alexander I are acceptable to it in Latin America as long as they remain under its control and do not fall under the influence of a European power.

The Marquis de Lafayette enthusiastically saluted the
Monroe Doctrine, against which, naturally, Metternich and
Czar Alexander directed their sharpest criticism. At that
time the United States did not have any military or naval
force capable of enforcing it. Such indeed was no longer the
case when President Kennedy invoked the Monroe Doctrine in 1962 in his efforts to compel the U.S.S.R. to remove the missiles it had installed in Cuba. However, at that
time, there clearly arose the strictly legal question of the
validity of a doctrine of which one component had been
abandoned; when contrary to Monroe's commitments, the
United States intervened not only in Europe, but also in
Asia and elsewhere in the world where it believed its intervention necessary, was it still justified in opposing any European intervention on the American continent? At the beginning, the Monroe Doctrine was a principle which the
United States did not have the means to enforce while a
century and a half later the United States commanded the
force to apply a doctrine that had become devoid of principle.

But meanwhile the doctrine played its role in the service
of United States policy. While in the throes of its Civil
War Spain re-established its control in the Dominican Republic in 1861 at the invitation of the President of that
country, and in 1863 France installed Maximilian in
Mexico. But those two adventures ended in 1865 and 1866
and indeed the doctrine did not prevent England from taking over the Falkland Islands claimed by Argentina and
part of British Honduras claimed by Guatemala. Those territories, however, were sparsely populated and considered
unimportant. The Monroe Doctrine has therefore effectively discouraged European powers from recolonizing
Latin America, which has remained wide open to the dominant influence of the United States.

This doctrine Theodore Roosevelt put in its final form by

distorting it. As a result of his "Corollary" to oppose all military interventions on the part of European powers anxious to collect payment from their debtors, the United States took the right to intervene upon itself in operations it would learn to turn to very great profit.

The first victim of the "Roosevelt Corollary" was the Dominican Republic. In that debt-ridden country, the corruption of the administration rendered any hope for the repayment of creditors unrealistic. The situation worsened after the death of President Heureaux (1899); so much so that in 1904, the same year that Theodore Roosevelt enunciated his "Corollary," Santo Domingo could not pay the interest on its debt. European powers protested but they were careful not to organize a naval expedition to obtain satisfaction as they had done two years earlier against Venezuela.

It was, however, by invoking the fear of an imaginary European intervention that Roosevelt decided to act. He concluded an agreement with the Dominican government (1905) granting to the United States charge of the finances of the country and the management of its debt. To that end, the United States took over the control of customs whose receipts were divided thus: 45 per cent to the Dominican Republic and 55 per cent for the repayment of foreign creditors. Such a system was the easier to implement since the United States represented the most important market to which Santo Domingo sold its principal product —sugar. By the same token, American interests took control of "the financial affairs of the country, one-third of the sugar industry, and other important resources." [16]

In 1907 Roosevelt tried to replace the 1905 agreement with a formal treaty. The Senate of the United States rejected the treaty, but Roosevelt nonetheless applied its principal clauses. While the Senators accused him of violating the Constitution, of trampling on the prerogatives of the legislative arm, and of openly scorning the members of Congress as well as the Dominican people, Roosevelt retorted that he himself intended to guide the foreign policy of the United States and he named an American as Customs Director in Santo Domingo. A year later, in 1908, the firm of Kuhn, Loeb & Co. of New York paid the debt ($20 million) and it was understood that the United States would receive 50 per cent of the Customs duties until repayment was completed.

In appearance, the Dominican Republic enjoyed full and complete sovereignty. It did not become a colony, not even a protectorate of the United States. Theoretically it kept its political independence but it was an independence made meaningless by the control Washington exercised over its financial resources.

Thus was born a particularly daring form of what no one yet called "neocolonialism." The system was profitable, as it did not result in the financial burden of direct colonization such as was then practiced by Great Britain and by France. The sovereignty of the Dominican Republic was no longer anything but a fiction. The reality of power belongs to whoever controls the finances and the economy of a country. An original formula for domination was born under the guise of democracy and self-determination. Financially advantageous, sparing the dominating power from being taxed with "colonialism," the Dominican experiment would be repeated in other Caribbean countries; half a century later it would be sufficiently perfected to be extended to other continents. Economic imperialism had shyly taken its first steps in the Dominican Republic.

Was an old dream, cherished by President Grant less than a century ago, about to be realized? In fact, only one Senate vote had prevented the White House from annexing the Dominican Republic in 1869. The affair, nonetheless, had been masterfully conducted by an adventuress who enjoyed the strongest support in Washington. That extraordinary woman had been a spy in Mexico and supported several uprisings in Cuba before her marriage to General William Cazneau. In 1862, with the help of Colonel Joseph W. Fabens, the couple founded the American West Indies Company in New York, which attracted immigrants for the exploitation of the natural wealth of the Dominican Republic. At the beginning of 1866, hardly recovered from the wounds he had sustained during the successful attempt made on President's Lincoln's life, Secretary of State Seward made an official visit to Santo Domingo, where the Cazneaus convinced him to annex the country. Although Congress had rejected his proposal to name General Cazneau United States Ambassador to the Dominican Republic, Seward remained in close contact with the two adventurers. In 1869 President Grant sent one of his close advisers, General Orville Babcock, to the island to study the possibilities of annexation. His conclusions, favoring the Cazneaus' wishes, were approved by Grant, who, the following year, even sent ships to protect the Dominican Republic from a possible aggression launched from Haiti. With that threat eliminated, the annexation treaty was negotiated between Grant and President Buenaventura Baez who, overthrown by three revolutions (1853, 1858, and 1866), was governing the country for the fourth time. A plebiscite was then organized to approve the treaty. Pressures and threats dispensed by President Baez were so effective that he had to stuff the boxes himself with a dozen ballots against annexation, in order to give the impression that voting had been entirely free. But to successfully complete the deal, it was still necessary to win the approval of the Senate of the United States, where the treaty was favorably considered by the southerners. The opposition was vigorously led by Senator Charles Summer, who won the support of a majority, and the treaty was rejected. Most of the Senators had understood that the transaction would have covered up the Cazneaus' shady operations at a time when several scandals tarnished General Grant's administration. That distant episode deserves to be recalled only because it brings to light the role played by adventurers, shows that the Senate can block the expansionist plans of the Executive, and finally because the affair suddenly rose from its ashes in 1960. General Arturo Espaillat, former head of secret services under the Trujillo dictatorship (1930–1961) revealed that during that period, an American Senator, having come into possession of certificates obtained a century earlier by the Cazneaus, tried to claim for himself the rights of the American West Indies Company. The claimant surrendered the documents when Trujillo had him billed for the arrears on the company's taxes.[17]

The attempt at annexation had failed, but in 1908 the United States, controlling customs and finances, kept a tight rein on the country without having to pay the price of a direct occupation, and without openly exposing itself to the accusation of colonialism. Revolutions, however, were constantly breaking out in the Dominican Republic, and made repayment of the debt to the European countries which Kuhn, Loeb & Co. of New York had redeemed increasingly more problematical. The "Roosevelt Corollary," in whose name the government in Washington opposed the intervention of European powers, thus risked becoming very costly. Trying to put an end to that embarrassing situation, Taft compelled the President of the Dominican Republic to resign in 1912, and Wilson ordered a landing of Marines under Caperton's command in 1916. The following year, a military occupation regime headed by Vice-Admiral Thomas Snowden was officially inaugurated in the Dominican Republic and continued until 1924. After the departure of American troops, President Horacio Vasquez held power in principle while the reality of it belonged more

and more to the Army's Chief of Staff, Rafael Leonidas
Trujillo Molina. In 1918, two years after the beginning of
the American occupation, Trujillo had enlisted in the National Guard, a corps of mercenaries entrusted with the
search for guerrillas who were fighting the Marines. In 1924,
as the last American was leaving, Lieutenant-Colonel Trujillo became, thanks to his protectors, head of the National
Guard, replacing Commandant Lora who had been mys-
teriously assassinated. Four years later, Trujillo, then thirty-
seven years old, was named Chief of Staff of the Army. In
1930 he succeeded Horacio Vasquez to the Presidency of
the Republic: The number of votes he received was greater
than the number of registered voters. When opposition
arose it was brutally repressed. One of the bloodiest dictatorships in South America maintained order in the Dominican Republic until May 30, 1961, when Trujillo himself was assassinated.

The Marines had occupied and administered the country
for eight years, leaving it in the hands of a "strong man"
whose training and rapid promotion in the military hierarchy they had ensured. "Trujillo has steadily cultivated the
friendship of the United States" the *Columbia Encyclopedia* observes without irony.[18] As for the control of Customs,
initiated in 1905, it continued for sixteen years after the departure of the Marines, until September 24, 1940, when an
agreement was concluded between Trujillo and Cordell
Hull, Franklin D. Roosevelt's Secretary of State. Before, as
after, that date, the dictator considered the country his personal property,[19] thus building an enormous fortune which
paid for his personal publicity in the United States, either
in the form of laudatory articles in the American press, or
speeches from American political figures completely devoted to his cause.

·   ·   ·

Having succeeded to the Presidency in 1901 after President McKinley's assassination, Roosevelt was elected three years later with a larger margin than that of his predecessor. His famous name got him 7,628,834 votes against 7,219,530 for McKinley in 1900. The Democrats had abandoned William Jennings Bryan, who had already met with two failures in 1896 and in 1900, replacing him with the very conservative New York judge, Alton Parker. The unionist Eugene V. Debs, who had converted to socialism while in prison, took populist votes away from the Democrat Parker who only got 5,084,491 votes as against 6,538,071 for Bryan in 1900.

Theodore Roosevelt thus found himself firmly in the saddle, powerful enough to brush off the criticisms that his adversaries launched against his "imperialist policy." His skill and his vigor in the Panama Canal affair, the firmness with which he opposed European interventions in South America, his dynamic foreign policy—all succeeded in earning him a great deal of sympathy and warm admiration in the public's eye. Domestically he inaugurated a "progressive" policy which gained him considerable popular support, and which after him would be applied by Presidents Taft and Wilson, and then in another style by John F. Kennedy and Lyndon Johnson. If he encouraged the rich to become richer, he also promised fair treatment to workers and farmers.

That Square Deal, which foreshadows the New Deal of Franklin Roosevelt and the Fair Deal of Harry Truman, was not an empty word. In 1902, the year after his coming to the White House, Theodore Roosevelt had to face a grave social crisis: the strike of the Pennsylvania coal miners. He gathered in conference the union heads and the mineowners—the former requesting arbitration from the President; the latter asking him to break the strike by force. Roosevelt could have sent the Army against the strikers, as

Cleveland had done eight years earlier during the railroad strike. Instead he decided, very skillfully, to publish the conference proceedings, and popular discontent obliged the owners to yield.

Such moves contributed strongly to the development of trade unions whose membership went from 868,000 to 2 million in four years. From 1880 to 1900 the average work week for an American worker had been reduced from sixty-four to sixty hours, but during the same period of time from 1900 to 1920 it would drop to forty-nine hours, thanks to the increased power of the unions and to encouragement from Roosevelt.

The social and economic problems gave rise to reform movements which inspired both the famous novel *The Jungle* by Upton Sinclair (1906) and the career of the Progressive, Robert LaFollette, who, in 1900, took control of Wisconsin from the Republicans. By denouncing the corruption of the local powers or the methods by which great enterprises acquired excessive political power, the newspapers widened their audience and politicians increased their prestige. Their targets were Standard Oil, as well as the Southern Pacific Railroad in California and insurance companies in New York. Neither Cleveland nor McKinley had invoked the Sherman Antitrust Law of 1890 against dumping, thanks to which John D. Rockefeller had managed to ruin his competitors and been able to pay 40 per cent dividends; likewise they had remained indifferent to the concentration effected by E. H. Harriman in the railroads or by J. P. Morgan. It was in 1901, the year Roosevelt entered the White House, that a new trust and one of the most powerful was born: the United States Steel Corporation with a capital of $1,400 million. Theodore Roosevelt felt powerless before that gigantic organization; he unceasingly urged a stronger antitrust law, which would only be voted in 1914 during Wilson's Presidency.

But meanwhile he tried to limit the excesses. The Supreme Court ruled for him in 1902 against the Northern Securities Company by which Hill, Morgan, and Harriman controlled four of the six transcontinental railroads. In 1906 he succeeded in obtaining a law for the regulation of freight rates. The same year, he had Congress vote the Pure Food and Drug Act, which imposed a minimum hygiene in the preparation and distribution of foodstuffs. The abuses of the forest exploiters who built enormous fortunes by dangerously deforesting the country were also curbed. The discovery of the Sugar Trust scandal which had robbed the Customs of $4 million by falsifying weights permitted Roosevelt to denounce "the speculative folly and flagrant dishonesty of a few men of great wealth." [20]

Naturally, like others after him, Roosevelt was accused of socialist tendencies and to such a point that the New York *Sun*'s publisher prohibited even the mention of his name in the columns of his newspaper. As later with John F. Kennedy, he was the idol of the young, cultivated the friendship of artists and scholars, and knew how to communicate his personal enthusiasm to crowds. Consequently his great popularity was not solely founded, far from it, on the vigor of his diplomacy. Rather, his progressivism in domestic affairs contributed to his popularity by ensuring indispensable support for his big-stick policy. His progressivism and imperialism thus sprang from the same spirit, fed on the same national dynamism and received in a somewhat contradictory way the same approbation. "While reforming the domestic social order, he wished America to flex her muscles and assert her strength abroad, as a world power. He seems to have had no vision of a new world order, but . . . did intend to make a strong, well-armed America a guarantor of world peace. Thus his place in history is that of the first of four presidents—himself, Wilson, the other Roosevelt, and Kennedy—who worked out a coherent domestic and foreign policy to meet the realities of the twentieth century."

Among these realities the most pressing were in the American hemisphere. Under Theodore Roosevelt's Presidency the United States took over some lands in Guatemala while the Northern Railway Company, an affiliate of the United Fruit Company, took control of the Costa Rica railroads thanks to the support from the United States legation there. The same year Mr. Squiers, the United States Ambassador to Cuba, tried unsuccessfully to dissuade the Cuban Senate from ratifying an Anglo-Cuban commercial treaty. On November 14, 1905, in the Isle of Pines, an integral part of Cuban national territory, three hundred American residents, owners of land and citrus plantations, tried to repeat the attempt which had worked so well in Hawaii a dozen years earlier. They fomented a revolution, declared that the Isle of Pines was separated from Cuba, and proclaimed its adhesion to the United States. They sent a delegation to Washington to have their decisions ratified. United States Ambassador Squiers requested the Cuban authorities to abandon the island and, in a telegram to Washington, asked that naval forces be sent to support his annexation plan. The Havana government, determined not to yield, declared him *persona non grata,* and the Ambassador was recalled on November 29. This operation had lasted only fifteen days, but the following year President Tomas Estrada Palma, faced with an insurrection of Cuban liberals, invoked the Platt Amendment to ask the United States to intervene. The country was then militarily occupied from 1906 to 1909 and Secretary of War Taft, accompanied by Under Secretary of State Robert Bacon, paid an official visit to Havana where he proclaimed himself "Governor-General of the Republic of Cuba."

Elihu Root, who had succeeded Hay as Roosevelt's Secretary of State, in 1908 justified United States intervention in Central America, "each time that the American capital invested in these countries is threatened." Such justifications were meaningless for the majority of Americans. They were especially aimed at foreign public opinion and more especially at Latin America, where hostility toward "Yankee Imperialism" was growing.

Had he chosen to seek a new mandate in 1908, Roosevelt, then fifty years old, would have been easily re-elected, especially since the Democrats—disappointed with the experiment they had tried with Judge Parker—had returned to their old candidate William Jennings Bryan. Though there is no doubt that Roosevelt's impetuosity had increased the number of his opponents, he remained popular. He had pursued the "open door" policy (see Chap. IV) toward China, inaugurated by John Hay in 1899. He had personally played the mediator in the Russo-Japanese War which was ended by the Treaty of Portsmouth (New Hampshire) on September 5, 1905. Two years later he had skillfully settled a dispute which had led the United States to the brink of war with Japan when racial segregation was introduced into the Los Angeles schools. Roosevelt had convinced the Mayor of the city to reverse his decision and at the same time he had obtained the assurance that Tokyo would discourage emigration. In 1908, through the Root-Takahira agreement, the United States and Japan pledged to maintain the status quo in the Pacific. In 1908–1909 Roosevelt displayed United States might to the world when he sent the Navy on an extensive tour of Latin American, Australian, New Zealand, and Japanese ports. In 1906, thanks to his good offices, the Algeciras Conference put a temporary end to the Moroccan crisis. But that last success was only partial, for, although the Senate ratified the Algeciras Conference, it affirmed, in an amendment similar to the Monroe Doctrine, that the role played by the United States in the situation strayed from "the traditional American foreign policy which forbids participation by the United States in the settlement of political questions which are entirely European in their scope." Congress, therefore, seemed reserved toward certain initiatives of Theodore Roosevelt, especially since his policy of prestige did not correspond with tangible benefits for the country. For instance, his role in the Algeciras Conference was much less approved than the manner in which he had taken over the Panama Canal. The Senate noticeably kept its distance, especially since Roosevelt in 1904 had publicly announced that "under no circumstances" would he be a candidate in 1908. In this way the favorites knew that they would have to look elsewhere for support and patronage. At the same time, because he had multiplied his attacks on big business and was more and more "progressive," an unbridled press accused him of socialism, treason, and even of insanity. But that did not at all prevent his popularity from increasing with the masses. In 1906 he answered one of his advisers who had asked him the secret of that extraordinary success: "[I express in] words what is in their hearts and minds but not their mouths." [21] The man who got that answer was a young lieutenant, who would be heard from later on, Douglas MacArthur.

At the Republican convention of 1908, Roosevelt had nominated his favorite candidate, William Howard Taft, who was elected on the first ballot. Former Governor of the Philippines (1901–1904), then Secretary of War, Taft had been closely associated with Roosevelt's foreign policy; in particular he had organized the military occupation of Cuba (1906–1909). The outgoing President could therefore announce with some serenity that he counted on his successor to pursue his policies and it is those policies that the voters ratified by 7,679,006 votes for Taft against 6,409,106 for William Jennings Bryan. Thus Taft got 50,000 more votes than Roosevelt in 1904, and the Democrat Bryan carried

only four states (Colorado, Nebraska, Nevada, and Oklahoma) outside of the Deep South. The stage was then
ready for the new President to continue asserting United
States power in the world and more especially at its doorstep in Latin America. Simultaneously, he would pursue
domestically the economic and social struggle against the
trusts and in that he would succeed better than his mentor,
gaining for himself an undeniably popular standing at least
during the first year of his administration. Basing himself
on the antitrust law, he initiated twice the legal actions in
four years that Roosevelt had in seven years. He had the
Sixteenth Amendment, which instituted the income tax,
added to the Constitution in 1913. "Progressivism" in domestic policy was therefore still balancing out among the
poorest classes the "imperialism" that McKinley had, despite himself, inaugurated with the Spanish-American War
of 1898 and which Roosevelt, won over by Admiral
Mahan's ideas and aided by his strong personality, was trying to give a concrete shape and style to be further refined
and developed.

The Monroe Doctrine (1823) represented the determination to keep the European powers out of Latin America.
It had naturally led to the Roosevelt Corollary (1904)
which justified armed intervention from the United States
under the pretext of preventing military expeditions from
European countries eager to obtain repayment of their
loans. But that big-stick policy had the great inconvenience
of arousing in all of Latin America a profound hostility
against "Yankee imperialism." At the time that he left the
War Department to enter the White House, Taft wanted
to find other means to have United States influence prevail
in the American hemisphere and if need be, beyond it.

"The diplomacy of the present administration," Taft explained in 1912, "has sought to respond to modern ideas of
commercial intercourse. This policy has been characterized
as substituting dollars for bullets." [22]

Many Republicans commented on what they themselves called *dollar diplomacy*. But its implementation promised to be tricky: after all, whatever his natural impetuousness, Theodore Roosevelt had not sent gunboats to the Dominican Republic; he had contented himself with taking over the finances and the customs of the country, and it was his successors, Taft and "a champion of peace" like Wilson, who would send in the Marines. The line between the big-stick policy and dollar diplomacy remained cloudy.

The man whom President Taft named as head of the State Department, Philander Chase Knox, had built a large personal fortune as a lawyer for powerful companies and in particular the Carnegie Steel Company. In the tradition of his predecessors Hay and Root, he tried to protect the financial interests of the United States, especially in Latin America and in China. With that strange form of idealism proper to American millionaires, he wanted to convince himself that by granting them credits and by increasing private investments, he would eliminate poverty in Central American countries and would stabilize their governments. That policy, which translates an unshakable confidence in the virtues of American capitalism, was coldly realistic, especially since Philander C. Knox—if Elihu Root is to be believed—was "antipathetic to all Spanish-American modes of thought and feelings." And, a historian notes, it is "a description which, unfortunately, fits many of its successors in the State department." [23]

Under the impetus from Knox, big-stick and dollar diplomacy were fused in Nicaragua in 1909. That country, since the revolution of 1894, was governed by President José Santos Zelaya, who during his Presidency, tried to create a central American Union of which he would be the head. The United States ensured the failure of that plan, but it discovered very quickly other reasons for discontent with Zelaya's policies. It offered President Zelaya, in effect, a loan of $15 million in exchange for the exclusive right to

build a possible transoceanic canal besides taking control of
the finances and customs of the country. When Roosevelt
had placed the finances and customs of the Dominican Republic in the hands of an American civil servant, there was
the matter of ensuring the repayment of European creditors. But the situation in Nicaragua was completely different: United States interest in Nicaragua had to do with its
gold mines and plantations operated mostly by American
companies and above all because it was geographically indispensable to the security of the Panama Canal then being
built. Besides, although the United States had chosen the
Panama route it had not forgotten that its inquiry commission had first favored a Nicaraguan canal whose construction would be facilitated by the San Juan River and by Lake
Nicaragua. At the beginning of the century and while the
building of the Panama Canal was still in progress, it did
not give up the idea of adding a second or replacing it by
another canal.

Relations between Nicaragua and the United States became embittered when President Zelaya in 1909 refused the
loan of $15 million which had been offered to him and, of
course, the conditions that went with it. Nicaragua wanted
to keep its independence, already quite endangered by
American companies which exploited its principal resources
and behaved toward the government like feudal powers. Zelaya's refusal had hardly reached Washington when a revolution broke out against him. The insurrection, inspired by
the conservatives Emiliano Chamorro and Juan Estrada,
and led by Adolfo Diaz, former bookkeeper in a Pittsburgh
firm, succeeded only thanks to the presence of an American
cruiser which had been sent into Nicaraguan waters to
"maintain order." The loyalist troops were in fact on the
point of crushing the rebels when the cruiser, under pretext of "protecting the lives and property of American nationals," landed Marines, who rushed to the rescue of the

insurgents and reversed the situation. The former Pittsburgh bookkeeper was modestly satisfied with the Vice-Presidency. "But new incidents soon permitted Diaz to proclaim himself president and he sent a dramatic appeal to the United States demanding the intervention of American troops to restore order. As they were already on the spot, order was effectively, rapidly, and very easily re-established." [24]

Adolfo Diaz secured diplomatic recognition by the United States only after accepting a loan from American bankers, (the $15 million refused by his predecessor) and the control of Customs by the United States. The economic colonization of the country provoked an uprising against Diaz in 1912. A thousand Marines under the command of Smedley D. Butler crushed the rebels at the battle of Cayotepeque, on October 4, 1912. But the victory did not suffice to stifle discontent and guarantee internal stability. The military occupation of Nicaragua by the United States continued until 1925. Washington then took advantage of this peculiar situation to conclude an agreement under Wilson's Presidency in 1916 which guaranteed to the United States the exclusive right to build a canal through the Isthmus, the use of the Islas del Maiz, and the establishment of a naval base in the Gulf of Fonseca. That agreement was signed by Bryan for America and by Chamorro for Nicaragua, the latter having been the principal instigator of the 1909 revolution against President Zelaya.

In his annual message of 1912, defending his dollar diplomacy—subjected to attacks from Democrats and Progressives—President Taft rejoiced that American bankers had contributed to the "financial rehabilitation" of a country which had simply needed "a measure of stability and the means of financial regeneration to enter upon an era of peace and prosperity." But he did not succeed in establishing a clear distinction between Roosevelt's big-stick policy

and his own dollar diplomacy. In fact, in the whole Nicaraguan affair dollars did at no time replace guns. The two
were used simultaneously. It was because he had refused
dollars that President Zelaya was overthrown in 1909,
thanks to the guns of the Marines. And in the two decades
to follow—we will see that the operation continued until
1933—the cooperation of dollars and cannons was indispensable to guarantee the United States hold over Nicaragua.

The interest inspired by Nicaragua in the United States
predated the twentieth century. Taft's innovation was to
have had the American government and its armed forces
intervene alongside private interests. That initiative had
been anticipated by Elihu Root, Theodore Roosevelt's Secretary of State, who declared in 1908, concerning armed interventions in Cuba and in the Dominican Republic, that
operations of the same type would happen in Haiti or in
Nicaragua if American interests in these two countries
reached similar scales. In fact, American historians have
conclusively shown that the expedition of Commander
Smedley D. Butler to Nicaragua in 1912 was conceived in
great part to protect the interest of two firms, Brown Brothers & Co. and J. & W. Seligman & Co.[25]

But as shown by the *a posteriori* Bryan-Chamorro Pact of
1916, the interests of the United States were not solely
financial: there was also here the matter of securing the authorization to build a canal and to establish a naval base, in
order to secure a strong strategic position. That objective
had been pursued by the United States since 1839, namely,
since Martin Van Buren's Presidency—but the United
States had to wait three-quarters of a century, with surprising perseverance, to achieve it. At first only powerful private
groups and adventurers were active. The history of their attempts, of their temporary successes, and finally of their
failure is indispensable to the comprehension of the great
operation which ensured Taft's final triumph.

At the start was the great figure of Cornelius Vanderbilt (1794–1877), founder of one of the most famous American dynasties. Born of poor parents in Staten Island, he transported passengers and merchandise across the bay to Manhattan as an adolescent; he then became the owner of several boats, and finally acquired control of most of the ferryboat lines of New York, to the point that he was known only by the title "Commodore." During the Civil War, he became President of the New York Central network. At his death, he donated a million dollars from his fortune to found a university in Nashville, Tennessee which bears his name.

How did that extraordinary man become interested in Central America? At the time of the gold rush, and four years before the completion of the Panama railroad which considerably shortened the voyage from the East coast to California, Commodore Vanderbilt had with the same purpose in mind opened the Accessory Transit Line in Nicaragua (1851), which brought passengers to Lake Nicaragua and to the Pacific. Vanderbilt thus owned the boats which left from New York and went up the San Juan river, and their logical complement, the railroad across the Isthmus.

It was at this moment that the famous filibuster William Walker came into the millionaire's life. Walker (1824–1860), a graduate of the University of Nashville, had studied medicine in Pennsylvania and law in New Orleans before settling down as a lawyer and newspaper publisher in California. In 1853, along with a few adventurers, he mounted an expedition against Baja California, which he did not succeed in wresting from Mexico. In order to compensate for that failure, he disembarked two years later in Nicaragua, on the "mosquito coast," with fifty-eight "soldiers of fortune," under the pretext of cultivating the land. Strengthened by the assurance of support from Jefferson Davis, Secretary of War and future President of· the Confederacy, he intervened in the civil war ravaging the country, allied himself with the liberals, got reinforcements from the United States, and victoriously attacked the conservatives in their stronghold of Granada. Walker had the liberal leader Patricio Rivas named provisional President of Nicaragua, while he himself became Commander in Chief of the Army. Emboldened by that success, the adventurer attacked Costa Rica, where he won an initial victory, but then had to face an alliance composed of Costa Rica, Salvador, and Guatemala.

Confronted with such events, Cornelius Vanderbilt remained neutral: his only concern was to accumulate the profits brought in by his railroad. But William Walker, in agreement with the minority stockholders of the Accessory Transit Line, seized the Commodore's steamboats which plied the San Juan River. In reprisal, Vanderbilt supplied money and arms to the Costa Ricans and their allies. Soon after, Walker and his men were besieged in the city of Rivas. The adventurer only escaped capture by taking refuge on board an American warship which brought him back to the United States. He made "a triumphant entrance into New Orleans to the enthusiastic acclaim of his countrymen," [26] and very quickly collected capital for another venture. The Indians from Roatan Island, a few dozen kilometers from the Honduras coast, appealed to Walker to "liberate" them. He established his headquarters on the island and launched an attack against the Honduran town of Trujillo, on the mainland. But the filibuster was beaten. To avoid falling into the hand of his enemies he surrendered to the English, who handed him over to Honduras. On September 12, 1860, William Walker, thirty-six years old, was shot near Tegucigalpa.

William Walker might have remained master of Nicaragua if he had not made the mistake of seizing Vanderbilt's boats. All that the American Navy did, in the circumstances, was to save him and take him back to the United

States. Washington was not interested in making a colony of Nicaragua. But half a century hence, the situation was quite different: with McKinley and Roosevelt, the United States entered the imperialist phase of its history; it had to protect the Panama Canal, establish a naval base in Nicaragua, secure the right to dig across the Isthmus in another location. Those strategic interests coincided with the private interests of the two firms, Brown and Seligman. The American government, with President Taft and Secretary of State Knox, hoped that the economic development of the country would stabilize its political regime. As it was important not to run any risks, control of the Customs served as guarantee for the $15 million loan. The Marines subsequently intervened, as only force could impose on Nicaragua those "golden chains" that President Zelaya obstinately refused. Taft made no secret of the connection between the actions of private groups seeking after their own profit and those of the government which in his eyes served the common interest of the country. "The United States," he declared in 1912, "has been glad to encourage and to support American bankers who are willing to lend a helping hand to the financial rehabilitation of such countries [of the Caribbean]." If, in his mind, that policy was to be profitable to the countries of South America, it was not, however, disinterested: "While our foreign policy should not be turned a hair's breadth from the straight path of justice, it may well be made to include active intervention to secure for our merchandise* and our capitalists opportunity for profitable investment which shall inure to the benefit of both countries concerned," Taft said.[27] The combined action of dollars and Marines is used in the service of the common good. Undoubtedly, "it is to be noted that Taft always attributes a moral significance to dollar diplomacy."[28]

---

* In 1913 the United States had a favored position in Nicaragua's foreign trade: 35 per cent of its imports and 56 per cent of its exports.

Men like Admiral Mahan, Senator Beveridge, and missionaries like Josiah Strong always exuded a moral idealism which intended to pull "backward" or "inferior" peoples out of their condition. The means of implementing that policy—naval power, establishment of bases, direct colonization in Puerto Rico or in the Philippines—could hardly seduce the banking or industrial tycoons, but enlisted the support of southern planters who dreamed of vast tracks of land cultivated by cheap labor. Washington, by leaving the doors open to the production and manpower of these "colonies" in everything but name, very quickly created deep disappointment. As to the industrialists, they remained hostile to this primary form of imperialism: there were still enough investments possible and money to be earned within the country's borders.

With Taft, the premises of the problem underwent a radical transformation. Dollar diplomacy appealed to the most powerful private groups and he proposed that they simultaneously serve their own interests and those of the country. In Nicaragua, American interests were protected by the Marines and by an autonomous government held tightly in rein by an important loan and the control over Customs. But the Star-Spangled Banner did not wave over the presidential palace of Managua, and Washington was not represented by a governor. Unless a coup overthrew an uncooperative President, the country retained all the attributes of political sovereignty. What it had lost was its economic sovereignty. That situation did not have the inconvenience of letting competitive goods and manpower freely enter the United States. Customs barriers remained as did limitations on immigration. It undoubtedly was the cleverest, the least costly, the most profitable type of colonization. It combined the economic, strategic, and political advantages of direct colonization without the counterpart of costs of administration, education, public health, and road upkeep, which remained the sole responsibility of Nicaragua. Thus, simultaneously, the United States strengthened its empire in Nicaragua and progressively brought the Philippines toward political independence. Apparently contradictory, those two actions were complementary. This was the time when France launched the conquest of Morocco, and in spite of the "protectorate" fiction and Lyautey's protest, placed the country in fact under its direct administration. The United States, ahead by half a century, was inventing the "neocolonialism" that the newly independent nations of Asia and Africa would denounce only in the wake of the Second World War.

The Spanish-American War had left the United States with the burden of the Philippines, which it hastened to unload, and of Puerto Rico, which still remains a burden. At that time (1898), American investments abroad only totaled $684 million. They reached $2,500 million when the intervention in Nicaragua took place, of which nearly half were in Latin America, predominantly in Mexico and the Caribbean. Thus, in fifteen years, American investments overseas had quadrupled. The table below gives a measure of the rapid development of American investments abroad during the seventeen years which separated the Spanish-American War and the First World War.

The 1940 figures, three times greater than those of 1914, demonstrate that the beginning of the century marks only the first timid exodus of capital out of the country which would henceforth accelerate. But their initial direction is confirmed: of these investments, the lion's share goes to the American hemisphere—from Canada to Tierra del Fuego—which, in 1914 as in 1940, received 72 per cent of the total. The trend conformed to the imperatives of geography and economy inasmuch as Europe had less need of foreign capital at the time. It also conformed to the political concept translated into the Monroe Doctrine during the preceding

INVESTMENTS ABROAD*
(in millions of dollars)

	1897	1908	1914	1940
Europe	151	489	691	2,006
Canada and				
Newfoundland	189	697	867	3,740
Mexico and				
Central America	270	938	1,283	1,510
South America	37.9	129	365	2,513
Africa	1	5	13	124
Asia	23	235	245	620
Oceania	1.5	10	17	233
TOTAL	673.4	2,503	3,481	10,746

* Direct investments and portfolio values, after H. U. Faulkner.

century: America for Americans, or more exactly, repeating the formula used to the south of the Rio Granade: America for the North Americans. The United States was not yet interested in Africa and Asia.

IV

━━━━━

Wilson, or The Mask
of Idealism

Lands taken from Indian tribes, the purchase of Louisiana
and Alaska, conquests achieved at the expense of Mexico:
United States Presidents acted irrespective of their political affiliation when it was a question of extending the
frontiers of the country to their present limits. But the Republicans did open the phase American historians classify
as "imperialist." They kept power for sixteen consecutive
years (1896–1912) and while McKinley was unwillingly led
to a course of conquest, his successors, Theodore Roosevelt
and William H. Taft, proudly represented themselves as
the champions of imperialism. They perfected its techniques while giving it a new juridical and moral basis. The
groups which attacked their schemes based their opposition
on various considerations, which cut across political arguments (colonial conquests undermine the foundations of
American democracy), economic arguments (distant adventures are onerous while the country needs capital), and
moral arguments.

But then the 1912 election brought to the White House
not only a Democrat but a man who came to stand in history as one of the most moving incarnations of American
idealism.

Was Woodrow Wilson going to change or even reverse the policies initiated by his predecessors? Because he presided over America's entry into the First World War on the side of England and France, Wilson retained a halo of generosity in the eyes of Europeans. But unavoidable realities and pressing material interests are imposed on any President, however fervent an idealist he might be. It was with particular brilliance that Wilson, verbally repudiating the methods of his predecessors, in fact pursued their policy of military and economic intervention in the small countries of the Caribbean. Drawing on the very sources of his idealism, he even added some new weapons to the arsenal, adorning them with all the respectability and the ineffable dignity of the moralist thrown into public affairs.

In fact, Wilson was to be responsible for more armed interventions in Latin America than Taft and Roosevelt combined. But for him idealism was not a hypocritical mask which he used to camouflage the real objectives of his policies. Only in the eyes of foreign observers did his sincere idealism conceal both narrow nationalist aspects of his policy and the constant pursuit of major material advantages for the United States. Examination of his Latin American policy, however, not only tears away the mask, it also shows how the most generous idealism does not succeed in shielding a President and his people from the compelling pressures of imperatives inscribed in the history of the nation. Others, after him, would have the same experience.

Wilson's interventions in Latin America throw a new light on his European policy. From 1914 to 1917, in order not to intervene in the First World War, Wilson invoked the neutrality of the United States and its desire for peace. A strange neutrality, a surprising desire for peace, especially since Wilson had Marines intervene in Mexico in 1914 and again in 1916. General Pershing, welcomed in France the following year as a liberator, was just back from Mexico where he had played the role of invader.

What interests made Wilson carry out more armed interventions than his two predecessors? What interests kept the United States out of the European conflict for three years? Why did it finally send troops to Europe in 1917? The answers to these questions leave little room for Wilsonian idealism. On the contrary, they show how idealism served—while it concealed—unchanging interests of an empire which increasingly asserted itself by widening its field of activity.

Taft's defeat in the 1912 presidential election cannot be interpreted as a repudiation of dollar diplomacy. Theodore Roosevelt came back to the United States in 1910 from great hunting expeditions in Africa and a triumphant tour of Europe. Fifty-two years old, he had kept all his fire, all his dynamism. He found an unsatisfied and discontented Republican Party. Progressive elements accused Taft of having become the prisoner of the conservative "old guard." The Supreme Court had annulled the social legislation enacted by several states. "I have been conscientiously trying to carry out your policies," [1] Taft wrote Roosevelt in 1910. But that same year the Republicans lost control of the House of Representatives. At the beginning of 1911 Senator LaFollette, leader of the "insurgent Republicans," founded the National Progressive Republican League with the intention of liberalizing the party, but he did not succeed in extending his popularity beyond the Mississippi valley. Theodore Roosevelt easily convinced himself that he alone could lead the Republican Party to victory by preserving its unity and its progressive character in economic and social areas. He therefore threw himself into the nomination race, but his radicalism lost him the support of notables like Cabot Lodge, Knox, Root, Stimson, while the Republican "machine" remained faithful to Taft. The Republican convention chose Taft as candidate for a second term.

But Theodore Roosevelt, who did not admit defeat, decided to run under the Progressive label. He had against him the conservatives, who supported Taft, and, because he had had amicable dealings with the black though very moderate leader Booker T. Washington, he did not succeed in breaking the southern bloc. The southerners more easily identified themselves with the Democrat Woodrow Wilson, fifty-six years old, born in Virginia, former President of Princeton University and elected Governor of New Jersey in 1910. Wilson had the support not only of the conservative south but also of a liberal wing based in the west and represented by former candidate William Jennings Bryan, the Irish who dominated Chicago and the great cities of the east and drew in their wake the recently naturalized immigrants, and the powerful newspaper chain of the demagogue William Randolph Hearst, who would have preferred another candidate, but supported him as well. But that coalition was so heterogeneous that the Democratic convention did not choose Wilson as its candidate until the forty-sixth ballot.

The presidential campaign took place in a troubled social climate. The red banners of the Industrial Workers of the World made their appearance during strikes. For many Americans the choice was between revolution and reforms. The socialist Eugene V. Debs, once more a candidate, got 6 per cent of the popular vote. Moderate Republicans were worried by Theodore Roosevelt's radicalism and, along with the conservatives, preferred Taft. In that context, Woodrow Wilson appeared as the reasonable candidate capable of bringing about calmly, indispensable reforms without violent shocks. He got 6,286,214 votes, 113,000 less than Bryan in 1908, or hardly 42 per cent of the total. But the opposition was divided between Theodore Roosevelt (4,216,000 or 27 per cent) and William H. Taft (3,483,922 or 23 per cent). Had they been united behind the name of one candidate, Roosevelt's and Taft's votes would have crushed Wilson.

Since the Civil War, the Democrats had had only one President, Grover Cleveland, who was elected twice. They had lost power in 1896, with McKinley's first election, on the eve of the imperialist venture. But when they recaptured the White House sixteen years later with Woodrow Wilson they not only benefited from the division of their opponents. They inaugurated a new era in American life, for, by one of those political turnabouts which often occur in history, they adopted the dynamic elements of Roosevelt's policy: the fight for greater socio-political justice, and a vigorous foreign policy which asserted the leadership of the United States in the world. Deprived of their Progressive ranks, of which Theodore Roosevelt was the symbol, the Republicans were to become set in their conservative positions, a fact which would still bring them brilliant electoral victories but which would leave them impotent before the great economic crises of 1929–1930. The Democrats, on the contrary, became the champions of interventionism under its three major forms:

a) United States intervention in the First World War with Wilson, in the Second with Franklin D. Roosevelt, and in all the trouble spots of the globe with Truman, Kennedy, and Johnson.

b) Intervention by the federal government in the economic life of the country, first with Wilson, who secured a strengthened antitrust law (Clayton Law) in 1914, then above all with Franklin D. Roosevelt during the New Deal, but also with Kennedy and Johnson, who fought against price rises and against certain trust abuses.

c) Finally, intervention of federal power against certain states of the Union, notably in cases of racial conflict.

The division between Taft and Theodore Roosevelt was indeed not the only cause of that evolution, but it perfectly and concretely spotlighted it and permitted the election of Woodrow Wilson, who took up the torch of domestic progressivism and of foreign interventionism.

Moreover, the transmission of this heritage took place without interruption, as is clearly shown by the affair with Mexico initiated by Taft and pursued by the Democrat Wilson despite his verbal repudiation of the dollar diplomacy of his predecessor.

The difficulties which the United States encountered in Mexico were already illustrative of the problems it would have to confront after 1945 everywhere in the world but especially in countries which had recently become independent. Not only did it have powerful economic interests in Mexico but that country was, under Porfirio Díaz as well as under Huerta, in the grip of a bloody dictatorship. Thus democratic idealism and economic realism were to confront each other, as would often happen henceforth. For that reason, American interventions in Mexico marked an important phase in the history of the empire and deserve to be related in detail.

The former seminarian turned lawyer, José de la Cruz Porfirio Díaz, had not come easily to the Presidency of Mexico. But once in power he remained there thirty-five years. His military exploits during the War of 1846–1848 during which two-fifths of Mexican territory was lost to the United States and the struggle against Maximilian (1864–1867) had earned him a certain fame which, however, did not prevent him from being beaten in the presidential elections of 1867 and 1871. Furious at his failure, he took up arms, but his partisans were crushed. Again defeated in the election of 1876 he seized power by force and it was equally by force that he was driven out in 1911, while Taft was President of the United States.

That long thirty-five-year reign permitted Mexico to build the basis of a more modern economy. Obviously, the most elementary democratic principles were systematically violated, the Indians were deprived of their communal lands and education stagnated; but order reigned, revolts were forcefully suppressed, banditry was decreasing, and foreign capital poured in to exploit the natural wealth of the country; finances were balanced, a minority benefited from the prosperity of the country, the network of railroads increased from 600 to 24,700 kilometers. This type of dictatorship was approved of in Washington, particularly by Republicans, since, as President Taft wrote to his wife, "We have two billions American capital in Mexico that will be greatly endangered if Díaz were to die."

Taft was mistaken. American capital in Mexico did not reach half of the figure he mentioned, but its $853 million represented 25 per cent of American investments abroad, or more than Mexico's total capital. The dollar grip formed around key sectors: 80 per cent of the capital invested in Mexican railroads was American, 70 per cent of the petroleum was then produced by American firms; $302 million was in the extraction and refining of metals ($140 million of which were for precious metals), $110 million in railroads, $85 million in oil, the rest in agriculture, cattle-raising, diverse industries, and commercial enterprises. Mexico thus received 52 per cent of American capital invested in all Latin America.

In the election of 1910, Porfirio Díaz faced a formidable opponent in Francisco Madero, who represented himself as the champion of democracy and social reform. The dictator jailed him and won an easy victory in the election. He then believed he could free Madero. However, as soon as he was out of prison Madero went to Texas, declared a revolution, again crossed the border and marched on Mexico, gathering troops of followers on his way. He seized the capital and was elected President in 1911. Porfirio Díaz took the road of exile. That was the beginning of an awkward period for the United States.

Henry Lane Wilson, the Ambassador named by Taft, thought of Madero as "a man of disordered intellect . . .

comparable to Nero." Reforms promised by the new President could be achieved only with the united support of a majority and an efficient administration. Madero did not possess those trump cards when he attacked powerful private interests, in particular when he started distributing land to the peons. In February 1913 the great landowners revolted and with them half the army. Madero's fate was settled when General Huerta, military commander of the capital, defected to the rebels. "At that juncture," wrote an American historian, "a super gangster, General Victoriano Huerta, won the support of Henry Lane Wilson [who] helped Huerta effect a coup d'etat against Madero and presented him to the diplomatic corps as the next president of Mexico. Huerta's henchmen promptly murdered both Madero and the vice-president. It remained for Woodrow Wilson to try to undo what Henry Lane Wilson had done." [2]

Taft, however, avoided the worst. On being requested, before the expiration of his mandate to intervene militarily in Mexico to re-establish order, he prudently declined, leaving the task of settling that problem to his successor. But dollar diplomacy and the role played by his Ambassador had created a situation which was to draw Woodrow Wilson into a dangerous venture.

The Democratic President at first took a position of watchful waiting. In 1895–1896 he had approved of Cleveland's firmness toward London in the frontier dispute between Venezuela and British Guiana. He had also approved the Spanish-American War, the conquest of the Philippines, the occupation of Puerto Rico and of Cuba. He was not hostile to colonization and agreed with Mahan and Beveridge that the flag must protect commerce. But he believed in the virtues of democracy. A few days after he entered the White House he repudiated dollar diplomacy as defined and exemplified by his predecessor and, in a great speech, tried to dispel the distrust that Roosevelt and Taft had inspired in all of Latin America. Displaying a concern which—albeit ineffectual—would be shared by most of his successors, he wanted to avoid tying American democracy to the dictatorships flowering on the continent. Soon after coming to the White House he declared: "Throughout the world the United States must always support constitutional regimes." Later, John F. Kennedy would use the same language in launching the Alliance for Progress. According to that principle, Wilson should not recognize the Huerta regime which had seized power by force. But the tradition of the United States, as of many other countries, was to recognize established regimes, thus avoiding the necessity of passing moral judgments on them—a realistic attitude, dictated by experience in international affairs, which Wilson opposed with idealistic concepts. And in Huerta's case, he expressed himself bluntly: "I will not recognize a government of butchers."

The problem was discussed at a meeting of the Cabinet on March 11, 1913. The ideas which were at the heart of the discussion would lead to confrontations in many later cases. Anxious to safeguard important investments, the advocates of large private interests preached diplomatic recognition, but, since the President had pledged to favor constitutional regimes, they suggested a compromise: all that was needed was a promise from Huerta to hold elections, a major concession as far as appearances were concerned—but minor in practice, as Huerta's predecessor Porfirio Díaz, who had been favored by American industrial and banking circles, had shown in demonstrating how predictable elections could be held. Wilson's top adviser, his *eminence grise*, Colonel House—"His thoughts and mine are one," the President had said about him—brought forth another argument, which, although not new, was to become popular. That clever politician, who had delivered the Texas votes to

Wilson, pointed out in a written memorandum that the refusal of diplomatic recognition would permit the British
and the Germans to supplant United States influence in
Mexico. Woodrow Wilson hung on to his idealistic concept. He was supported by former presidential candidate
William Jennings Bryan, whom he had made his Secretary
of State. Finally, in May 1913, he decided not to recognize
the Huerta regime, and in August he recalled Ambassador
Henry Lane Wilson.

Thus, from the onset, the break between Wilson's policy
and that of his predecessors, the big-stick diplomacy of
Roosevelt or the dollar diplomacy of Taft, seemed complete and radical. The Democratic President wanted to reverse the tide, tear down the wall of distrust that the Republicans had erected between Washington and Latin
America. "The United States," he solemnly proclaimed in
March 1913, "has nothing to gain in Central or South
America except the permanent interests of the people of
those two continents." He reiterated the same theme in
October of the same year. "The United States will never
again seek one additional foot of territory by conquest. . . .
We dare not turn from the principle that morality and not
expediency is the thing that must guide us, and that we will
never condone iniquity because it is most convenient to do
so." [3]

Such statements represented disapproval of Great Britain
and the other European powers that had recognized
Huerta, indifferent to great idealistic principles but anxious
to have access to Mexican oil and to develop their trade.
Wilson tried to change the attitude of the European chan-
celleries, and he succeeded as far as London was concerned.
It happened that a law voted by Congress in 1912 exempted
American ships using the Panama Canal from all fees. That
law violated the Hay-Pauncefote Treaty, which guaranteed
equality of treatment to all users of the canal, and England

vigorously protested. Wilson saw in that situation a means of having his idealism triumph simultaneously on two fronts. A secret agreement between Colonel House and Sir William Tyrrell, Secretary of the Foreign Office, anticipated that Wilson would get Congress to abrogate the law favoring American ships; in return, Great Britain would withdraw the diplomatic recognition it had granted Huerta, and would support American policy in Mexico.

But that success did not prevent the Mexican crisis from worsening. In October 1913 Huerta disappointed big business in the United States, which was waiting for at least a promise of elections, and had 110 deputies arrested, establishing a bare-faced dictatorship. Then he provoked an incident by giving the order to arrest the sailors from the ship *Dolphin*, one of Admiral Henry Mayo's fleet, in Tampico, on the Atlantic coast. Notwithstanding their prompt release, the Admiral demanded apologies and a ceremonial salute to the American flag. Huerta refused.

Wilson's riposte was threefold. First he made contact with Venustiano Carranza, who had taken part in the revolution started by Madero against Porfirio Díaz. Carranza was fighting to return to the Indians their lands and to nationalize the petroleum deposits, and did not inspire blind confidence from the United States. Put into effect, his program would have seriously hurt American interests. But, while it might be useful to overthrow Huerta, there was no proof that a victorious Carranza would be able to keep his promises. Wilson, therefore, sent him an offer of "arms and advice on ways to make the country democratic. Carranza accepted the arms but refused the advice." [4]

Second, under Wilson's orders, Admiral Frank F. Fletcher landed his Marines at Vera Cruz, on the Atlantic coast, on April 21, 1914. That port had been chosen because a shipment of German arms destined for Huerta was expected there. Furthermore, if Huerta's troops occupied the city, Carranza's partisans would attack it. Vera Cruz was the most important Mexican Atlantic port: by taking it, the Marines would economically smother the Huerta regime.

Finally, Wilson strove to get the support of other Latin American countries. Argentina, Brazil, and Chile agreed to participate in a conference as mediators. But that move failed, as Carranza, seeing victory within his reach, refused mediation.

In fact, three months after the landing of the Marines at Vera Cruz, Huerta fled. In August 1914 Carranza entered the capital. The long fight he had been waging since Madero's assassination finally triumphed, thanks to the support of American arms.

Carranza's success over Huerta represented "a victory for Wilson apparently; but Huerta's departure made matters worse, because all Mexican political elements splintered into factions under rival leaders, each printing money, raising soldiers, killing, looting, and destroying property." [5]

What could Wilson do, faced with such chaos which menaced American investments? Convinced that the United States had a "civilizing mission," he dreamed of helping Mexico enter the road to democracy and progress. The man he could count on for such a task was the same Carranza whom he had permitted to overthrow Huerta. But we have seen that the new President of Mexico would not accept any interference. He had promised the nationalization of the subsoil and an agrarian reform—out of 15 million Mexicans, 10 million were then deprived of land, while the rural population represented 75 per cent of the total [6]— and to carry out such programs would affect unfavorably American interests in the oil and mining industries, agriculture and cattle-raising. He had clearly shown his attitude toward the United States when he protested the occupation of Vera Cruz by American forces.

Seeing that it was difficult to negotiate with Carranza, Wilson turned toward those who, having been on his side, were now fighting Carranza. The famous Pancho Villa, who had first helped Madero, then Carranza, was now on his own. Thanks to the courage and devotion of his followers, he seized the cities of Juarez and Torrien and even occupied the capital for a few weeks at the end of 1914 and in January 1915. Having established his domain in the north of the country, he sometimes went on joint expeditions with Emiliano Zapata, the Indian revolutionary who had also distinguished himself in the fight against Porfirio Díaz, and whose renowned "legion of death" was strongly established in the south of Mexico. For landowners as well as for foreigners, Pancho Villa and Emiliano Zapata were nothing but common bandits. They seized lands, even if they were the property of American companies, and gave them back to the Indians, after having destroyed property deeds. Between these two formidable guerrilleros, Carranza felt threatened. He had to recapture his capital three times. Drawn into an ambush, Zapata would be killed in April 1919, but the fight would continue after his death. The greatest difficulties however arose with Pancho Villa. After a defeat by government troops he moved his forces to his northern asylum and let Washington know that he would welcome a democracy on the American model. Wilson and Bryan, without suspecting a maneuver, were seduced by his advances. After having helped Carranza triumph over Huerta they refused him diplomatic recognition until the time, they said, when the new President would be constitutionally elected. Through his program Carranza represented the desire for progress but also for national independence vis-à-vis Washington and powerful private American interests. In everything he was and did, Pancho Villa represented the miserable illiterate peasant masses and here he was soliciting American "advice," which Carranza did not want to hear. During the first ten months of 1915 American hesitation contributed to the spread of anarchy in Mexico. Carranza and Pancho Villa having refused mediation, the United States and six Latin American countries finally resigned themselves in October 1915 to give the Carranza government *de facto* recognition.

That belated gesture irritated Pancho Villa, especially since the Mexican Army was authorized to move into American territory to ferret out rebellious bands. Determined to create an incident, Pancho Villa in January 1916 stopped a train at Santa Ysabel, captured sixteen Americans who were traveling on it, and had them shot. Most historians credit him also with a raid in March 1916 on the other side of the frontier, in Columbus, New Mexico, where nineteen Americans were killed. But, more cautiously, the *Columbia Encyclopedia* simply notes that "the circumstances of the raid and even Villa's participation in it are still unsettled: it is only certain that Mexican soldiers made the raid and Villa was universally considered responsible."

The incident in any case occurred at the right time to furnish a decisive argument to the numerous partisans of military intervention in Mexico. In the forefront stood Theodore Roosevelt who heaped sarcasm on the hesitation and the softness of the Wilson government. The Hearst newspapers attacked Wilson after having supported him in his electoral campaign and also demanded an expedition. When, seventeen years earlier, he was preaching war against Spain to "liberate Cuba," Hearst was seeking above all to increase his papers' circulation by inflaming the minds of his readers. He had now other motives. "One reason was his and his mother's holdings of ranch, oil, mining, timber and chicle property in Mexico which he later valued at 4,000,-000 dollars but was probably worth more," his biographer wrote. "Under the iron regime of his good friend Porfirio Díaz, this property had been protected, but since the exile of Díaz in 1911 governmental authority had crumbled and the country was in chaos for many years. There were threats among the revolutionists to drive out the Yankee imperialists who had taken so much of the land and its resources. . . . Hearst's Babicora ranch in Chihuahua was caught in a whipsaw and cruelly treated. It was taken over and looted by the irregulars of Pancho Villa, one employee being reported killed and four held prisoner. Villa, it was said, stole 60,000 of Hearst's cattle. Later the ranch was occupied for a time by Carranza forces. . . . Babicora vaqueros at length formed their own 100-man 'army' and were reported to have killed more than twenty bandits in one pitched battle. . . . Feeling it the duty of the United States government to restore order in Mexico, he stepped up his propaganda campaign. His newspapers sprouted inflammatory headlines: 'Bandits join Carranza to fight US' and 'Mexicans prepare for war with US.' "

Hearst would again demand an expedition to Mexico in 1921. On this matter, his biographer wrote that "It was true that his father had originally got his millions of Mexican acres from the dictatorial Porfirio Díaz for a song and that Díaz's careless sale of land resources had resulted in a flock of Yankee capitalists fattening in Mexico while peons were in the most abject poverty." [7] However, following a talk with President Obregon, Hearst declared that his properties were not threatened and that he had only praise for the new President. The situation worsened again under the Presidency of Calles (1924–1928) who wanted to "give Mexico back to the Mexicans." In November 1927 Hearst published "documents" which purported to prove that Mexico was mounting a vast plot against the United States and was buying four American Senators for $1,115,000. It was easily proved that these "documents" were complete forgeries.

Theodore Roosevelt and the powerful Hearst press were not the only ones preaching a crusade against Mexico. With them was Albert B. Fall, Senator from Arizona, (later Secretary of the Interior during Harding's Presidency, 1921–1923), who represented oil interests and was known to belong to the "Ohio gang." Senator Fall called for the occupation of Mexico by an army of 500,000 men. Compelled to resign during the Coolidge Presidency, he was tried, condemned, and jailed for having embezzled for private companies, petroleum deposits kept in reserve for the Navy. The scheme, which earned him at least $400,000, defrauded the government of $6 million. Naturally that shady gentleman did not act on his own initiative: the oil companies whose interests he served hoped for the downfall of Carranza who was guilty of wanting to nationalize Mexican petroleum. But when the Senator heightened his attacks against the President of Mexico, it was, he said, because Carranza was "more despotic than Peter the Great" and that his despotism was a menace to American democracy.

The war partisans also numbered among them Senator Slayden of Texas and Chief of Staff General Hugh L. Scott. After having led many operations against the Indians, General Scott had served on the staff of the American troops in Cuba (1898–1903), then he had taken command in the Philippines before becoming Commandant at West Point (1906–1910). Entrusted with the surveillance of the Texas frontier in 1915, he got Pancho Villa's promise to respect American lives and property. That move led President Wilson to defer diplomatic recognition of the Carranza government and to negotiate with Pancho Villa.

Further, Carranza proposed to curtail the temporal powers of the Catholic Church, which earned him determined hostility in American Catholic circles.

The news of the bloody incidents of January and March 1916 at Santa Ysabel and Columbus—which cost a total of thirty-five American lives—was received in the United States by a public opinion already cleverly prejudiced against Carranza. The partisans of military intervention finally found favorable echoes in the population. If he had continued to hesitate, Wilson would have seen his prestige severely affected. He therefore ordered a "punitive expedition" whose command was entrusted to General John J. Pershing, who had already served in Cuba in 1898 and twice in the Philippines. Pershing's mission was to capture Pancho Villa and put an end to his plunderings. American troops crossed the Mexican border March 15, 1916, six days after the raid against Columbus. "This was unilateral military intervention by the United States, unmistakable and on a grand scale. . . . At first the expedition consisted of 5,000 men, by June it numbered 11,000. As early as April it had penetrated about 300 miles into the interior, but Villa could not be seized." [8]

For Carranza, as for most Mexicans, the invasion of American troops was a national affront. His regime had been recognized by Washington five months earlier, and that move had exasperated Pancho Villa with whom General Hugh Scott and President Wilson had at first agreed to negotiate. But the rivalry between Carranza and Pancho Villa took second place as soon as a foreign power intervened in Mexican affairs. Carranza demanded the withdrawal of American troops to whom his Army refused passage. Captain Boyd, of the American cavalry, attacked. He lost ten killed and twenty-four wounded. The United States was then ready to transform its "punitive expedition" into a general war against Mexico.

But the "clamor of the peace faction," which at the end of the previous century used to irritate Theodore Roosevelt and Beveridge, rose again. Most of the Protestant churches, Jewish circles, and pacifist organizations demanded a truce, a mediation, a compromise. The campaign was led by the eminent Samuel Gompers, founder and first President of the American Federation of Labor, whose power was constantly making itself felt. Finally, Gompers succeeded in having Carranza free the prisoners. That move contributed to relaxing tensions in the United States. The United States was now ten months away from entering the First World War. Wilson, absorbed by other problems, agreed that a joint commission study the withdrawal of American troops.

The work of the commission dragged on. For Carranza, there could be no satisfactory solution other than the unconditional withdrawal of the "invaders." As for the Americans, they were trying to secure guarantees not only for the inviolability of their frontiers and the personal security of their nationals, but also and above all for their investments, especially in the petroleum industry. Those talks proved to the Mexicans that the "punitive expedition" led by General John J. Pershing did not have as its sole objective the capture of Pancho Villa. That is why the protocol already worked out by the commission and signed in November was rejected by Carranza in December 1916.

Meanwhile, Carranza had held elections for the Constituent Assembly (October 1916) which enacted the 1917 Constitution, still in force today. In apparent fulfillment of his promise to support democratically elected governments, Wilson withdrew the expeditionary corps on January 18, 1917, and on March 13 gave *de jure* recognition to the Carranza government, in office since August 1914 but accorded only *de facto* recognition in October 1915. Industrial and financial groups with powerful interests in Mexico were still dissatisfied. They tried to provoke another military intervention, as the 1917 Constitution hardly suited them. Not only did it nationalize clerical property and proclaim the soil and subsoil of the country the property of the Mexican people, but it also regulated the acquisition of land in Mexico; however the government had the option to grant that right to certain foreigners, on condition that they agree "to be considered as Mexicans as it concerned real estate, and consequently not to invoke, under penalty of forfeiture, the protection of their government in the matter." The "Calvo Doctrine" (see p. 99) was thus an integral part of the 1917 Mexican Constitution. The latter was not retroactive. It was, nonetheless, fought by private American interests in Mexico, which did not, however, succeed in having Washington intervene directly.

The two military interventions in Mexico, although the most spectacular, were not the only ones during Woodrow Wilson's Presidency. In 1914, as reparation for the damages caused by the Panama revolution that Theodore Roosevelt had provoked, Wilson offered Colombia an indemnity of $25 million, but the treaty was not ratified until 1921 (see p. 96). The belated gesture testified to his good intentions, to his desire for establishing relations of natural trust between the United States and the Latin American republics. But it did not erase the memory left by the big stick, and many people even thought that the offer of indemnity was another manifestation of dollar diplomacy. Furthermore, Wilson had also inherited from his predecessors an explosive situation in Nicaragua, where Taft's dollar diplomacy had brought about the fall of President Zelaya and tied golden chains around President Adolfo Diaz's neck. Taking advantage of the occupation of Nicaragua by the Marines, Wilson secured an option from that country for the eventual construction of a second canal, a lease on the Islas del Maiz, and the installation of naval bases on the Gulf of Fonseca by means of the Bryan-Chamorro Treaty of 1916 (see p. 121).

Similarly, in the Dominican Republic, where the Customs and finances were already under American control, Wilson took a hard line: he landed troops in 1916 to put an end to the anarchy that endangered the repayment of American creditors, especially Kuhn, Loeb & Co. (see p. 108). The military occupation lasted for eight years before leaving the field to dictator Trujillo.

The previous year Woodrow Wilson had ordered the

military occupation of Haiti without recourse to the excuse that his Republican predecessors had created the troubled situation. Haiti was heavily in debt to France, Germany, and the United States, which jointly demanded reorganization of the finances of that small, poor, and wretched country, whose economic production had been steadily decreasing since its independence, while its population constantly increased. The situation was worsened by internal dissensions and by the instability of governments which succeeded each other at a dizzy pace. Washington proposed a treaty of military aid, which Haiti rejected. President Guillaume Sam had some two hundred of his political enemies executed. A popular revolt erupted, the insurgents invaded the palace and finding the President hiding under his bed, killed him. Several American ships were on alert at Port-au-Prince. Two Marine companies and three infantry companies immediately received the order to land. The indignation of the Haitians and the protests of American liberals did not change anything. Order was re-established and the military occupation continued. American officers took over Customs, finances, education, road-building, and public health. At the same time, the United States gave Haiti a new Constitution nullifying the clause contained in the preceding one which prohibited foreigners from owning or leasing lands in the country. Major improvements were made, but most of the American officers were Southerners and their attitude toward the blacks provoked numerous incidents. From 1915 to 1922 the Marines had to suppress many revolts. In 1916 Wilson imposed a treaty on Haiti which established American military rule. That regime continued until 1933 with the United States retaining control of Haitian Customs thereafter.[9] In Washington, the Secretary of State adopted "sanctimonious language" to justify that policy: "The United States government has no purpose of aggression and is entirely disinterested in promoting this protectorate." [10] Spontaneously, the Democrats in power thus rediscovered the moralizing vocabulary of the Republican McKinley. They pretended to ignore and they profited from the fact that "for a number of years, American bankers had been interested in Haitian finances, and the First World War gave an opportunity for government intervention. Professing to believe that Germany had designs upon Haiti and determined that no European nation should assume control of it. . . ." Wilson had ordered a military occupation which added "another protectorate . . . to the American Empire." [11]

Under Wilson the Marines also landed in Cuba relying on certain provisions of the "Platt Amendment" that was included in the Cuban Constitution by authority of the United States Congress. General Mario G. Menocal had been elected President of Cuba in 1913 and, like his predecessors, he freely welcomed to the country American advisers and administrators. Four years later he sought re-election. The Liberals, under the leadership of former President José Miguel Gomez, revolted and seized power February 7, 1917. The United States declared that it would not recognize a government created by an armed coup, and on March 8 its troops landed at Santiago de Cuba. Gomez was overthrown and Menocal was "re-elected" under the protection of American soldiers. Four years later the Cuban people went to the polls again on March 15, 1921, after the United States through General Enoch H. Crowder had the elections of the preceding November annulled and rewrote the electoral law—an intervention which remained without practical results, as Doctor Alfredo Zayas was elected in March 1921 just as he had been in November 1920. The American General, Crowder, after having served in the Philippines (1899–1901) became Secretary of State of Cuba (1906–08) during the occupation and then Wilson's personal representative to that country from 1919–1921.

From 1923 to 1927, he would serve as the first United States Ambassador to Havana. Meanwhile he sent President Wilson a telegram in 1921 advising him to delay approval of a loan expected by Cuba until the Cuban government recognized the American Ambassador's right to revise Cuba's annual budget and all supplementary credits and tax laws.

Wilson's "great maneuvers" in Mexico, Nicaragua, the Dominican Republic, Haiti, and Cuba overshadow other interventions of less scope which went almost unnoticed in Europe and to which the great majority of the American public itself gave scant attention but which were not forgotten in Latin America. Thus in 1917 the United States intervened in Costa Rica to secure petroleum concessions. The same year, it engaged in a show of force in Nicaragua, already occupied by the Marines: The cruisers *Chattanooga* and *San Diego* watched over the election of President Emiliano Chamorro, who had shown his sympathy for the United States. On March 2, 1917, the Jones Law made Puerto Rico a "territory" of the United States and granted American citizenship to its inhabitants. In 1918 American troops suppressed an insurrection organized by Charlemagne Perlate in Haiti. The same year, in the young Panamanian Republic that they had so greatly helped to separate from Colombia, American troops occupied the capital and the city of Colon while a regiment under command of Major Page invaded the province of Chiriqui, over which he exercised control for two years: officially, he was helping the authorities to protect the property of American residents; one of these, a landowner, Gerald Chase, took advantage of the situation and considerably enlarged his domain. In 1919 American troops landed twice in Honduras, and managed to "protect" the election of President Julio Acosta, whose regime was immediately recognized by Washington. In 1920 American troops intervened in Guatemala in order to protect the legation of the United States and seized the Empresa Electrica Nacional. The same year, the military attaché of the United States in Guatemala requested— without success—10,000 Marines to support the dictator, President Manuel Estrada Cabrera, who was facing an insurrection; overthrown by Carlos Herrera, Estrada Cabrera shelled the capital in an attempt to recapture it; defeated, he was jailed despite official protest from Washington, which had nothing but praise for his dictatorship installed twenty-two years earlier. On September 5, 1920, General Alvaro Obregon was elected President of Mexico, but Wilson did not grant him diplomatic recognition (President Coolidge was to recognize Obregon on August 31, 1923, after he had promised to "respect the property titles of lands acquired before 1917"). In October 1920—the Haitian government refused to give up control over its National Bank and Wilson sent Admiral Knapp to Port-au-Prince with full powers to "settle the dispute." The following year, General John H. Russell was named High Commissioner to Haiti. Meanwhile, Wilson in 1917, had bought from Denmark for $25 million the Virgin Islands (St. Thomas, St. John, St. Croix) to the east of Puerto Rico, to protect the access route to Panama.

In his *American Economic History*, Harold Underwood Faulkner comments: "Whatever the objectives, it was clear that by the end of the First World War the United States had achieved a 'sphere of influence' in the Caribbean which virtually made that area an 'American lake.' Puerto Rico had been annexed, the Virgin islands purchased, Cuba, Panama, the Dominican Republic, Nicaragua, and Haiti reduced to the status of protectorates, and naval bases scattered strategically at various points in the Caribbean. The development of this control had occurred during the two decades 1898–1918. Of the chief executives, only Theodore Roosevelt could be described as an expansionist. Taft was an exponent of 'dollar diplomacy,' on the theory that American economic penetration would be a distinct aid to less developed countries and a stabilizing influence. Wilson was neither an expansionist nor a dollar diplomatist, but his Caribbean policy differed little from that of his predecessors." [12]

Another American historian, Samuel Eliot Morison, simply notes that Wilson pursued Roosevelt's and Taft's policies even "after it had been demonstrated that dollars and Marines could not cure Caribbean instability." [13]

This was so because the big stick and dollar diplomacy did not propose solely to bring order and prosperity to the countries that were subject to that harsh experience. Wilson was animated by a sincere idealism, but he had to consider other aspects of the problem. Franck L. Schoell rightly observes that Wilson "certainly was not himself an imperialist, but the situation, the particular combination of circumstances that he had inherited, and above all his desire to assure his country's security . . . had the effect of little matching his principles of respect towards small nations." [14]

That explanation is still insufficient. The installation of naval bases in the Caribbean met the necessity of assuring the security of the Panama Canal which was vital to Americans. But the two interventions in Mexico, the occupation of the Dominican Republic and Haiti, the often-repeated interference in the internal affairs of other countries of the region did not serve at all the national security of the United States. Their only justification was the protection of important private economic interests. Nevertheless, in his inaugural address Wilson had declared: "There has been something crude and heartless and unfeeling in our haste to succeed and be great. . . . We have come now to sober second thought. The scales of heedlessness have fallen from our eyes. We have made up our minds to square every process of our natural life with the standards we so proudly set up at the beginning and have always carried in our hearts." [15]

Such were Wilson's intentions when he entered the White House, but the experience of power imposed on him restraints which he had not thought of, or which he had underestimated. The pressure of public opinion, for example, was decisive in convincing him to intervene in Mexico. And the interests of special groups were no less powerful each time that investments were involved. That's why "his administration was responsible for a greater number of interventions than all those made by Roosevelt and Taft." [16]

Arthur P. Whitaker was even more critical, as he remarked that Wilson, after having condemned imperialism, dollar diplomacy and military intervention, "went on to more armed interventions in Latin America than Roosevelt and Taft put together, revived and developed dollar diplomacy and even invented a new form of intervention by transforming the American policy with regard to the recognition of governments." [17] By refusing diplomatic recognition, he showed an attitude which encouraged the elements hostile to the established regime. He also knew how to use recognition to bargain for useful concessions.

From the Republicans to the Democrats the tone and the content of declarations of principles had undergone an evident evolution, the methods and style had changed, the techniques of intervention had been transformed, but the main thread of a particular policy and its basic inspiration had remained unchanged on a certain number of essential points: Americans knew that their country had joined the ranks of the great powers—and that its power had to be asserted in the whole world, with primary attention to be paid to Latin America which was crucial to the security of the United States; American vitality manifested itself politically, through intervention by Washington, and economically through the exportation of capital, the search for new markets and a powerful tariff barrier to protect its expanding production; finally, government policy could not fail to concern itself with private investments abroad. In that multifaceted effort Latin America occupied a central place: at the time of the First World War, the Monroe Doctrine (1823) was almost one hundred years old and had been expressed with singular vigor for about thirty years. A simple theoretical formulation at the outset, the doctrine grew in scope and significance as a result of the big-stick policy, the Roosevelt Corollary, and dollar diplomacy, that Wilsonian idealism not only failed to reject but, to the contrary, invested with a high degree of virulence. Through four Presidents with strongly contrasting personalities an extraordinary continuity marked the policy which succeeded in installing a series of American protectorates in Central America which certainly had no such legal status and which neither Washington nor the American people wanted to recognize as such, which, however, were for that no less real.

Washington's interest, however, was not limited to Latin America; it also extended to the Far East and more especially to China. Although perhaps little known, the resources of Asia were to become an object of fascination for the masters of the empire.

But the American penetration of Asia was going to stumble on difficulties that the United States had not met in Latin America. Two major obstacles rose in its path. Geographically, while the Caribbean was at its doorstep, the United States needed a powerful Navy to approach

Asia's coast line. Historically, the European powers had preceded the United States in Asia, and furthermore, competition from Japan would have to be expected. Yet, geography and history inspired United States interest in Asia. From the time when the pioneers, in their rush to the west, reached the Pacific coast, America began to look beyond that vast ocean, for nothing could stop it in its continuous search for new frontiers. And in 1898, when the United States declared war against Spain, its strategy carried it not only to the West Indies but also to the Philippines, which became its Asian beachhead.

The advance in Asia was slower than the penetration of Latin America but American dynamism made it unavoidable. In 1785 a boat from Canton unloaded merchandise in New York, and in 1853 warships opened the doors of Japan to the United States. The pattern therefore was well established. And, from the outset, cold economic calculations cloaked in moral considerations played the prime role for that continent as for the others. The half successes and failures of the first American attempts in Asia were a lesson that the empire would profit from to subsequently assert its power on a continent where it nonetheless would meet its most serious disappointments.

Japan had had an inward-looking policy for two hundred years when on July 8, 1853, an American ship dropped anchor in Yedo Bay. Commodore Matthew Calbraith Perry, chief of the expedition, was under orders from President Fillmore to conclude a treaty of friendship and trade with the Japanese government. From his trip to China, Marco Polo had brought fabulous tales of the wealth of "Cipango," which six centuries later preoccupied the Commodore. Japan was surrounded by mystery since the Shogun had prohibited trade with Spain in 1624, and with Portugal in 1638. Except for a few very limited exchanges with the Dutch, the Japanese archipelago had practically cut itself off from the West. Matthew C. Perry was ready to use force to compel it to renew communications. But the Shogun understood that any resistance would be useless and he opened Japan to American trade by the Treaty of Kanagawa (1854).

When Christopher Columbus sailed on August 3, 1492, on the *Santa Maria* he was looking for the road to the Indies but he also dreamed of "Cathay" and carried letters of introduction from Ferdinand V and Isabella of Castile for the Great Khan, Emperor of China. Three centuries later, coming from Canton, the *Empress of China* dropped anchor in the port of New York in 1785, and the *Grand Turk*, also coming from Canton, touched port in Salem (1787). From 1787 to 1790 Captain Gray's voyages to Oregon and China inaugurated a three-way exchange: manufactured products from New England were bartered against furs from the American northwest and in turn exchanged for oriental products in China.

In 1789 forty-six vessels arrived in Canton: eighteen of them were American. To encourage the development of the Merchant Marine, Washington had reduced duties on merchandise imported on board American ships by 10 per cent. To stimulate commerce with the Far East the same law (July 4, 1789) cut in half duties on tea that came directly from the Orient. Several fiscal measures encouraged the birth of a national Merchant Marine of ships built in the United States and owned by American citizens. The great rush westward had not yet begun when enterprising Americans would take to the sea for distant lands rather than set forth on foot through the vast forests and deserts of the continent. As for the tonnage and value of foreign commerce, the United States was then second only to England. Between 1795 and 1801 profits from the American Merchant Marine were valued at $32 million annually. American ships went to China for tea, silk, porcelain, and spices.

The invention of the cotton gin had increased the production of cotton from 60 million to 1,300 million pounds between 1800 and 1850—and cotton, of which China was the major buyer, headed the list of exported products. Its soaring economic growth made the United States turn toward Asia.

During that first half of the nineteenth century the population of the United States rose from 5 to 23 million and capital invested in industry leaped from $50 million to $1 billion. Thanks to the increase in manpower (28½ million immigrants between 1860 and 1920), but also thanks to the progress of mechanization and to large investments, production increased prodigiously at the end of the nineteenth century and the beginning of the twentieth (figures below in thousands of dollars):

	1880	1919
Agriculture	2,460,107	23,783,200
Industry	9,372,379	62,418,079
TOTAL	11,832,486	86,201,279

Foreign trade showed a parallel surge (also in thousands of dollars):

	Exports	Imports	Surplus
1860	400,122	362,166	37,956
1900	1,499,462	929,771	569,691
1920	8,663,723	5,783,609	2,880,114

In other words, during that period, exports multiplied twenty-two times, imports sixteen times, and the balance-of-trade surplus seventy-five times. As Europe remained the principal partner of the United States, trade with Asia at first developed slowly. Between 1870 and 1900 exports to Asia rose from 2.07 per cent to 4.66 per cent of the total and imports from Asia increased from 6.8 per cent to 16.5

per cent. Trade accelerated during the first three decades of the twentieth century to the point when in 1929 Asia received 12.3 per cent of exports from the United States and supplied 32 per cent of its imports. Thus the turn of the century marked a decisive stage in the United States interest in Asia. Burgeoning economic power called for a parallel development in foreign commerce. And, three favorable factors interacted at the right moment: Admiral Mahan's aspirations took shape with the annexation of the Philippines (1898) and offered the United States a platform in the Pacific; Japan was becoming a world power, fifty years after Commodore Perry's first visit; finally, Japanese and European plans for China led to active United States intervention.

Japan gave the signal by taking over Korea, Formosa, and the Pescadores Islands (1895). China paid Japan a large indemnity and opened its territory to Japanese industries. Then Russia obtained the right to construct a railroad through Manchuria in 1896 and the lease of the Liaotung Peninsula and Port Arthur (1898). German forces established themselves in the Shantung Peninsula while England extended its hold in the Yangtze-Kiang Basin. France, which had already conquered Tonkin, extended its influence in the south and leased Kwangchowan. Thus the Western powers were dividing the Middle Empire among themselves. What was the United States going to do?

Washington could not see its nationals failing to share in the spoils. It wanted to guarantee them equal rights with Europeans in industry and commerce. John Hay, Secretary of State, sent the European powers a note (1899) in which he enunciated the principles of the "open door" policy: each country would respect the interests of other powers within its own zone of influence in China; a commission headed by Europeans and Americans would collect customs duties at the entrance of Chinese ports. European capitals responded courteously, without committing themselves. Americans, who did not at the time have a strong position in China, had a warm friendship for the Chinese, nourished by the tales of Protestant missionaries.

As a powerful wave of xenophobia spread through the empire, which had been delivered over to the cupidity of the "barbarians from the west," anger erupted into the Boxer Rebellion. In August 1900, to protect their legations and their nationals, the Western powers sent an international army made up of British, French, Russian, German, Japanese, and American troops.

From Washington, John Hay (McKinley's, and then Theodore Roosevelt's Secretary of State), sent another note (July 1900) to the European powers explaining the attitude of the United States, which participated in the international expedition against the Boxers but had as its objective to "preserve [the] Chinese territorial and administrative entity . . . and safeguard for the world the principle of an equal and impartial trade with all parts of the Chinese Empire." [18]

The international army arrived in Peking just in time to rescue the outnumbered Westerners. Disguised as a peasant, Empress Tsen-si left the capital, to return only eighteen months later when she reigned over a country placed in trusteeship by the 1901 Protocol, which extended the facilities granted to Western trade, placed the legation quarters under the permanent protection of an international army, and obliged China to pay an enormous war indemnity: $320 million or almost 2 billion gold francs. The payment of that sum was guaranteed by the customs revenues: the system which had been unilaterally applied by the United States in several countries of Latin America was organized on an international basis in China with joint participation of Japan, the European powers, and the United States. Customs control by foreigners hardly respected the "administrative entity" of China, hoped for by John Hay. Violating the same principle, warships from each country patrolled China's territorial waters and even the Yangtze-Kiang Basin. Nor did the increase in concessions respect the "territorial entity" of the Middle Empire. The "open door" policy, however, did succeed—in return for American military participation in the fight against the Boxers—in giving satisfaction to John Hay on one point: the commercial rights of the United States were recognized.

In February 1904 the Japanese fleet attacked a Russian squadron in Port Arthur, and in May 1905 Admiral Togo sank half the Russian Baltic fleet which was going toward Vladivostok after an eight-month voyage through the Atlantic, the Cape of Good Hope, the Indian Ocean, and the China Sea. John Hay protested that the Japanese attack in Manchuria violated the "open door" policy. Theodore Roosevelt offered his mediation to Japan and Russia. His position may not have been completely impartial, for at the same time he sent his Secretary of War, William Howard Taft, on a mission to Japan. The warring parties signed a treaty in Portsmouth, New Hampshire, in 1905 which gave Japan the southern part of Sakhalin, the peninsula of Liaotung, and complete freedom of action in Korea. Russia furthermore withdrew from southern Manchuria and surrendered part of the railroad which terminated at Port Arthur. Because he had furthered the signing of that treaty, favorable to a victorious Japan, Theodore Roosevelt received the Nobel Peace Prize. Five years later Japan invaded Korea, in violation of the Portsmouth Treaty.

The "open door" policy inaugurated by John Hay and pursued after his death encouraged the movement of a certain amount of capital. American investments in Asia which did not exceed $23 million in 1897, increased to $235 million in 1908 and reached $245 million in 1914. But these figures represented only a very small part of American capital invested abroad, which soared to a total of almost $3½ billion by 1914 (see table, p. 128). On the other hand, most of the $23 million invested in 1897 was represented by commercial operations and not by industrial enterprises. The progress shown subsequently was due mostly to the Philippines, which had recently been conquered. In 1914, almost half of the $245 million invested in Asia was represented by holdings related to loans to the Japanese government. China, for which it is difficult to secure accurate figures, therefore occupied but a very modest place in the enterprise of American capitalists. Theodore Roosevelt, however, encouraged the America–China Development Company, organized by Edward H. Harriman and J. Pierpont Morgan, to undertake railroad construction in China. But the Peking authorities were not easily convinced; they made many dilatory responses and played up European and Japanese competitors. Finally, the American group became discouraged and to Roosevelt's dismay gave up the deal. It was only during Taft's Presidency that the group was recognized. Under pressure from the State Department the America–China Development Company finally was admitted to an international consortium to which the Chinese government entrusted construction of the railroads. "The consistent purpose of the present administration has been to encourage the use of American capital in the development of China," Taft declared to Congress on December 3, 1912.[19] But Woodrow Wilson, who had just replaced Taft in the White House, against the advice of the State Department made public on March 18, 1913, a note hostile to the consortium which in his eyes was guilty of threatening "to touch very nearly the administrative independence of China itself . . . just now awakening to a consciousness of its power and of its obligations to its people. . . . Our interests," Wilson continued, "are those of the Open Door—a door of friendship and mutual advantage."

Thus, the efforts of Theodore Roosevelt and of Taft, who wanted to make of the "open door" an instrument of their imperialist policy in China, were practically nullified by Wilsonian idealism. Republican Presidents had not succeeded in attracting important American capital to China: "First, American capitalists were busy with investments elsewhere, including some reorganization of the American economic system. Second, Americans, as in the case of the Chinese trade, met the continuous, bitter, and successful rivalry of Japan and the European nations." [20] Soon after, moreover, the Morgan Bank, acting for the Allies, was asked to finance the purchase of military materiel during the First World War and that undertaking relegated its Chinese projects to last place. Therefore the consortium continued without American participation. The United States encouraged another attempt after the First World War, but without success, because China refused to negotiate with the new consortium. When hostilities ceased in Europe the portion of American capital invested in China was very small and that country received only 0.6 per cent of American exports. Japan and European countries had taken over the market—which remained unimportant anyway—before the United States. Because the Monroe Doctrine corresponded to profound realities, the American continent retained priority in the attention of the United States, which devoted to it more than half of its foreign investments.

Ultimately, the history of the "open door" policy was the history of a failure. American historians do not agree on the motives which induced John Hay in 1899 to take up an idea which was not his. Some see in it an initiative inspired by the idealism and by the democratic spirit of Americans, hostile in principle to the establishment of "zones of influence" in a country which had a right to its territorial integrity. But George Kennan has clearly shown that the "open

door" was part of the diplomatic baggage of England, skill-
ful in preserving a position which permitted it to control 80
per cent of Chinese trade. In the United States, by contrast,
the State Department at that time did not even have a section assigned to the Far East. London, dreading the competition of other powers, may even have renounced the
"open door" policy, which ran the risk after all of going
against its interests. Rockhill, who had served in China, and
the Englishman Hippisley, employed by the Chinese Imperial Service of Maritime Customs, had suggested to John
Hay, who knew nothing of the Far East, that the United
States endorse the idea. Japan and the European powers
gave lip service to the beautiful principles enunciated by
John Hay, but they continued nonetheless to strengthen
their positions in China. The military intervention against
the Boxer Rebellion, Kennan notes, "was bound to lead to a
net increase, rather than decrease, in the authority exerted
by foreign governments in China." Besides, was John Hay
really completely disinterested? ". . . in December, 1900,"
Kennan also points out, "only five months after his proclamation of devotion to the principle of upholding Chinese
territorial and administrative 'entity,' [John Hay] secretly
instructed our minister in Peking to try to obtain for the
United States a naval coaling station at Samsah Bay in the
Chinese province of Fukien." Moreover the United States
was not resolved to enforce the principles whose cause it
pleaded: that is what it politely replied when Japan was
concerned about the Russian advance in Manchuria. Kennan points out that the United States rebelled against being
discriminated against in the China trade, at the time that it
inaugurated in the commerce of the Philippines and of
Puerto Rico discrimination in its favor. The "open door"
policy was nonetheless presented to the American public as
a great and noble endeavor. "The popularity of the administration's foreign policy was materially improved just at the

time of the coming presidential elections," George Kennan notes.

In any case, with Roosevelt and Taft the "open door" policy had another significance, as is shown by their efforts to bring the Harriman and Morgan groups into the competition waged by the railroad companies in China. But these efforts remained very cautious, for, as Roosevelt wrote to Senator Henry Cabot Lodge, it was important to preserve some balance between Russia and Japan in the Far East. Furthermore, because of distance, China occupied a secondary place in the preoccupations of the American government, which did not yet have the means of establishing a grand policy on a world scale. Although he dreamed of conquest and greatness, Theodore Roosevelt knew the limits of his capabilities. "And as regards Manchuria," he said for example, "if the Japanese choose to follow a course of conduct to which we are adverse, we cannot stop it unless we are prepared to go to war, and a successful war about Manchuria would require a fleet as good as that of England, plus an army as good as that of Germany." [21] Realism led Roosevelt and his Secretary of War Taft to conclude the Taft-Katzura (1905) and Root-Takahira (1908) accords, which the Japanese could only interpret as implicit approval of their expansionism in Manchuria and Korea, which violated John Hay's principles. Although highly anti-imperialistic in its formulation, the "open door" policy thus remained ambiguous when John Hay endeavored to obtain a naval station and to have the commercial rights of the United States recognized in China. But all ambiguity disappeared when Roosevelt's big stick was not big enough for the Middle Empire, and Taft's dollar diplomacy, so fruitful in Latin America, could not triumph in China where other powers were already too solidly entrenched to yield a free hand to Harriman and Morgan. When Wilson disavowed the efforts of the State Department in support of these two groups, his sincerest idealism was the other side of a material inability to introduce American imperialism in China. From the Republican McKinley to the Democrat Wilson, the United States role in investments in China and in that country's foreign trade remained modest. Its field of action in Asia was almost wholly confined to the Philippines, which it had conquered, and to Japan which was in the process of being industrialized, while China had not yet undertaken to modernize its economy.

V

———

Nationalism and
the Empire

The "idealism" which, half a century later, still preserves a halo around him did not dissuade Woodrow Wilson from intervening drastically a number of times in Latin America. It was above all for economic reasons that he sent troops to Mexico, the Dominican Republic, Haiti, Cuba, Nicaragua, Panama, Honduras, Guatemala, and that he exerted strong pressure on many other countries. But other economic considerations were to take America much further on the road of empire. For America was prosperous and determined to develop the prosperity by which it let itself be intoxicated while devoting to it the best of its efforts. At the same time, forgetting that—without too much concern for democracy or self-determination—it bore down on its close neighbors, it continued to consider itself the refuge of liberty in the world. Freedom and prosperity thus fed a powerful and understandable nationalistic trend. For such a brilliant success strikingly confirmed the sentiment of John Adams, who looked upon the formation of America as a great "design of Providence" conceived to enlighten the rest of humanity.

That nationalist trend was to find a thousand ways to

manifest itself and two world wars would permit it to carry its ambitions to the ends of the earth. The empire did not conceive of itself on a strictly economic basis. It was necessary also for it to have an indomitable nationalist fervor, faith in a special mission to be filled in the world. And if the fulfillment of that mission strengthened the prosperity of America, it would only show that the end pursued and the means used were completely consistent. Thus was found again the old ambiguity of an empire simultaneously generous and profitable, highly disinterested and also greatly advantageous. But only very concrete decisions, not altruistic dreams, were going to put into effect the last decisive stages of imperialist expansion.

Nationalist manifestations occurred in many areas. Intervention in Latin America served powerful economic interests, but to develop its prosperity, America had to barricade itself behind a double protective barrier: against the competition of foreign industries and against too great an influx of immigrants threatening domestic equilibrium. Tariff protectionism and an ostracism directed at certain categories of people both extended over a long period, well before the First World War and lasting well after. We will show how nationalism, the mainspring of empire, was translated into a tariff policy and into laws on immigration.

In the aftermath of the First World War President Harding formulated with great vigor "the nationalist gospel" of the United States: *America first*. But that naked nationalism also dominated a long period of the First World War. That nationalism kept the United States, between 1914 and 1917, out of the conflict that ravaged Europe. America was moreover much less tempted to "fly to the rescue of democracies," since its neutrality permitted it to grow in wealth while the war exhausted the European democracies. It developed its productive facilities, expanded its foreign markets, profited from a rise in prices and strengthened its Merchant Marine and, finally, New York replaced London as the world financial center. As will be seen, only when it felt threatened in its territorial integrity did America resign itself to a belated entry into the war. A strict conception of national interest, which Wilsonian "idealism" could not change, had dictated first a policy of neutrality, then a declaration of war.

But enriching America remained the major goal. When peace returned, the United States isolated itself to permit its affairs to continue to prosper. Reinforcing its tariff barriers, it had little interest in the outside world except to develop its exports. It is thanks to the First World War that its balance of trade finally showed a large surplus. And that expansion continued until the great crisis of 1929–1930 in which the United States dragged the world down after it.

Nationalism still remained a dominant trait of American policy when the European democracies entered the war against Nazi Germany. And the experience of the First World War was repeated: first a neutrality made the more profitable by supplies to "allies" which provided the American economy with precious help to get out of the crisis that paralyzed it; then, when America was threatened no longer only in its territorial integrity, but directly struck at Pearl Harbor—the entry into war on a fraternal, shoulder-to-shoulder basis with the severely exhausted democracies.

From one war to the other, in a quarter of a century, that nationalist evolution brought the American empire to a degree of power which it had not dared dream of. When Japan and Germany capitulated, the empire was very near its apogee. Then began its real problems in a world in which it was inextricably involved. From the beginning and end of that quarter-century Europe remembered two very different but equally memorable faces of America, both stamped with an idealism that was unyielding before economic imperatives and the harsh realities of war. Between the two

Democrats who had sought refuge in neutrality before taking America into war, between Woodrow Wilson and Franklin D. Roosevelt is a journey that we now want to retrace. The voyage is brief, but it deeply affected the history of America. Men and events of that period anticipated the power of the empire which reaches far beyond the American continent.

America developed, grew rich, asserted its power. While the population of France remained almost stationary, that of the United States rose from 76 to 106 million between 1900 and 1920. During the same period, the budget of the federal government increased from $698 to $6,454 million and the gross national product from $28 to more than $61 billion, the First World War playing a major role in that soaring progress. Foreign investments quintupled since the beginning of the century to reach $3,500 million in 1914. But at the same time America, intoxicated with its prosperity, closed its doors to the outside world.

First, against foreign competition, the Dingley Tariff of 1897 remained in effect until 1909; it set a general level of Customs duties at 57 per cent, higher duties on raw and manufactured wool, and took skins off the list of exempted products. The Republican program of 1908 in which public opinion saw a plan for the lowering of tariffs strongly contributed to the Republican defeat in the midterm elections of 1910 and in the presidential election of 1912. Wilson's victory was followed in 1913 by passage of the Underwood-Simmons Bill, which compensated for the exemptions granted iron, steel, raw wool, and later sugar, by a rise in duties on chemical products and various articles. After the First World War, the return of Republicans to power (1920) was followed in 1921 by protective measures against agricultural products and in 1922 by the Fordney-

McCumber Tariff which exceeded all earlier tariffs: duties on iron and steel were re-established and duties on textiles and agricultural products greatly increased.

Second, against immigration, between 1900 and 1910 the United States welcomed the largest contingent of immigrants, in absolute numbers and in percentage of the total, as is shown by the following table.

Decade	Total Population	Immigrants	% of Total
1880–1890	62,947,000	5,246,000	8.3%
1890–1900	75,994,000	3,687,000	4.8%
1900–1910	91,972,000	8,795,000	9.5%
1910–1920	105,710,000	5,735,000	5.4%
1920–1930	122,775,000	4,107,000	3.3%
1930–1940	131,669,000	1,528,000	1.1%
1940–1950	151,683,000	1,035,000	0.6%

In general terms, immigration was encouraged all through the nineteenth century in spite of some campaigns against the granting of the vote to foreigners. A law in 1875 prohibited entry into the country only to prostitutes and criminals. In violation of a treaty signed in 1868 between the United States and China, the United States in 1882 closed the door to the Chinese; the law was adopted under pressure from workers who complained of the competition of Chinese laborers, but the exclusion did not prevent the government, sixteen years later, from advocating the "open door" policy in order to ensure the participation of American businessmen in Chinese trade. The treaty of 1868 specified, however, that in no circumstances could Chinese immigrants apply for American citizenship: the right to vote was therefore automatically and in advance refused to them. At the request of the trade unions, Congress enacted a law in 1885, strengthened in 1887 and 1888, requiring that any candidate for immigration have a work contract: it was important to fight the importation of cheap manpower which would break strikes and lower wages. A law in 1891 prohibited immigration of polygamists, indigents, and persons with various diseases. Those laws contributed to reducing the number of immigrants between 1890 and 1900: compared to the preceding decade the number fell from 5.2 to 3.6 million and from 8.3 per cent to 4.8 per cent of the total population (see table, p. 170). Anarchists were excluded in 1903 after the assassination of President McKinley, then tubercular and mental patients in 1907. But the whole of those restrictive measures was fought both by idealists who wanted to make of the United States a land of refuge and by representatives of clearly defined interests: shipping and railroad lines which undertook the transportation of immigrants, industrialists in search of cheap labor, renegade union leaders who supplied contractors with laborers prepared to accept low wages. A whole "racket" was organized to attract foreigners, make them promises which were not kept, and shamelessly exploit them. These efforts succeeded in having the largest contingent of immigrants in any decade enter the United States between 1900 and 1910.

Against them rose up one of the major prophets of imperialism, Senator Henry Cabot Lodge, in whose eyes massive immigration threatened Republican institutions. He proposed to close the door to illiterates. Trade unions warmly approved his position. "So far as I remember, this is the only issue upon which I have ever found myself in accord with Senator Lodge," wrote Samuel Gompers, founder and President of the American Federation of Labor, who was soon playing a major role against Woodrow Wilson's "imperialist" policy in Mexico.[1] In 1912 Congress voted a law against admission of illiterates but Taft vetoed it. Congress did it again in 1913 and Wilson also vetoed the law but Congress was determined to override his veto. And, gathering the required two-thirds majority, in February 1917 it voted a law which no longer had need of the President's signature. That law was aimed above all at immigrants from southern and eastern Europe, also at Asians, for America willingly welcomed only immigrants of Anglo-Saxon, German, and Scandinavian origin. The First World War had brought an influx which threatened to reach a new high once peace was restored. Therefore a 1921 law established quotas: for each country 3 per cent of the total number born in that country and settled in the United States at the time of the 1910 census. Quotas were again reduced in 1924, bringing down to 154,000 the number of European immigrants admitted each year. Thus is explained mathematically the fact that 1,528,000 foreigners could settle in the United States between 1930 and 1940. The same law gave satisfaction to trade unions by prohibiting immigration of Japanese workers. At the entrance to the port of New York the Statue of Liberty, unveiled in 1886, is no longer anything but the symbol of a forgotten dream and a disowned ideal:

> Give me your tired, your poor,
> Your huddled masses yearning to breathe free,
> The wretched refuse of your teeming shore,
> Send these, the homeless, tempest-tossed to me:
> I lift my lamp beside the golden door.

In March 1920, by rejecting the Versailles Treaty and the Pact of the League of Nations, the United States, confirming a basic tendency, entered the road of isolationism. America withdrew within its national egoism. However controversial, the role played by Senator Henry Cabot Lodge was a determining factor in the refusal to ratify the treaty and the pact. The champions of imperialism now became the most ardent advocates of economic protectionism, of Draconian restrictions to immigration, and of political isolationism. Their objective had not changed: It was always a matter of making the United States into a rich and powerful country. In order to do that, it was important to protect America against foreign competition and from a massive influx of population; it was just as important to keep it out of European disputes. In 1916 the voters gave Woodrow Wilson 9,129,606 votes against 8,538,221 to Republican Charles E. Hughes. The Democratic slogan "He kept us out of war" was certainly responsible for the fact that Wilson had won over 3 million more votes than in 1912. But after the war Republicans came back to power in force. In 1920 Warren G. Harding got 16,152,200 votes against 9,147,353 for Democrat James M. Cox. In January 1920 Harding expressed the deep feelings which for years had been shared by the large majority of his compatriots when he declared: "I have confidence in our America that requires no council of foreign powers to point the way to American duty. . . . Call it the selfishness of nationality if you will, I think it an inspiration to patriotic devotion. To safeguard America first—to think of America first—to exalt America first." [2]

Although not new, the nationalist gospel had never been formulated with such force, but it was the same nationalism which had dictated the actions of Harding's predecessors in the White House. Subsequently, the slogan *America first* was to resound often on the American political scene. In the same way that the will for power and greatness had launched the Republicans Theodore Roosevelt and Taft into the imperialist adventure, it dictated neutrality to Woodrow Wilson at the beginning of the First World War, then inspired isolation in the Republican contemporaries of Harding. Their concern was throughout the vigor and strength of the United States and the openly imperialistic period provided striking confirmation of it to the rest of the world. After the disappointments which followed the First World War, that vigor and strength had to be consolidated behind the protective wall of tariff barriers and stringent restrictions to immigration by concentrating all energies on domestic development, far from the European conflicts and world whirlpools whose echoes resounded in the League of Nations in which the United States had refused to participate. National pride involved the United States in the conquest of the Philippines and of Puerto Rico, in armed interventions in Cuba, Panama, Nicaragua, the Dominican Republic, Haiti and Mexico, and in the strengthening of the "Monroe Doctrine" which was to make sure that the will and the interests of the United States prevailed on the American continent. National egoism, after having caused the policy of neutrality to triumph from 1914 to 1917, compelled the United States to retrench within its frontiers beginning in 1920, to enjoy in all tranquillity an exceptional prosperity, and to devote itself exclusively to the accumulation of more material wealth. Whether it took the form of Theodore Roosevelt's swagger, Wilson's indecision, or Harding's mediocrity, imperialism and isolation proceeded from the same nationalist fervor. America was a big enough power to speak loudly and intervene in world affairs—or to ignore them.

Harding and his successors refused to be distracted by military operations, but nonetheless extended the economic empire of the United States: American investments abroad rose from $3,481 million in 1914 to $9,090 million in 1924, the largest share in Latin America ($4,040 million) and in Canada ($2,460 million), Europe receiving only $1,900 million. The U.S. was getting richer. "The census of 1900 placed the total wealth of the nation at approximately 88,500,000,000 dollars. This had more than doubled by 1914 and with it had come an increase in per capita wealth. Significant increases are also to be noted during these years in the national income." [3] With Europe at war, the neutrality of the United States was to increase that prosperity even more.

Indeed America was completely absorbed by the accumulation of wealth when the drama exploded in Europe. President Wilson proclaimed the neutrality of the United States as early as August 4, 1914, and took care to renew that declaration the next day. Neutrality could not, like a miracle, relax the tensions which became apparent in the country between citizens of English origin who wished for an Allied victory, German-Americans devoted to their fatherland, profoundly anti-British Irishmen, and Jews who had suffered in Russia. Wilson also asked his countrymen to observe neutrality not only in their actions but also in their minds. "Every man who really loves America," he declared, "will act and speak in the true spirit of neutrality." [4]

That attitude may seem surprising on the part of a President who did not hesitate on April 21, 1914, to intervene in Mexico with Marines who occupied Vera Cruz. Likewise, while he waited until April 1917 to put the United States on the side of the democracies fighting in Europe, Wilson had sent thirteen months earlier, again in Mexico, a "punitive expedition" led by the same General Pershing who would disembark in Europe at the head of American troops. Obviously the two ventures did not have the same scope, but both divided American public opinion. Wilson hardly hesitated in the case of Mexico because it was a neighboring country where great interests were involved, a country within the zone covered by the Monroe Doctrine, the doctrine by which the United States pledged not to intervene in European disputes. Be that as it may, United States neutrality appeared to be a very flexible principle when Latin America was involved, but very rigid in its application to Europe.

In 1913–1914 the United States was going through a minor crisis, heightened by the economic disorders which marked the first months of the war in Europe. But in 1915 a prodigious period of industrial and agricultural expansion began which continued for five years. For the duration of the war, the total production of the United States increased by 15 per cent, naturally at a much higher rate for war production. The production of petroleum rose from 265 to 335 million barrels, that of iron ore from 41 to 75 million tons, that of copper from 1,150 to 1,886 million pounds, etc. And agriculture followed the trend: wheat production in spite of a slight weakening in 1916 and 1917 increased from 763 to 900 million bushels between 1914 and 1918 but above all, the price of wheat, exported in great quantities, rose from 97 cents to $2.73 per bushel, or tripled, while the price of cotton quadrupled—climbing from 8.5 cents to 35.9 cents a pound in 1920. And, cut off from some of its sources of supply, America began producing at home on a large scale articles that had previously been imported. Born under cover of neutrality the American chemical industry was the most remarkable of those "war babies," but precision instruments and optical instruments should be added to the list.

War gave American foreign commerce a prodigious spurt in spite of the risks that German submarines posed for the merchant fleet. Exports tripled from 1914 to 1920, rising from $2,329 to $8,080 million. The surplus of exports over imports which had been fluctuating between $400 and $500 million in the years preceding the war, reached $3,845 million in 1919. Exports were mostly war material and food products. Thus the value of the explosives exported went from $6 million to $802 million between 1914 and 1917, that of chemical products from $21 to $181 million, that of iron and steel from $251 to $1,133 million. During the same period, export of meat more than doubled and that of wheat more than tripled.

America, in neutrality as in war, remained the great supplier of the Allies who, in order to meet increasing needs, began to liquidate $2 billion in American stocks, then arranged large loans first with private banks, then with the

American government when the latter finally entered the war. At the end of hostilities the United States had loaned more than $9 billion to the Allies. During the conflict, the United States had taken the place left vacant by European powers in the markets of Latin America and Asia. Thanks to that combination of circumstances it reached a position which was completely new for it: it had become a lending nation and New York had supplanted London as financial center of the world.

Admiral Mahan had dreamed of a powerful Merchant Marine, indispensable for the development of international trade. While the United States owned the second largest fleet in the world a century earlier, in 1914 it had a capacity reaching hardly a million tons. But the war in the Atlantic sent many European ships to the bottom, while others were reassigned to military transport. The scarcity of ships was soon felt and the American government took several measures to encourage its Merchant Marine; it created a Shipping Board in 1916, whose duties comprised among others an important program of naval construction. In 1917 the Shipping Board launched the Emergency Fleet Corporation with a capital of $50 million. In two years the number of shipyards rose from 61 to 341. Results were spectacular: tonnage assigned to foreign trade reached 2,185,000 tons in 1916, then 8,694,000 at the time of the armistice and, the effort being continued after the war, more than 11 million in 1921.

Notwithstanding several laws designed to encourage its development, the Merchant Marine increasingly declined from that date until the Second World War, falling to 3,312,000 tons in 1939. Only the war effort, which permitted the intervention of the federal government, explains the temporary spectacular rise of the Merchant Marine. Between 1916 and 1918 Congress had voted credits of $4 billion to that effect, and the number of workers employed in the shipyards rose from 45,000 to 380,000. When America came back to business as usual, private capital, hardly anxious to take on the capital expenditures of the state, preferred to turn to other activities. In 1925 the tonnage launched in the United States did not reach one-eighth the tonnage launched by Great Britain or one-third the tonnage launched by Italy. Increasingly, American freight sailed under foreign flags. In 1935 the percentage of freight transported under the American flag fell back to the level of 1870. Lacking orders, important shipyards had to close their doors. For the cost of maritime construction in the United States was abnormally high and, furthermore, the whole of the economic situation was marked by anarchy which, among other causes, led to the great economic crisis of 1929–1930.

As it was, it took the Second World War to see the powerful rise of the Merchant Marine again. Hardly greater than 3 million tons on the eve of the conflict, capacity had already tripled by 1943. Once more, war had forced government intervention in the domain of production, thus ensuring the development of a powerful Merchant Marine without which no empire can expand and prosper.

Some authors have relied on oversimplifications and a hasty definition of "imperialism," to explain the entrance of the United States into the First World War by the pressures that big business, always in search of profits, exercised on President Wilson. Such a dogmatic interpretation does not stand a study of the facts. Of course, in 1917, private loans taken by the Allies in the United States rose to $2,500 million, against only $45 million in German loans. But that was not a sufficient reason for the United States to fly to the rescue of its principal debtor. The theory according to which big bankers and American munitions merchants, violating the spirit and letter of neutrality, acted as "warmongers" seemed justified by the publication in 1936 of a report

by a Senate commission of inquiry headed by Gerald P.
Nye. That report inspired, in particular, C. A. Beard's article titled "Solving Domestic Crises by War" published in
the *New Republic*, March 11, 1936.

The authors of the theory should have recognized what
would be, in their own eyes, a most serious contradiction:
the influence of big business would have had to be very
weak indeed if it had taken three years to convince the federal government to enter the war. In fact, a serious inquiry,
based on a detailed analysis of the most influential commercial and financial newspapers, showed that American businessmen were warm partisans of neutrality.[5] Figures
previously cited (see pp. 175–176) prove conclusively that
neutrality had greatly favored the economic prosperity of
the United States. For that reason, it was widely supported
in business circles. Soon after the outbreak of the conflict, a
businessman as eminent as Henry Ford, ridiculed by the
eastern press but warmly supported by the west, chartered a
boat, which he filled with preachers and pacifists, and took
them to Europe to try to convince the governments to "get
the boys out of the trenches by Christmas." The avowed
imperialists, who sixteen years before had drawn McKinley
into the little war against Spain, intended to remain neutral
in a conflict of much greater scope. Theodore Roosevelt was
not dreaming of charging at the head of his Rough Riders
on any point of the European front. To the contrary, in the
Outlook of August 22, 1914, he solemnly proclaimed: "I am
not now taking sides." Furthermore, the following month,
he paid homage to the German people, "stern, virile and
masterful," but declared that it would be "folly to jump
into the war." He no longer appeared as the fiery war advocate outraged before 1898 by the clamor of the pacifist clan.
No one dreamed now of "regenerating savage and senile
peoples" confronting each other in such a bloody conflict.
For the First World War had nothing in common with the

"splendid little war" that Secretary of State John Hay regarded complacently a few years earlier.

Only a minority actively took sides for England and France: sons of well-to-do families, Francophiles since Lafayette, volunteered for the Lafayette Esquadrille, for the Foreign Legion, or the Ambulance Service. The great mass of the country, "and working people in general, were both neutral and pacifist. Even recent immigrants embraced American isolationism with fervor; the European war represented part of what they had come over to get away from," notes Morison.[6] The Progressives saw in the war an obstacle to scientific and human progress. Many others felt that both camps were equally guilty. The Hearst newspapers, which had done so much to rouse public opinion in the war of 1898, now led pacifist campaigns in 1914, as indeed most of the other newspapers did. Inciting to war, this war, was not at that time a good way of winning readers or of increasing circulation.

Like big business, public opinion was hostile to the war. For, Morison remarks, "The business and financial interests who followed their pocketbooks, and Wall Street generally, remained strong for neutrality until early 1917, because that status offered them all the profits of war without the corresponding sacrifices." The choice was clear: Thanks to neutrality during the war, production increased by 15 per cent, the volume of exports more than doubled ($2,329 million in 1914 and $6,227 million in 1917), and average wages went from $100 a month in 1913 to $162 in 1918. It would take a powerful psychological shock for America to enter the war.

That shock was not provoked by the British blockade, which, however, hurt American commercial interests, especially when London added cereals and cotton to the list of forbidden products. Nor was it any more provoked when Germany, increasing the damage caused to the commercial rights of neutrals, therefore the United States, declared in 1915 that waters surrounding Great Britain were in the war zone. Each of these measures provoked a simple diplomatic protest on the part of the United States. Finally, the shock was not even provoked by the torpedoing of the *Lusitania* on May 7, 1915, by a German submarine, although more than one hundred Americans died in the sinking. The *Lusitania* had not only transported American passengers, but also munitions for the Allies. Feeling ran high in the United States but did not last. This time, Theodore Roosevelt launched an appeal to enter the war and the Hearst press did not fail to follow in his footsteps. But the fever quickly subsided, for America was not ready to fight. And why risk thousands of American victims because some one hundred Americans had drowned? Three days after the sinking of the *Lusitania*, President Wilson declared: "There is such a thing as a man being too proud to fight." However, on May 13 Wilson sent a protest to Germany which was ignored. On June 9, in another note Wilson became more stern. But Bryan, his Secretary of State, judging that the wording of the new note was too strong and fearful that it might be taken as an ultimatum and risk drawing the United States into the war, resigned rather than sign it. For he believed that the government should not concern itself with the fate of Americans who traveled on board belligerent ships. Alluding to the fact that the *Lusitania* transported munitions, Bryan added: "Germany has a right to prevent contraband from going to the Allies, and a ship carrying contraband should not rely upon passengers to protect her from an attack—it would be like putting women and children in front of an army."

The myth of automatic solidarity between American democracy and the English and French democracies has tended to blur the long delay of two years between the sinking of the *Lusitania* (May 7, 1915) and the entry of the

United States into the war (April 6, 1917). In any case, there is no direct link between the two events, in spite of the agitation generated by Theodore Roosevelt and Hearst on the occasion of the sinking. Ten months after the *Lusitania*, the French ship *Sussex* was sunk by a German submarine (March 24, 1916), resulting in the death of eighty civilians. Washington informed Germany that such war tactics were "utterly incompatible with the principles of humanity." [7]

In France, French troops sacrificed some 350,000 men from February to December 1916 to repulse German attacks on Verdun. The battle of the Somme, which cost the French 200,000 men, and the British almost 400,000, began at the beginning of July. At that moment President Wilson, in spite of all the care that he took to preserve United States neutrality, ordered General Pershing to intervene not in Europe but in Mexico in a vain attempt to capture Pancho Villa. However, the elections which took place in the fall of the same year did not leave any doubt as to the state of mind which largely prevailed in the United States. Democrats stumped the country exalting in passionate speeches "the splendid diplomatic victories of our great President who has preserved the vital interests of our government and its citizens and kept us out of war." On that platform, Wilson got 49.3 per cent of the vote and 277 electoral votes. The Republicans had nominated Charles Evans Hughes, who declared: "We desire peace, the peace of justice and right, and believe in maintaining a straight and honest neutrality between the belligerents in the great war in Europe." On that platform Hughes got 46 per cent of the vote and 254 electoral votes.[8] The Democratic New York *World* had even believed on November 7, 1916, that it could assign victory to the Republicans: the California results were not yet known. When they were Wilson had won by 4,000 votes, which finally gave him victory. The two candidates had campaigned for neutrality. Without a shadow of a doubt, the American people did not want to hurl themselves into the war. Protected by its neutrality, the empire, already powerful, intended to pursue its economic expansion, to develop its industry and its commerce, to increase its exports while the prices of raw materials and industrial products rose. It not only sold those products in Europe but also in markets that the warring powers could no longer supply. To ensure this thrust toward its new markets it built up a Merchant Marine (highly inadequate on the eve of the conflict), while internally, new industries to meet the deficiency of European supplies were born and grew. Prices rose but wages rose also. The minor recession of 1913–1914 was forgotten. A welcome prosperity returned and was received, in this era of cyclical crises, with great optimism and unshakable confidence in the duration of any period of expansion. America was neutral and intended to remain so. That will was confirmed by the results of the presidential election on November 6, 1916. Nevertheless, six months later the United States was going to hurl its forces into the conflict on the side of the British and French democracies. What happened between November 1916 and April 1917 to explain such a turnabout?

The event which profoundly changed the mood of the people and of the empire's government had no relation to the unfolding of military operations in Europe. At the beginning of 1917 several facts confirmed that America was solidly attached to a lucrative neutrality. On January 22 President Wilson made his "peace without victory" proposal to the Senate, which no belligerent was disposed to accept. On January 31 Germany made known its conditions for peace, also unacceptable, and at the same time announced that it was going to wage merciless submarine warfare from which no neutral ship could escape. That blow to the "rights" of neutrals provoked a sharp reaction in the United States, which on February 3 broke off diplomatic relations with Germany. On February 22 Congress adopted a military budget similar to that of the preceding year which, by its small size ($250 million), confirmed a strong desire not to make preparations for entering the war. Furthermore, Congress had authorized expenditures for the construction of some new destroyers, but the Secretary of the Navy, Josephus Daniels, refused to sign the contracts, for he feared that such a move would be interpreted as a "provocation" by Germany and risk drawing the United States into the conflict. Wilson told Colonel House, "This country has no intention of letting itself be drawn into a war. To engage in it would be, on our part, a crime against civilization." On February 3, 1917, Wilson went to the Capitol to tell Congress of his decision to break off diplomatic relations with Berlin following Germany's decision to wage unrestricted submarine warfare. And, said the President that afternoon, "I refuse to believe that it is the intention of the German authorities to do in fact what they have warned us they will feel at liberty to do." The same evening, in Berlin, German Minister of Foreign Affairs Zimmermann was dining with United States Ambassador Gerard and told him, "You will see, everything will be all right. America will do nothing because Wilson is for peace and nothing else." And, as a matter of fact, it was not the submarine war which made Wilson change his mind.

On January 16 the German Ambassador to Washington, Bernstorff, had been informed of the decision concerning unrestricted submarine warfare, a decision which he had to communicate to the American government on January 31. That message was followed by a note from Zimmermann to Bernstorff, which he was to transmit to the German Ambassador to Mexico, Eckhardt. Here is the astonishing text of that note.

We intend to begin unrestricted submarine warfare on the first of February. We shall endeavor in spite of this to keep the United States neutral. In the event of this not succeeding, we make Mexico a proposal of alliance on the following basis: make war together, make peace together, generous financial support, and an understanding on our part that Mexico is to reconquer the lost territory in Texas, New Mexico and Arizona. The settlement in detail is left to you.

You will inform the President [of Mexico] of the above most secretly as soon as the outbreak of war with the United States is certain and add the suggestion that he should, on his own initiative, invite Japan to immediate adherence and at the same time mediate between Japan and ourselves.

Please call the President's attention to the fact that the unrestricted employment of our submarines now offers the prospect of compelling England to make peace within a few months. Acknowledge receipt.

(signed) Zimmermann[9]

This plan was at once too Machiavellian and too naïve. Should unrestricted submarine warfare make the United States abandon its neutrality, Mexico—by declaring war on Washington—would immobilize a large part of America's troops. In return, after the inevitable German victory, Mexico would take back Texas, New Mexico, and Arizona that the United States had taken from it the preceding century. Mexico had good relations with Japan, from which it had bought arms and a munitions factory, and was capable of persuading it to change camps in return for the promise that it would get Hawaii. When Wilson had sent Admiral Fletcher's Marines to occupy the port of Vera Cruz in 1914, it was primarily to prevent the delivery to Mexico by boat of two hundred machine guns and 15 million shells from Germany. German agents, among them von Papen, had spent some $27 million in the United States—half for propaganda, espionage, the organization of strikes and half to incite the Mexican Huerta to foment an uprising against Carranza. That scandal, uncovered by American intelligence, broke out in the *New York Times* on December 8, 1915. After the attack against the small American city of Columbus, New Mexico, on March 9, 1916, an attack which was ascribed to Pancho Villa and which triggered the United States intervention in Mexico, the American Ambassador to Berlin, James Gerard, cabled the State Department: AM SURE VILLA'S ATTACKS ARE MADE IN GERMANY.[10] That opinion was confirmed by several American journalists in Mexico who were convinced that Germany wanted to dissuade the United States from intervening in the European conflict by keeping it on the alert on its southern frontier. An American news service informed the government that the German arms destined for Huerta, who had just died on January 14, 1916, had gone to Pancho Villa to incite United States' intervention in Mexico. Using in particular the intermediacy of German-Americans, German propaganda in the United States kept reiterating that American forces should occupy all the territory between Texas and Panama to ensure the safety of the canal. Some newspapers were completely convinced of it, like the *Chicago Tribune* which wrote: "Fate offers us a golden apple in Mexico and only bitter fruits in Flanders. If we win a war with Mexico we know what we get out of it—a secure continent. And it is practically impossible for us to lose." President Carranza himself sent a cordial letter to Zimmermann assuring him of his pro-German sympathies and of his desire to strengthen political, military, and naval cooperation with Germany. The affair was especially promising, since the Mexican concessions belonging to a single English owner, Lord Cowdray, supplied more than half of the petroleum necessary to the English fleet. The plan was Machiavellian, but not insane.

The whole affair was nevertheless bizarre, since communications between Zimmermann and the German embassy in Washington took place over the cable used by—the State Department. The English had cut German cables at the beginning of the war. At the suggestion of Colonel House, President Wilson had accepted an unbelievable deal in the fallacious hope that his peace plans, transmitted more rapidly to Berlin, would have a greater chance of success: messages went from the German embassy to the State Department, which transmitted them to the American embassy in Berlin, which delivered them to Zimmermann. On January 24, 1917, Wilson, filled with misgivings, wrote Colonel House to ask him whether he was sure that messages thus transmitted really served the cause of peace, and whether there was in those dispatches anything "which it would be unneutral for us to transmit." Belated doubt, for the famous "Zimmermann note" which offered Mexico part of U.S. territory had already left Berlin January 16, had reached the American State Department on the 17th, and had been immediately delivered to the German Ambassador, Bernstorff. The latter sent it on the 19th to Eckhardt, Ambassador to Mexico, by Western Union. Thus the United States, unknowingly, became the accomplice of a plot hatched against itself.

The announcement that Germany was going to intensify the submarine war was then according to plan communicated on January 31 by Bernstorff to the American government, which, three days later, broke off diplomatic relations with Berlin. But Wilson did not yet know that the same message received two weeks earlier by Bernstorff proposed to deliver to Mexico an important part of the territory of the United States. Had he known it, his reaction would undoubtedly have been stronger.

On February 5 Zimmermann asked Eckhardt to go into action to convince Mexico to declare war against the United States. That message was transmitted through the intermediacy of the Swedish embassy in Mexico. But it was too late: Carranza had been deprived of his principal grievance against the United States, as the withdrawal of General Pershing's "punitive expedition" in Mexico had been ordered on January 25. Mexico was not going to attack the United States at the precise moment when American troops were evacuating its territory. Wilson had no inkling of what had been plotted behind his back with his unintentional cooperation. He believed that he had done everything he should have by breaking off diplomatic relations with Berlin and now he morosely shut himself away in the White House where, Ambassador Page noted, "He engaged in what he called 'thought,' and the air currents of the world never ventilated his mind."

This entire grotesque affair would have been of no consequence if it had been known only by German diplomats. But it was known by people who had interests in being well informed and in cleverly using the information at their disposal: a long time before, British intelligence services had broken the German code; they had intercepted messages and immediately decoded them. As Germany had an interest in immobilizing United States troops in America, England had an interest in drawing the United States into the war. And, with the Zimmermann note, the English held dynamite in their hands. Their sole problem was to use it at the opportune time to shock American public opinion into the turnabout that neither the bloodshed on the European front, nor the blockade which hampered but did not eliminate United States commerce, nor the torpedoing of the *Lusitania* had been able to cause.

"We can no longer refuse to play our part . . . in favor of Democracy against Absolutism," Secretary of State Lansing noted. But for Wilson and for the majority of his countrymen neutrality remained adorned with all its moral virtues and with all its material advantages. Naturally, Theodore Roosevelt was in the minority which agitated in favor of armed intervention. He wrote his old friend Senator Cabot Lodge: "I don't believe Wilson will go to war unless Germany literally kicks him into it." Zimmermann's note to Bernstorff and Eckhardt was going to be that "kick."

On February 23, 1917, Balfour received the United States Ambassador in London and handed him the decoded note. It was, he later said, "the most dramatic [moment] in all my life." The next day, Page transmitted the text with all necessary information to the State Department. It was met with stupefaction and indignation, for the German plot had been hatched in mid-January while Berlin was talking of peace. The State Department succeeded in securing the copy of the message sent by Bernstorff to Eckhardt through Western Union. But in Congress a debate was begun on the urgency of arming the merchant ships that were threatened by the unrestricted German submarine warfare. Senator Stone, Democrat from Missouri and chairman of the Foreign Affairs Committee, was asked to sponsor the proposal, but he had just joined the camp of its opponents. The proposal therefore was to be sponsored by Senator Hitchcock of Nebraska whose pacifism could be called pro-German. It was to him that Secretary of State Lansing communicated the text of the Zimmermann note on February 28, and Hitchcock, exploding with anger, saw in it immediately a "dastardly plot" that shocked his pacifism. Then Lansing notified a journalist of the Associated Press, E. M. Hood. The newspapers of March 1 devoted front pages to that momentous affair. The country was in an uproar but impenitent pacifists questioned the authenticity of the Zimmermann note, which could have been invented by the British to draw the United States into the war. Senator Stone asked if the information had come from London, and his question was posed in such a way that Lansing could have no doubt: an affirmative answer would imply that it was the result of a dark British machination. Mississippi's Senator Williams was not interested in the source of the information but solely in the authenticity of the note. For Arkansas's Senator Tillman the whole affair was nothing but a lie. A trick from perfidious Albion, said the Irish O'Gorman, Senator from New York. "A forgery and a sham born in the brain of a scoundrel and a fool," Senator Smith of Michigan called it. Among the few who did not doubt was Senator Fall of New Mexico—of unlamented memory —the oil tycoon paid to provoke an intervention in Mexico and who would be condemned in court (see p. 194). But Senator Cabot Lodge gloated: the news "would arouse the country."

Faced with requests for an explanation, Wilson personally guaranteed the authenticity of the note which led Cabot Lodge to say: "He does not mean to go to war but I think he is in the grip of events." The Hearst papers spoke of the note as "in all probability a fake and a forgery." For G. S. Viereck, publisher of the pro-German newspaper *The Fatherhood* and German agent, it was naturally nothing but a "brazen forgery planted by British agents." That opinion also prevailed in New York's high society.

But doubts were going to disappear. On March 2 Zimmermann had a press conference in Berlin. Among the journalists present was William Bayard Hale, correspondent of the Hearst chain, former clergyman, but recipient of a $15,000-yearly stipend from the Germans. He tried to give Zimmermann an out:

"Of course," he asked him, "Your Excellency will deny this story."

And the minister's answer came like a bombshell: "I cannot deny it, it is true."

Indignation exploded on the other side of the Atlantic. Germany admitted that it had wanted to take away from the United States part of its national territory. Threatened in its very being, America was ready to go into action. From east to west, the American press rose in wrath and swore to make Germany pay dearly for its arrogance. Somewhat boastfully, the Texan editor of the *San Antonio Light* wrote that if a German-Mexican army invaded the country, Texans would give their lives to the last man, at least until the moment when the aggressor has been pushed back to the other side of the frontier. The *Sacramento Bee* denounced the "treacherous enmity, underhanded, nasty intriguing." The *Buffalo Express* quickly evoked the "hordes of Mexicans under German officers, sweeping into Texas, New Mexico and Arizona."

But the most remarkable was the reaction of the newspapers of the middle west, seat of pro-German sentiment. The *Chicago Tribune* informed its readers that "Germany recognizes us as an enemy." The *Cleveland Plain Dealer* believed that neutrality offered "neither virtue nor dignity." The *Minneapolis Journal* confessed that German-Americans must now choose between their country of origin and their country of adoption. German-language newspapers like the Chicago *Staats-Zeitung*, the Detroit *Abend-Post*, the St. Louis *Amerika*, the Cincinnati *Volksblatt*, after having denounced the note as a shameless forgery, proclaimed their loyalty to the United States.

Theodore Roosevelt wrote to Cabot Lodge: "If Wilson does not go to war now, I shall skin him alive." That would not become necessary.[11]

Speaking one day to the United States Ambassador to Berlin, Zimmermann had said: "In case of trouble, there are half a million trained Germans in America who will join the Irish and start a revolution." To which Gerard had answered: "In that case, there are half a million lamp-posts to hang them on." But the lamp-posts were not necessary either.

To complete the picture, it should be recalled that Zimmermann, to the greatest possible joy of English intelligence officers, continued to communicate with Eckhardt by using the same code.

"Had the telegram never been intercepted or never been published, inevitably the Germans would have done something else that would have brought us in eventually," Barbara Tuchman notes.[12] "So Wilson waited, hoping for something to turn up," Samuel Eliot Morison also wrote. "What did turn up was a diplomatic bombshell—the 'Zimmermann note'." [13] Secretary of State Lansing remarked that it changed the apathy of the western states into "intense hostility to Germany." It was certainly not the only reason for United States entry into the war, but it was the determining factor which conditioned public opinion. National territory had been threatened. The American people therefore accepted the idea of war. Twenty-three years later it would also be necessary to wait until the national interest was not only threatened but directly struck by the Japanese attack on Pearl Harbor for the United States finally to decide to enter a war which had been going on for two years.

The only thing left to Wilson was to supply the American people with noble reasons for fighting, and he did it in a magnificent way. "Neutrality is no longer feasible or desirable when the peace of the world is involved and the freedom of its peoples, and the menace to that peace and freedom lies in the existence of autocratic governments backed by organized force which is controlled wholly by their will," Wilson declared.[14]

Democracy was clearly involved since the two camps were now clearly differentiated: On one side, "autocratic regimes," on the other, the English and French democracies and, thanks to the abdication of the Czar (March 15, 1917), the democracy born, in Wilson's words before Congress, of that "wonderful and heartening" Russian revolution. That revolution which, a quarter of a century later,

America would confront determined to defend the frontiers of democracy against Communism.

Woodrow Wilson insisted only that "the world must be made safe for democracy. Its peace must be planted upon the tested foundations of political liberty. We have no selfish ends to serve. We desire no conquest, no dominion. We seek no indemnities for ourselves, no national compensations for the sacrifices we shall freely make. We are but one of the champions of the rights of mankind."

Wilson summed up his concepts in the "Fourteen Points" which he presented to Congress January 8, 1918. Had they been proclaimed in 1914 or 1915, they would have spared the European democracies from being bled to death, now they did not survive the postwar disappointments, the tedious transactions of Versailles, or the Senate's incomprehension of the treaty and of the pact. The First World War cost the United States four times less men than the Civil War (1861–1865) and three-and-a-half times less than the Second World War.

During the midterm elections of November 5, 1918, Wilson urged the citizens to elect a Democratic majority to support his policies. But the popular verdict left no doubt as to the sentiments of the nation. The war had not yet ended and the Republicans won the majority in the House as well as in the Senate. Two years later the presidential contest had Warren Harding with Calvin Coolidge as Vice-President on the Republican side, and James Cox and Franklin D. Roosevelt on the Democratic side. The 1918 verdict was strikingly confirmed: the Democrats got only 9,147,000 votes while the Republicans triumphed with 16,150,000 votes. As for the Socialists, they got almost 1 million votes for Eugene V. Debs.

If Wilson had not been able to obtain the ratification of the Versailles Treaty and the League of Nations Pact, he at least convinced Congress to vote for the Webb Law in

1918, which softened the Sherman Antitrust Law and permitted authorized American exporters to form associations to more efficiently combat foreign competitors in world markets. The passage of the Webb Law revealed America's preoccupation better than the refusal to ratify the Versailles Treaty and the League of Nations Pact. The surge of prosperity created by the war in Europe had to be maintained. In spite of the fact that foreign competitors emerged greatly weakened from the conflict America wanted to protect its exporters' interests against them. That concern, which became evident before the end of Wilson's mandate, was to dominate the policy of the Republicans who kept the power they regained thanks to Harding for twelve years. In 1924, Calvin Coolidge got 15,725,016 votes against 8,395,586 for the Democrat Davis and 4,822,856 for the Progressive La-Follette. Then Hoover in 1928 received 21,392,190 votes against 15,016,443 to the Democrat Alfred E. Smith. That period, C. and M. Beard wrote, "was marked by a foreign policy that practically ignored the League of Nations, though 'observers' were sent to its headquarters at Geneva from time to time. Imperialist activities conceived as in the interest of trade were pushed everywhere. Former associates in the war were urged to pay the war debts they owed to the United States. The tariffs on imported manufactures were twice raised." [15]

The love of money, evident throughout the country, did not naturally spare the ruling circles. In less than two years, a member of the Cabinet went to prison for corruption and influence-peddling, while two others barely escaped. They were personal cronies of the President, named to their offices not because of their competence but only through friendship. The scandal touched the Veterans' Bureau and the Interior Department in charge of natural resources. Harding died, which spared him from seeing two of his men brought to justice: Albert B. Fall, Secretary of the Interior, and Harry H. Daugherty, Attorney-General. Various federal civil servants suspected of influence-peddling had to resign. Harding's government is considered one of the most corrupt in the history of the United States. The beginning of the Coolidge administration was marked by scandals that the press revealed following a Senate inquiry into the theft of important oil reserves during Harding's Presidency. The ties between businessmen and Republican politicians were completely exposed.

The government did not hide the fact that it leaned on big business. A power plant built by the government with public funds during the war became the center of a sharp debate. That installation had been built at Muscle Shoals in the Tennessee valley for the manufacture of chemical products necessary to the munitions industry. Republicans and conservative Democrats urged that it be sold or leased at a minimum price to a private company, a project which was approved by Presidents Harding, Coolidge, and Hoover. At the end of a seven year effort, the progressives in Congress secured enough votes for a resolution keeping the Muscle Shoals plant in the hands of the government. In order to please the business sector Coolidge vetoed the resolution. For the second time, in 1931, the progressives voted a similar resolution, and it was Hoover who this time vetoed it. It would take the New Deal to organize the Tennessee Valley Authority around that installation. Private industry would be more successful after the Second World War when the atomic plants, built by the government with public funds, were turned over to it.

Republicans revived the old McKinley doctrine: "More business in government and less government in business." Coolidge, expressing the great aspirations of the period, forged a new slogan of which his countrymen were very proud: "The business of America is business." [16] And business prospered. The principal federal authorities of economic control, created to ensure more production, were eliminated one after the other. In 1930, 50 per cent of the industrial wealth of the country was in the hands of two hundred corporations. Concentration increased: 89 mergers involving 438 enterprises took place in 1919 and 221 mergers affecting 1,038 enterprises in 1928. According to the Federal Trade Commission, the sixteen most important groups controlled approximately 22.8 per cent of the electric power capacity in 1915; in 1925 it would be 53 per cent. The concentration process extended to the automobile industry, to canning, to banking, to the retail trade. For example, the Great Atlantic and Pacific Tea Company owned 5,000 stores in 1922 and 17,500 in 1928. The number of banks fell from 30,812 in 1921 to 22,000 ten years later. The merger of the Chase National Bank and the Equitable Trust Company made Chase at that time the largest bank in the world. Enormous ingenuity was used to circumvent the antitrust laws by all kinds of schemes leading to the concentration of economic and financial power. "By 1930," H. U. Faulkner wrote, "the 200 largest corporations controlled nearly half of all non-banking corporate wealth (probably 38 percent of all business wealth), received 43.2 percent of the income of all non-banking corporations, and were controlled by approximately 2,000 individuals."

President Coolidge did not fight concentration; far from it. The Supreme Court showed the same concern by refusing, for example, in 1920 to dissolve United States Steel, which, however, according to Faulkner, "virtually dictated price." [17]

Why worry about concentration when there seemed to be general prosperity? Based on an index of 100 as the mean for the years between 1933 and 1939, industrial production went from 58 to 110 between 1921 and 1929. During the same period, gross national product leaped from $59.4 to $87.2 billion and the per capita income from $522 to $716.

Savings went from $8 to $23 billion between 1914 and 1925. However, some sectors did not show any progress: coal, cotton, ship-building, shoes, agriculture. But the automobile industry built 569,054 cars in 1914 and 5,621,715 in 1929. Between those two dates the number of registered cars soared from 1,258,062 to 26,501,443—or one car for every five people. Signs of prosperity were evident in most areas. And that prosperity, born of the First World War, was naturally evident in the increase of American investments abroad.

Between the Spanish-American War (1898) and the First World War, American foreign investment rose from $684.5 million to $3,513.8 million. But its volume increased much more rapidly thereafter as it went from $3,513.8 million in 1914 to $17,009.6 million in 1929 without counting government loans. In round figures, foreign investment had therefore quintupled between 1898 and 1914 and again quintupled between 1914 and 1929. The empire extended its ramifications a little everywhere in the world with a clear emphasis on Canada, Latin America, and Europe. Thanks to the war, the United States ceased to be a debtor, and became a creditor. In 1914 foreign investment in the United States rose to $7,200 million, or a little more than double the American investment abroad. The United States therefore showed a deficit of $3,686 million. The war quickly reversed that situation. First, $2,000 million in American stocks held in Europe came back to the United States to finance the military effort between 1914 and 1917. That movement affected England and France first and it was increased by the dollar loans of $2,600 million that the American government granted the Allies. Henceforth, America became Europe's creditor. And the trend continued when Europe, by virtue of the Liberty Loan Act of 1917, borrowed from the United States $9,581 million, which would be reduced to $9,386.6 million when the labo-

rious negotiations for the repayment of war debts opened in
1922. The Americans had become the world's bankers.

The end of the war left Europe in search of capital, and
naturally Europe turned to the United States, then in the
midst of a broad economic expansion. In 1929 the 17,009
million American dollars invested abroad divided, according to the Commerce Department, half into stocks held in
portfolios, and half into direct investments made by American companies in mines, industry, agriculture, and commerce. Added to the debts of European governments was
the fact that part of their economy came under the control
of American capital. The political isolationism which convinced the Senate to reject the Versailles Treaty and the
League of Nations Pact was therefore accompanied by economic interventionism. The Senate had a Republican majority, as did business circles. In the name of the slogan
America first the same political family was disinterested in
political settlements in postwar Europe, but extended its
economic empire in a ravaged Europe as well as in Latin
America and in Canada. For, as H. U. Faulkner remarks,
"It came in part because American economic interests were
stretching far and wide to extend business. Most of the big
American concerns, such as the Ford Motor Company,
General Motors, General Electric, Standard Oil, International Telephone and Telegraph, and International Harves-
ter, set up their own plants or bought control of foreign
companies. Many economic factors led to this movement of
capital into foreign industries, and of these the high tariffs
which developed rapidly in the 1920's were one of the most
important." [18]

The expansion of the empire did not take place through a
miraculous succession of felicitous accidents. Business
circles and the governments of Harding, Coolidge, and
Hoover which leaned on them showed identical concerns.
Since business was America's business each one willingly

took part in it, the government taking the responsibility to supply the necessary tariff protection to the operation. For that reason Europe would find itself at a dead end. In order to repay its war debts it needed dollars. To get dollars it was necessary that it send its exports to the United States or that it supply services to the United States. By raising its customs barriers, the United States deprived Europe of a flow of exports which would help it to redeem its debt. For, although the American delegates had signed the report of the International Economic Conference of 1927, which stated that "the time had come to put an end to the increase of customs tariffs," Hoover, in contradiction to that document, did not hesitate for a moment to support the Hawley-Smoot Tariff, higher still (52.2 per cent average) than the 1897 Dingley Tariff (46.5 per cent). Failing to export merchandise, Europe could have supplied services payable in dollars to the United States, among those services the most important being the transport of American products under European flags, but this possibility was almost nullified by the development of the American Merchant Marine, whose capacity went from 2 to 11 million tons between 1916 and 1921. But Europe was not the only victim of that situation. Latin America borrowed more than it could repay, and since at that time the development of Canada coincided with the financial exhaustion of England, the Canadian economy rested primarily on American investments.

During the war and the immediate postwar years the prodigious development of American foreign trade became one of the decisive factors in the increased wealth of the United States. The surplus of exports over imports doubled from 1914 to 1915, then doubled again from 1915 to 1916 to almost double again the following year. Between 1914 and 1921, the surplus balance reached a total of $18,530 million (see table below), a sum considerably greater than the

A LARGE SURPLUS BALANCE OF TRADE
(in millions of dollars)

	Exports	Imports	Surplus
1914	2,329.7	1,893.9	435.8
1915	2,716.2	1,674.2	1,042.0
1916	4,272.2	2,197.9	2,074.3
1917	6,227.2	2,659.4	3,567.8
1918	5,838.7	2,945.7	2,893.0
1919	7,749.8	3,904.4	3,845.4
1920	8,080.5	5,278.5	2,802.0
1921	4,378.9	2,509.1	1,869.8
TOTAL SURPLUS 1914–1921			18,530.1

loans granted to the Allies, which had facilitated their financing. The striking fact is that the surplus balance was maintained after the end of hostilities; the surplus of the years 1919, 1920, and 1921 approximately corresponded to the total of the Allied debts, which had been themselves contracted to buy American products from the United States. The long quarrel over the repayment of debts never drained that abscess. On the contrary, resentments were built up on both sides. The debate led Congress to vote three neutrality laws (1937) in the hope of avoiding the return of similar circumstances. But thirty years later many voices in the United States were raised to ask a recalcitrant ally, France, for the repayment of debts whose validity still remains open to discussion.

The foreign trade of the United States was naturally affected by the great economic crisis of 1929–1930, but the balance remained highly favorable (table below showing millions of dollars).

Yearly Average	Exports	Imports	Surplus
1921–1925	4,397	3,450	947
1926–1930	4,777	4,033	744
1931–1935	2,025	1,713	312
1936–1940	3,220	2,482	738

Reflecting internal economic developments, the nature of exports had changed: while in 1900 finished products represented only 24 per cent of the total exports, they reached 49 per cent in 1929. The industrialization of the United States changed the flow of trade: in 1914 Europe absorbed 63 per cent of American exports, and in 1929 only 44 per cent. At that time Latin America and Canada received 37 per cent of the exports of the United States to which they also supplied 37 per cent of its imports. As much as being a political aim, the Monroe Doctrine therefore responds to an economic reality: the underdeveloped countries of the American continent supplied the raw materials to the United States, and bought its industrialized products from it, while American investments multiplied in Canada and in Latin America. A largely undeveloped continent like Asia bought little from the United States (12 per cent of American exports) and *a fortiori* Oceania (3.7 per cent) and Africa (2.5 per cent), but the underdeveloped continents are rich in raw materials, and Asia supplied one-third of the rubber and raw silk imports of the United States. A major consumer of raw materials, the United States, on the eve of the economic crisis, ranked after Great Britain as the principal importing nation of the world, and yet its balance of trade was favorable every year. Under those conditions, "Gold was largely disappearing from the debtor nations and the free flow of goods was obstructed by high tariffs. In such a situation the balances due the creditor lead generally to foreign loans or to investments abroad. This was what was happening in the 1920's when American trade was to no small extent supported by such loans. This could not go on indefinitely for the continued export of capital by the creditor nation merely accentuated an already unhealthy situation. Conditions were in the making which led to the almost complete debacle of international trade at the end of the decade." [19]

In spite of a few solemn warnings voiced by experts, the American people were unconcerned; they had let their increasing wealth go to their heads. The great new industries (automobiles, telephones, electrical equipment, aviation, chemical products, etc.) ceaselessly expanded the horizons of prosperity. The Hearst and Pulitzer empires had consolidated and developed an unprincipled and unscrupulous "yellow press" which offered to their readers entertainment, emotionalism, and continuously fresh rations of optimism. Prohibition, introduced by the Eighteenth Amendment (1920), opened up an unlimited field to the traffic in alcohol thanks to which gangsterism developed, but during the same period women won the vote, another reason for optimism in a society wide open to all forms of progress. Motion-picture producers, taking advantage of the closing of the European studios during the war, secured almost exclusive control of the world market. Gambling, in spite of many state laws on betting, was widely popular. The empire was powerful and confident. Speculation on the Stock Exchange, and the unhealthy state of international trade, were not yet throwing the empire into the economic crisis that would shake the very dogmas of Americanism and have repercussion that would be felt by the whole world. Babbitt (1922) was at this time happy and unconcerned.

Another danger unsuspected by Americans was undermining the empire. While they were discovering syncopated ragtime, dancing to jazz tunes and cheering Bessie Smith, Duke Ellington and the young Louis Armstrong, war production and the expansion of new industries was creating jobs numerous enough to increase union membership by 37 per cent and to offer blacks opportunities that would change the foundations of the racial problem. By tens of thousands blacks left the plantations, the small farms, the southern villages, and settled down in the great northern cities where they took over whole sections and a combination of racism and real estate speculation soon spawned real ghettos. A result of economic prosperity and the shortsightedness of the public, this is the historic cause of the bloody riots which were to break out in Detroit twenty years later and then in most American cities between 1960–1969, shaking the internal foundations of the empire.

Self-righteousness and blind optimism were at that time the major weakness of an apparently invincible nation. Prosperity fed a strong self-confidence, especially since the Puritan heritage regarded fortune as a sign of Divine protection. That self-confidence was translated into a natural mix of unfailing amiability and a clear feeling of superiority. Idealism easily gave way to the xenophobia and intolerance against which the Founding Fathers had rebelled. The wealth of the empire could not have been built without hurting the interests of other nations and continents. But that wealth, already compromised internally through the mistakes of economic leaders and the lack of foresight in regard to the black problem, was it not also threatened from the outside? That is what the majority of Americans thought. Therefore they closed their frontiers to immigration and discovered false threats of subversion at home. By its very nature, the empire bred several forms of ostracism.

The most violent was represented by the action taken by Attorney General Mitchell Palmer. In 1917, he seized German and Austrian property worth $600 million, then, when those properties were to be sold, he saw to it without scruples that his personal friends made profitable deals. But, after the war, he quickly discovered a new danger: the Bolsheviks. In April 1920, during a cabinet meeting President Wilson told him: "Palmer, do not let this country see red!" But that is exactly what he did and being a Cabinet member he was much better placed to do it than Senator Joe McCarthy would be when he exploited the "witch hunt" immediately after the Second World War. He started the famous "Palmer raids": In a single night he had more than 4,000 alleged communists arrested in 33 cities. The results did not at all justify that haul but Palmer nevertheless became a national hero: he knew how to protect the security of the nation. In New York, the five elected socialist members, although innocent, were thrown out of the State Assembly. Deportation orders were delivered to 5,000 immigrants. The trial of Sacco and Vanzetti, falsely accused of a murder attributed to anarchists, took place in a climate of violent xenophobia and the two defendants were condemned to die in the electric chair in 1927. In a famous law book, a Supreme Court judge would describe that execution as a typical case of judicial error provoked by the pressure of an aroused public opinion, but Sacco and Vanzetti could never be rehabilitated so as not to undermine the confidence of the citizens of the empire in their institutions. At the same time the periodical *Dearborn* spread anti-Semitism. Dormant since the beginning of the century, the Ku Klux Klan claimed 4 million members in 1924 and unceasingly hunted down blacks, Jews and Catholics. In a race riot, 47 people, blacks for the most part, were killed in East St. Louis in 1917. In July 1919 after Wilson had just come back from the Paris conference blacks and whites fought in Washington, and the police separated them, leaving six dead on the street. The same month three days of race riots in Chicago caused 36 deaths. There were also incidents in New York, Omaha, in the south, each time that black veterans demanded recognition of their civil rights. Of course the xenophobic and racist demagoguery did not yet shake the empire, but it did subject its democratic foundations to a severe test, one that would worsen in times to come (see Chapter 11).

The euphoria had not been affected by the slow decline which began on Wall Street at the beginning of October

1929. But, on the 24th, there was panic. Sixteen million securities changed hands and fifty blue-chip stocks made dizzy plunges which reached some forty points a day. For many, it was ruin and suicide. However, the leaders watching over the interests of the empire did not panic. Hoover was convinced that the crisis would fade away in less than two months. Mellon, Secretary of the Treasury, predicted that 1930 would be a "normal year." The big financier, with a fortune inherited from his father, had organized corporations for the exploitation of coal and iron-ore mines. He soon became one of the foremost bankers while at the same time he controlled aluminum and petroleum trusts. In 1921, Harding had nominated him for the Treasury post, which he kept during the presidencies of Coolidge and Hoover. He made a proposal, obviously welcome in business circles, for a reduction in the income tax. In 1935 the origin of his fortune was the subject of a federal inquiry. But, in the meantime, he was the guardian of the Treasury's gold. How could anyone not trust a man when his fortune was a monument to his competence and to his acumen in financial and economic matters? America was not threatened by the blacks, the Communists, the anarchists or the Jews. It was about to collapse through the faults of the "Wasps," the businessmen whose personal success was the ideal incarnate of America.

In the beginning of 1932 the National Bureau of Economic Research drew a somber picture of the situation. Securities had gone down 83 per cent, production 40 per cent, wages 60 per cent, dividends 57 per cent; approximately thirteen million unemployed walked the streets or stood in line in front of soup kitchens. In the country, farmers greeted with gunfire the marshals who came to repossess their mortgaged farms, chattels, and equipment. "Credit froze at the source, money depreciated to half its value. The carnival of the twenties was over." [20]

"People will work harder, live a more moral life," Mellon said and everything would be straightened out again. The National Association of Manufacturers distributed a poster showing a seductive Miss Columbia: "Business is good, keep it good. Nothing can stop the U.S." And President Hoover himself stated May 1, 1930, "We have now passed the worst." [21]

But exorcisms and autosuggestion did not stop the crisis. In the presidential election of 1932, the Republicans adopted an austere platform and chose Hoover for another mandate. The Democrats chose the Governor of New York, Franklin D. Roosevelt. The solution of new problems is incumbent on those who want to remain free, he said. He asked the citizens to fight against the "new despotism," against the "industrial dictatorship," against the "economic royalists." Private enterprise had given birth to monopolies which struck at the very principle of the equality of opportunity. The country had too many poor, not enough rich. "Throughout the nation, men and women, forgotten in the political philosophy of the government of the last years, look to us here for a more equitable opportunity to share in the distribution of national wealth. I pledge you, I pledge myself to a new deal for the American people." [22] The Socialists had nominated Norman Thomas to replace Debs, who had died in 1926. The Great Depression brought Thomas the support of intellectuals like Paul Douglas, John Dewey, Elmer Davis, the theologian Reinhold Niebuhr, while the novelist John Dos Passos and fifty-one eminent writers supported the Communist candidate, William Z. Foster. Many thoughtful men doubted the virtues of free enterprise and liberal democracy. Some were drawn toward Fascist organizations which played on xenophobia and racism. Faith in the empire was threatened.

Roosevelt was elected by 22,821,857 votes or 57.3 per cent of the total, while Hoover got only 15,761,841 (39.6

per cent). More than one-third of the voters therefore kept their confidence in the man who had steered the ship to shipwreck. Less than a million votes went to the Socialists and to the Communists. Only some intellectuals no longer had faith in the economic and political dogmas of liberalism. The majority wanted a man able to start up again a system whose excesses and turbulences alone had led to failure. It was on Roosevelt that the task of accomplishing that miracle fell. He did not have any pre-established plan to do it. He did not know himself what would be the content of his New Deal. A pragmatist, he was going to strive to repair the damage. And he was going to succeed in saving the cracked structure of the empire.

"Only a foolish optimist can deny the dark realities of the moment," Roosevelt said on entering the White House on March 4, 1933, and he added: "This nation asks for action, and action now!" [23] This is not the place to analyze in detail the great measures which mark the New Deal.[24] Banks were subjected to stricter federal control, the convertibility of paper money into gold or silver was abandoned, credit was reorganized, interest rates lowered, subsidies helped to normalize agriculture, great programs of public works created jobs for the unemployed, the law on reciprocal trade agreements gave more flexibility to international trade, speculation was gradually strangled, trade unions were encouraged and collective bargaining became obligatory, standard wages and hours were introduced in various industries, insurance and pension systems became widespread, etc. None of these measures developed from a completely new idea. The general orientation could be found in the Progressives' proposals dating back several decades. But Wilson, greatly absorbed by international affairs and deceived by a prosperity born of neutrality in wartime, had scarcely promoted reforms, and the three Republicans who had succeeded him in the White House were not men to worry about achieving a better distribution of wealth in order to build a healthier base for the economy. Franklin Roosevelt drew from forgotten traditions, improvised, put things in motion again, stimulated. He refused to nationalize and adopted a new capitalist orthodoxy to repair the damage that the abuses of almost unbridled liberalism had caused. His popularity was enormous. In the 1936 elections he got 27,751,597 votes against 16,679,583 for the Republican Alfred Landon. The number of unemployed had fallen from 12.8 to 9 million, hope was reborn and the percentage differential in popular votes garnered by the two candidates (60.7 per cent and 36 per cent) showed a wider margin than in 1932.

Facing the problems which remained yet to be solved, America more than ever concentrated on its internal difficulties. The word "isolationism" had been forged with a clearly pejorative meaning, to define the attitude of the opponents of Woodrow Wilson's internationalism and interventionism. The word was suddenly applied by its opponents to the Roosevelt New Deal. The President, though, had proposed participation of the United States in the International Court of Justice at The Hague, and when the Senate rejected the proposal the White House did not take umbrage. Scandals involving fortunes built on the armaments industries threw a sordid light on a war which had been presented as a struggle for democracy and permanent peace. The refusal of the Allies to repay their debts increased a profound distrust of any international enterprise. Accused of isolationism, Roosevelt answered: "We are not isolationists except insofar as we seek to isolate ourselves completely from war." The 1934 Johnson Bill prohibited any future loans to governments which had not repaid their previous debts. America felt that a new conflict was being prepared on the European horizon. Not only did it stay out of the League of Nations, which was beginning to meet with its most serious difficulties, but two years after Hitler's coming to power it voted a neutrality law which prohibited the sale of arms, munitions, and weapons of war to possible belligerents. The same document (1935) stated that American citizens who traveled by sea in wartime would do so at their own risk. The 1937 neutrality law reinforced the then-existing regulations. All these laws were voted by overwhelming majorities. In the same spirit Roosevelt withdrew from the London conference which, in 1933, was trying to put an end to the general depression through a series of international economic and monetary accords. "We can keep out of war if those who watch and decide have a sufficiently detailed understanding of international affairs to make certain that the small decisions of each day do not lead toward the war and if, at the same time, they possess the courage to say 'no' to those who selfishly or unwisely would let us go to war." [25]

But no one thought of drawing the United States into a war that had not yet erupted and "small decisions of each day" would not keep America out of the imminent conflict. On the contrary, great solemn decisions were going to hurl the United States into the worldwide conflagration: dramatically, Roosevelt in 1933 had condemned to failure the economic conference held in London; spectacularly, Roosevelt had been re-elected in 1936 on a promise of neutrality; ostentatiously, the Senate had voted and Roosevelt had signed the laws establishing a reinforced neutrality. *America first*; the troubled world did not have top priority among the concerns of the President, far from it. The resounding affirmations of the neutrality of the United States in an eventual conflict could only encourage Nazism in preparing its great offensive against the democracies. As Roosevelt remarked later, "Our arms embargo played right into the hands of the aggressor nations." Germany, Japan, and Italy took a considerable lead over England, France, and the U.S.S.R. in building their military power. "American neu-

trality legislation assured the Axis that when they got ready
to strike, their victims would be shut off from obtaining im-
plements of war from America," Samuel Eliot Morison
observes.[26]

When war broke out in Europe, the American empire
was still far from having overcome its crisis. A recession
marked the year 1937 and more than 10 million unemployed were registered in 1938. There were still 9 million in
1939 and 8,120,000, or 15 per cent of the working force, in
1940. Foreign trade had fallen to a very low level compared
to 1920; then slowly it climbed in 1939 to barely the level of
the crash year of 1930 (three tables below are in millions
of dollars).

	Exports	Imports	Surplus
1920	8,228	5,278	2,950
1929	5,241	4,399	842
1930	3,843	3,061	782
1931	2,424	2,091	333
1932	1,611	1,323	288
1939	3,177	3,192	−15

Just as during the First World War, it was the conflict
which was going to give the United States a new surge—
tripling exports and increasing imports by 50 per cent.

Average	Export	Import	Surplus
1936–1940	3,220	2,482	738
1941–1945	10,051	3,514	6,537

The evolution of the balance of payments followed a similar curve, the year 1940 hardly reaching the plateau of
1930, while 1945 showed a surplus almost twice as great as
in 1920, a year of prosperity par excellence.

Projections issued in 1939 and 1940 make it clear that,
with increasing recovery, America would have come out of
the crisis in several years. The Second World War was not

	Exports	Imports	Surplus
1920	10,264	6,741	3,523
1925	6,348	5,261	1,087
1930	5,448	4,416	1,032
1935	3,265	3,137	128
1940	5,355	3,636	1,719
1945	16,273	10,232	6,041

indispensable to cure the ills of the American economy, but five years of war in Europe and in Asia were more effective than all the economic and fiscal measures inspired by the New Deal between 1932 and 1939. American historians agree in noting that until Pearl Harbor (December 7, 1941) most Americans hoped that their country could remain out of the war. But at the same time the public understood that for reasons at once political, strategic, and economic, it could not remain indifferent to the conflict which had just erupted. Three weeks after the declaration of war in Europe, Roosevelt convened Congress in special session to submit to it a revision of the neutrality laws. Belligerents were allowed to make purchases in the United States on a cash-and-carry basis—of paying cash and guaranteeing transport on their own ships, a condition which favored England, mistress of the seas. Then, eight months after the defeat of France, Roosevelt asked for the repeal of the neutrality laws and the authorization to sell or loan any war equipment to any nation whose defense he would judge vital for the security of the United States. That was a recognition that the defense of Great Britain was vital for America, but nevertheless the latter intended to remain out of the war and let the English carry the burden of the conflict alone. Two months of impassioned debate were necessary for Congress to vote the Lend-Lease bill which, put into effect in March 1941, practically repealed the previous cash-and-carry provision and the 1934 law which refused loans to any nation not having repaid its debts from the first war.

Lend-Lease was of considerable scope, since it accounted in 1941 for $750 million worth of merchandise sold to the Allies. "The demands of lend-lease added new impetus to the development of war economy already stimulated by a defense program which had begun seriously in 1938. This program was stepped up after the European war began and particularly after the evacuation of Dunkirk and the fall of France." [27]

Congress voted $1,498 million for defense in 1940, and $6,054 million in 1941, but those figures kept increasing until the end of the war, representing a greater and greater part of the federal budget (table below in millions of dollars).

	Total	Defense	% of the total
1930	3,320	734	22.1
1934	6,645	540	8.1
1938	6,765	1,030	15.2
1939	8,841	1,075	12.2
1940	9,055	1,498	16.5
1941	13,255	6,054	45.7
1942	34,037	23,216	70.4
1943	79,368	63,216	79.6
1944	94,303	76,757	80.8
1945	98,303	81,277	82.7

Between the onset of the war in Europe (August 1939) and the entry of the United States into the war (December 1941), industrial production doubled, and exports rose from $3,177 million to $5,147 million in 1941. The "sky rocketing of industrial production" did not correspond solely to the increase of war production. But the latter was responsible for the creation of new jobs and also for a rise in wages, those two elements combining increase by 25 per cent the production of consumer goods between August 1939 and August 1941. Unemployment, indeed, was not yet entirely eliminated but the number of nonagricultural workers rose from 35,321,000 in April 1940 to 41,036,000 in December 1941. Thanks to the war taking place in Europe, the economic situation in the United States was the more favorable, since incomes increased more rapidly than prices. The average hourly wage went from 73 cents in 1940 to 87 cents in December 1941, and the average weekly wage from $29.88 to $38.62 while prices increased by only 10 per cent.

Mining production, which represented an average of $2,463 million for the period 1931–1935, reached $5,107 million in 1941 and $6,310 million in 1944. If industrial production doubled between 1939 and 1941, that progress was not yet sufficient and the federal government, thanks to the War Production Board, whose chairmanship had been given to Donald Nelson, was going to spend $16,000 million for the construction of war factories, with the Defense Plants Corporation acting as intermediary. Hence Donald Nelson could say in May 1942: "The United States is actually doing things today which were unthinkable a year ago. It is executing programs which sounded utterly fantastic no more than six months ago." [28] All that, thanks above all to federal loans. The federal government built steel plants, chemical plants, oil refineries, not to mention 6,000 kilometers of pipeline to bring oil to the coast. Thus, at the end of the war, the government owned more than 90 per cent of the capacity for the production of airplanes, ships, synthetic rubber, magnesium; 70 per cent of capacity for aluminum production; 50 per cent of that of machine tools. All that would go back to the private sector after the end of hostilities.

Industrial installations in the United States were appraised at $40,000 million in 1939 and at $60,000 million in 1945 or a prodigious increase of 50 per cent in six years. In reality $26,000 million had been added to the industrial capacity but only $20,000 million could be used for peacetime production. But the combined strength of the giants of industry would not have sufficed to ensure that effort—two-thirds of it had to be financed by the federal government. State intervention had favored the industrial giants while it helped only indirectly the small and middle-sized enterprises to which the larger ones subcontracted part of their production. In 1939 the 250 most powerful companies owned 65 per cent of industrial installations; during the war, they profited from the 79 per cent of production capacity newly created by the government and received 78 per cent of government contracts. The war and the state financing thus accelerated the trend to industrial concentration. After the war 135 companies controlled 45 per cent of the industrial installations of the United States and those 135 companies produced more than one-quarter of the goods manufactured in the whole world.

The word "empire" must be used here in two different senses. On the one hand, the war had given an irresistible impetus to a nation which had 9 million unemployed in 1939 and made it by far the greatest industrial power in the world with the highest standard of living. The empire extended its economic influence, directly or indirectly, to all the countries of the world—whether it traded with them or refused to recognize them—to all the sectors of productions either through the purchase of raw materials, of which it was the greatest consumer, or through the sale of industrial products, of which it was the major producer. On the other hand, the war had considerably expanded within the country the power of giant enterprises constituting the industrial empire which exercised a preponderant influence on the lives of its citizens and the political scene (see Chap. X). The industrial empire weighs heavily on the nation which in turn rules its empire in the world.

Thanks to the giants of industry, strengthened by government investments and orders, the index of industrial production, figured on the basis of 100 for the years 1935–1939, reached 239 in 1943. Machinery production quadrupled in the same period and the means of transport (automobiles, airplanes, ships, railroad equipment) increased seven-fold. In 1944 production of coal and oil reached 145 on the index, while farm production reached 136. At the time of Pearl Harbor, the United States had only 1,157 airplanes battle-ready at its disposal: it built 297,000 in five years; it had a little more than 1,000 tanks in 1941 and produced 86,338 in five years, as well as 17,400,000 small arms. Aluminum becoming scarce, the government itself constructed installations whose exploitation was turned over to private enterprise in such a way that production—meeting essential needs at the end of 1942—quadrupled as compared with production before the war. The advance of the Japanese in Southeast Asia caused a scarcity of rubber, but six months after Pearl Harbor the production of synthetic rubber was organized. Before the war, imports of natural rubber fluctuated between 550,000 and 650,000 tons and in 1944 the production of synthetic rubber reached 836,000 tons. The tonnage of the Merchant Marine tripled in a year, going from 3 million to 9 million tons between 1942 and 1943. Thanks to the war, the empire had recovered its drive.

More than 11 million men and women were mobilized, the number of workers rose from 54 to 64 million between 1940 and 1945, which not only took care of the unemployment problem but put 5 million women on the production line as well as several hundred thousand retired people and young students. Management was not alone in benefitting from the war effort. Union leaders understood, and during December 1941 Roosevelt signed a "social armistice" with six leaders of the American Federation of Labor and six leaders of the Congress of Industrial Organizations. The signers pledged to avoid strikes and lockouts until the end of the war. Practically alone, the President of the Miners

Union, John L. Lewis, violated the pact, but the time lost through these illegal strikes represented only 0.1 per cent of the work total. The nation participated unanimously in a gigantic effort which increased the wages of workers as well as management's productive capacity. A few years before, the foundations of the empire had been cracking everywhere. It increased its power and reinforced its social as well as its structural foundations. The effort was financed through taxes but also through loans which totaled $156.9 billion, of which $102 billion were subscribed by corporations and, more significantly, more than $43 billion by individuals.

With prosperity recovered thanks to the war, population increased, not only through immigration, strictly reduced and controlled, but thanks to a high birth rate. In the years of crisis from 1930 to 1940, the population increased only by 9 million, going from 122 to 131 million, but during the following decade and despite mobilization, it increased by 19 million, going from 131 to 150 million in 1950. Growth continued to accelerate, reaching 178 million in 1960 and 200 million at the end of 1967, or an increase of 52 per cent in a quarter century. Among other causes, the high birth rate expressed the optimism in which a people whom war had liberated from the nightmare of economic crisis basked. And the birth rate was in itself cause for optimism in business circles, which saw in it each year the promise of increased production to satisfy the needs of a domestic market in the full flush of expansion. But external markets too were in full expansion.

The balance of trade does not show the complete picture, in particular because of American foreign aid and of the heavy military burdens that the United States carried almost everywhere in the world. It shows, nevertheless, the economic vitality of a country which, banker to the world and in quest of new commercial markets as well as new

BALANCE OF TRADE

(in millions of dollars)

	Exports	Imports	Surplus
Average 1941–1945	10,051	3,514	6,537
Average 1946–1950	11,829	6,659	5,170
Average 1951–1955	15,333	10,832	4,501
Average 1956–1960	19,204	13,650	5,554
1961	20,962	14,713	6,249
1962	21,359	16,387	4,972
1963	23,347	17,138	6,209
1964	26,489	18,684	7,805
1965	24,478	21,366	3,112
1966	30,336	25,550	4,786

sources of supply of raw materials, multiplied its overseas investments.

Numerous indicators permit us to measure the wealth of the empire since 1929, the year preceding the Great Depression. Evaluated during 1952, the average per capita annual income went from $1,000 in 1929 to $1,500 in 1952. In the same period the production of goods and services rose from $72 billion in 1929 to $345 billion in 1952. Industrial production had doubled, farm production had increased 50 per cent. During the same period, while the number of workers went from 48 to 61 million, the work week had been reduced from forty-eight to forty hours.[29]

Thus the Second World War permitted the empire to solve an economic crisis infinitely more grave than the recession of 1913–1914 that was overcome thanks to the First World War. In both conflicts, a period of neutrality (1914–1917, 1939–1941) had powerfully contributed to an eco-

FOREIGN INVESTMENTS

(in millions of dollars)

1940	12,275	1957	54,388
1945	16,818	1958	59,335
1950	32,844	1959	64,852
1955	44,947	1960	71,497

nomic recovery, accelerated afterward by the entrance of the United States into the war. The empire emerged from its neutrality when it saw itself threatened in its territorial integrity in 1917 through the dealings between Zimmermann and Mexico, and when it was directly and brutally attacked by Japan in 1941 at Pearl Harbor.

In the course of two wars, the United States had considerably developed its productive capacity, while taking over the foreign markets that the European powers could no longer supply.

In the aftermath of two wars, the immediate temptation had been to demobilize and to go back to "business as usual." But what could be done in 1918 was no longer possible in 1945. For, henceforth, the empire had a serious competitor: the U.S.S.R. of Stalin, also dreaming of expansion and pushing back the boundaries of its zone of influence. America, which did not want to accept the responsibilities of a major world power in 1918, could not evade them in 1945. It had disdained the League of Nations, but it plays a major role in the United Nations, whose budget it largely finances and where it exercises a preponderant influence on large problems (Korean War, nonadmission of China, etc.) and on smaller ones.

In the name of its primordial interests and of "America first," America had been able to choose either isolationism or interventionism; but henceforth, in spite of a fleeting temptation to seek refuge inside an "American fortress," the United States is condemned to intervene, always in the name of "America first," in any part of the world where its economic and strategic interests are threatened. Reaching to the four corners of the earth, the empire has its sources of raw materials, its commercial outlets, its allies and its clients, its networks of military bases, its atomic aircraft carriers and submarines. No part of the world is free from the influence of the American economy, the American dollar,

American diplomacy, American missiles. Through refusal or granting of diplomatic recognition, as well as through refusal or agreement to sign accords and treaties, to give economic and financial aid, to engage in commercial transactions, it influences friends, neutrals, and adversaries. It extends its net over the whole planet. Naturally, the empire can reinforce its positions, defend them more or less skillfully, jeopardize them by its inaction or by untimely initiatives. But, through the thousand means at its disposal, its weight is felt by its neighbors as it is in the most distant countries, by those who admire it as by those which are jealous or fearful of it. The empire is everywhere.

Part Two

———

THE EMPIRE TODAY

VI

———

The Economic
Empire

The moral obligation of commercial intercourse between nations "is most emphatically enjoined by the Christian precept to love your neighbor as yourself. But China, not being a Christian nation, its inhabitants do not consider themselves bound by the Christian precept to love their neighbor as themselves. . . . This is a churlish and unsocial system. . . . The fundamental principal of the Chinese Empire is anti-commercial. . . . It admits no obligation to hold commercial intercourse with others. . . . It is time that this enormous outrage upon the rights of human nature, and upon the first principle of the rights of nations, should cease." [1]

There is a venerable tradition which confers a sacred character to commerce in America. In these incredible terms it was formulated in 1842, during the Opium War, by John Quincy Adams (1767–1848), successively diplomat, Secretary of State in Monroe's Presidency, then President of the United States and member of the House of Representatives. At the time the United States was not a large importer of raw materials and had no capital to export. Commerce, however, seemed to it the highest mani-

festation of the Christian ideal. And, just as Lyndon John-
son would obtain support from high ecclesiastical personages
who blessed the war in Vietnam, the American Board of
Commissioners for Foreign Missions portrayed the Opium
War as "the result of a great design of Providence" to put
China in "contact with Western and Christian nations."

Although formulated in less outlandish terms, the mission assigned today to commercial transactions is no less
elevated. It tends toward several objectives which, in fact,
are so closely related as to be virtually identical:

1. On the one hand, commercial transactions serve the
national interest of the United States, which has a vital
need to import raw materials and to export manufactured
products as well as capital. For example, in his inaugural
address of January 20, 1953, President Eisenhower declared,
"We know that we are linked to all free peoples not merely
by a noble idea but by a simple need. No free people can for
long cling to any privilege or enjoy any safety in economic
solitude. For all our own material might, even we need markets in the world for the surpluses of our farms and factories. Equally, we need for the same farms and factories vital
materials and products of distant lands. This basic law of
interdependence, so manifest in the commerce of peace, applies with thousandfold intensity in the event of war." [2]

2. But commercial transactions are also profitable to
other countries of the free world which can sell the United
States their raw materials and buy from it the equipment
they need. That function is of prime importance for it tends
"to help make a historical demonstration that in the twentieth century, as in the nineteenth—in the southern half of
the globe as in the north—economic growth and political
democracy can develop hand in hand." Such a demonstration will give the people of the world a clearcut choice since
"the last decade has proved that those who sell their souls
to the Communist system under the mistaken belief that

the Communist system offers a quick and sure road to economic prosperity have been proven wholly wrong." For "it is now apparent that this system is incapable in today's world of achieving the organization of agriculture, the satisfying of consumer demands and the attainment of lasting prosperity." [3]

3. The interests of American private enterprise thus closely coincide with those of a government which assumes the leadership of the free world in resisting Communism. On November 9, 1964, Fred J. Borch, President of the General Electric Company, stated to the Economic Club of New York: "Overriding both the common purposes and cross-purposes of business and government, there is a broader pattern—a 'consensus' if you will, where public and private interest come together, cooperate, interact, and become the national interest." [4] And John D. Lockton, General Electric's treasurer, had been still more explicit when he said on April 22, 1964, "thus our search for profits places us squarely in line with the national policy of stepping up international trade as a means of strengthening the free world in the Cold War confrontation with Communism." [5] Whatever the form of the action taken by the United States, whatever the area in which it operates, it always tends toward a single and similar objective. There can be no fundamental contradictions between the government's initiatives and the initiatives of private enterprise or, more explicitly, if differences do appear it is because the common objective has been lost sight of. That's why Bernard Baruch insisted upon the "essential one-ness of United States economic, political and strategic interests." [6]

4. Private interests and national interests being related, their interventions abroad must be coordinated. There is no conflict between private foreign investments and government programs of foreign aid. The former President of the World Bank, Eugene R. Black, explained why: "Our for-

eign aid programs constitute a distinct benefit to American business. The three major benefits are: a) Foreign aid provides a substantial and immediate market for U.S. goods and services; b) Foreign aid stimulates the development of new overseas markets for U.S. companies; c) Foreign aid orients national economics toward a free enterprise system in which U.S. firms can prosper." [7] The "substantial and immediate" market is opened up by a clause which obliges the beneficiary country to apply an average of 80 per cent of the aid received to purchases in the United States. The two other advantages of foreign aid are less directly felt, but are nonetheless real to the extent to which private American firms export finished products and capital.

5. The system of free enterprise thus encouraged by the joint action of private capital and government aid calls for military protection. Andrew F. Brimmer, Under Secretary of Commerce, speaking before the Tax Foundation, insisted on that point. If the aid programs, economic as well as military, were suspended, he declared, "private investments might be a waste because it would not be safe enough for you to make them." [8] The representatives of private enterprises are even more explicit when they deal with that problem. For example, Alfred Wentworth, Vice-President of the Chase Manhattan Bank in charge of the Far East area, declared: "In the past, foreign investors have been somewhat wary of the over-all political prospect for the [Southeast Asia] region. I must say, though, that the U.S. actions in Vietnam this year—which have demonstrated that the U.S. will continue to give effective protection to the free nations of the region—have considerably reassured both Asian and Western investors. In fact, I see some reason for hope that the same sort of economic growth may take place in the free economies of Asia that took place in Europe after the Truman Doctrine and after NATO provided a protective shield. The same thing also took place in Japan after the U.S. intervention in Korea re-

moved investors' doubts." [9] Without adequate military protection, private capital will not take the risk of investing in exposed regions. But economic penetration is also indispensable to the military security of the United States, for, as John F. Kennedy said: "If India were to fall, if Latin America turned away, and if the Middle East slid behind the Iron Curtain, then no amount of missiles, no amount of space satellites or nuclear-powered planes or atomic submarines could save us." [10]

Thus clearly emerges what Bernard Baruch called "the essential one-ness" of American interests, be they political, economic, or military. These different aspects are so closely intertwined that no one of them can predominate. Each is indispensable to the others. Let one of them weaken and the whole edifice is threatened. The American empire cannot be purely economic. Its economic base is inseparable from its political base and from its military base, neither is more nor less important than the others, and all three find their justification in the same ideal that Lyndon Johnson summarized this way: "If we who serve free men today are to differ from the tyrants of this age, we must balance the powers in our hands with God in our hearts." [11]

The United States cannot have an imperialist economic policy because its productive apparatus is essentially oriented toward domestic consumption. At first glance this argument appears convincing, for the United States is probably the country which devotes the lowest percentage of its gross national product to exports: hardly 5 per cent, against 37 per cent for Belgium, 21 per cent for Canada, 15 per cent for France, 20 per cent for West Germany, 17 per cent for Italy, 11 per cent for Japan, 12 per cent for Spain.[12] But the gross national product of the United States is 2½ times greater than the six countries of the Common Market and its proportion of exports, although small, nevertheless reached $30,336 million in 1966—against $25,550 million for imports, or a trade surplus of $4,786 million.

If total American exports represent a small percentage of production (5 per cent), official statistics list forty-four sectors in which exports exceed both $10 million yearly and 15 per cent of production. The table below gives a few examples of those industrial sectors whose production is, in large part, intended for export.

PERCENTAGE OF PRODUCTION
INTENDED FOR EXPORT

	1960	1964
Cotton	41%	26%
Molybdenum	46	42
Coal	15	15
Synthetic rubber	25	19
Agricultural chemicals	18	16
Turbines, etc.	7	23
Agricultural equipment	11	15
Construction equipment	33	35
Petroleum equipment	31	23
Machine tools	22	24
Adding machines	13	18
Sewing machines	28	36
Aviation engines	11	18
Surgical implements	17	16

These forty-four sectors, which exported at least 15 per cent of their output in 1964 totaled more than $11,285 million in foreign sales, or 43 per cent of total exports. Thus we can see that in selected key sectors American production is, in large part, oriented toward export. Deprived of their foreign markets, those sectors would have to reduce their activities by 15 to 30 per cent or even more, a decline that would be felt in all areas of industrial production.

But, above all, the empire is indispensable to U.S. prosperity for the procurement of raw materials. The same official statistics list 53 products where imports represent in each case more than $10 million yearly, or more than 50 per cent of the quantity available on the American market. It is sufficient to recall (see Chapter I) that the United States imports 34 per cent of the iron ore that it consumes, 88 per cent of its bauxite, 92 per cent of its nickel, 99 per cent of its manganese, 100 per cent of its chrome, 25 per cent of its tungsten, 21 per cent of its copper, 44 per cent of its zinc, 28 per cent of its lead, 66 per cent of its tin, 14 per cent of its petroleum, 85 per cent of its asbestos, 26 per cent of potash, 100 per cent of natural rubber and tropical products: coffee, cocoa, bananas, etc., 40 per cent of its sugar. Deprived of those external sources the United States would jeopardize its industry—especially its basic industries, major consumers of rare metals indispensable to the manufacture of special steels.

The dependence on raw materials mostly located in countries of the Third World is particularly striking because the United States consumes more of them than anyone in the world. For, with 6 per cent of the world's population, the United States consumes 33 per cent of the bauxite produced in the entire world, 40 per cent of the nickel, 13 per cent of the manganese, 36 per cent of the chrome, 25 per cent of the tungsten, the asbestos, and the copper, 41 per cent of the tin, 23 per cent of the zinc, 14 per cent of the iron and lead, 28 per cent of the potash, 50 per cent of the coffee. It is thus that a privileged minority, representing hardly one out of seventeen inhabitants of the planet, consumes a quarter or a third or even a half of the raw materials necessary to modern life. The affluent society is built on a very unequal division of the resources available in the world. The myth is often entertained that American prosperity is founded both on an advanced technology—which is true—and on the abundance of the soil and subsoil of the United States—which is no longer true. The same facts dispel any mirage of an American-type prosperity being accessible to all the earth's inhabitants. It is said that if the latter do not enjoy these benefits, the reason is essentially that there is a technological gap compounded by a management gap. The differences in technology and in management methods are real, but they are infinitely less significant than the difference in aptitude between the United States and other countries in exploiting the raw materials of the world for their own benefit.

If American public opinion is not generally aware of this fact, the nation's leaders are not ignorant of it. For example, Lyndon Johnson declared: "It has been estimated that if everyone in the world were to rise to the level of living of those in the United States, we would then have to extract about 20 billion tons of iron, 300 million tons of copper, 300 million tons of lead, and 200 million tons of zinc. These totals are well over a hundred times the world present annual rate of production." [13] Not only are world reserves not inexhaustible, but American industry increasingly depends on rare minerals that it buys abroad. Its imports of bauxite rose from 79 per cent to 88 per cent between 1960 and 1964, its imports of chrome increased from 1,304,000 tons to 1,864,000 tons between 1960 and 1966. Its imports of nickel leaped from 91,347 to 141,000 tons between 1950 and 1966—or an increase of more than half.

The myth of an American-style prosperity within the reach of anyone willing to adopt American methods collapses under statistical examination. America consumes more and more iron, aluminum, chrome, nickel, etc., and the known deposits of those minerals are not sufficient to permit Europeans, Asians, Africans, and Latin Americans to consume as much as the inhabitants of the United States. The day may come when synthetic products will permit the reduction of the consumption of natural resources, but at the moment that is not true for anything except textile fibers and rubber, and even then the United States imports sizable quantities of wool, silk, and natural rubber. While it knows how to dangle before the eyes of the Third World the glittering and seductive visions created by the science of synthetic products, it multiplies at the same time its efforts to increase and to tighten the control it exercises over the available natural resources of the world. Its policies of foreign investments and economic aid clearly show the importance it attaches to this raw materials strategy.

In the very spirit of the Monroe Doctrine and by virtue of its "Manifest Destiny" which compels the United States to extend its influence over the whole of the continent, American private foreign investments were first attracted to Canada and Latin America where they found abundant raw materials to exploit. In 1940, 72 per cent of American private foreign investments were in Canada and Latin America. That proportion fell to 68 per cent in 1957 and to 53 per cent in 1965. For—starting with the Second World War—while American investments increased slowly in the extractive industries, they were massively directed into manufacturing industries. And that trend created a new geographic distribution which also corresponds to the world vocation of the United States. The attack on Pearl Harbor drew the United States out of its retreat within the confines of the American continent. But its investments were selective: it broadened its access to raw materials in Canada and Latin America, the Middle East, Africa and then, more cautiously, in Southeast Asia; it also strengthened its influence in industrialized countries. Canada and Europe were the first targets of an expansion which, from 1957 to 1965, doubled the value of private foreign investments:

INVESTMENTS BY CONTINENTS

(in millions of dollars)

	1957	1965
Canada	8,769	15,172
Europe	4,151	13,894
Latin America	7,434	9,371
Asia	2,019	3,611
Africa	664	1,904
Oceania	698	1,811
TOTAL	23,735	45,763

Investments increased still relatively little in the world's underdeveloped regions, the producers of raw materials over which the United States had already established firm control. But in a few years they doubled in Canada and tripled in Europe, where they flowed into manufacturing industries. Here, in millions of dollars, is their division into the major sectors of economic activity:

	1961	1965	+ %
Mines	3,061	3,794	24
Petroleum	12,151	15,320	26
Industry and commerce	19,472	30,104	54

Yet these figures are misleading, for in 1965 $3,429 million was invested in European petroleum facilities, but largely in refining and distribution which are far less profitable than extraction. In any case, the slight increase in investments in mines and petroleum should not hide the fact that they produce the largest profits. Here is, in fact, the division of profits:

PROFITS BY AREA OF ACTIVITY

(in millions of dollars)

	1961	1965
Mining	296	443
Petroleum	1,303	1,798
Industry and trade	1,074	1,720
TOTAL	2,673	3,961

Thus, in 1965, $15 billion invested in petroleum brought in as much as $30 billion invested in manufacturing industries and in commerce. But the $29 billion invested in Europe and in Canada have a double advantage in those countries: a skilled labor force and the protection of the NATO shield. They must, indeed, take into account an economic and social structure which forces them to pay wages and taxes higher than in Third World countries. But they weave increasingly closer links between the rich countries whose industrialization is already quite advanced and which enjoy a high standard of living. The 1965 figures show that capital invested in the exploitation of raw materials in Latin America, Asia and Africa is infinitely more profitable than capital invested in industry in these same regions, and more profitable also than capital invested in Europe and in Canada (see table below).

INVESTMENTS IN MINING AND PETROLEUM
IN THE THIRD WORLD ARE, BY FAR,
THE MOST PROFITABLE

	Mines and Petroleum		Industry		Total	
	Investments	Profits	Investments	Profits	Investments	Profits
Latin America	4,148	653	5,223	236	9,371	889
Africa	1,381	288	523	43	1,094	331
Asia	2,421	923	1,190	110	3,611	1,033
	7,950	1,864	6,936	389	14,886	2,253
Canada	5,075	232	10,097	360	15,172	692
Europe	3,484	25	10,411	735	13,895	760
	8,559	257	20,508	1,195	29,067	1,452

The table shows that American private investments are nearly twice as large in industrialized countries as in the Third World, but only produce profits of $1,452 million as against $2,253 million. In proportion to the capital invested, the most profitable operations are, by far, mining and petroleum in the Third World. But profits repatriated from

Latin America and Asia are each year greater than new investments made in those countries. In Europe on the other hand, new American investments are each year much larger than profits realized there. Exploitation of natural resources in the Third World thus permits the United States not only to have access to rich deposits of raw materials which ensure it a very high level of consumption, but also to obtain the necessary capital to invest in industrialized countries.

For example, as is shown by the table below, American private investments in Latin America rose from $8,120 million to $9,371 million between 1959 and 1965, or an increase of $1,251 million, while profits during the same period totaled $5,297 million. Each year, the contributions of new capital are less than profit repatriated to the United States, and in this seven-year period repatriated profits were more than four times greater than new investments.

INVESTMENTS AND PROFITS IN LATIN AMERICA

(in millions of dollars)

	Investments	Profits
1959	8,120	600
1960		641
1961		711
1962		761
1963		801
1964		895
1965	9,371	888
INCREASE	1,251	
TOTAL PROFITS		5,297

Asia, in that respect, is not in a more favorable position than Latin America. Between 1959 and 1965 profits realized by American capital in Asia were five times larger than new investments:

INVESTMENTS AND PROFITS IN ASIA

(in millions of dollars)

	Investments	Profits
1959	2,237	732
1960		853
1961		893
1962		1,017
1963		1,017
1964		983
1965	3,611	1,033
INCREASE	1,374	
TOTAL		6,528

On the other hand, private American investments in Europe are each year greater than published profits:

INVESTMENTS AND PROFITS IN EUROPE

(in millions of dollars)

	Investments	Profits
1959	5,323	393
1960		397
1961		511
1962		526
1963		507
1964		654
1965	13,894	760
INCREASE	8,571	
TOTAL		3,748

A detailed analysis of the flow of investments ought naturally to take into account the movements of capital by the largest American companies and consider them sector by sector. But gross investments by American private enterprise in Europe have exceeded profits by $4,823 million while they showed profits in Latin America and Asia that surpassed investment in those two continents by $9,200 million. In Canada, investments and profits are almost in balance: The former rose from $11,804 million to $15,172 million between 1959 and 1965—or an increase of $3,368 million—while profits totaled $3,372 million. Still in gross figures, the enormous surplus of profits over new investments in Latin America and Asia ($9,200 million) largely compensates for the "deficit" ($4,823 million) of investment over profits in Europe. The very high financial return on American investments in Latin America and Asia furnishes the United States with a major part of the capital necessary for its massive investments in Europe and for its export of capital to Africa and Oceania, where it is relatively still not very profitable. Here is, for the major regions of the world, the comparative table of new investments and profits between 1959 and 1965:

	Europe	Africa	Oceania	Canada	Latin America	Asia
New Investments	8,571	1,071	932	3,368	1,251	1,374
Profits	3,748	657	398	3,372	5,297	6,528
	−4,823	−414	−534	+4	+4,046	+5,154

Thus the United States received from Canada, Latin America, and Asia $9,204 million more than it had invested, which permitted it to invest $5,771 million more than its profits in Europe, Africa, and Oceania. The large profits that the United States draws from two underdeveloped continents gives it the means gradually to "colonize" the European economy and to extend its empire toward Africa and Oceania. There is nothing to prove that such a policy corresponds to a pre-established plan. American capitalism does not develop according to a planned concept, but responds to the sole law of profit in its most elementary form. It is purely a matter of profit which leads the United States to repatriate from Latin America and Asia capital which, invested there, would be very useful in the development of those continents. And those profits are themselves in turn invested in Canada and in Europe, where they reinforce the economic and political influence of the United States. The "noble idea" hailed by President Eisenhower and the great dream of John F. Kennedy, who wanted to show that in the Third World "economic expansion and democracy go hand in hand" are thus far removed from reality. The President of General Electric, quoted earlier, lives in an illusion. It is not true that "public and private interests come together . . . and become the national interest." The national interest of the United States would be to reduce the already considerable gap which is increasing between it and Latin America, and not to realize profits in Latin America to be invested elsewhere.

Is it true that aid granted by the American government to countries of the Third World compensates for the profits repatriated to the United States? Taking the example of Latin America, here is for recent years a comparison between government aid and profits realized by private investments:

	Government Aid	Private Profits
	(in millions of dollars)	
1960	194	641
1961	710	711
1962	587	761
1963	576	801
1964	447	895
1965	632	888
	3,146	4,697

Smaller than the profits of private American investments, which are largely repatriated to the United States, government aid granted by Washington is, in part, devoted to debt repayment and cannot alleviate the hemorrhaging of capital from Latin America. Latin America's annual debt rose from $455 million in 1956 to $2,100 million in 1965. Thus when, under the guise of investments or loans, $1,814 million goes into Brazil, the flow toward the United States (profits and interest) represents $2,459 million to which must be added $1 billion of clandestine transfers. Thus the poor countries help to finance the rich countries, led by the United States. When John F. Kennedy launched the Alliance for Progress he envisaged for Latin America annual credits of a billion dollars for ten years, or thirty times less than the price of the Vietnam War in 1968 alone. He thought that Latin America would thus achieve an economic growth-rate of 5 per cent per year. The real rate has been 2 per cent, while the rate of demographic expansion has been 2.4 per cent. But the most serious result is that Latin America, by furnishing capital to the United States, contributed to the enrichment of the empire to which it is subject and which weighs so heavily on its economic and political life. Only a vigorous revision of our policy toward Latin America can still contain the rise of poverty and discontent of that continent, Senator Robert F. Kennedy declared. But such a revision, favored by certain political realists, would seriously impair the internal prosperity of the United States and the external power of its empire. "One dollar in 14 of the national income of the United States comes from abroad. In the IBM Company it is 1 dollar in 4," stated Thomas J. Watson, President of International Business Machines (IBM). But he fully realized that such a situation was abnormal, therefore he added: "If the Europeans do not find a way to slow us down politely, and if we ourselves in our enlightened self-interest do not find methods of making our operations abroad more acceptable to the nationals of the countries in which we operate, Europeans in simple self-defense will throw up new barriers against further penetration of American industry on their continent, and will begin to restrict the positions we already have." [14] Obviously Europe was more on Thomas J. Watson's mind than the continents where American firms make profits several times their investments. The shrewdest American businessmen well understand that the United States cannot—without danger—continue to enrich itself by expanding its empire on all continents. But the ruling circles are less clearheaded and continue to confuse the notions of generosity, national interest, and prestige to justify a policy of foreign aid that is always tied to private investments. For example, Lyndon Johnson declared: "We are distributing in the form of aid and military assistance about one half of one per cent of our Gross National Product. This investment is not only one of the most noble acts that a great country could perform, but it is an act of necessity if we are to preserve our leadership in the world. We must help developing countries because our own welfare demands it. It takes no great gift of foresight to realize that unless there is progress, there will be discontent." [15]

It is not clear that that "enlightened self-interest" adds to the prestige of the United States, much to the contrary, in many cases economic aid has fueled strong animosities. What is certain, on the other hand, is that aid in all its forms greatly contributes to the prosperity of the United States. Does it offer a solution to the countries of the Third World? John F. Kennedy supplied the answer in his *Strategy for Peace:* "And so, among the nations of the world, the rich grow richer as the poor grow poorer—with less capital and more people and fewer hopes. It is this kind of atmosphere which increases the appeal of a narrow nationalism and dictatorship, which argues that economic interpendence with foreign nations is ominous. The United States of America, the richest nation on earth, has not given the poorer nations new hope." [16]

However harsh, that judgment does not take into account the whole reality. In fact, it is not enough to say that the United States has failed to give poor countries new reasons for hope: Figures cited above show that the United States enriches itself to the detriment of poor countries. It is not enough to say that poor countries have less and less capital: It must be added that thanks to the poor countries the United States has at its disposal more and more capital to extend the reaches of its empire toward the rich countries of Europe and toward the poor countries of more distant and exposed regions into which American capital has until now hesitated to venture. It is not enough to say that the poor countries consider any economic tie with the United States a "threat": It must also be remembered that those economic ties have quite often permitted the American government to intervene in the internal political life of these countries. There is no attempt here to draw up a complete list of interventions, but a few striking facts are cited to show to what political and economic ends Washington uses the power given it by private foreign investments and governments grant of economic and military aid.

American intervention in the internal problems of foreign countries takes different forms depending on the type of government these countries have; depending also on their degree of economic dependence. There is only one common denominator: no one is able to avoid intervention. And when pressure or threats are not sufficient, the empire resorts to economic reprisals. The actions cited here are simply intended to illustrate the variety of means at the disposal of the United States.

Thus, officially only the best relations exist between Washington and Ottawa, but Canada depends on the United States for 52 per cent of its exports and 68 per cent of its imports. Besides, American capital controls 60 per cent of Canadian industry. The two countries are so closely related economically that fluctuations of the American dollar are immediately reflected—as in 1967–1968—in the Canadian dollar. A wave of prosperity in the United States, during the Korean War, gave new impetus to Canadian industry. A recession in the United States, a downturn of production, immediately affects black Americans—the last to be hired, the first to be fired—but also Canadian workers employed in the American affiliated firms in Canada.

Such a situation allows the United States to intervene vigorously in Canadian affairs. When the Pentagon wanted to install Bomarc missiles with nuclear warheads in Canada, the decision was imposed on Ottawa.

When Lester B. Pearson, the Liberal Prime Minister, came to power in 1963 he inherited from his Conservative predecessor, John Diefenbaker, an issue which was to provoke a serious crisis: American periodicals distributed in Canada were offering English-Canadian business advertising space at rock-bottom prices, which deprived Canadian periodicals of an important part of their income. As a safeguard, a commission proposed a special 40 per cent tax on those contracts, and the project was approved by Pearson as it had been by Diefenbaker. Immediately, John F. Kennedy telephoned Pearson from the White House and laid it on the line: either the publications of the *Time-Life* group and the *Reader's Digest* would be exempt from the 40 per cent tax, or the United States would slash a $420 million contract intended for the Canadair firm in Montreal; that, added Kennedy, would throw 16,000 men out of work.

There are numerous cases of the United States government intervening all over the world through its highest representatives, to defend not the national interest of the United States but the private interests of a particular group. To wit: in 1967 President Johnson threatened the Canadian government with economic reprisals if Ottawa did not rescind a new law on bank controls which, naturally, also applied to American banks in Canada.

Prime Minister Lester Pearson was publicly rebuked by

President Johnson for having advocated a bombing halt for North Vietnam and he openly stated that "we can't ignore the fact that a first result of any open breach with the United States over Vietnam . . . would be a more critical examination by Washington of certain special aspects of our relationship from which we, as well as they, get great benefit . . . it's not a comforting thought but in the economic sphere, when you have 60 per cent or so of your trade with one country, you are in a position of considerable economic dependence." [17]

In the same vein, Washington intervened with threats to prevent Canada from selling uranium to France. Strong pressure dissuaded Canada, and also Belgium and Italy, who had decided to act jointly, from voting for the admission of Peking to the United Nations and from normalizing their relations with Communist China.

If the United States took the liberty of acting this way with a developed country like Canada, it took fewer precautions with weaker countries which it was accustomed to treat as protectorates. In this regard the example of Cuba is particularly enlightening, because—after as before the revolution—Washington believed that it could impose its will on that country. After Fidel Castro came to power, Earl E. T. Smith, former United States Ambassador to Cuba, declared in September 1960, before a subcommittee of the House of the Representatives, that until the revolution the American Ambassador was "the second most important man in Cuba."

His power rested on the fact that Cuba sold more than half of its sugar crop to the United States and was firmly tied to the American economy by a series of agreements—in particular a tariff agreement which placed Washington in a quasi-monopolistic position.[18] A full-blown propaganda campaign spread the idea that this system was particularly profitable to Cuba. But John F. Kennedy was not taken in.

He noted for instance: "Ninety-eight cents of every American dollar spent to purchase sugar from Cuba, for example, is spent by the Cubans to buy American exports." And he added: "Our recession cut the prices received for commodities the underdeveloped nations must sell, while our inflation continued to boost the prices they paid for our machinery." [19]

Cuba's close economic dependence vis-à-vis the United States resulted in a serious disadvantage: Washington furnished Batista with the financial and military aid necessary to maintain his bloody dictatorship. And it permitted the United States to control and, if need be, to slow down the economic development of Cuba.

For example, before the fall of Batista, France wanted to build a flour mill in Cuba which would have had several advantages: besides giving work to Cubans, it would have permitted Cuba to import wheat rather than flour from the United States—wheat being less expensive and easier to transship. As soon as the flour-dealers' lobby in Washington learned of the project, it went into action. The State Department took the position that it could not interfere in Franco-Cuban relations. But it suggested the strategy the lobby could follow. Wheat being cheaper than flour, installation of a flour mill would permit Cuba to reduce the dollar value of its imports from the United States; the latter, in order to adjust its trade balance, would reduce its imports of Cuban sugar. It would be enough to pass this information on to the Cuban sugar producers, who would then pressure their own government to prevent the installation of the French flour mill to protect their interests.

This scenario was carefully followed and the desired result was obtained. The American flour-dealers had prevailed. Washington could be satisfied: it was maintaining intact its influence in Cuba. In this way the empire finds natural allies in many countries, namely, the economic groups closely tied to the American market which do not hesitate to put their group interests ahead of their country's interests. There are many examples of this, particularly in countries whose economy is based on one or two products, of which the United States is a principal buyer. Officially, Washington does not intervene; its "clients" take care of the matter. Such is the case, for example, with the coffee producers in Brazil and Colombia who know that the United States consumes half the world's output.

The situation in Cuba after the revolution illustrates just as clearly the empire's methods and strategy. The verbal violence of the controversy between Havana and Washington, the bitterness of the conflict between the two countries, may obscure the real cause of their break. Fourteen months after the fall of Batista, Mikoyan's visit created the first official contact between the Castro regime and the U.S.S.R. The Cuban revolutionaries were then involved with buying agricultural equipment from the United States, which they paid for in dollars. Mikoyan proposed a way to stretch their foreign currency reserves. All they needed to do was to replace American oil with Soviet oil, which was much less expensive and could be paid for in local currency.

When, eighteen months after Batista's fall, the first oil tanker loaded with Soviet crude oil arrived in Havana, the three refineries on the island refused to process it. One of the refineries belonged to Shell and the other two were American—Texaco and Standard. Fidel Castro could not, obviously, allow his plans to be checkmated by three private companies. When the latter rejected any compromise, they were nationalized by the Cuban government. In reprisal, President Eisenhower, defending not the national interest of the United States but the interests of private groups, reduced Cuban sugar purchases by 700,000 tons. Thus, the economic war began because Washington could not allow a country to buy oil that was less expensive than American oil. Fidel Castro retaliated by nationalizing other American companies and Eisenhower, in return, completely cut off Cuban sugar purchases. At the end of the year diplomatic relations were broken. In the spring of 1961, the CIA launched its attempted invasion at the Bay of Pigs and Fidel Castro declared himself a Socialist.

This chain of events does not irrefutably prove that the attitude of the United States compelled Cuba to turn toward Communism and that a more conciliatory attitude would have avoided such an outcome. However, it does show that private American firms can remain aloof from the authority of a country in which they are established and that they can count on Washington's support. It also shows that as far as the White House is concerned, the concept of the country's national interest is closely tied, abroad, to that of the great private interests.

In the specific case of Cuba the only way Washington could have avoided the crisis and the break would have been to compel Texaco and Standard to refine Soviet crude oil. This would have been in the interests not, indeed, of the refineries but of the United States, to the extent that it wanted to maintain its relations with the government of Cuba in the eventual hope of moderating some of its initiatives. But, many other countries would then have been tempted to buy Soviet oil—and that would have been a great blow to an American oil empire accustomed to fix world prices at its pleasure.

Although the United States government can, within its frontiers, take on powerful private interests in certain cases, its authority often does not extend to American private interests abroad. Whether it wants the role or not. Washington is the guardian of investments which compromise the empire's outposts or bridgeheads in countries near and far. It thus experiences great difficulty in making a distinction between American private interests and the national interest of the United States, these being closely intertwined. On the other hand, in dealing with a foreign country, Washington can see quite clearly the necessary distinction between special interests and the general interest whose sole judge and protector it is. That is why, for example, the United States does not have the same attitude to the Panama Canal, which concerns it directly, and the Suez Canal Company, which it rightly considers a relic of Franco-British imperialism. To have its ideas prevail in the Suez crisis, it put the full weight of its economic empire behind its diplomatic efforts.

When Nasser nationalized the canal on July 26, 1956, Eisenhower and John Foster Dulles treated it as "a business dispute over the control of an international public utility." Dulles told Christian Pineau, French Foreign Affairs Minister, "I had no idea I would run into such strong emotions here. I just can't understand why you people are willing to risk so much for the sake of this damn canal." But, from the 9th to the 12th of January, 1964, so that the Star-Spangled Banner would continue to wave over the schools of the Panama Canal Zone, General O'Meara's troops killed twenty-four Panamian students and wounded almost four hundred. That use of force certainly cannot be compared to the means used during the Suez expedition. But the absolute control of the United States over the Panama Canal was not even being challenged by the demonstrators. In contrast, when the Suez Canal was involved, President Eisenhower, who two years earlier had launched an armed expedition against Guatemala (see Chap. IX), told Hervé Alphand, French Ambassador to Washington: "You must stop this war. . . . Life is a ladder which mounts up to Heaven. I am near the top of that ladder, and I wish to present myself with clean hands before my Creator." [20] In order to impose his point of view on London he emphasized the fact that Great Britain was closely dependent on the

American economic empire. In Washington, the State Department let the British Ambassador understand that if the pound sterling continued to decline, Great Britain could not avoid bankruptcy. And to back up that statement Washington kept "selling the pound left and right." [21] Later, Eden would discreetly note in his memoirs: "The United States . . . used every resource at their command, and there were many." [22]

But the economic power of the American empire permits it to operate on two levels. To prevail, the United States had first hastened the fall of the pound sterling. Then it offered to save it. André Fontaine writes: "Eden was informed by Washington that a loan of $1 billion would be authorized if he ordered a cease-fire by midnight." [23] This double-pronged intervention was decisive and Eden immediately summoned his ministers to inform them that there was no other course of action left but to halt the Suez expedition.

The American empire, which at the time was cultivating the friendship of the Arab states, had to exert similar pressure on the Tel Aviv government for Israeli troops to evacuate the Sinai peninsula. The United States took official as well as unofficial action.

Officially, Eisenhower wrote to Ben Gurion, on November 8, 1956, that the United States "viewed . . . with the deepest concern" his declaration that Israeli troops would not submit to the United Nations resolution on the Sinai evacuation. At the same time, Hoover, acting Secretary of State, wrote much more explicitly, to Golda Meir, Israeli Foreign Affairs Minister, speaking of a "complete severance of United States-Israel relations and a powerful movement within the United Nations to expel Israel." [24]

Unofficially Washington let Israel know what economic sanctions would consist of. Michael Bar-Zohar writes on that subject: "Goldmann, the president of the World Jewish Congress, informed Ben Gurion that American Jewry . . .

would not stand behind Israel if she persisted in keeping the conquered territory. He added that collections for the Nation Jewish Funds [sic] might be forbidden. And Germany too, under American pressure, might stop paying reparations" owed by Bonn to the victims of Nazi persecution. Threatened with being deprived of outside resource, Ben Gurion had to yield, but he tried delaying tactics during conversations with the interested capitals. There again he had to give in, because the empire increased its economic pressure. "The United States," wrote Michael Bar-Zohar, "had in fact already started to apply sanctions by blocking a loan promised to Israel some time previously." [25]

Thus, the economic pressure of the United States on England and on Israel resolved a crisis started by a "gamble" of John Foster Dulles who had believed that he could apply economic pressure on Nasser with impunity by withdrawing the American offer to grant Egypt $70 million for the construction of the Aswan dam. All during the crisis, Dulles insisted on the necessity of not questioning the principle of nationalization and of only assuring the right of passage in the canal. "The Secretary of State," notes André Fontaine, "was afraid that any other approach might be extended to the Panama Canal, leased in perpetuity to the United States, and which the Americans did not for one moment consider abandoning." [26] For, however well or poorly they are understood, the national interests of the United States become, in Washington's eyes, the interests of the "free world" of which it is the leader, while—well or poorly understood—the national interests of allies of the United States are subject to Washington's approval.

Through a unilateral decision, without consulting its allies, the United States decided to give legal support to its interventions in the form of the Eisenhower Doctrine that the President proposed to Congress on January 5, 1957. By means of the Monroe Doctrine the United States affirmed its rights over the whole of the American continent. Through the Truman Doctrine it took the initiative in Greece and Turkey. Through the Eisenhower Doctrine it designated itself as the policeman of the Middle East, over which the Sixth Fleet was watching. By virtue of this new doctrine, unilaterally proclaimed without any international agreement, the President of the United States was authorized by Congress to "help develop the economic strength of and enter into military assistance programs with any nation or group of nations in the area which desired such help." The resolution authorized the President "to use armed forces to assist any such nation or group of nations requesting assistance." [27] Three months later, faced with the disorders in Jordan, Eisenhower ordered the movement of the Sixth Fleet and then made an initial $10 million grant to King Hussein. In June of the same year, to support the election of President Chamoun in Lebanon, who was known for his pro-Western sympathies, the United States provided him with economic aid on the eve of the second ballot. In January 1958 Egypt and Syria decided to merge and form the United Arab Republic. Then, on July 14 General Kassem overthrew the monarchy in Iraq, while President Chamoun complained of "outside aggression against Lebanon," for which no observer could find the slightest evidence. Dulles, deciding it was time "to bring a halt to the deterioration in our position in the Middle East," [28] landed 10,000 Marines in Lebanon. Their presence and the activities of Robert Murphy, who had been sent by Eisenhower, dissuaded Chamoun, whom they had caused to be elected the first time, from seeking another mandate.

The list of American interventions in different countries of the Middle East is long. When General Kassem in Iraq promulgated Law No. 81 by which he gave the state 95 per cent of the concessions held by the Iraq Petroleum Company, Washington protested vigorously. Then Iraq withdrew from the Bagdad Pact. General Kassem was overthrown and assassinated in February 1963 by General Aref with the help of the CIA. That "revolution" was followed by what amounted to a massacre of Communists and progressive elements, with the United States Ambassador in Bagdad even supplying the militia with lists of undesirables.

Naturally, Egypt was not spared United States interference. In 1965, in collusion with the CIA, the ultra-conservative Moslem Brotherhood organized a vast plot to overthrow the Nasser regime, but the responsible principals were arrested. In October of the same year Washington refused to renew the triennial accord on wheat shipments by which Egypt was supplied with $879 million of wheat by the United States over a ten-year period. These shipments were payable in local currency, which was the only means Washington had at its disposal to sell the enormous agricultural surpluses (whose storage in 1960 alone cost $576 million) without ruining American farmers. The sale of those surpluses had become an excellent means of applying pressure on countries proving to be more or less recalcitrant toward Washington. Cairo had often attacked American policy in Vietnam, the intervention in the Congo, the sending of troops to the Dominican Republic, etc. On January 3, 1966, the United States, after having left Egypt without wheat for several months, agreed to sell it $56 million of grain, but on less favorable terms. Then in 1967 it spelled out for Nasser its conditions for the renewal of shipments: withdrawal of support from the nationalists in Aden, halting Egyptian propaganda against Saudi Arabia, etc. Nasser rejected these conditions and the American wheat.[29] Finally, on the eve of the Israeli-Egyptian conflict, the American Ambassador in Cairo threatened Nasser with the intervention of the Sixth Fleet if he opened hostilities. A similar warning was not given to Israel, which started the fighting. Innumerable forms of pressure have thus been exercised in the hope of bringing down a regime that the United States had looked upon favorably when it first came to power.

Thanks to long-standing tradition, United States intervention in Latin America is extremely frequent and quite open. The most glaring example was the sending of more than 20,000 Marines to the Dominican Republic in 1965 on the pretext of protecting the lives of American nationals. The dictator Trujillo had been assassinated on May 30, 1961, and, after many vicissitudes, the reform-minded democrat Juan Bosch had been elected President of the Republic in 1963. He was overthrown in September of the same year, without the United States feeling the need to come to his aid, although it had pledged in the Alliance for Progress to support constitutional regimes. That abstention by Washington would retrospectively have had an entirely different significance if the United States had not massively intervened two years later to save, *in extremis*, the troops of General Wessin y Wessin, which Colonel Cammano's constitutional forces had practically defeated. In order to justify this action, which again plunged the Dominican Republic into a dictatorship, the State Department published a list of "53 Communist figures" suspected of wanting to seize power.[30] A firm resolution to have democracy in the Dominican Republic would have led the United States in 1963 to support Juan Bosch and not to rush to the rescue in 1965 of a military clique bequeathed to the country by Trujillo's dictatorship. However, the last intervention, which provoked profound indignation in Latin America, particularly in Chile and in Uruguay, is hardly surprising. When the United States halted its sugar purchases from Cuba in 1960, the Dominican Republic, under Trujillo's dictatorship, was one of the first countries to which the United State gave priority for additional sugar orders. Trujillo could hardly have hoped for a more concrete gesture of support. Thirty years before, he had come to power in the wake of the American Marines who had been occupying the country. Since that time Washington had not spared its support and it was natural that the United States, which had done nothing to help the democrat Juan Bosch, would massively intervene to save military leaders trained in the school of dictatorship.

For sometimes complex reasons the United States has maintained the best of relations with the dictatorships of Latin America. Thus Paraguay, subject to General Stroessner's dictatorship, received United States government assistance of $66.8 million between 1948 and 1956—this to a country with 1,900,000 inhabitants, while the democracy of Uruguay, with 2,600,000 inhabitants, received only $35.2 million. As a general rule, the United States has had no reason to complain about the dictatorships of Stroessner in Paraguay, Somoza in Nicaragua, Perez Jimenez in Venezuela, Trujillo in the Dominican Republic, Batista in Cuba, Odria in Peru, Rojas Pinilla in Colombia, etc. That was true for the period before John F. Kennedy became President and launched his Alliance for Progress, which proposed not only to assure Latin America's economic development, but also to favor democratic regimes. The principle remained the same under the Alliance for Progress.

The United States, which rarely hesitates to intervene in any country of the continent, has done nothing to uproot the dictatorships holding power—for they know how to respect American private interests. On the other hand, against Fidel Castro's Socialist regime, which has tampered with American investments, the United States has triggered a very powerful propaganda war, a diplomatic boycott in which only Mexico refused to participate, an embargo which imposes a heavy burden on the Cuban economy, an armed invasion which ended in the failure of the Bay of Pigs, commando operations aimed at sabotaging the Cuban economy and assassinating Fidel Castro, and a grand strategy to make sure that Cuba would be expelled from the Organization of American States (OAS). That last move required a two-thirds majority vote—or fourteen votes. But the fourteenth was lacking. Washington bought it at a high price in 1962 by promising the recalcitrant country the necessary aid to build a jet airport. That deal was made with Haiti, a country ruled by the bloody and insane Duvalier dictatorship. The dictatorships keep their seats and their votes in the OAS and nothing is done to weaken them, for they are subservient to the interests of the economic empire.

In fact, the Alliance for Progress seems to have encouraged Latin American military coups against constitutionally elected governments. A report of the Foreign Affairs Committee of the Senate stated in 1967: "Over the past 5 years a new wave of militarism has been sweeping across Latin America. Between March 1962 and June 1966 nine duly elected, constitutional, civilian presidents were deposed by military coups." In Argentina, the military overthrew President Frondizi in 1962 and President Ilia in 1966 when the election results, which showed the strength of Peronism, did not suit them. In Peru the military overthrew President Prado in July 1962 to annul elections which had taken place the preceeding month. But the military are not satisfied in intervening *after* elections whose results disturb them. They also go into action *before* the voting when they foresee that the verdict of the ballot box will be unfavorable to them. This was the case in 1963 in Guatemala, to prevent the return to power of former President Juan José Arevalo, whose previous government (1945–1950) had allowed Jacobo Arbenz, overthrown in 1954 by the CIA, to come to power. The same year, the report of the Senate committee continued, "The Ecuadorean military acted to prevent the expected return of the populist leader José Maria Velasco Ibarra whom they had deposed two years before, and the Honduran military intervened to prevent the expected triumph of the populist Liberal Party candidate Rojas Alvarado." [31]

By according a *de facto* priority to the fight against Communism, Washington has supplied the military of Latin America with an easy pretext to violate democratic legality. All that is required is that they present their designated victim as guilty of playing the game of a Communist pawn. In many cases, however, the men thus denied power were both pro-American and proponents of the prudent reforms recommended by the Alliance for Progress. But those men disturbed not only the Army but also the real masters of the economy—be they native companies or American companies established there. A contradiction thus appeared between the two objectives—democracy and economic progress—of the Alliance for Progress. A democratic champion of reforms indispensable to economic progress quickly becomes a dangerous revolutionary in the eyes of reactionary forces which decide to overthrow him. Thus parliamentary democracy and economic progress both recede at the same time. In reaction to these coups, Washington does not intervene, except through a temporary recall of its Ambassador or the suspension of aid, but these measures are themselves rescinded a few weeks later, after a vague promise of return to democratic practices. In this way the economic empire of the United States in Latin America preserves its power intact. The military know that even if they are not always appreciated, they have nothing to fear from Washington. Quite the contrary, the United States gives them considerable aid (see Chap. VII) so that they can become occupied with fighting guerrillas—for the guerrilla is, as a matter of fact, the only serious threat to an economic empire which, in six years, supplied the United States with more than $4 billion in repatriated profits. In each country the empire knows how to make use of its "natural allies," even though they remain steadfast opponents of the proclaimed ideal of the United States.

But that ideal is perverted when it crosses the frontiers of the United States, for it is immediately subordinated to imperatives even beyond fighting Communism. Outside, still more than within the United States, the highest law is determined by the most powerful interests. In Brazil, for example, Washington was not satisfied to merely stand by during the 1964 coup which overthrew President Goulart or later to maintain the best of relations with the military regimes of Marshal Castelo Branco and then of Marshal Costa e Silva. As it happened the government of President Goulart was compelled to grant important advantages in the Brazilian petrochemical field to an American company to obtain a United States government loan. Similarly when Lionel Brizzola was Governor of the State of Rio Grande do Sul, he was summoned to Brasilia where the representatives of an American telephone company that he had just nationalized were waiting for him in the President's office. At the same moment the author of this book was in Washington, in the office of the Under Secretary of State for Latin America. When informed by telephone that the Governor had signed the nationalization order, the latter answered, undisturbed by the presence of his visitor: "Brizzola will have to be kicked out." Again, when the Hanna Mining Corporation had not succeeded in its efforts to obtain from the Goulart government a long-term concession for the exploitation and sale of iron ore in Minas Gerais, it had no difficulty in being granted that monopoly following a conversation between the United States Ambassador in Rio and Marshal Castelo Branco who had become President following the military *coup d'état* against Goulart. Subsequently the Hanna Mining Corporation decided to resell its rights to the Brazilian group Antunes, which was linked to the Bethlehem Steel Corporation which already controlled the very rich manganese deposits of the Amapa. When João Goulart refused to satisfy the demands of the American company Bond & Share, he was told by telephone to go to Rome, where President John F. Kennedy was visiting, in order to settle that unpleasant affair which was proving harmful to relations between the United States and Brazil.

These few examples concerning Brazil certainly do not give a complete picture of Washington interventions in Latin America in the service of its economic empire. They illustrate, however, what has become classic procedure. For a century, through many ups and downs, American private interests have given priority to Latin America under the protection of the Monroe Doctrine and the Roosevelt Corollary. While exploiting raw materials that are indispensable to the prosperity of the United States, they have locally acquired considerable influence over poor and often weak governments. At the same time, they have found allies in each country among certain sectors of the propertied classes which are all the more powerful because they exercise a generally decisive influence over politics. They, furthermore, enjoy the support of the armed forces in these various countries which are traditionally hostile to any change in the status quo and pampered by the Pentagon, which sees in them the necessary barrier against "subversion"—Communist or not. In addition, the large American companies which have invested in Latin America have at their command lobbies in Washington and most members of Congress and the government consider them missionaries of progress in economically underdeveloped countries. Washington encourages private investments in the conviction that government aid is not sufficient to ensure a rapid enough rate of development. Congress approves of that policy, which allows it to vote smaller appropriations for aid programs—necessarily unpopular in the eyes of the taxpaying voter. At the same time, government and Congress feel they are the guardians of those investments, which can be threatened by possible revolutions or nationalization. They also know that those investments are indispensable to the American standard of living, that they guarantee freedom of access to rich raw materials deposits which the United States economy cannot do without, and that they provide repatriated yearly profits much greater than new investments which can be reinvested elsewhere. At the same time, American programs of economic aid open the way to influencing Latin American governments, which do not want to deprive their countries of these credits, however much smaller they are than the profits repatriated by American companies.

In a very complimentary analysis of the Alliance for Progress, William D. Rogers described United States interference in the election campaigns in Argentina and in Chile.[32] In this way a tight network has gradually been created, reinforced by the training given to officers, engineers, technicians, etc. in the United States, who all become faithful servants of the empire. The United States has further established in Latin America strong control over the press, television, and the movies (see Chap. VIII) to condition public opinion.

So we see that the system has been greatly perfected since the proclamation of the Monroe Doctrine in 1823. The latter remains in force, as John F. Kennedy demonstrated during the Cuban missile crisis in 1962. The big-stick policy, initiated by Theodore Roosevelt, was continued in the second half of the twentieth century with the coup in Guatemala (1954), the Bay of Pigs landing (1961), the occupation of the Dominican Republic by the Marines (1965), and the training of antiguerrilla forces in the other countries. The dollar diplomacy inaugurated by President Taft is revealed in the pressures which accompany government aid and in the direct intervention of the White House and State Department on behalf of American private interests. The good neighbor policy of Franklin Roosevelt always inspires official proclamations—under Kennedy as much as under his successors, although its principle is denied by the facts. The Alliance for Progress synthesizes, more or less harmoniously, these diverse inheritances, whose effects combine to maintain and reinforce the influence of the United States over Latin America, a bastion essential to the survival of the empire.

To keep a firm grasp on the nations of the continent, Washington has at its disposal the Organization of American States, where it sooner or later prevails, especially since the United States guarantees 66 per cent of its budget. The State Department carefully watches over the choice of the person who occupies the general secretariat of the Organization. The latest example was furnished by the election to that post, in February, 1968, of Galo Plaza Lasso. A former President of Ecuador, he was born in New York and speaks English without an accent. He had been sent by the United Nations to Lebanon, the Congo, and Cyprus during the crises that shook these countries. Galo Plaza—who was not elected until the sixth ballot, so great was the suspicion he inspired—only declared his candidacy after having discussed it with Secretary of State Dean Rusk. The too-obvious support of Galo Plaza by American officials was at the back of Senator Fulbright's denunciation of "inept diplomacy" incapable of acting "with a minimum of discretion." And the American delegate, Sol M. Linowitz, replied that he had done nothing other than to make clear that Plaza was the man chosen by Washington. In this way the OAS continues to protect this vital sector of the American economic empire, although the member countries of the Organization are poorly recompensed for the support they give United States policy. The President of Colombia, Carlos Lleras Restrepo, went unheeded when he declared that a jeep could be imported in 1950 for the price of seventeen bales of coffee and that it took fifty-seven in 1967. Totally impotent to resolve the economic problems of Latin America, the OAS remains a useful instrument in the service of the empire to "cover" the operations mounted against Cuba, or the sending of Marines to the Dominican Republic, and to control recalcitrant governments by subjecting them to the rule of a majority.

However, President Kennedy had clearly seen that it was desirable to encourage Latin America's economic development—particularly by stabilizing the prices of the raw materials that it exports. Thus an international agreement on coffee was concluded, and was renewed in February 1968. The advantage of such an accord is to ensure producer countries (especially Brazil and Colombia) stable revenues by putting an end to the speculations of commodity importers. The renewal of the accord was particularly difficult owing to the position taken by the United States, which intended to import raw coffee, while Brazil had made plans to create a major instant coffee industry. Once more Washington hindered the transformation of a raw material in the country producing it. Obviously, the American government was concerned not to harm the interests of its importers, and the problem was not settled to the advantage of the producers. This happens because any disagreement will be submitted to arbitration by a three-judge tribunal, which will hardly be in a position to make the country which consumes half the world's production yield.

A similar situation is found with cocoa. There again, the opposition to a reasonable international accord comes from the United States. Once more the interests of the producer countries are sacrificed to those of American importers who do not hesitate to build up stockpiles so that they can reduce purchases and bring prices down and then take advantage of importing when prices are at their lowest. An agreement failed because the United States was acutely sensitive to business pressures at home in an election year.[33]

If dictatorships remain solidly entrenched, if military regimes have a tendency to multiply, if the different Latin
American governments are maintained along the lines indicated by Washington—these results have not been obtained without vigorous intervention beyond Latin America.
For the game which is played on this continent is inseparable from the vaster, worldwide confrontation. In its
desire to control the markets for raw materials, of which it
is the largest consumer, the United States has exerted
strong pressure on its European allies. One example is furnished by the "nickel war." In 1965 Le Nickel, a French
company controlled by the Rothschild group and the third
largest producer of this extremely rare ore, concluded a tri-
angular agreement: the French company would buy nickel
in Cuba and sell to Communist China a large part of its
output in New Caledonia. In August 1965 the America
government prohibited the importation of all products con-
taining metal supplied by Le Nickel. Six French ships trans-
porting stainless steel were detained in the port of New
York. The paradox is that the company, Le Nickel, before
buying Cuban ore had tried to buy some from the United
States, where the government had a stockpile of 166,761
tons. But Washington categorically rejected the proposal.
The French government strongly protested the detention of
the boats but as *Time* magazine wrote:"The U.S. does not
seem to be in any hurry to compromise, however, as long
as General de Gaulle continues to make trouble for NATO,
the Common Market, the Kennedy Round tariff talks." [34]
A compromise was finally reached when French authorities
agreed to guarantee that products sold in the United States
would not contain any nickel coming from Cuba. But the
affair was to have a sequel with the creation in France of a
new company, heavily backed by American capital, to compete with Le Nickel, which had dared to buy in Cuba and
sell to Communist China.

Such an incident must be compared with the United States sanctions against Western European freighters which carry cargo between Europe and Cuba: be they French, English, Greek, or Swedish, access to American ports is denied them. Washington always tries to impose its own political decisions on foreign firms. A French automobile manufacturing company gave up the idea of installing an assembly plant in several countries because the Quai d'Orsay had been informed that the company would then lose its United States market. A French seed company gave up contracts concluded with certain countries, including Cuba, because the United States consulate informed it that its American suppliers would refuse its orders. An already signed Franco-Haitian commercial accord, which offered the means of balancing Franco-Haitian trade, was revoked following a visit of the United States Ambassador to President Duvalier. Any government receiving official aid from the United States is threatened with its loss if it tries to replace an American supplier with a European or Japanese supplier offering more advantageous terms. American Presidents of affiliates of American companies abroad are subject to the legislation of the United States Congress. This means that they cannot work out their commercial policies in relation to the interests of the country where they are located, but must, as for example, in the sale of so-called "strategic" products, submit to decisions from Washington. And, needless to say, countries economically or financially dependent on the United States lose their freedom of political and diplomatic initiative. That is why the government of Harold Wilson, going against the wishes of the Labour Party which opposed the bombing of North Vietnam, refused to dissociate itself from President Johnson's Vietnam policy.

. . .

Only access to the diplomatic archives of the great powers would enable one to compile a list of interventions of the United States government which, secure in its economic power, feels free to intervene in the political life and diplomatic policies of other countries. But the number of known facts is sufficient to suggest the scope of those interventions. All governments, provided they have the means, act in the same manner. But no government possesses the means at the disposal of Washington. And the problem, by changing scale, changes its nature—for only the government of the United States can intervene throughout the world. The old colonial powers enjoyed geographically determined spheres of influence. France and England held in their hands the destiny of a good part of Africa, but the United States imposes its weight on an empire which knows no frontiers, on Europe and on Latin America, as well as on Asia, the Middle East, and Africa. Some supply it with raw materials, others with outlets for its capital, and all guarantee its profits without which the prosperity of the Americans, who constitute 6 per cent of the world's population, would not be enjoying living standards so greatly superior to those of the rest of humanity. America drains the entire world of the elements that make it the economic power which permits it to intervene on all continents.

This politico-economic action is made possible by the fact that it takes place in the shadow of United States military power. Countries tempted to resist Washington's economic and political interventions often hesitate to do so because they know they are protected by the American arsenal. The fear of Communism thus plays an essential role in the service of the United States, which in the final analysis, considers itself sole judge of its own interests and of the interests of a "free world" whose guardian it chooses to be through a kind of one-sided solidarity. Its economic empire, impressive as it is, would have its weak spots were it not joined to a no less formidable military empire.

VII

The Military Empire

The military apparatus of the empire is the United States' mightiest economic enterprise. Its power and its efficiency are a measure not of its national territory, or of its population, but of the exceptional wealth over which it is empowered to watch. Through the interplay of importing raw materials at advantageous prices and exporting capital at very profitable rates, its wealth becomes more or less entrenched everywhere in the world. Its protection requires more than the defense of 9,385,000 square kilometers between the Atlantic and the Pacific, between the Mexican and Canadian borders. It requires the defense of mines and plantations in Latin America and Southeast Asia, of oil deposits in the Middle East, of the fabulous natural resources of the Canadian Shield, of the still barely exploited wealth of Africa, and of the industrial potential of Western Europe into which American capital flows. In addition, the freedom of navigation must be assured on all oceans and seas. The military apparatus therefore matches in scale an empire without frontiers. And, like it, it stands second to none.

Receiving more than $70 billion in 1968, the military absorbs 56 per cent of the federal budget or 8 per cent of a gross national product which would hardly reach its present level if the wealth of the Third World were not primarily channeled into a country representing only 6 per cent of the world's population. No point on the globe escapes the protection or the threat of this prodigious arsenal. At the start of 1968, the United States had four times more intercontinental bombers than the U.S.S.R., 1,054 intercontinental ballistic missiles against 720 for the U.S.S.R., and ten times more submarine-launched nuclear missiles than the U.S.S.R.

That fantastic firepower, enough to kill all life on the planet several times over, is not intended only to protect the wealth of the world's richest country. Because of its high cost and the price of the Vietnam War, the military apparatus certainly contributes to the deficit in the American balance of payments, but at the same time it opens up vast fields of activity for an economy which discovered in war industry a source of dynamic growth. With the country still at 9 million unemployed, only the Second World War, was able to put an end to the major economic depression that had started ten years earlier. What would happen if a large number of the 5,141,000 civilians and military directly employed by the Pentagon were added to the 2,964,000 unemployed in 1967? Besides, 66 per cent of the defense budget, or approximately $49 billion in 1968, is contracted out to private industry. Every sector of industrial activity would have to reduce its output if large and small companies alike did not receive manna from the Pentagon, each year more generously than the year before. Any large-scale reduction of the defense budget would throw a few million unemployed on the labor market and lower the standard of living. The large companies which divide among themselves the biggest Pentagon contracts would not be the only ones affected, for they subcontract to hundreds of thousands of small and middle-sized companies.

Under the pseudonym of H. McLandress, a former economic adviser to President Kennedy and former Ambassador to India, John Kenneth Galbraith, in a style that is easily recognizable, wrote a humorous preface to a book. The book, satirically offered as a report written at the request of the American government, concludes that peace is undesirable. Among other reasons, it suggests that no one had been able to propose an economic program which could replace military expenditures. Alluding to a ten-year social welfare program whose cost was estimated at $185 billion, the "report" makes the point that some people would be tempted to reject it because it was "far too costly." But, on the contrary, "as an economic substitute for war, it is inadequate because it would be far too cheap." [1] This macabre satire perfectly points out the weakness of an economy which can no longer do without a military output that consumes tens of billions of dollars.

A few examples cited later show how military contracts contribute to the prosperity of certain industries and certain regions in the United States. Furthermore, the arms the United States sells abroad average $3 billion a year. These sales are often made through credits offered by the United States to buyer governments. Nonetheless they constitute a sizable element in the output of specialized industries.

The American defense budget rose from $1,498 million in 1940 to $75,487 million in 1968, thus increasing from 1.5 per cent to 8.1 per cent of the gross national product. It was as important in 1968 as in 1944 when American forces were simultaneously fighting on every war front, for the United States must have the capability to intervene anywhere in the world where the need for its military presence is felt. The withdrawal of French forces from Indochina in 1954 already foreshadowed the first symbolic and then massive appearance of American forces in a small country, insufficient though they were to assure victory. In the same way, Great Britain's decision to evacuate its bases east of Suez conferred on the United States a decisive role in the Indian

Ocean. It is a repetition on a vaster scale of what had already happened in Greece in 1947.

The United States has treaties with forty-four countries,* in which it pledges to intervene in the event that their security is threatened. Should the promise made to any one of these countries not be kept, the others' confidence in the word of the American government would be seriously shaken. But, in fact, the involvement of the United States extends far beyond the zones covered by the pacts and treaties it has concluded. Countries like India, Indonesia, Saudi Arabia, Egypt, Ethiopia, etc., and the countries of North Africa and black Africa are not tied to the United States by military agreements, but no one in Moscow or Peking doubts that, in case of need, American forces would intervene in those countries. And the countries that are proudest of their neutrality know that their security is based primarily on the will of the United States to contain Communism, to oppose any expansion of a system which threatens not only a particular country near or far, but also the prosperity and security of the United States and its influence in the world.

The Pentagon estimates that in order to be effective deterrence must have the capability of destroying, within a few moments, one-third of the population and two-thirds of the industrial capacity of a possible aggressor. Accordingly, a surprise attack by the Soviet Union would incur an American retaliatory strike resulting in the loss of 100 million people and 80 per cent of the Soviet productive potential. By the end of 1970 the United States will have operative

* Namely, its fourteen allies in NATO: Belgium, Canada, Denmark, West Germany, France, Greece, Iceland, Italy, Luxembourg, the Netherlands, Norway, Portugal, Turkey, Great Britain; its seven allies in SEATO: Australia, France, New Zealand, Pakistan, the Philippines, Thailand, Great Britain; its two allies in ANZUS: Australia and New Zealand; its four allies in CENTO: Iran, Pakistan, Turkey, Great Britain; its twenty Latin American allies, signatories of the Rio Pact; South Korea, Taiwan, the Philippines, and Japan, with which it has concluded bilateral treaties.

700 Minutemen II missiles with a range of 14,000 kilometers and a 10-megaton warhead, and 300 Minutemen III missiles of a more powerful type. The Strategic Air Command has 590 B-52's and 80 B-58's which can remain airborne and carry respectively 24- and 13-megaton loads. Each of forty-one atomic submarines is equipped with sixteen Polaris missiles, which are gradually being replaced by Poseidon missiles. Twenty-five aircraft carriers cruise the Atlantic, the Pacific, and the Mediterranean, along with their escorts of nuclear-propelled attack submarines, of cruisers, destroyers, missile-launching frigates, landing ships, etc. All these forces, together with a ground army equipped with tactical atomic artillery, can reach any target at any time.

This enormous military apparatus employs under Pentagon direction more than 5 million people, to whom must be added another 5 million employees working in private industry directly in the production of military equipment. The modern world's most powerful war machine is thus in terms of its budget, its labor force, and the amount of wages paid, the most important industry in the United States. Its military assets are three times greater than the sum of the assets of five great corporations: United States Steel, American Telephone and Telegraph, Metropolitan Life Insurance, General Motors, and Standard Oil of New Jersey. But though this military "trust" is by far the most powerful in the United States, no antitrust law will force it to be dismantled. For with all the continents and all the oceans within range of its firepower, it protects the prosperity of all Americans and it ensures regular income for some 10 million employees and their families, who represent a very high percentage of the working population of the United States.

Thus a real revolution has taken place in American society. In 1935 the United States devoted only 10.9 per cent of the federal budget to defense; after the 1918 victory, and its refusal to ratify the Versailles Treaty, America once again surrendered to its isolationist tendencies, withdrew within itself and did not feel the need of maintaining a large army. Following the great economic crisis of 1929–1930, when the country had some 10 million unemployed, it wanted to devote all its resources to revitalizing production. And so, during the period of prosperity from 1918 to 1929, as well as later on during the depression, the military appeared to be an economic and social parasite.

By contrast, after the Japanese attack on Pearl Harbor, the military became in everyone's eyes the guardian of the American way of life. Military costs absorbed 80.8 per cent of the federal budget in 1944 and 55.9 per cent in 1968. For, though Nazi Germany and Japan had capitulated, another more specific and at the same time more insidious threat made its weight felt against the American way of life: the Communist threat. The military was no longer a parasite. In the popular mind, it became a hero leading the crusade against Communism in Korea and in Vietnam, as it had against the antidemocratic forces in the Pacific in 1941 and on the beaches of Normandy in 1944. It watched over the American republic as over the ramparts of the free world.

But quite naturally it also became integrated into the country's economic machinery and has stimulated production by granting private companies contracts larger than the total volume of the automobile industry. Out of total sales of $17,296 million in 1965, the aeronautical industry's sales to the government, that is to say the Pentagon, totalled $13,708 million. Out of total sales of $8,691 million for the telecommunications industry, $5,070 million were in sales to the Pentagon. The shipyards, on sales of $3,516 million, received Pentagon contracts amounting to $2,446 million.[2] Obviously, not only has the military ceased to be a parasite, it has become one of the factors of American prosperity. In California 23.3 per cent of industrial jobs depend on the Pentagon, in Kansas 30.2 per cent, in Arizona 20.6 per cent, in Connecticut 21.1 per cent, in New Mexico 23.8 per cent, in Utah 20.4 per cent, etc.

Thanks to the military budget, key industries and various regions in the United States have undergone exceptional growth. Just as America's powerful industrial empire had developed within its borders before it expanded into Latin America, Europe, and Asia, so its military empire, which has sent the Seventh Fleet to the Far East and the Sixth Fleet into the eastern Mediterranean, exercises its influence over the principal economic segments and regions of the United States. As distant deposits of raw materials and distant investments nourish American prosperity, the worldwide military apparatus creates employment and stimulates the industrial machinery of the United States.

The empire, military or economic, is neither an accident nor an accessory. Without it, American society would be compelled to make an "agonizing reappraisal" not only of its objectives but of its means of subsistence. Founded on the economic empire, protected and strengthened by the military empire, the American way of life would probably not survive a withdrawal within national boundaries. That is why the Presidents of the United States rightly say that the "national security" of the United States is involved in the Vietnam conflict, as it was in the Korean War, or in the landing of Marines in the Dominican Republic, or even yet in the fate of the Cuban revolution. There is no point on the globe where the empire's soldiers can afford to drop their guard.

The United States did not want it this way. This was not the result of a carefully considered decision coldly taken by the masters of the empire. During his second term, Franklin D. Roosevelt could have chosen to resolve the economic

crisis by starting a vast program of arms production. He did
not do that. The Second World War showed America's
leaders and electorate that their military effort had triggered an unprecedented expansion, but their principal concern when hostilities ended was to reconvert industry from
war to peacetime production. The Korean War throttled a
recession, but it was not for economic reasons that the
United States has kept its defense budget at a high level.
The great force which propelled it on that course was anti-
Communism, the vital need to oppose any attempt at territorial conquest, to contain Communism within its boundaries.

Of course, demagogues have played on this fear of Communism, have exacerbated it to provide an electoral
launching pad, and have raised it to its highest pitch. But
the noisiest and most frenetic of these demagogues, the late
Senator Joseph McCarthy, never obtained the smallest increase in the military budget. Anti-Communism may have
inflamed the Cold War, ruined opportunities at international detente, and led to questionable decisions—it did
not completely create what was an unavoidable confrontation. When the Soviets orbited their first Sputnik, Secretary
of Defense Charles Wilson naïvely declared that he preferred to see the Russians on the moon rather than in Detroit. But the United States could not stay out of the race
and the space-research budget rose from $430 million in
1959 to $7,230 million in 1968. The competition between
East and West imposed what no pressure group had been
able to obtain from the government and the Congress in
Washington.

But, in that competition, private industry quickly saw
where its interests lay. Washington was pouring funds into
all industrial sectors having to do with the development
and construction of space vehicles, missiles, atomic weapons, submarines, aircraft carriers, bombers, electronic

equipment, arms of all kinds. They feed research, stimulate production, create millions of new jobs at a time when automation tends to eliminate them, assure higher profits. At the same time they strengthened the forces within the United States whose influence radiates all over the world.

This unparalleled military might is based on an economic power which also knows no rival and is imposed alike on allies and adversaries of the United States. President Johnson was convinced that the United States must bring its own concept of freedom to "everyone, whether rich or poor, whether they agree with us or not, no matter what their race or the color of their skin." Such is, indeed, the old dream, America's messianic role, exalted for two centuries by men like John Adams and Herman Melville. And quite often events seemed to justify them: "There are those who ask why this responsibility [in Vietnam] should be ours," said President Johnson. "The answer is simple. There is no one else who can do the job." Because it alone in the West wields such power, the United States feels obliged to intervene everywhere, to become the policeman of the world.

Some American statesmen, more astute and more capable of appreciating world complexities, objected to that conception. "Great as is our strength, we are not omnipotent. We cannot, by fiat, produce the kind of world we want. Even nations which depend greatly upon us do not always follow what we believe to be the right course. . . . We cannot deal in absolutes." [3] But that statement was made by the late Secretary of State, John Foster Dulles, and it hardly guided his actions. For Dulles, probably more than any other man, was determined to forge networks of alliances and pacts intended to encircle "international Communism" with an allegedly insurmountable barrier. It was he who strengthened the anti-Communist clauses of the Organization of American States (OAS) before the intervention in Guatemala, who thought up the SEATO and CENTO pacts for Southeast Asia and the Middle East, the treaty with Australia and New Zealand (ANZUS) and bilateral accords with Spain, Japan, etc. And Dulles actively endeavored to draw unwilling allies into "what we believe to be the right course." The task was made easier by the fact that those countries "depend greatly upon us," which alone could assure them of atomic protection in the case of aggression. It was Dulles who imposed on reluctant Europeans the rearmament of Germany by threatening them with an "agonizing reappraisal" of American strategy if they did not comply. On the one hand, he agreed that the United States "cannot deal in absolutes," but, on the other hand, he did not hesitate to say that neutralism was "immoral," for no one can refuse to choose between the Absolute Evil which is Communism and the Absolute Good which has been entrusted to the United States.

Do the policies of the United States show a conscious determination to use its military power to impose its point of view on partners whom it repeatedly calls real allies and not satellites? Certainly not. The allies of the United States often take liberties toward the United States that satellites would not dare take. France and England have conducted colonial policies which displeased Washington. Countries such as Canada and Japan have disregarded warnings and built up trade with China which is vital for them. In Latin America various countries have dissociated themselves from the United States in certain votes on the subject of Cuba or the Dominican Republic. And, even within NATO, many projects, such as the multilateral force, were not accepted by the United States' allies and have been returned to the back of the State Department's files.

But in the final analysis those deviations remain insignificant and, on the whole, the forty-four countries linked to the United States by military agreements have followed the course charted by Washington. For only the United States has at its disposal an atomic potential sufficient to dissuade any possible adversary, and that monopoly has as much weight in the allied capitals as in the Communist capitals. No Western country is ready to dispense with the atomic protection of the United States. But is this sufficient reason to comply with Washington's slightest wish? Governments which have attempted to rebel against this tutelage have quickly had to deal with violent internal protests from an "American party" or an "Atlantic party" which the United States government certainly had not created from whole cloth, but which was supported by American subsidies to certain newspapers and to certain political organizations (see Chap. IX).

However, the determinant fact is that the alliances in which the United States participates group together countries of unequal power; not only because of the United States economic superiority, but also because of its atomic monopoly. In spite of the waywardness of several Latin American countries which opposed certain resolutions proposed by the United States, the OAS has always supplied the United States with the legal framework and the international support it needed for its moves against the Arbenz government in Guatemala, or against Cuba, or the resolution in 1965 of the Dominican crisis. In spite of numerous disagreements within NATO, the voice of Washington has prevailed in the definition of strategy as well as in the allocation of arms contracts. In the same way, the countries allied to the United States in the Vietnam conflict can create political and diplomatic complications, but they are not capable of opposing decisions from Washington.

The power that the United States enjoys thanks to its atomic monopoly stems less from its military superiority than from a faulty analysis of the situation by its allies. Europe, in particular, has wanted a lasting alliance with the United States and an integrated command in order not to find itself again, one day, in the situation France faced in 1940, when Paul Reynaud's appeals to America remained unanswered. Europe does not see that conditions have radically changed, that isolationism would henceforth be impracticable for the United States and that with or without NATO Washington could not abandon the economic potential of Western Europe to a possible adversary. Above all Europe does not understand that even within NATO nothing obliges it to yield to American pressure. Even if it were neutral, Europe would still remain under the atomic protection of the United States. The power of the American empire, like that of all empires, is also based on the weaknesses of the countries which submit to its rule.

The military empire nonetheless remains a useful instrument to back up the policy and to reinforce the links that bind the United States to its client states. Each of these states has accepted aid from the United States to equip its national Army. A candidate for the Democratic Party's nomination in the 1968 presidential election, Senator Eugene McCarthy, wrote: "The United States is today the principal source of conventional weapons throughout the world. The United States government . . . is the world's leading supplier of arms. The United States government itself has assumed the role filled by the widely scorned munitions makers during the interwar period." [4] He added that between 1950 and 1966 the United States had given or sold to other countries $35 billion in military equipment, and that the average per year since 1961 was estimated at $3 billion.

The program of military aid is, naturally, intended to strengthen the forces of the free world against Communism, but its effectiveness in that regard, however tangible it may be in a particular case, remains secondary—for the primary task of defense rests on the overwhelming superiority of the armed forces of the United States. The case of

Vietnam is particularly clear: $1,511,700,000 in military aid did not save the United States from having to send half a million men into that country. It is doubtful that the $5,665,600,000 granted in the years 1950 to 1967 to various Middle East countries would be any more efficacious in the event of war in that region where only the American Sixth Fleet is in a position to discourage a possible aggressor. As for the $925,300,000 furnished to Latin America, it principally serves to flatter the military and to provide them with modern equipment which they unhesitatingly use to overthrow elected governments and to seize power for themselves. In the same way, the $2,493,300,000 supplied Taiwan has often permitted the United States to control a sometimes difficult ally. In the event of war an enormous part of the $35 billion already distributed would prove of questionable value, the only real defense being assured by American intercontinental ballistic missiles, by American strategic bombers, by American aircraft carriers, by American submarines equipped with nuclear warhead missiles.

If, however, the program of military aid succeeds in creating and equipping supplementary forces, it also and above all achieves two objectives in the eyes of American leaders: it tightens the bonds between the United States and the empire's client states, and it permits the unloading of an important share of military production in foreign markets.

This is not an unforeseen consequence of the decision to help allies but the result of deliberate calculation. In fact, each year the budget includes a specific figure for the promotion of arms sales. This sum reached, for example, $500,-000 in 1965 and, the year before, General Robert Wood, director of the program of military aid, explained to a committee of the House of Representatives that the program of military training was the key to arms sales: "We bring officers over here from other countries with a view to looking at equipment which they might buy. . . . Then we have a

program to train certain countries in some of our equipment in the expectation they will buy the equipment. This
is really sales promotion."

The objective is to secure markets, and that consideration is not necessarily subordinated to higher objectives of
American diplomacy acting as guardian of the world's freedom. The $1,489 million given to Greece between 1950
and 1967 strengthened a military system which finally ex-
tinguished whatever democracy existed in that country. The
$1,036,800,000 given to Iran has scarcely transformed that
country's feudal structure—quite the opposite. Nonetheless, the government of the empire sometimes has scruples.
Thus in 1965 it agreed to supply fifty Skyhawk jets to Argentina: "It is said we hoped to appease the Argentine military so that they would be less inclined to overthrow the
civilian government," wrote Senator Eugene McCarthy.
But the military launched their *coup d'état* on June 28,
1966, and the United States decided—to reduce the
number of Skyhawks furnished the Argentine air force from
fifty to twenty-five.

Furnishing jets to the Argentine military did not discourage them from seizing power, which they seem quite determined to keep. In turn, that sale started a new phase in the
Latin American arms race. The Argentine example urged
Chilean military leaders on to acquire equally modern
planes. The United States rejected their order, although the
Chilean Army had traditionally respected democracy more
than the Argentine Army. Chile then turned to Great Britain, and Venezuela, Peru, and Brazil followed suit. It was
then that France entered the race, offering its own jets.
Prompted by the Pentagon and the State Department, numerous articles were published in leading American and
European newspapers that accused General de Gaulle of
triggering a frenzied arms race in Latin America.

The case of military aid to India and Pakistan was both

tragic and absurd. A U.S. ally in SEATO, Pakistan received military aid from Washington estimated at between $1,500 million and $2 billion—and then, more recently, aid from Communist China. India was refusing American military aid until the outbreak of hostilities on its frontier with China, but it was already receiving arms from Great Britain. Finally, in the Indian-Pakistani conflict, American arms were used by each country against the other. Deliveries were halted during the fighting, but were resumed when the Tashkent accord was signed, thanks to the good offices of the Soviet Union.

The arms race has also reached into Africa. In 1956 Ethiopia was the only African country to receive military aid from the United States, which granted it $4.8 million that year. But seven African countries were receiving American military aid in 1961, and fourteen in 1962. Ethiopia's share had by then more than doubled, to $10.9 million and total United States military aid to Africa rose from $4.8 million in 1956 to $26 million in 1963 and then to $31.9 million in 1967.

Senator Eugene McCarthy remarked that these military programs had their diplomatic effects: "United States military aid is usually, if not invariably, accompanied by the stationing of U.S. military personnel in the country receiving the arms to supervise, advise, assist, and draw up plans, in accordance with Defense Department procedures, for the utilization by the country of additional U.S. equipment. In essence, the U.S. military advisers act as on-the-spot salesmen, attempting to make certain that the country concerned obtains its military equipment from the United States and not from a competitor, political or commercial. These military advisers sometimes assume more direct roles."

The advisers on the scene establish friendly ties with officers who will one day be in charge of foreign purchases, or who may become members of a military junta seizing power from civilians. The best prospects are invited to come to the United States to take courses or be trained, in order for them to appreciate at first hand the power of the American war machine and the advantages of the American way of life. Military aid cannot be exclusively technical and material; it is always accompanied by a certain amount of indoctrination, for, according to Robert McNamara, when he headed the Pentagon: "Military assistance provides essential arms, training, and related support to some 5 million men in allied and other friendly forces, who help us hold the line against aggression in all its forms and guises. These men are critical to our forward strategy." If the empire reserves to itself the power to decide where and how it will eventually use its most formidable weapons, it believes it cannot do without the cooperation of allied troops who are almost twice as numerous as its own Army scattered throughout the world. On those allied forces falls the task of holding the very ground from which the empire draws its raw materials and into which it pours its investments— ground which must be protected by the military. They are in the front line of the resistance to Communism. Their military efficacy cannot be compared to that of the two super-powers, but they represent an indispensable cog in the larger apparatus whose control panel is in the Pentagon. Destined to play a minor role in any possible international conflict, they are nevertheless the principal defenders of order within their own national frontiers, even if that works to the detriment of the very democracy the United States wants to defend against Communism.

But their role in the service of the empire is also an economic one. Henry Kuss, head of the Department of Arms Sales, declared in 1966 before the Foreign Affairs Committee of the House of Representatives: "Military sales are . . . small in terms of our total annual defense spending, accounting for less than 4 per cent of the total. However, at the same time, receipts from military sales account for about one-half of the deployment costs of our forces, measured in balance-of-payments terms. The ability of this country to follow a forward strategy is heavily influenced by the balance-of-payments costs attributable to such a strategy. Thus, foreign military sales are of major interest to the Nation because they facilitate arrangements for our security throughout the world." In 1966 the Senate Foreign Affairs Committee criticized this concept, which consisted of "taking blood money from poorer countries" in order to improve the American balance of payments.

Arms sales to underdeveloped countries are generally made on credit. They are considered so important in the over-all policy of the United States that the Pentagon budget includes appropriations, taken from public funds, to promote these sales of arms manufactured by private companies. Furthermore, the Pentagon offers buyers credit facilities and furnishes a government guarantee making it ultimately responsible should a defaulting buyer be unable to pay his debt to the private company. This is how certain countries considered insolvent by commercial organizations or by the Export-Import Bank can buy American arms. In 1967 the Pentagon had at its disposal for that purpose an insurance fund of $300 million. Obliged by law to "cover" one-quarter of the credit sales, it could thus make arms sales of $1,200 million to insolvent clients. The Export-Import Bank does not become involved in these operations: it closes its eyes, which is hardly its custom with more normal contracts, and gives the Pentagon practically a blank check.

Here again the empire lives off the weakness of other countries. Some governments that consider the Export-Import Bank's 3 per cent interest rate for the financing of productive economic undertakings too high, agree to pay through the same financial channels a rate of 5.5 per cent for the purchase of American arms. And naturally the countries in question are already carrying a heavy foreign debt.

In January 1967 the Senate Foreign Relations Committee published a report criticizing the American government for encouraging arms sales in spite of the White House's publicly stated intention to contain the arms race in certain parts of the world, notably in Latin America and the Middle East. According to that report, arms sales in 1966 were seven times larger than the average in the years 1952–1961. A special body, the International Logistic Negotiations Bureau, was created in 1961 to stimulate those sales. The report added that the first director of that Bureau, Henry Kuss, had been rewarded for his efficiency by being nominated as assistant to the Under Secretary of Defense in 1964. Between 1962 and 1966, the report continued, the Pentagon secured foreign orders for arms amounting to $11 billion. An equally high figure had been cited by Robert McNamara, who, on September 16, 1965, estimated that arms sales for the shorter period from June 1961 to August 1965 reached $9 billion.

It is clear, as Henry Kuss stated, that those sales improved the American balance of payments. But at the same time they tightened the control the United States exerted over certain countries trapped in the meshes of the empire. "The primary goal of military assistance now seems to be to develop client states, to erect military-political bastions, to preserve (or to upset) regional balances of power," wrote Senator Eugene McCarthy. That is clearly a political objective, vital to the expansion of the empire. In addition to the economic ties which bind them closely to a country that is a major importer of cheaply priced raw materials and a major exporter of capital which is profitable because wages abroad are lower and taxation is less onerous, these client states find themselves entangled by new bonds spun by the military empire: the installation of bases, "military" advisers, arms purchases which increase their foreign debt.

A popular image is that this policy can be credited to a few warmongers supported by the "arms merchants" and "hawks" of the Pentagon. In reality, the problem is more complex. Close working relations have been developed between big business, military leaders, and politicians (see Chap. X): one example will suffice to illustrate that fact. On August 9, 1967, by a vote of forty-eight to forty, the United States Senate defeated an amendment offered by Democratic Senator Allen Ellender which would have resulted in prohibiting the Export-Import Bank from making loans for the sale of arms to poor countries. This vote thus allowed the continuation of a policy burdensome to underdeveloped countries, but one economically and politically profitable to the United States in search of client states. And, needless to say, the amendment was vigorously contested by the government. The final tally and the slim eight-vote margin (out of ninety voting) clearly illustrates one of the tragedies of American democracy: the "arms merchants" lobby obtained the necessary votes, and no competing lobby was there to get five Senators to change sides— five Senators who would have made it possible to put an end to such a questionable practice.

A Democratic Senator, Daniel Brewster, took this occasion to criticize the government's policy: he recalled that the United States had armed Israel, as well as various Arab countries, and he could have cited other cases, such as India and Pakistan. He noted that an enormous percentage, 36 per cent, of the loans granted by the Export-Import Bank were for the purchase of American arms. Finally Senator Brewster declared, "It is very unfortunate that this [Export-Import] bank which started with such excellent aims, should have to suffer a loss of prestige and reputation by involving itself in shady arms dealing. Fourteen developing countries received $591 million in country X or secret, unidentified loans. The amazing part of these so-called country X loans is that not even the director of the bank knows where this money is going." [5]

Although forty Senators had used their votes to denounce sales which they deemed reprehensible, their protest was meaningless in a country which by its very power is forever led to increase its economic-military potential and its political influence over friendly allied or neutral countries. In that drive it draws its principal strength from the championing of resistance to Communism. Official speeches, the press, radio, and television daily remind America that it is entrusted with a sacred role. In such a climate the elected representatives of public opinion have sometimes been encouraged to go further even than the government. For, obviously, the system possesses its own internal dynamics. Just as John Foster Dulles had to abandon the idea of establishing diplomatic relations with Peking—such a gesture being considered political suicide— the complex interaction of propaganda and public opinion sometimes pushes the machinery of government and its military apparatus further than some might desire. Thus when Secretary of Defense Robert McNamara reiterated his grave doubts in August 1967 on the military effectiveness of the bombing of North Vietnam, the Senate Subcommittee on National Defense Preparedness asked, that it be intensified.[6] Members of the subcommittee were encouraged to take that position by the statements of certain military leaders and by the arms lobby, and also by a public opinion which did not quite understand why the whole weight of the military empire was not thrown into the balance "to block the road to Communism in Asia." It is easier to create an apparatus than to control it. And the voices which attempt at times to appeal to reason are stifled.

The example of Latin America demonstrates how the empire's military apparatus functions in a given region. In December 1967 seventy-two Green Berets were parachuted into the jungles of Panama. Their assignment was to organize guerrillas in support of a pro-American government leader who had been deposed by a military *coup d'état*. It was only a training mission but the training corresponded faithfully to the task assigned to the "Special Forces" which is counterinsurgency in Latin America and elsewhere. The only difference is that, in five years, nine duly elected civilian governments in Latin America have been overthrown by military *coups d'état* and the Green Berets have not intervened to re-establish constitutional legality. The Panamanian training mission is pure fiction: the Special Forces are not defending democracy but fighting Communism.

During the 1960's, the military strategy of the empire vis-à-vis Latin America has been modified. In 1959 an Under Secretary of Defense stated before a Congressional committee that the most serious threat in that area was created by "submarine action [of the Soviets] in the Caribbean Sea and along the coast of Latin America." And, to be sure, from time to time there were stories—which were not entirely fantasy—about sightings of mysterious submarines at the mouth of the Rio de la Plata or in the Caribbean. During the Second World War, counterespionage and the United States Navy had mounted an all-out attack on the German submarines in that zone. Now, Russian submarines had taken over, and it was also necessary to maintain observation of the Soviet "fishing fleet" along the western shore of the Atlantic. The great preoccupation had been to protect the continent from external attack. But a revolution in Cuba succeeded without any Soviet submarines having supplied Fidel Castro's *barbudos*, without any Russian or Czech guns having reached the Sierra Maestra. From that time on, during John F. Kennedy's Presidency, American strategy was revised to protect the continent not from external aggression but from internal subversion. Or, more exactly, from a single type of internal subversion: that which could push a country into the other camp. Any other form of subversion, in the interests of conservative forces say, was cautiously tolerated. Robert McNamara indicated this new orientation when he stated before Congress, in 1967: "The primary objective in Latin America is to aid, where necessary, in the continued development of indigenous military and paramilitary forces capable of providing, in conjunction with police and other security forces, needed domestic security." [7]

The influence of the "military and paramilitary forces" and the political role which they played in most Latin American countries are known (see Chap. VI). But Washington's primary goal is to stop subversion rather than effectively fight the basic causes of subversion, in particular the foreign exploitation of Latin America's natural resources. The military apparatus, besides providing in the usual manner for the defense of the Panama Canal, established three further means for immediate and future intervention: (a) an American military school was established in the Panama Canal Zone which graduates each year 1,400 Latin American officers; (b) the 8th Special Forces Group, composed of eight hundred Green Berets, stationed at Fort Gulick on the Atlantic side of the Canal Zone, is prepared to intervene at any moment and any place on the continent; (c) a military aid program supports forty-three missions in seventeen Latin American countries.

The presence of the school and the Green Berets violates the 1903 treaty with Panama which stipulated that troops could be stationed in the Zone solely to assure the defense of the canal and not in order to intervene in another country.

The eight hundred Green Berets belong to the Special Action Force for Latin America which is comprised of seventeen "mobile training teams" capable of being quickly transported into any Latin American country at the request of its government. Those teams are supposed to give armed support to the "military advisers" stationed in seventeen countries. Since their arrival in the Canal Zone in 1962, they have intervened in every country, with the exception of Cuba, Haiti, and Mexico. Specialists in war against revolutionary movements, their stay in various Latin American countries has been of variable duration. One of the teams, comprised of sixteen men, was responsible for the training of the Bolivian Rangers battalion which finally encircled Ernesto "Che" Guevara's guerrillas and killed him. The Commander of the 8th Special Forces Group personally went to Bolivia to supervise the operation which, needless to say, Washington considered of the greatest importance. Arriving on April 14, 1967, the team trained the 2nd Bolivian Rangers battalion in the problems of logistics and intelligence, as well as in the use of communications equipment which played a major role in the success of its undertaking. Soon after, another team of twelve men was sent into Honduras, where guerrillas had been reported. Other teams were, at the same time, located in Colombia, Argentina, Guatemala, Chile, Peru, Panama, and Uruguay.

Near the Special Forces base at Fort Gulick is the U.S. School of the Americas. Established in 1955 at a former Second World War hospital, it has on its staff 215 American military instructors who are attached to the U.S. Southern Command. Since its establishment the school has given diplomas, on completion of training, to 21,294 Latin American officers. The length of training varies from two to forty weeks. Naturally, all the courses are given in Spanish. Among the school's former pupils are the Defense Ministers of Colombia and Bolivia, as well as a large number of high-ranking officers. The school represents an effective means of tightening the close personal bonds existing between American officers and Latin American officers, who often, following their schooling, enjoy rapid promotions in their particular armies and who may one day achieve high command posts—perhaps even at the ministerial level.

This effort is complemented and furthered by the work of forty-three American military missions stationed in seventeen Latin American countries. These missions, which comprise a total of eight hundred men, can vary from five officers in Panama to 103 officers in Brazil. Ninety per cent of the financial outlay in this area is concentrated in six countries: Argentina, Brazil, Chile, Venezuela, Peru and Colombia.

In 1967 Congress decided that this program of military aid was too extensive and reduced its budget from $85 million to $75 million. But the activities of the Green Berets and the U.S. School of the Americas and the military missions are nevertheless maintained at about the same level. Naturally, the program entails the supply of equipment, such as the three helicopters sent in 1967 to the thirty-one-man mission assigned to "advise" the army hunting down Guatemalan guerrillas.

During their stay at the U.S. School of the Americas, Latin American officers are able to experiment with American-made equipment, whose technical qualities the military missions in the different countries know how to extol. The commercial pump is thus primed. The military missions then attend training maneuvers of the national Army which they can "advise" in the use of the equipment. Some carefully chosen officers are invited to spend time in the United States where they visit the Pentagon, the principal military bases, the arms factories, etc. When such military leaders later use the forces at their disposal to overthrow an elected government, they know they can count on the trust and even the friendship of American officers ready to provide assurances that the new regime will not be soft on "Communism." The State Department may hesitate a few days, or even make a symbolic gesture of disapproval, but a few weeks later everything is back to normal. Back to normal, for the empire knows its survival depends on the effectiveness of its military apparatus.

VIII

The Cultural Empire

Under the protection of its formidable military apparatus the empire is not satisfied to just import raw materials at low cost, to export capital and then repatriate profits which permit it to make other productive investments. It well knows that a brain can yield—in dollar terms—far more than an oil well. As shown already by an earlier example it also knows that while, for industry as a whole, one out of every fourteen dollars of the gross national product comes from abroad, the return is three times greater for a firm like IBM, which is enjoying the benefits of a massive investment in research. Science and culture are not merely one of the glories of the empire, they are also one of the major sources of its wealth and power.

The glory though, is considerable. For a long time Americans suffered from an inferiority complex in regard to the older nations which had a rich and broad cultural heritage. The feelings of Americans were hurt by widespread stereotypes which presented them as a people accomplished in business but poorly endowed in higher qualities. The barb was unfair because, ever since its founding, America has had its men of science and of culture. But the criticism was also absurd because the people of old countries do not all have equal access to culture, and furthermore money made in business—honestly or not—is exactly what permits the building of universities and museums, laboratories and concert halls, the subsidization of schools and artists, the importation of works of art, and the wide distribution of books and records. While it was getting rich America developed its cultural facilities, and its intellectual accomplishments quickly spread throughout the world and gained it everywhere a little more respect, esteem and admiration, factors surely as important as the fear inspired by its arms, or the self-seeking solidarity bought with its economic power.

The United States is not unaware of the fact that its literature translated into all languages, its films projected on all screens, its wire services widely disseminating news, its lecturers criss-crossing the world, its scientific achievements, etc., all add to the glory and power of the empire. America cannot neglect any means of asserting its intellectual and artistic vitality. Furthermore, the export of books, of records, of films for the cinema or television, the sale of patents, etc., represents an important source of revenue which makes possible new research and new creative activities. Undoubtedly the empire needs bankers and engineers, businessmen and soldiers, but it cannot do without scientists and teachers, writers and actors. Its overseas cultural centers are hardly less important than its military bases. Its arms sales do not prevent it from exporting its films. Its imports of raw materials do not at all prevent it from encouraging the immigration of scientists and technicians.

Cultural imperialism is subject to the same principles that brought about the birth of the economic and military empires. Like them, the cultural empire fulfills a need. Society not only consumes rare metals, petroleum, or tropical products; it also hungers for works of art, science and literature, and it imports them according to its needs. Further, it needs to export: it sells its films, it invests capital abroad to publish books or newspapers. The cultural empire also benefits from favorable circumstances that the United States did not create: Nazism and Communism, for example, have compelled countless gifted people to go into exile, and they have wanted to get as far away as possible from the political regimes they were fleeing. In the realm of culture as of economics, power begets power, and the vitality of the United States has attracted a great many brains who find better opportunities in their adopted country than in their own. In the cultural domain as well as in other sectors, the empire naturally encourages and favors currents which add to its power: it deliberately attracts foreign scientists, it exploits its cultural potential to benefit its prestige and project its image to the world—indispensable complements of its political and diplomatic policies.

James A. Perkins, the President of Cornell University, estimated that 43,000 engineers and scientists emigrated to the United States between 1949 and 1961. Of that number, a large but unspecified proportion came from underdeveloped countries which may not have offered the best conditions for employment although they had great need of their abilities. Another particularly striking example: in 1964–1965 American hospitals employed some 41,000 interns and residents, of that total 11,000 were graduates of foreign medical schools, and 8,000 came from underdeveloped nations. In other words, foreign countries had financed the training of more than a quarter of the interns practicing in the United States. The empire siphons off brains and specialists in the same way that it siphons exorbitant profits off capital invested in the Third World which has long since been amortized. According to the calculations of Professor Kelly M. West of the School of Medicine of the University of Oklahoma, the United States would have to build and endow twelve new schools of medicine if it wanted to provide the training of the 1,200 or so physicians who immigrate each year.

The situation is so abnormal that Great Britain, for example, loses 16 per cent of the doctors it trains. And yet, like most European countries, it too drains the Third World of large numbers of talented people who have come to study. In effect, the exodus takes place either directly from the Third World (above all, Latin America, Taiwan, and Korea) to the United States, or from the Third World to European countries which, in turn, lose part of their brains to the United States. That is why Kenneth Robinson, British Minister of Public Health, declared that "Great Britain simply cannot afford the luxury of training physicians in order to enlarge the American Medical Association."

Between 1962 and 1966 the immigration of highly trained personnel to the United States reached 59,851, of whom 37,818 came from developed countries and 22,033 from underdeveloped countries. The table below shows that the flow of immigration coming from underdeveloped countries increased more rapidly than that from developed countries:

	Developed Countries	Underdeveloped Countries
1962	6,447	3,401
1963	7,903	4,579
1964	7,885	4,438
1965	7,953	3,796
1966	7,630	5,819
TOTAL	37,818	22,033

Note: From *L'Exode des cerveaux*, Centre de recherches européenne, Lausanne, 1968.

In other words, from 1962 to 1966 the annual contingent of highly trained immigrants increased at the rate of 18 per cent for developed countries and 71 per cent for underdeveloped countries. This situation somewhat recalls the comparative profitability of American investments abroad. Just as Latin America and Asia supply capital to the United

States through repatriated profits, so the whole world, and increasingly the poor countries, supply it with brains. In the return on invested capital, as in the brain drain, Latin America and Asia are the two underdeveloped continents which make the most important contribution to the United States. Of 5,819 highly trained immigrants who entered the United States from underdeveloped countries in 1966, 2,820 came from Asia and 2,472 from Latin America. In this respect, as in others, Africa is still not yet exploited by the empire. This phenomenon is not surprising. Immigration is much higher from countries over which the United States exercises a greater political, diplomatic, or military influence. In Asia, therefore, two of the empire's bastions—South Korea and Taiwan—supplied the greatest number of immigrants.

But it is Europe which makes the greatest contribution to the empire. Here are some figures, also cited in the Center for European Research study which, for 1962 and 1966, show the number of engineers, scientists, doctors, dentists, etc. who have come to the United States from the principal Western European countries:

	1962	1966
Great Britain	1,488	2,015
West Germany	574	615
France	102	180
Italy	126	185
Netherlands	213	129
Belgium	50	63
Sweden	148	195
Switzerland	157	297
Greece	103	142
Spain	87	116
Austria	44	117

In the name of its national interest and of "America first," the United States has slowly closed its frontiers (see Chap. V, p. 170), first to several categories of undesirable or feeble-minded immigrants and then gradually through a strict quota system. Intellectuals and scientists can enter the United States with greater facility: government intervention on their behalf, contracts with universities or large companies. However, American authorities are now concerned that certain legislative restrictions block the entry of highly trained immigrants. On December 12, 1967, the chairman of the Immigration Committee of the House of Representatives, Michael Feighan, announced the start of an inquiry which would help pinpoint which modifications of the law were necessary to remove obstacles to the immigration of scientists and technicians.[1] He brought out that on June 30, 1967, there was a waiting list of 48,000 applicants in that category. But the quota system only permits the entry of 17,000 yearly. Why restrict, asked Michael Feighan, the immigration of scientists which the United States needs?

While Congress was thus preoccupied with increasing the brain drain, the American government, on the other hand, had to defend itself against criticism from friendly or allied countries for taking their most competent nationals away from them. An official spokesman then asserted that the brain drain to the United States had been overestimated but to the extent that it existed, American authorities could not prevent it.[2] He even supplied incorrect statistics to minimize the harm done by the brain drain to underdeveloped countries: he went so far as to say that Latin America did not account for more than 8.4 per cent, whereas the true figure was 18.3 per cent. In fact, from 1962 to 1966, the underdeveloped countries have supplied 36 per cent of the highly qualified labor which emigrated to the United States. And, as we have seen, their contribution increased more rapidly than that of industrialized countries.

In 1965 President Johnson signed a new bill which liberalized the admission of engineers, doctors, etc., and Congressional concern leads one to believe that further liberalization is in the offing.[3] If the United States wants to help the countries of the Third World to develop, one of the most urgent measures would be to reduce the exodus of brains. This is not the intention of the empire's government. On the contrary, Dean Rusk, Secretary of State, was pleased with a situation which was highly beneficial to the strengthening of the empire when he declared that ". . . the United States has a rare opportunity to draw immigrants of high intelligence and ability from abroad; and immigration, if well administered, can be one of our greatest national resources . . ." [4]

In the natural course of the empire's development, the brain trade has, in much more attractive ways, taken the place of the slave trade; there is no further need for brutal coercion; advantageous contracts and good work and research opportunities offer sufficient enticement; the fact is that this only contributes to impoverishing the poor countries to further enrich a rich country which pretends to wanting to help them. However, Europe does not behave any differently toward the countries of the Third World still under its influence. In seeking to imitate the United States in everything, Europe will be increasingly inclined to intensify the brain-drain for its own advantage in the fallacious hope that it will compensate for the similar loss it suffers at the hands of the United States. Without, however, attaining the American level, Europe will thus widen the cultural and scientific gap between rich and poor countries. It dissipates its strength in trying to imitate a "model" of which it is only a pale reflection, thus condemning itself to become, increasingly, the satellite of the United States. In this area, as in others, Europe does not want to recognize that it too is being exploited by the empire, much as the nonindustrialized countries. The techniques used on it are, although different, no less effective. The desire to conform to the American "model" ties it more closely to the imperialist enterprise, without giving it the hope of becoming equal to the master. Thus Europe loses either way. This has always been the role and destiny of vassals up to the day when their suzerain seizes the fief which had been temporarily subject to their rule.

The suzerain displays the splendor of his court and, if need be, rattles his arms. In order to find protection beside him, or in the hope of rivaling him, the vassal maintains order in his fief or exploits material and human resources. If he performs his tasks reasonably well, he will be admitted to the court of the suzerain, who eventually will offer him the protection of his arms. The more powerful his arms and the more brilliant his court, the more submissive the vassal will be. The masters of the empire have clearly shown their military strength, just as they ostentatiously exhibit the advantages offered scientists and artists invited to live at court.

The court is dazzling, and the empire could not do without it. There is no longer any need of building palaces, of designing gardens, of planning *fêtes de nuit*. The modern palaces are the chemistry and physics laboratories, electronics factories, think tanks, the installations at Cape Kennedy, the RAND Corporation, the major universities. Architects, sculptors, painters, playwrights, and musicians play a role there, but also—and above all—scientists and engineers. The empire needs them to build its scientific, military, and economic power. It does not neglect anything which might attract them. It devotes larger and larger amounts to their activities.

Between 1957 and 1965 the funds allotted to research by all American industry doubled—rising from $7,731 million to $14,197 million. And of that amount the percentage financed by the federal government was 56.1 per cent in 1957 and 54.7 per cent in 1965. Between those two dates the number of researchers employed rose to 115,100—or an increase of 47 per cent. The table below shows how—in dollars spent, in federal subsidies and in number of researchers—the lion's share very clearly belongs to the war industries: electronics, telecommunications, aircraft, and missiles (dollars shown below in millions).

	1957		1965		
	Total Research Funds	*Fed- eral Funds*	*Total Research Funds*	*Fed- eral Funds*	*Increase in Number of Researchers*
	$	%	$	%	
Electronics and telecommunica- tions	1,804	66.3	3,167	62.5	+43,300 90
Aircraft and missiles	2,574	88.4	5,120	87.9	+42,100 72
Motor vehicles and transport equip- ment	707	26.9	1,238	26.3	+9,700 65
Chemical products	705	12.6	1,377	13.8	+10,400 34
Machinery and plant	669	40.7	1,129	22.9	+6,700 24
Other industries	1,272	24.5	2,166	23.4	+2,900 5
All industries	7,731	56.1	14,197	54.7	+115,000 47

Note: From *Reviews of Data on Science Resources,* National Science Foundation 66–33, No. 10, December 1966.

The two key sectors (electronics and telecommunications, aircraft and missiles) have benefited from the largest Pentagon subsidies (62.5 per cent and 87.9 per cent). They also recruited the largest number of new researchers (90 per cent and 72 per cent), reaching a total of 85,400—which is three-fourths of the 115,100 new researchers recruited by all industry between 1957 and 1965. National Science Foundation charts show how close the relationship is between the military budget for research and the immigration of highly trained personnel. The different sectors of the empire cannot be separated: pure science leads to discoveries which find their applications in war industry and in civilian production, one drawing on the other so as to establish on a broader basis an increased prosperity which, in turn, permits the training of new scientists and accelerates the brain drain.

Businessmen and private industry would not be equal to the task, and the empire's government understands that it must play a vigorous part. The most effective means at its disposal to attain its goals is the military budget. Official projections show that the needs are immense and that only vast resources will satisfy them. The government commands such resources, thanks, especially, to the profits it reaps from its empire without frontiers.

The Department of Labor in Washington has estimated that the working population in the United States will rise from 72.2 million to 88.7 million between 1965 and 1975. That represents an increase of 16.5 million, of which one-quarter, or 4.3 million, will be highly trained scientific personnel. The same estimate foresees that, of those 16.5 million new workers, immigration will supply 1,700,000, of which 23 per cent, or 380,000, will fall into the category of highly trained scientific personnel. Immigration therefore is not equally open to all kinds of workers, and clearly favored are those who are most qualified to add to the scientific potential of the United States. For the empire there is a twofold advantage: It throws open the doors of its court to those who can make the most valuable contribution to its scientific growth—and it leaves to other countries the responsibility for their training.

Washington anticipates that the flow of highly trained scientific personnel should be increasing. In 1965 the United States actually welcomed 16,000 immigrants in that category, while it ought to be receiving 380,000 between 1965 and 1975—or 38,000 annually. In order to meet the

Department of Labor projections, the United States would have to welcome in 1975 some 60,000 highly trained scientific workers. Their annual inflow will then have almost quadrupled between 1965 and 1975. And yet official estimates are moderate, and the experience of the last years has shown that projections quickly fall behind actual needs. Thus, for example, in 1965 the American Institute of Physics anticipated that the United States would have a shortage of some 20,000 physicists in 1970. The same institute has already published another report showing that the shortage will be even greater.

Under such conditions the American government increases its efforts to intensify the "brain trade." Its stakes are vital. It does not matter that it deprives other countries, be they faithful allies or not, of particularly competent individuals, or that it welcomes them at the moment when, having barely terminated their training in their own countries, they have become "productive." It is of no concern that it increases the gap between rich and poor countries, a gap which, as the White House admits, represents one of the greatest dangers in the contemporary world. For that pillage of brains is indispensable in the great competition between the free world and the Communist world. Besides, it is effective because foreign scientists are offered greater advantages than they could find in their own countries. And if the United States acts this way, it is not merely to serve its vanity of national glory, or to increase its own power, for America is charged with a world mission and it serves the entire world by attracting the best talents. Other countries may establish their policy on strictly nationalistic considerations, but America, because of its world responsibilities, is beyond such petty designs. And if some countries of Europe, of America, or of Asia do not travel as rapidly as the United States along the road of scientific progress they would be at fault if they complained about it. Because the

United States works for them, and those countries will always have the opportunity to buy American patents, American machinery, American scientific equipment, all the while benefiting from the protection of American arms. Therefore, let them trust in America and stop criticizing when they see their scientists leaving. Their protests expose their narrow nationalistic outlook. Ever since Woodrow Wilson, America has understood that American nationalism was the higher form of liberal internationalism (see Introduction). The partners of the United States may be fearful of falling still more deeply under the domination of a giant who, thanks to its own scientists but also thanks to the Scientists of the whole world, will ever more strikingly demonstrate its scientific, technological, and industrial superiority. But their fears are groundless, for, since the time of McKinley, the world has known that "no imperialist design lurks within the American heart."

The empire's government, therefore, does not hesitate to increase the funds granted to scientific research. Here are, in millions of dollars, the contributions of the federal government as compared to private industry's.

	1960	1963	1964	1965
Federal government	6,081	7,270	7,720	7,759
Private industry	4,428	5,360	5,792	6,438
TOTAL	10,509	12,630	13,512	14,197

Note: From *Statistical Abstract of the United States,* 1967 (p. 539).

The funds devoted to research by private industry naturally go to sectors directly concerned with commercial production, where federal subsidies are likely to be less important. On the other hand, the governmental effort gives of course priority to the sectors which are keyed to military production—these offer the best returns and later result in a great variety of extremely profitable commercial applications (see Chap. VII). Here, as an example, are a few figures for the year 1965 (in millions of dollars).

	Federal Funds	Private Funds	Total
Food products	1	148	149
Paper	0	76	76
Chemical products	190	1,187	1,377
Petroleum	69	366	435
Rubber	25	141	166
Machinery	258	870	1,128
Electr. and telecom- munications	1,978	1,189	3,167
Motors and transports	326	913	1,239
Aviation and missiles	4,500	620	5,120
Scientific instruments	125	261	386

Note: From *Statistical Abstract of the United States,* 1967 (p. 539).

Closely linked to the economic empire, the military empire therefore plays the determining role in the building of the scientific empire which permits the United States to import highly trained personnel who—in turn—help to strengthen the power of the empire and more firmly establish its influence in a world whose intellectual resources it exploits in the same way that it plunders its raw materials.

Thus the empire's internal cohesion increases year by year. The sums allotted to scientific research increase at the same rate as the growth in military spending. The Pentagon's budget determines the economic vitality of various and closely interdependent sectors of the empire: it enables the United States to perfect and to multiply the weapons which can at a moment's notice reach any point on the globe; it keeps at a respectful distance any possible adversary while encouraging compliance by allies and neutrals somewhat tempted to show signs of independence; it assures outlets for industrial production that internal consumption could not guarantee alone; throughout the whole world it protects reserves of raw materials which the United

States consumes in frightening quantities; it stimulates scientific research which benefits civilian industry as well as war production; and last but not least it stands as the principal factor behind the brain drain and the scientific thrust of the United States.

The powerful magnet with which the United States attracts tens of thousands of scientific minds trained abroad is matched by a drive to export its scientific and intellectual output in order to extend its influence in the world. Every sector of the empire is affected by these currents and their interaction: the economic empire imports raw materials in order to export industrial products and capital, itself the source of profits which enable the purchase of increasingly more raw materials; likewise the cultural empire imports scientists and researchers in order to export a rising output, itself a source of wealth which enhances the U.S. role in the brain trade.

For several years the American government had thought the best way to expand its cultural empire was to organize and finance, itself, institutions abroad which would add to its prestige. But considerations of economy and efficiency soon convinced it to reduce an effort which was both too conspicuous and too onerous. Thus the personnel of the United States Information Service (USIS) in Western Europe was cut by one-third between 1956 and 1960. This was only a first step. Between 1960 and 1967 the American personnel of USIS was reduced from 238 to 155, and the European personnel from 1,674 to 723. During the same period the number of American cultural centers in Western Europe shrank by half. In 1962 USIS maintained eight libraries in France: two in Paris and six in the provinces. The six in the provinces were closed in 1963 and one in Paris two years later. Since 1960 nine American cultural centers have been closed in West Germany, nine in Italy, and similar action was taken in Spain, in Iceland, in Norway, in Portugal, etc.

It would be wrong to conclude from this that the cultural empire was weakened. The cultural centers subsidized by the government were very expensive and their official character restricted their real influence. The all-too-visible fronts have disappeared, but much more subtle and effective ways to influence remain: the press, motion pictures, television, radio.

Throughout the non-Communist world hundreds of millions of people every day read newspapers printed in their own languages and in their own countries, but often written according to the dispatches of American press agencies. In Europe this invasion of news-dissemination is contained within reasonable boundaries by the existence of European press agencies. But it is quite different in regions like Latin America, in spite of Chile's half-hearted attempts to create an agency and of the efforts of a Cuban agency with limited technical equipment and distribution.

Furthermore, Latin American newspapers are offered, at cut rates, a vast quantity of articles translated from English into Spanish and Portuguese: editorials by American columnists, miscellaneous articles, cartoons, reportage. In this way news and commentaries come directly from the United States, with an American bias, and offer readers one particular view of the war in Vietnam, the crisis in the Middle East, the turmoil in Africa, Gaullist diplomacy, the situation in the U.S.S.R. or in China, etc. Gradually an American concept of the world is surreptitiously imposed on millions of readers who have not the slightest reason to agree with the analyses made by Americans but who possess no other basis for comparison, no other source of information.

The influence that the United States exercises through the intermediacy of nominally "national" newspapers is augmented by more direct forms of influence. In Latin America, but also in Europe, American capital is invested in publishing enterprises. Magazines like *Vision* (in Spanish) and *Visao* (in Portuguese, in Brazil) do not reveal that they are directly controlled by American companies. In them readers never find articles or photographs which might influence them in forming troublesome political attitudes. And *Life*'s Spanish edition, which does not conceal its origin, is not for that reason any less influential. However, certain articles in the American edition of *Life* are never included in the Spanish edition. The most blatant is *Reader's Digest*, whose "selections" in several languages peddle throughout the world the picture of a moral and generous America, full of good intentions and human qualities. This is particularly believable, since it corresponds to a real aspect of America—but to only one aspect: the picture's shadings are blurred or erased and the war in Vietnam, for instance, becomes a heroic crusade in which kindly black G.I.'s pass out chewing gum to Vietnamese children cared for by American military M.D.'s.

In Europe, the readers of this made-in-U.S.A. news have no cause to complain, for no one obliges them to feed on such literature. European publications offer them a wide choice of viewpoints, unless they are themselves joined to American publishing enterprises, either directly through financing or through agreements which permit them to use American reportage or yet again through substantial advertising contracts.

Well-known European journalists will often place their pen in the service of the empire. One of them, whose prolific prose fills a widely distributed weekly, was quite surprised when, after a long stay in the United States, he was refused American citizenship. On reflection, however, he realized that his articles would be of more use to the cause of the empire if he preserved his own nationality. Week after week such publications produce an idyllic picture of America and of its role in the world. They must, however, take into account reactions from their readers—if they have access to other sources of information. This is why they often find themselves forced to make spectacular turn-abouts. One magazine with an unquestioned reputation told its readers in categorical statements that Julius and Ethel Rosenberg, condemned for "atomic espionage" in the United States, were guilty beyond the shadow of a doubt. But the magazine had to change its tune when, in the weeks preceding the execution of the Rosenbergs in the electric chair at Sing-Sing, public opinion swung to their side following interventions from Pius XII, numerous prelates, outstanding members of the bar, intellectuals, political leaders and the most respected professors, to working girls and hairdressers.

That was only one example, but many publications project into the minds of their readers a picture of America which many Americans themselves no longer believe in. Those publications, however, remain subject to market considerations which prevent them from ignoring certain events in America or from refusing photographs earth-shaking enough to stimulate sales. They therefore keep on explaining the wonderful progress made in the field of racial integration in the United States right up to the moment when photos of armored cars in the streets of Detroit, of fires in Washington, of police brutality in Harlem or Watts oblige them to reveal an unsuspected side of the drama. This makes it hard for their readers to understand the black revolution. But the game is not lost, because reports on the racial riots prove the impartiality of the publications and thereby authenticate articles to the glory of America.

It does not matter that each time a particular European professor returns from a series of lectures in the United States, he publishes a masterly article denouncing the ingratitude of anyone attacking various aspects of American policy. No one suspects him of thus catering to useful contacts he can use to take other trips to the United States. He does not suspect that some of his American colleagues are subjected to very strong official pressure to discourage them from publishing their articles in European newspapers. The empire jealously watches over the image its nationals and foreigners spread about it throughout the world.

And the situation is much more delicate in regions like Latin America. From Mexico to Argentina the entire press is suffocating from looking at the universe through a single window. Several major newspapers, in Brazil for instance, have attempted to sign agreements with independent European publications to offer their readers another view of the world. But that is only a halfway measure: a few articles translated here or there to supply information not available in the American press, an unorthodox analysis or point of view. The information services department of the United States embassy quickly sends out a luncheon invitation and attempts to convince the culprit that his documentation is inaccurate or incomplete. Pressures are exerted from every side. It can even lead to the cancellation of advertising contracts for the newspaper from American firms operating in the country.

The most serious point is that these newspapers seldom have the necessary resources to ensure their independence. At the start of 1968 a leading newspaper of a major Latin American country, for the first time, sent a reporter to Vietnam. Until then it had kept its readers informed through dispatches and stories sold inexpensively by American news agencies and newspapers. A special correspondent in a distant country costs five hundred times more than the price of a Joseph Alsop article resold to a Rio or a Buenos Aires newspaper. The Brazilian or Argentine reader has probably nothing in common with Joseph Alsop who, well-connected in the Pentagon, has since 1964 several times announced that Hanoi and the Vietcong would capitulate in the next dry season. But Joseph Alsop is a respected commentator whose categorical judgments are spread over every continent in every language.

As important as it is, the influence of a press outfitted by American suppliers has a lesser effect than the pictures spread by the movies and by television. Through advertising, the American economy offers the press and television large revenues which increase rapidly from year to year and constitute a powerful resource for newspapers and television stations. Here, in millions of dollars, is the growth of advertising budgets, as given in *Statistical Abstract of the United States*, 1967 (p. 806).

1940	2,088	1960	11,932
1945	2,875	1965	15,255
1950	5,710	1966	16,545
1955	9,194		

These advertising funds follow the curve of economic expansion. Relatively small before the entry of the United States into the war, while the country still had millions of unemployed, they surged upward thanks to postwar prosperity, increased again with the industrial expansion due to the Korean War, and got another boost during the war in Vietnam. Of course, television's share is constantly increasing (in millions of dollars).

	1950		1966	
Newspapers	2,076	36.3%	4,876	29.5%
Radio	605	10.6%	1,001	6.1%
Television	171	3.0%	2,765	16.7%
Magazines	515	9.0%	1,295	7.8%
Others	2,343	41.1%	6,608	39.9%
TOTAL	5,710	100.0%	16,545	100.0%

Note: From *Statistical Abstracts of the United States*, 1967 (p. 807).

With advertising revenues of $2,765 million in 1966, the major American television networks had financial resources unavailable to any other country in the world. They produced reports, serials, children's programs, etc., which are resold throughout the world. Even in countries suspected of anti-Americanism, like France, national television every day broadcasts a large percentage of American telecasts. Of course, cuts can be made in some tapes, and their commentaries changed. Fairly often these tapes even show the least appealing aspects of American life. Nevertheless, and especially in countries of limited means, they disseminate in millions of homes one particular presentation of the problems facing the world and completely ignore other serious problems.

This is not necessarily a deliberately partial view of the world. Many television journalists have, on the contrary, a well-deserved reputation for independence and nonconformity. But, actually, they cater to a very limited public, and the average American in the middle west does not share the concerns of the farmer in Brittany or the Netherlands, the Moroccan fellah, the Chilean miner, or the Formosan peasant.

The impact of the image is probably even greater in the case of motion pictures. For American industry exports its films throughout the world and controls an increasingly large portion of the distribution outlets. In every capital a good many theaters show American films which, naturally, include important works as well as junk. German, French, and Spanish producers, to name only a few, find holding out against American competition more and more difficult. Obviously, their commercial growth depends on receipts from their own productions. Faced with the influx of American films, national production in most countries of the world either declines or tries to assure its commercial success by the choice of subjects, through well-known stars, etc.—and increasingly at the expense of quality. Thanks to motion pictures, American fashions or fads can infiltrate the whole Western world within a few weeks. American "values" are very rapidly disseminated, showing both the best and the worst but almost always holding up (even unconsciously and even in the form of social criticism) the advantages and blessings of the high standard of living provided by the American way of life. But what those films do not say is that the civilization of the automobile and the private swimming pool, of air conditioning and the private plane, of material comfort and waste is based not only on an ideal of progress and the virtues of free enterprise, but also on the exploitation of mines and plantations in the Third World, where meager wages and low selling prices are the ransom paid for the prosperity of 200 million Americans.

A false image is thus provided for the admiration of the crowd. But that golden image reminds one of a double-edged sword: granted, it inspires great admiration and a desire to attain the American way of life, but at the same time it emphasizes the contrast between the wretched living conditions of the immense majority of humanity and the privileges of the minority which lives in the United States. In spite of vigorous "anti-imperialist" campaigns, the populations of continents economically exploited by the empire are certainly not aware of the specific techniques by which America assures its own prosperity. But television and cinema, by picturing for them a way of life whose splendors they had not suspected, reveal more harshly the burden of their own poverty and misery. And the feeling that this inspires in them is closer to hatred than to admiration. The cultural empire thus carries within itself the seeds of its own destruction.

Meanwhile, like all imperialism, it speeds up the process of acculturation which tends to deprive humanity of rich potentialities. Wherever it can strongly assert itself it eliminates indigenous cultural traditions and substitutes for them the American "mold." Puerto Rico represents a caricature of this situation, where one is faced not with a symbiosis of Hispanic and American culture, but with the obliteration of the former in the face of the latter. Of course all of Latin America is not as deeply involved in that process—far from it. But the Latin American student rebellions are directed not only against dictatorial, corrupt or ineffectual regimes, not only against the foreign exploitation of the economic and human resources of their country, but also against a cultural colonization which strikes at their heart. And that is why perhaps their revolts are more violent than those of labor or peasant organizations which above all resent economic colonization.

The empire thought it would command the loyalty of the students by offering them many opportunities to study in American universities. In a few years a trend was reversed: the number of European students in the United States remained almost constant, while the number of Asian or Latin American students increased. In 1953 a quarter of the foreign students registered in American universities were European, but that fell to 12 per cent in 1963. The number of Fulbright scholarships given to French students decreased from 220 in 1950 to 130 in 1963; to English students, from 175 to 83. But those Fulbright scholars represent only a small part of the European students registered in American universities: their total went from 7,800 in 1953 to 7,923 in 1963. During the same period, the number coming from the Third World increased considerably. From 1953 to 1963 the number of Asian students in the United States climbed from 7,585 to 23,768 and the number of Latin American students, from 7,615 to 11,021. This trend has accelerated during the last few years.

The intention is clear: the United States intensified its efforts to train cadres in the underdeveloped continents. And the priority of these efforts is directed toward Asia and Latin America, since Africa, in this respect, receives sizable aid from France and England. But this policy is ineffective for two main reasons.

1. As we have already seen, out of 5,819 highly qualified immigrants who entered the United States in 1966 and who came from underdeveloped continents, 5,292 came from Asia and Latin America. The statistics do not show how many among them had received American diplomas, but an immigrant visa and a work contract are more easily granted to foreigners who are graduates of an American university. They know the language and the customs of the country, their studies have kept them one or more years in the United States, and they can be tempted to settle permanently; finally, American companies know they will be more easily assimilated. The welcome extended to students from Asia and Latin America facilitates the brain drain of which those continents are the victims.

2. Many students educated in the United States eventually go back to their country of origin. Some of them make up the personnel of American companies located in those countries. Others work for domestic firms if they can find employment commensurate with their qualifications. Whoever their employer, either they will be solely concerned with making a living in the best possible way, that is, preoccupied with their own material comfort, or they will make a political choice. Some will become avowed champions of the American cause and thus serve the interests of the empire which has permitted them to finish their university training; others will take the position of José Martí, the hero of Cuban independence at the end of the last century. After having lived in the United States—"inside the monster"—he specifically attacked the threat it posed to his country. Without being more precise, it is sufficient to mention that a good many of the students who died in the revolutionary *maquis* of Peru and Venezuela had attended American universities, just as did many Cubans who are serving the Castro revolution. This is a classic phenomenon. Many African nationalists had received English or French diplomas. The empire itself trains not only the cadres

which will serve it more or less loyally, but also the revolutionary leaders who will struggle against it. This is an ineluctable law and its effectiveness is proportionate to the cultural effort made by the empire.

Every empire itself generates its self-destruction. Although it does not conform to the classic definition, the empire without frontiers founded by the United States is no exception to the rule. While it exploits the material and human resources of countries subject to its rule, it provides increasingly more cause for revolt among the least educated social groups and guarantees the intellectual training of a certain number of revolutionary leaders whom it will one day have to fight.

The cultural empire makes use not only of the press, television, motion pictures, and foreign students invited to the United States; books remain one of its favorite weapons. Two organizations of the federal government with large financial resources share the task of spreading American propaganda throughout the world. One was especially created for this purpose—the United States Information Agency (USIA), [or, as it is known abroad, the United States Information Service (USIS)]. The other, and one is more surprised to find it involved in this drama, is the American espionage service, the Central Intelligence Agency (CIA).

Since 1947, students all over the world have burned or wrecked ninety-seven American libraries or cultural centers. They wanted to protest against "cultural colonialism" whose dangers they well perceived. For among the literary or scientific works destroyed were books of pure propaganda, written to order for the American government to justify its policies, without any regard whatever for historical truth.

In 1965, for example, USIS spent several million dollars to distribute 14,453,000 books throughout the world. This large market was naturally appealing to American publishers, some of whom agreed to publish books whose authors were paid by the USIS and whose texts were reviewed and revised by the same agency without, needless to say, its name being mentioned. Other publishers brought out books whose contents were such that they believed USIS would order several thousand copies to be used for propaganda purposes.

The written-to-order books, naturally, were published under the imprint of a publisher who would carefully fail to specify that such-and-such a book had been subsidized by the empire's government. These books could either be distributed gratis abroad for propaganda purposes or be sold within the United States where they would equally well serve as propaganda for the government. The latter is what offended the American lawmakers' curious concept of integrity. Appearing before a committee of the House of Representatives, Leonard Marks, Director of the United States Information Agency, provided interesting details. Questioned by Glenard Lipscomb, Republican Congressman from California, Marks explained that a book bearing the imprint of the government rather than that of a known and respected publisher would be viewed abroad with understandable suspicion. Lipscomb replied that he warmly approved of Marks's efforts abroad, but not inside the United States. Then this surprising dialogue took place between the two men.

> Lipscomb: "I assume you are distributing [these books] overseas, for lack of a better word, for propaganda purposes?"
> Marks: "Yes, definitely."
> Lipscomb: "Is it being sold in the United States for propaganda purposes?"
> Marks: "No." [5]

And the *New York Times* humorously commented: "In other words, what is meant to manipulate a foreign reader is

believed by Mr. Marks to be a fair and objective account to
an American reader." But that remark does not go to the
heart of the matter. In fact, the truth is to be found elsewhere. Marks knew he could admit without risking criticism that his organization was spreading propaganda
abroad. There was no harm in that, since the empire's best
interests demanded it. But since the American citizen was
of a privileged or, in any case, different breed, Marks knew
it was not proper to subject him to overt propaganda. Lipscomb, furthermore, agreed with him. He approved of propaganda abroad, but disapproved of propaganda in the
United States. Not because the agency's statutes defined its
field of action as beyond the nation's borders, but because it
is natural to conceal from a foreign reader the fact that a
book is published by the government, while an American
reader has the right to be informed of it. No matter how
unselfish, a colonial power is condemned to create a distinction of nature and quality between its own nationals and
colonized peoples.

The debate about this which took place in the United
States brought to light certain facts which were considered
particularly outrageous. In its April 1966 issue, a publication as respected as *Foreign Affairs*, sponsored by the New
York Council on Foreign Relations, published an article entitled "The Faceless Viet Cong" by George A. Carver. The
author was identified as a specialist in political theory and
Asian affairs, a graduate of Yale and Oxford who had served
with the American aid mission in Saigon and, above all, as
the author of a scholarly book: *Aesthetics and the Problems
of Meaning*. George A. Carver thus appeared to be a respectable scholar writing objectively on a subject he knew
well. His article asserted that the Vietcong was only a
Hanoi puppet, and vindicated from start to finish American policy in Vietnam. Then what was outrageous? American newspapers waxed indignant because *Foreign Affairs*

had not told its readers that George A. Carver was a CIA agent. The American public had been deceived. Only foreign readers may be the target of such insidious propaganda.

In truth, foreign readers are very well treated. In 1966 Praeger published *Why Vietnam* by Frank N. Trager. Advance publicity said: "Professor Trager's account of the struggle that has torn Vietnam apart offers compelling reasons for that [U.S.] involvement and shows why the United States commitment—a commitment of three Presidents—must still stand. It also seeks to show why, after a succession of unstable governments, the administration of Premier Nguyen Cao Ky offers new hope for a secure and free South Vietnam." Once again, what was outrageous? The USIA had paid Professor Trager $2,500 to write the book and had bought two thousand copies for $5,750 from the publisher for distribution abroad. All that was perfectly acceptable according to American values. But what was intolerable was that the same publisher sold the same book inside the United States, with *Newsweek* magazine warmly recommending it without informing the American reading public that the book had been written on government order and was not an objective study but a propaganda device.

The USIA's objectives had been defined in March 1964 by Reed Harris, who, though eleven years earlier a victim of McCarthyism, nevertheless used arguments worthy of the notorious "witch-hunter." He explained, in effect, that this "[is a program under which we can have] books written to our own specifications, books that would not otherwise be put out, especially those books that have strong anti-Communist content. . . . We control the thing from the very idea down to the final edited manuscript." One of his associates explained: "We try to reach outside commercial writers who have stature in the literary world, we try to get them to do books. This results in greater credibility, sir." [6]

Two different systems were used for that purpose. In

1956 the USIA allotted $570,850 to subsidize 104 books "that would not be written or published for the commercial market without Agency encouragement." The same year, USIA spent $183,905 to have forty-six other books published at its request, according to its specifications and under its control. These two types of contracts obligated the author and the publisher not to reveal under any circumstances the agency's role.

Among the books written to order for USIA was *The Truth about the Dominican Republic*, by Jay Mallin, a correspondent of *Time* magazine, and published by Doubleday under the title *Caribbean Crisis: Subversion Fails in the Dominican Republic*. The same Jay Mallin received $4,946 from USIA for writing *Terror in Vietnam*, published by D. Van Nostrand. The graver the crisis, the greater the efforts of the USIA to sing the praises of American policies. It was therefore to be expected that the Dominican Republic and Vietnam would be objects of its attention. Besides the two books by Trager and Mallin, written to order and at its expense, USIA subsidized another book on Vietnam: *The Vietnam War: Why?* written by Mr. Sivaram, an Indian journalist. That book was first published by Charles E. Tuttle in hard cover, and the USIA ordered 460 copies for distribution abroad. The book explained that "the war in Vietnam can only be ended by the retreat of the aggressor," i.e., North Vietnam. Later Macfadden brought out the same book in paperback, and USIA ordered 25,000 copies in English and then bought the translation rights in thirty-one languages.

In American eyes, the problem lay in the fact that the same publisher released books by independent authors and by USIA-paid authors without the American reader—once again, the foreign reader did not count—being able to distinguish one from the other. Praeger, for example, brought out books by Bernard Fall that criticized American policy in

Vietnam, and a book by Philip Geyelin, *Lyndon B. Johnson and the World*, which in not concealing Washington's weaknesses and failures showed an impartiality that discredited it in the eyes of the USIA. But Praeger also brought out sixteen books in 1965 that were subsidized or ordered by the USIA, and even admitted publishing fifteen or sixteen books that were paid for by the espionage agency, the CIA. In spite of such important financial aid, Praeger could not survive as an independent publisher and was bought by the *Encyclopaedia Britannica*, which, contrary to its name, is an American enterprise. The *Encyclopaedia Britannica* in association with the Club Français du Livre launched the *Encylopaedia Universalis* in Paris.

A few years ago the USIA paid the formerly leftist weekly the *New Leader* $16,500 to draft *The Strategy of Deception: A Study in Worldwide Communist Tactics*, published in 1963 by Farrar, Straus. The author was Mrs. Kirkpatrick, wife of a former intelligence agent who became director of the American Political Science Association and an organization called Operations and Policy Research which received funds from the USIA and from two "foundations" serving as fronts for the CIA. The book sold 25,000 copies and was selected by the Book of the Month Club, which assured it an enormous distribution.

The USIA has a simple way of getting sensational books which serve its propaganda purposes written and published. It gets the State Department or the CIA to classify documents on current problems. Then it comes to terms with an author for whom the documents will be declassified on condition that USIA will have absolute control over the manuscript. Many journalists and writers cannot resist the dual temptation of earning money and acquiring the dubious glory of revealing "secret" dossiers. Only one price is exacted of them: they surrender their freedom of judgment and their intellectual integrity in agreeing to put their names to works whose contents are censored and slanted.

The *New York Times* summed up the problem as follows: "There is much evidence that books are used increasingly as engines of propaganda, that highly placed persons are pre-censoring books they find repellent or embarrassing, and that they are commissioning and controlling the writing of books without disclosing the facts of such control." [7]

In the United States, as in foreign countries, some "intellectuals" have been unable to resist the financial blandishments of the USIA. Others have not considered it compromising to make "study trips" at the expense of the State Department. But their conclusions on their return were so obliging—at least as they publicly expressed them—that their sponsors did not need to exercise the slightest direct pressure. The great "foundations" have often played a similar role, and with more skill, since a large portion of the projects financed by them are politically neutral. Besides, as will be seen in the following chapter, some of these foundations were only a camouflage for the CIA. The espionage agency sometimes intervened under cover of the USIA to effect the writing and publication of books. Anyhow whether the money comes from the USIA or the CIA, the distinction is academic. It is always a question of money from a government entrusted with the task of watching over the interests of the empire.

"Archeologists and journalists, freelance writers and editors of academic journals are not normally very wealthy. Some of them are vulnerable to money corruption, and the CIA has not hesitated to use them when it could," wrote James Reston in the *New York Times*.[8]

The cancer of minds corrupted by money can spread far and fast. It acts simultaneously within American society and abroad: internally because it needs the intellectual warranty of certain figures to be more effective abroad. The two worlds are inextricably bound together, something which

forcefully shows once again that the empire's dramas touch
not only the colonized, but also the colonizers. American
liberals were wildly indignant when they learned in 1967
that the CIA had financed certain university activities.
They believed the "tainted" origin of the money compromised their reputation at home and abroad. But is there
such a difference between Michigan State University accepting money from the CIA to organize police forces in
Vietnam, and the University of California receiving $363
million in 1965 from the Pentagon with $246,470,000 going
into atomic research for military purposes? According to the
Reston article, already cited, 53 per cent of the budget of
the University of California in 1965 came from the government. And he added: "The Government contracts are so
valuable that some universities have paid lobbyists in
Washington to see that they get their fair share."

But that aspect is an internal American problem. It is a
different matter when the efforts of the USIA, CIA, and
certain foundations, with the more or less conscious conniv-
ance of American intellectuals, deal specifically with intellectual activities abroad. Then this kind of corruption is
even more widespread because it is not limited to venality.
Quite often, as Jason Epstein writes, "It was not a matter of
buying off and subverting individual writers and scholars,
but of setting up an arbitrary and factitious system of values
by which academic personnel were advanced, magazine editors appointed, and scholars subsidized and published, not
necessarily on their merits, though these were sometimes
considerable, but because of their allegiances." He adds:
"The CIA and the Ford Foundation, among other agencies,
had set up and were financing an apparatus of intellectuals
selected for their correct cold-war positions." [9]

Although peaceful coexistence has now officially succeeded the Cold War, the same policy is pursued by the
same methods, for the Communist threat continues and to

conquer minds is always as important as to have access to reserves of raw materials and to retain military supremacy. It may seem surprising that the CIA and the Ford Foundation can be spoken of in the same breath. But any surprise could only be due to an underestimation of the collective will to serve America and its mission in the world.

Where, in fact, is the dividing line between the university, diplomacy, government, the CIA and the foundations? After having been High Commissioner in Occupied Germany, John J. McCloy became President of the Ford Foundation. Going the other way, John Foster Dulles and Dean Rusk had been Presidents of the Rockefeller Foundation before becoming Secretaries of State. When McGeorge Bundy, special assistant for National Security affairs to Presidents Kennedy and Johnson and among other things, in charge of liaison with the CIA, left the White House, John J. McCloy had him named head of the Ford Foundation. Shepard Stone, a former officer in the espionage service and McCloy's assistant in Germany, became director of international affairs for the Ford Foundation. And once the scandal had exploded, and the CIA was no longer able to subsidize the Congress for Cultural Freedom (and its publications: *Preuves, Encounter, Quadernos*) it was naturally the Ford Foundation which took over and assured its financing. All foundation activities certainly are not politically motivated nor do they exclusively serve the empire's interests. But foundation heads approve of the major objectives of American diplomacy. Naturally they are interested in certain activities which they judge worthy of their financial support. The CIA in that respect does not operate differently. It would be wrong to believe that foundations act "honorably" while the CIA, by its nature and functions, is "Machiavellian." The secret intentions and motivations of the masters of the empire are of less concern than the powerful methods they command on behalf of America's cause.

Whether their offices are located at the headquarters of the CIA or a foundation, the people who occupy eminent positions in American society are convinced that their country represents a model to be envied by the world, and must be strengthened, and even defended at times by questionable means. Of course they recognize that their society is not perfect, and they know of its faults and shortcomings. But they do not doubt its fundamental justice, or that its failings can be corrected given time, intelligence, will power, and competence. Meanwhile, the struggle must continue against the dark forces at home or abroad which attack this society without regard for the fact that its prosperity is tied to the poverty of three-quarters of mankind. These men believe in their virtue success, that they can solve domestic and international problems and that, one day, all the world will be enjoying the advantages of the American way of life. It need only be patient, learn from America's success and use its formulas.

The formulas are known. Books have been devoted to them, explaining the merits and efficacy of American methods of management, advertising, public relations, marketing, etc. American books on these subjects, which deserve to be better known, have been supplemented by foreign works confirming America's genuine superiority in these matters; American technology will solve everything. The USIA buys translation rights to these books and has them published everywhere by foreign publishers. They are available in many languages. Slipped in among them are several books of straight propaganda on the Dominican Republic and Vietnam, and other books which are meant only to testify to the high quality of American intellectual efforts. American publishers even acquire large financial interests in foreign publishing houses; an example is Time, Inc.'s purchase of 46 per cent of the shares of the French publisher Robert Laffont.

But what the USIA, the foundations, and the CIA do not make known in any of the world's languages is the volume of profits repatriated to the United States from the Third World, the fabulous amount of raw materials which the empire can waste because they are cheaply bought, the political and cultural weight of the economic empire and its brutal interventions in the lives of other countries, the number of dictatorships on which the empire rests in Latin America and elsewhere.

In this gigantic effort, the CIA is not limited only to propaganda operations or the spreading of America's intellectual influence. It undertakes much more complex and delicate tasks. The detailed story of one CIA intervention, in Iran, will enable us to better understand the functioning of the secular arm of the empire that is in charge of America's dirty work. It will also show how police activities are related to the political, economic, and military interests of the empire. Finally, it will help sketch the secret interventions of the United States in allied as in enemy countries.

IX

In the Service of the Empire: The CIA

In the second paragraph of the first page of his memoirs, Dwight D. Eisenhower expressed his concern about a certain country: "Iran seemed to be almost ready to fall into Communist hands." Three months after entering the White House, faced with Senator Taft's opposition to his proposed budget, he decided to meet with him in an effort to win him over. The meeting took place on April 30, 1953. "I referred to the dangers in Iran," noted Ike, "and pointed out that Western Europe and the oil of the Middle East must in no circumstances fall to Communism." Then, in the next-to-last page of the same first volume of his memoirs, Eisenhower assessed his actions and pointed to the termination of the wars in Korea and Indochina, adding: "The march of Communism had been halted and in some parts of the world, as in Iran and Guatemala, certain of its tentacles had been cut off." [1]

These persistent references to Iran are not surprising, since the activities of the United States in that country fully reveal, almost to the point of parody, the close connection between the government, its intelligence service, and private enterprise in strengthening the empire's position and, more specifically, its control over sources of raw materials. The history of the Central Intelligence Agency's (CIA) intervention in Iran is known in outline, but it has never been told completely. A detailed recounting brings out the exact techniques the empire uses to extend its strategic and economic position. The case of Iran shows what role is played by the President of the United States, how the CIA operates, and what pressures are exerted to overthrow a legitimately elected government. It also demonstrates that in the "struggle for democracy" the United States, if need be, appeals to former Nazis or their collaborators, in this instance General Zahedi. And, finally, since the operation succeeded, the American oil companies, which had never been able to operate in Iran, were able to spread their net of exploitation to that country. On that point, Iran's case provides a model.

In 1951, a few weeks after having married Princess Soraya, the Shah of Iran faced the most serious crisis of his reign. On the initiative of the Prime Minister, Mossadegh, the Majlis (Parliament) voted to nationalize Iran's oil (13 per cent of world reserves), which until then had been exploited by the Anglo-Iranian Oil Company (AIOC) which was controlled by the British government with 52 per cent of the stock. Two years before, the company had negotiated an agreement with the Iranian government by which it paid royalties of between 25 and 30 per cent. Deciding that that rate was inadequate the Teheran Parliament had rejected the agreement. Ultimately, the oil industry was nationalized, and in October 1951 the British shut down the Abadan refinery. The Iranians then turned to other Western oil companies to sell their petroleum in world markets. Supported by the governments of London and Washington, the AIOC systematically intervened to block such transactions because they would have destroyed its hopes of recovering its property. Despite several rulings in favor of the Iranian position by Italian and Japanese courts, no company dared run the risk of standing up to the AIOC. Moreover, "The State Department gave these companies little encouragement—which is to say it told them 'hands off.' " [2]

In the United States, General Eisenhower, President of Columbia University, had just been elected President of the United States in November 1952 but had not yet taken office. He received a visit from the Shah of Iran, who voiced his complaints against Mossadegh. Mossadegh then wrote Ike: "It is my hope that the new administration which you will head will obtain at the outset a true understanding of the vital struggle in which the Iranian people have been engaging . . . [against] a company inspired by covetousness and a desire for profit supported by the British government." The President-elect replied that he did not as yet have an opinion on the dispute. In January 1953 the Iranian Parliament extended Mossadegh's powers for one year. On February 28 the Shah announced his intention to abdicate "for reasons of health." This tactic only partially achieved the expected result: although it provoked a few demonstrations by the Shah's supporters, Mossadegh emerged victorious from this test of strength. He was backed by the nationalist bourgeoisie and the masses, which were both hoping that Iran could derive more from the exploitation of its oil. Needless to say, the Communists of the Tudeh Party supported Mossadegh, and Washington was going to make use of that fact. The Shah reversed his decision to abdicate.

On May 28, 1953, Mossadegh again wrote Eisenhower, asking for his political help in order "to remove the obstacles placed in the way of sale of Iranian oil," and for economic aid. But Ike, as he wrote in his memoirs, refused to "pour more American money into a country in turmoil."

He replied to Mossadegh that the American taxpayer would not understand if he granted aid to a country which "could have access to funds derived from the sale of its oil." Ike's false ingenuousness is somewhat disarming, for he himself explained his objective, which was based on a plan drawn up by Loy Henderson, his Ambassador in Teheran. It had to do with replacing the AIOC with an international consortium which would include American oil companies.

Meanwhile, the agents of the CIA were not wasting their time. They did not doubt that Mossadegh was a Communist puppet and they used every possible device to substantiate their thesis. They were already very active in Teheran, trying to regroup Mossadegh's opponents. On July 19, 1953, Mossadegh retaliated by announcing a referendum for August 2. Immediately, wrote Eisenhower, "reports were coming in that Mossadegh was moving closer and closer to the Communists." And he added, without being any more specific, "one report said he was looking forward to receiving 20 million dollars from the Soviet Union." [3] As a matter of fact, Moscow was waiting for the results of the referendum before declaring itself. The results were clear-cut: On August 2 Mossadegh received 99.4 per cent of the votes. Malenkov stated before the Supreme Soviet that negotiations with Iran had begun on August 8.

"The time had come for the United States to embark on an international gamble," wrote Andrew Tully.[4] On August 10, on the pretext of joining his wife on a vacation, Allen Dulles, Director of the CIA and brother of Secretary of State John Foster Dulles, flew to Switzerland. Before his departure he had seen Princess Ashraf, the Shah's sister, who relayed the plans to the sovereign and then also left for Switzerland. It is from that splendidly neutral country that all the moves of the coup were directed.

At the same time, General H. Norman Schwartzkopf, a top CIA agent, took a "sightseeing" trip that included Pak-

istan, Syria, and Lebanon, and then brought him to Iran.
Why there? To visit with old friends. But if Americans
thought of General Schwartzkopf as the man who, as head
of the New Jersey police, had directed the inquiry into the
Lindbergh kidnapping (1932), the Iranians knew him primarily as the expert who had reorganized the Shah's police
between 1942 and 1948. At that time he had the opportunity to take stock of General Zahedi, one of his more
energetic colleagues in the Iranian police. On August 13,
eleven days after the referendum when speed was of the essence, the Shah signed an illegal decree deposing Mossadegh and appointing General Zahedi Prime Minister. The
sovereign had prudently left his capital to vacation on the
shores of the Caspian Sea, ready to flee if the game went
against him. He sent the Colonel of his bodyguard to deliver
the decree removing Mossadegh. But Mossadegh took the
decree and had the Colonel imprisoned. The Shah and
Soraya took refuge in Italy.

What happened then? Here is the sequence of events,
which Eisenhower tells in the manner of a fairy tale:
"Then, suddenly and dramatically, the opposition to Mossadegh and the Communists began to work. The Iranian
Army turned against officers whom Mossadegh had installed. The Army drove all pro-Mossadegh demonstrators
off the streets," etc. But the President of the United States
is less naïve than he would like us to believe, since he himself noted: "I conferred daily with officials of the State and
Defense departments and the Central Intelligence Agency
and saw reports from our representatives on the spot who
were working actively with the Shah's supporters." [5]

The Ambassador being in Switzerland, those "representatives on the spot" were in fact CIA agents. Among them
was General Schwartzkopf, who directed the operation.
The latter, wrote Andrew Tully, "took over as unofficial
paymaster for the Mossadegh-Must-Go clique. Certain

Iranians started to get rich, and the word later was that in a period of a few days Schwartzkopf supervised the careful spending of more than ten million of CIA's dollars. Mossadegh suddenly lost a great many supporters." [6]

To whom did those millions of dollars go? In a thoroughly documented article, obviously stemming from the CIA and designed to raise its standing in the eyes of Congress, the *Saturday Evening Post* reported as follows fifteen months after the events:

"On Wednesday, August nineteenth, with the army standing close guard around the uneasy capital, a grotesque procession made its way along the street leading to the heart of Teheran. There were tumblers turning handsprings, weight lifters twirling iron bars and wrestlers flexing their biceps. As spectators grew in number, the bizarre assortment of performers began shouting pro-shah slogans in unison. The crowd took up the chant and there, after one precarious moment, the balance of public psychology swung against Mossadegh.

"Upon signal, it seemed, army forces on the shah's side began an attack. The fighting lasted nine hours. By nightfall, following American-style military strategy and logistics, loyalist troops drove Mossadegh's elements into a tight cordon around the premier's palace. They surrendered and Mossadegh was captured. . . . In Rome, a bewildered young shah prepared to fly home and install Zahedi as premier, and to give Iran a pro-Western regime." [7]

The circus parade which had swept out of the slums of Teheran was led by a big fellow named Shaban Jafari, whom we'll come across again a little later. Here is what *Le Monde* (September 17, 1953) wrote on the subject:

"The southern district of Teheran is an appalling shantytown. Half the city's population is packed in there amid labyrinths of putrid hovels teeming with poverty, sickness, drugs, and vice. From those lower depths, on Wednesday,

August 19, a crowd began marching toward the center of the city, starting the revolution which brought about Mossadegh's fall. This was proof, proclaimed the new regime's partisans, that the revolution had been the work of the people. Completely false, retorted Mossadegh's followers; it was from the *lumpenproletariat* of the southern part of the city that the hirelings and the *tcheroukech*, or hatchet men as they are called, had been recruited. The revolution, they added, had been financed by the Americans. The mollahs had distributed more than four million tomans ($400,000) to people willing to do anything. The Tudeh Party's clandestine paper, *Mardom*, even gave the number of the cashier's check allegedly used by American agents to obtain Iranian currency: check #703,352 drawn on the Melly Bank for 32,643,000 rials—or $390,000—to the order of Mr. Edward G. Donnaly."

As a matter of fact, that check for $390,000 was only part of the amount spend by General Schwartzkopf and his associates to organize the "spontaneous uprising" thanks to which officers faithful to the Shah overthrew Mossadegh. For the "loyalist" Army was not about to take risks for a sovereign who had prudently found refuge in Italy, and it was the military that got the major part of the $10 million which Andrew Tully, according to his informants within the CIA, reckoned to be the total cost of the operation.

None of this prevented the *Saturday Evening Post* from asserting in the article already cited that "the physical overthrow of Mossadegh was accomplished by the Iranians themselves. It is the guiding premise of CIA's third force that we must develop and nurture indigenous freedom legions among captive or threatened people who stand ready to take personal risks for their own liberty."

The explanation was always the same: the Iranians who, in the August 2 referendum, had shown their confidence in Mossadegh "themselves" overthrew him on August 19.

Eight years later, Adlai Stevenson would maintain at the United Nations with an equally clear conscience that the fighting then taking place in the Bay of Pigs was a conflict "between Cubans"—up to the moment when President Kennedy would assume entire responsibility for the operation carried out, from beginning to end, by the CIA. Iran is just one of several examples.

"The next day Mossadegh, in pajamas, surrendered. He was placed under arrest. Zahedi's forces rounded up and jailed the Tudeh leaders. It was all over," noted Eisenhower in his memoirs.

Actually, this was only the beginning. Political repression crushed all opposition, of which only a small part was Communist. There were many victims among the middleclass bazaar tradesmen, who constituted in large measure Mossadegh's National Front, and also among the students and even among the tribes that refused to recognize the authority of the Shah or of his representatives—mere bandits who had been given official powers, just like the governors of the provinces who, in ancient Persia, were called satraps. But because repression was unable to re-establish order, sympathy, loyalty, and support had to be bought.

"Throughout the crisis the United States government had done everything it possibly could to back up the Shah," wrote Eisenhower. Mossadegh's fall was not sufficient to establish the sovereign's authority. The American government therefore decided to grant Zahedi the financial aid it had refused Mossadegh.

"On the 4th of September," Eisenhower wrote "Ambassador Loy Henderson and Premier Zahedi exchanged letters to the effect that the United States could now continue its planned technical-aid program of 23.4 million dollars for the current fiscal year. Largely as a result of a letter which I had received from Premier Zahedi on August 25, outlining the country's difficulties and need for aid and desire to align itself with the freedom-loving countries of the world, I decided that under the circumstances the technical-aid program as planned was insufficient. I announced on September 5 an additional 45 million dollars for emergency economic assistance. In all, American aid to Iran that fiscal year came to nearly 85 million dollars." [8]

But this figure was also only a modest beginning. Between 1953 and 1961 American aid to Iran totaled nearly a billion dollars. But it was squandered so openly that the House of Representatives in Washington voiced its concern. In a 1957 report it noted that the hundreds of millions of dollars given Iran had been used in such a "loose, slipshod and unbusinesslike manner that it is now impossible— with any accuracy—to tell what became of these funds." American aid was to have been used for, among other projects, the construction of a large dam estimated to cost several million dollars. But this project, the committee's report noted, achieved only one thing: "the relocation at a cost to the United States government of nearly three million dollars, of a road around the proposed site" of the dam. With some bitterness, the committee added that despite all the aid provided, the country was still 93 per cent illiterate.

But who was General Zahedi that he was chosen by both the Shah and General Schwartzkopf to organize the coup against Mossadegh and to succeed him as Prime Minister? Zahedi was known not only as the former head of the Shah's national police in the years 1942 to 1948 when Schwartzkopf was reorganizing it. During the Second World War he had starred in a cloak-and-dagger story that is told by the principal hero of the adventure, Fitzroy Mac-Lean, a British agent who had been on assignments in Moscow, Cirenaica, and Iran, was parachuted to join Tito's *maquis* in Yugoslavia, etc., and, when peace came, was elected a Conservative member of Parliament. His story and his "encounter" with General Zahedi deserve to be mentioned, for CIA historians never make the slightest allusion to this event which they prefer to ignore or conceal. What it reveals is that General Zahedi was cooperating with the Germans at the same time that General Schwartzkopf was in Iran. The CIA, therefore, knew perfectly well what kind of a man they were dealing with.

Fitzroy MacLean arrived in Teheran at the end of 1942. He was welcomed at the British legation by General Baillon, General Wilson's chief of staff, and by the British Minister, Sir Reader Bullard. Wrote MacLean: "They told me that they had a job for me. For some time past, they said, there had been signs that some kind of trouble was brewing in South Persia. The tribes, the Qashgai and the Bakhtiari, had German agents living amongst them and seemed likely to rise at any moment, just as they had in 1916 when their rebellion had caused us a disproportionate amount of trouble. Were this to happen, our supply route to the Persian Gulf might be cut. There was also discontent in Isfahan and other towns, largely caused by the hoarding of grain by speculators, which we were unable to prevent. This discontent might at any moment flare up into open rebellion. Worse still, if there were trouble, the Persian troops in south Persia were likely to take the side of the rioters."

Those troops were led by General Zahedi. Wrote MacLean: "A sinister part was being played in all this by a certain General Zahedi." And MacLean continued: "Zahedi was known to be one of the worst grain-hoarders in the country. But there was also good reason to believe that he was acting in cooperation with the tribal leaders and, finally, that he was in touch with the German agents who were living in the hills and, through them, with the German High Command in the Caucasus. Indeed, reports from secret sources showed that he was planning a general rising against the Allied occupation force, in which his troops and

those of the Persian General in the Soviet-occupied northern zone would take part, and which would coincide with a
German airborne attack on the Tenth Army, followed by a
general German offensive on the Caucasus front. In short,
General Zahedi appeared to be behind most of the troubles
in south Persia."

This was the situation General Baillon and Sir Reader
Bullard described to Fitzroy MacLean. They decided that
"it was essential to nip the trouble in the bud. . . . General Baillon and Sir Reader Bullard had decided that this
could best be achieved by the removal of General Zahedi,
and it was this task that they had decided to entrust to me.
How it was to be done, they left me to work out for myself.
Only two conditions were made: I was to take him alive
and I was to do so without creating a disturbance."

With a thousand juicy details, Fitzroy MacLean told the
sequel to that delicate operation. He went to Isfahan,
where the British Consul, John Gault, confirmed that General Zahedi was "a really bad lot." He showed him Zahedi's
residence. Despite the closeness of the barracks where an
Iranian garrison was stationed, General Zahedi was arrested
in his own house by Fitzroy MacLean, who kidnapped him
in a car under his guard's noses, took him to the desert, and
put him on board a plane. "In the General's bedroom I
found a collection of automatic weapons of German manufacture, a good deal of silk underwear, some opium, an illustrated register of the prostitutes of Isfahan and a large
number of letters and papers which I took with me to the
Consulate. . . . One of the first letters that caught our eye
was a recent communication from a gentleman styling himself 'German Consul-General for South Persia' and apparently resident in the hills somewhere to the South. He
spoke of Zahedi's activities in terms of general approval and
asked for more supplies. His letter left no doubt that the
General's arrest had not come a moment too soon." [9]

This was the man the CIA called upon, in the name of democracy, to overthrow Mossadegh and form a new government in Teheran. And Eisenhower wrote in his memoirs "I cabled General Zahedi my congratulations," and was delighted with the good intentions shown by the new Iranian Prime Minister. At least, he said, that is what he was assured of in "a memorandum prepared by an American in Iran, unidentified to me." The head of the most powerful state in the world was satisfied with a report whose author he did not know, and who could only have been a CIA agent. That informant also wrote Ike: "The Shah is a new man. For the first time, he believes in himself because he feels that he is King of his people's choice and not by arbitrary decision of a foreign power." This is how the empire treats its tools, even though they have the title Shah-in-Shah, "King of Kings."

Eisenhower recounts in his memoirs that on October 8, 1963, he noted in his private diary his intention to aid General Zahedi "both financially and with wise counsel." This was just the way, in 1913, Woodrow Wilson had offered the Mexican, Carranza, "arms and advice on ways to make the country democratic" and, more than half a century later, Lyndon Johnson offered Generals Thieu and Ky—beyond weapons and money—advice on the way to build South Vietnamese democracy. We know what happened in Vietnam. We saw how Carranza accepted the weapons and refused the advice. Here is what General Zahedi did in Iran after having accepted American aid.

Seven months after the fall of Mossadegh, General Zahedi held elections. The rest of the story is to be found in *Time* magazine: "For three days the city [of Teheran] had been voting for its twelve Deputies to the National Majlis. . . . As is the custom in Iranian elections, it was all pretty much fraud. The twelve lucky winners had been decided before the first voter dropped his scrap of paper into the metal box. All were supporters of Premier Fazlollah Zahedi's government . . . One Teheran elector dropped his ballot in the box, then salaamed deeply three times to the container. Asked why, he retorted: 'This box is magic. One drops in a bulletin for Mohammed [Mossadegh] and lo, when the box is opened, it becomes a vote for Fazlollah [Zahedi].' "

Time continues its story by stressing the role played by Shaban Jafari, the hireling who had led the parade which, the preceding August 19, triggered the mass demonstration and the fall of Mossadegh. The American magazine wrote: "Without waiting for the government to solicit his services, a fierce, black bearded giant named Shaban Jafari cruised the polling places through the week with his ragged associates—The Society of Gallant Men—to flex his muscles on behalf of Zahedi candidates. Tough, rough Shaban, who is called the 'Brainless One,' came out of Teheran's slums, was once Iran's national wrestling champion. In the past he put his brawn to work for Mohammed Mossadegh and in his behalf used to sack opposition newspaper offices. Now professing loyalty to Zahedi, . . . Brainless led his knife-armed toughs on tours of the polling places. Systematically, Brainless pulled voters out of line, searched their pockets for an anti-government ballot. When he found one, the voter was cuffed or stabbed, then turned over to the nearest policeman to be arrested and carted off to jail. Occasionally Shaban sheared off the hair of the victim." *Time*'s story ends this way: "At the end of one busy day Shaban eased his bulk into a cafe chair and poked at his dish of ice-cream. His score for two days was 50 hospitalized, 'mostly Communists.' 'We did better than the police and the soldiers together,' Brainless boasted. 'I know Shaban is a little rough,' said Ardashin Zahedi, U.S.-educated son of the premier, 'but . . . he is against the Communists.' " [10]

This election account in the Iranian capital is all the more remarkable because all the opposition leaders were then in prison. That year, Loy Henderson received the Distinguished Service Award from the State Department in Washington. This was to reward a diplomat who not only re-established democracy in Iran and barred the way to Communism, but also extended the empire's oil interests into Iran.

It does not come as a surprise that one of the first acts of the government that followed Mossadegh was to settle the oil dispute and to conclude an agreement with the consortium which, as Eisenhower reports, took the place of the Anglo-Iranian Oil Company,—just as Loy Henderson had proposed following nationalization. In gratitude for the decisive role played by the United States in the settlement of the crisis, Standard Oil, already a stockholder in ARAMCO* in Saudi Arabia, was allowed to participate in the consortium whose shares were thus divided: Anglo-Iranian Oil Company, 40 per cent; Royal Dutch-Shell, 14 per cent; Compagnie Française des Pétroles, 6 per cent; American companies, 40 per cent. The American companies were Standard Oil of California, Standard Oil of New Jersey, Texaco, and Socony Vacuum Oil Company, namely, the same ones which made up ARAMCO.

The arrangement was of course favorable to the American companies, but also to AIOC for two reasons: first, it received from the United States $70 million in lieu of compensation and, second, although it was only one of the active members of the consortium, the latter was within a few years to quadruple production, a fact which resulted in dividends for AIOC larger than it had received when it was the only company in control. Here are the facts: Iranian production reached 155 million barrels in 1947, fell to 21.5 million in 1954—the year that followed the crisis—then

---

* ARAMCO was owned by Standard Oil of California, 30 per cent; Standard Oil of New Jersey, 30 per cent; Texaco, 30 per cent; Socony Vacuum, 10 per cent.

climbed to 301 million in 1958, then to 345 million in 1959, to 538 million in 1963, to 618 million in 1964. The arrangement was also profitable to the Iranian government, which received payments of 50 per cent from the consortium, instead of the 25 to 30 per cent that AIOC had offered Mossadegh. But given Iran's power structure, the mass of the people did not share in that prosperity.

The very creation of the consortium posed a delicate legal problem for Washington because of the joint participation of American companies which, by working together, were subject to the antitrust laws. But the highest government officials intervened to remove that obstacle to the expansion of America's oil empire in the world. Eisenhower wrote in his memoirs: "Under a special ruling by the Department of Justice, based on the national-security needs of the United States, American oil companies participated in this consortium without fear of prosecution under antitrust laws." [11]

Thus everything returned to normal. An elected regime had been overthrown by a "popular" *coup d'état* which had been legitimatized by "free" elections. The Iranian Communists were imprisoned, tortured, executed and, along with them, many nationalists who were not in the slightest Communist. A "pro-Western" sovereign was put back on his throne. The most important thing had been to prevent nationalization, for the example could have inspired imitators in other countries. England, which Mossadegh wanted to expel, lost its exclusive position but regained a foothold in the country. The American oil companies were, in advance, absolved of any violation of the antitrust laws so that they could extend their spheres of activity and influence for the greater good of the United States. The government in Washington had shown the watching world that it was capable of driving back "Communism" in a troubled region. The good of the cause coming first, it did not matter that Mossadegh, pursuing a strictly nationalist policy, had been portrayed as a Communist puppet seeing that the Communists supported him.

The entire operation had been carried off with perfect agreement between President Eisenhower, Secretary of State John Foster Dulles, Director of the CIA Allen Dulles, and the American oil companies. This coordination of government, secret service, and large private enterprise is typical. Its methods are familiar: corruption ($10 million); subversion by appealing to the most vicious elements (whether a General Zahedi or a Shaban Jafari); rigged elections. The empire, naturally, had no choice in the selection of methods.

The ill-defined concept of "national security" plays a large role in the empire's growth. "The national-security needs of the United States" were invoked to "authorize" the American oil companies' participation in the international consortium set up to exploit Iranian oil, although they would be violating antitrust laws. John Peurifoy, United States Ambassador to Guatemala, rationalized the coup organized by the CIA against that country by asserting on October 8, 1954, before the House of Representatives, that Colonel Arbenz Guzman's government "represented a menace to the security of the United States." In 1967 President Johnson used the same language about Vietnam.

But what was at issue in Guatemala? Colonel Arbenz came to power in 1950. His predecessor had bequeathed him a very modest agrarian reform program calling for the distribution of uncultivated lands. It did not seem possible that such a plan could provoke any serious opposition.

"Expropriation in itself does not, of course, prove Communism," noted Eisenhower in his memoirs. But he added that Arbenz's actions make it very easy to suspect him of being a Communist tool. The agrarian reform law was promulgated on June 17, 1952. Then, on February 24, 1953,

Eisenhower wrote: "The Arbenz government announced its intention to seize about 225,000 acres of unused United Fruit Company land. . . . The company was to receive the woefully inadequate compensation of 600,000 dollars in long-term non-negotiable agrarian bonds." Washington immediately decided to be represented in Guatemala by a hard-liner, John Peurifoy, who had proved his worth during the Greek civil war. For now the "banana empire" was threatened.

The new Ambassador himself tells how in his first conversation with President Arbenz, which lasted six hours, "he listened while I counted off the leading Communists in his regime." [12] The procedure was rather curious, but not extraordinary. The political parties supporting Arbenz comprised forty-five deputies, of whom only four were Communists. Yet against Arbenz would be unleashed a vast diplomatic effort, a vigorous propaganda campaign in the press, and finally a military coup. The whole operation was directed by the CIA, with the support of the State Department, the White House and, naturally, private enterprise, in this case the United Fruit Company. The CIA director's brother, Secretary of State John Foster Dulles, had worked before the war for the New York law firm of Sullivan & Cromwell, which in 1930 and 1936 had drawn up the contracts between United Fruit and the Guatemalan government. But the United Fruit empire also extended to most of the countries of Central America, over which it exercised considerable economic and political influence. Just as the nationalization of Iranian oil risked being imitated elsewhere, was not agrarian reform in Guatemala going to be contagious in Latin America?

While American newspapers were attacking the "Communist" activities of the Arbenz government, the meeting of the Organization of American States (OAS) in Caracas adopted a resolution on March 26, 1954 condemning any intervention of Communism in the hemisphere. Guatemala voted against, Argentina and Mexico abstained, Costa Rica was absent. In the event of a Communist threat the final text called for consultations between the member countries. The United States would have liked immediate action. But to make its proposal acceptable to the other countries it had to modify it and be satisfied with the consultation procedure. This was the resolution which the United States was going to violate by fomenting a unilateral attack through mercenaries.

Plans for the military operation had yet to be completed. The man chosen to head it was Colonel Castillo Armas, exiled in Honduras where he was trying to procure arms. Naturally United Fruit gave him financial help. While the attack against Guatemala was being prepared, Honduras and El Salvador accused Guatemala of wanting to invade them and recalled their ambassadors. Andrew Tully wrote: "There was concern felt that, should Arbenz gather added strength in these countries, he might even make a thrust at the Panama Canal." [13] But Arbenz, who knew he was in danger, did not plan to invade any country and was, above all, preoccupied with his agrarian reform program. At the same time, in the face of the preparations being made against him, he tried to buy arms, first in Western Europe where he did not find any sellers, and then in Eastern Europe. On May 17, 1954, John Foster Dulles announced that the Swedish ship *Alfhem*, coming from Stettin, was unloading in Guatemala two thousand tons of arms and munitions from the Skoda factories. The CIA had closely followed the progress of the boat and transmitted the information through its agents in Paris. On May 19, at Washington's instigation and to create the impression that there was a real international threat to the peace, Nicaragua broke off diplomatic relations with the Arbenz government.

"Five days later," wrote Eisenhower, "we announced

that the United States were airlifting arms to Honduras and Nicaragua"[14] to protect them against the nonexistent aggression Guatemala was planning. Two Globemasters were used to ship fifty tons of guns, machine guns, and ammunitions. "Most of these arms found their way to the headquarters of Colonel Castillo Armas," wrote Andrew Tully.[15]

The Arbenz government decreed a state of siege. On June 17, 1954, the forces of Castillo Armas entered Guatemala, but that invasion was not disclosed until the following day. Armas had three old American B-26 bombers. On June 22 Allen Dulles, Director of the CIA, told Eisenhower that Castillo Armas had lost two of his three bombers. The President of the United States calmly recorded in his memoirs: "The country which had originally supplied this equipment to Castillo [Armas] was willing now to supply him two P-51 fighter-bombers if the United States would agree to replace them."

It would be hard to imagine a clearer way of exposing the intrigues then being brewed in Central America with the complicity of several governments whose intention was to prevent an agrarian reform program which would have deprived United Fruit of 225,000 acres not under cultivation. Henry F. Holland, in charge of the Latin American desk in the State Department, opposed this transaction while Allen Dulles supported it. Eisenhower decided in favor of the latter because "Castillo Armas was obviously the only hope of restoring freedom in Guatemala." The intervention of the planes,* together with President Arbenz's vacillation, was decisive. Castillo Armas entered the capital on June 27. "He proved to be far more than mere rebel. . . . He enjoyed the devotion of his people." So much so that, three years later, on July 23, 1957, Castillo Armas was assassinated in his palace. In the meantime he had abrogated the

* Marcel Niedergang, *Les 20 Amériques latines* (Paris: Plon, 1965) p. 456 notes that "the pilots were mostly Americans."

agrarian reform law and returned to United Fruit its lands.

A week after the fall of the elected President, Arbenz, on June 30, John Foster Dulles, Secretary of State, said on television: "Now the future of Guatemala lies at the disposal of the Guatemalan people themselves." [16] In 1957 President Ydigoras Fuentes was elected President. He depended on the Army to maintain a "strongman regime" until 1963. He was succeeded by Colonel Enrique Peralta, who suspended all political activities "to save the nation from the permanent threat of Communist subversion."

But the "threat of subversion" did not arise from the activities of political parties. Essentially it thrives on the fact that 0.3 per cent of the proprietors own more than half of the agricultural land of which a large part is left fallow. Exactly why Arbenz had begun the distribution of uncultivated lands. The task he had started and which had been annulled by Castillo Armas and the CIA was especially urgent because the number of unemployed was rising in the countryside. Between 1950 and 1962 their number had increased from 789,000 to 1,195,000 or, in percentages, from 73.2 per cent to 78 per cent of the population. Since 1955 the very modest land-distribution program had benefited an average of 2,676 families per year, while the number of unemployed in the fields increased yearly by 30,000. The race against unemployment could be won only by rapid agrarian reform. Washington had brought it to a standstill. And it is naturally among the landless and unemployed peasants that the guerrillas find the welcome and sympathy without which their struggle would be bound to fail. Thus the basic causes of popular discontent were aggravated and order was only temporarily restored.

The United Fruit Company's empire was not saved. Its political interference in those countries of Central America where it was operating was so transparent that it fomented anti-American feelings. Although the company built schools, it paid its workers such meager wages ($1.80 per day in 1955) that it became the object of popular hatred. Throughout Latin America it was known as *El Pulpo*, the octopus, which wound its tentacles around several countries and a fairly large number of unrelated enterprises. The *Frutera* had a bad reputation, and it tarnished the image of the United States. The White House, the State Department, the CIA, and the Pentagon (which had supplied the planes) had just saved it. The American government was thus in a position to ask the company to transform itself and put on a public face less vulnerable to criticism. The Justice Department, armed with the same antitrust laws whose application had just been suspended in favor of a few oil companies in Iran, intervened and applied pressure. In Guatemala the empire's interests required that the antitrust laws compel a company to soften its policies. Even Samuel Zamurray, its former President who had retired in 1951, acknowledged that changes were necessary. To achieve the necessary metamorphosis so that the company would no longer seem to be a voracious monster, the Justice Department began to exert pressure. In 1958 United Fruit agreed to sell its railroad interests, to give up certain ancillary activities, in short to dismantle an empire whose too-obvious power had become a symbol. According to *Fortune* magazine "United [Fruit] has had to alter its policies in Latin America, for one reason because of developments in the policies of the United States Government, on whose good offices it must often depend."

The Eisenhower administration was still in office, as it had been at the time of the Castillo Armas *coup* against Arbenz, but this time it appreciated that "modifications of its policies" were necessary to maintain Washington's influence in Latin America.

United Fruit's size and operations amply justified the application of the antitrust laws. As *Fortune* magazine pointed out, "in Guatemala, Costa Rica and Honduras, it is the largest single private land-owner, largest single business, and largest corporate employer" [17] with 10,500 employees who are U.S. citizens and 69,000 recruited locally. In Panama it was the largest business after the Canal Company. It owned or leased 800,000 hectares, had a fleet of some sixty boats and 2,500 kilometers of railroad lines for the transportation of bananas, plus 40 per cent of the stock of the American-owned Central American Railroad with 1,300 kilometers of tracks. It also ran a radio station and a radio-telephone network, engaged in cattle raising, owned cocoa and palm tree plantations, and, in Cuba, 36,000 hectares of sugar cane. But bananas accounted for 80 per cent of its profits. That was *El Pulpo,* and its profits rose from $18.9 million in 1945 to $52.7 million in 1948 and $66 million in 1950.

But in 1958, when it began to yield to pressure from the Justice Department, the company was not in such good shape. During that year hurricanes had done $20 million worth of damage to its plantations—$19 million the year before. The excessive use of chemical products destroyed the ecological balance and caused insects to proliferate and diseases to attack the banana trees. United Fruit's profits fell from 33.4 per cent in 1950 to 15.4 per cent in 1957. The price of each of its 9 million shares fell from $73 in 1951 to $43 in 1959, and dividends per share declined from $4.50 to $2. A very conservative management had neglected basic research, leaving the company defenseless before the epidemics that ravaged its crops. A research laboratory was not opened until 1957 when younger men were gradually coming into executive positions.

Pressure from the Justice Department and the impetus provided by a more dynamic management changed the image of the company. It disposed of several holdings and "no longer dictates policy to Central American governments at least not openly and directly," commented the London *Economist*, "but the burden of action rests clearly with the American government today and not with the 'octopus arms' of corporate enterprise." [18]

United Fruit began to invest in other areas. In 1960 it bought a palm oil factory in Costa Rica. In 1966, in the United States, it bought J. Hungerford Smith & Co. and one of its affiliates, a chain of drive-in stores. At the start of 1967 it bought an ice cream factory with a network of five hundred distributors, in the hope of finding a new market for banana custard. Its management also invested in tourism in the form of hotels and motels in Western Europe and the United States. By diversifying not only in economic activity but in geographical location, the company does appear less and less as a monster dominating the political and economic life of Central America. The intervention of the Justice Department had compelled the monster to assume a less repugnant face. If need be, the empire can show flexibility to avoid an ostentatious display that invites criticism.

But United Fruit remains powerful and may become even more powerful than it had been before. The shares which paid $4.50 dividends in 1951 paid only 25 cents in 1960; but the dividend rose again in 1967 to $3.06. According to *Fortune* United Fruit had once supplied 66 per cent of the bananas consumed by the European market, then in 1959 only 10 per cent; but in 1967 its share rose again to 35 per cent, serious competition for African countries linked by various agreements to the Common Market. The banana empire adapts itself, raises wages, is less arrogant in Central American politics. It does not surrender. It does not give up, because giving up is not a characteristic of power. On the contrary, by extending its operations into other areas it strengthens its corporate structure, and thus is better able to withstand the blows which might be directed against it in Central America. The antitrust laws have never brought an economic empire to its knees. The example of United Fruit shows, on the contrary, how those very laws were used to save it, by shattering the old-fashioned methods and attitudes of an anachronistic management which had a knack for attracting the hostility of the people of Latin America.

A year after having brought about the fall of the Arbenz government with the complicity of the CIA and the American government, United Fruit elected General Walter Bedell Smith, then sixty years old, to its Board of Directors. Eisenhower's Chief of Staff during the Second World War, Ambassador to Moscow from 1946 to 1949, Director of the CIA from 1950 to 1953, and Under Secretary of State in 1953–1954, General Walter Bedell Smith had retired from public life after having headed the American delegation to the Geneva Conference on Indochina in 1954. Then United Fruit invited him to become a Director and he held the post until his death in August 1961. This choice of Director was typical of the old management's policies. Saved by the CIA, United Fruit had no scruples about bringing into the company the very man who had preceded Allen Dulles. Besides, General Bedell Smith was also a Vice-President of the American Machine & Foundry Co. and of its atomic subsidiary—two posts in which his retired-General's stars could be useful in negotiating lucrative contracts with the Pentagon. Such policies are still embraced, even increasingly with the passage of time, by the large companies which deal with the Defense Department. But United Fruit does not today have any former top executives of the CIA on its Board of Directors. Its management is in the hands of competent and dynamic businessmen. Washington's control over Central America is exercised through other channels.

.   .   .

Naturally, in spite of some changes, the CIA has not surrendered its role. The choice of methods is dictated by circumstances, and circumstances often make the CIA the appropriate instrument. Here is an example which shows the CIA not in collusion with a giant commercial and industrial company but with a labor union—the objective always being the overthrow of a government judged to be too revolutionary.

In April 1967 Harold Wilson, the British Prime Minister, had to answer a rather delicate question in the House of Commons. Posed by Stan Newens, Labourite member from Epping, this is how the question was phrased: "Will the Prime Minister make a statement on his policy towards efforts which are being made by the United States Central Intelligence Agency and other intelligence organizations to infiltrate and influence organizations which function in British administered territories, for purposes of subversion of law and order?"

The territory in question was Guyana, the former British Guiana (bordering on Venezuela, Dutch Guiana, and Brazil) and the organization infiltrated by the CIA was a union affiliated with Public Services International, whose headquarters is in London. The 1964 operation aimed at overthrowing the Guyanese Prime Minister Cheddy Jagan, and it cost the CIA £250,000, or $600,000. But it cost Guyana 170 dead, hundreds of wounded, and some £10,000,000 in damages.

The first elections held in British Guiana in 1953 brought to power Cheddy Jagan who is of Indian extraction and won handily over his black opponent, Forbes Burnham. Guyana has 600,000 inhabitants, of whom 300,000 are Indian and 200,000 black, and the votes received by the two candidates were roughly divided according to the two ethnic groups represented by the voters. But, at the same time, while Forbes Burnham was clearly conservative and tied to the

American AFL-CIO, Cheddy Jagan was a progressive (therefore "Communist" to his opponents and to Washington); his wife was always called "Red Janet" in the United States press. Surprised by the election of Cheddy Jagan after a dynamic campaign, and by his first policy statements which made clear that he planned to carry out his intentions, the government in London sent a warship to Georgetown and announced that new elections would be held in 1957. But Cheddy Jagan won in 1957 as handily as he had four years earlier.

That is when the CIA went into action. It made use of the Guyanese unions, which had altogether 40,000 members in both ethnic groups and political parties. The two major Guyanese unions, the sugar workers' union and the civil servants' union, were rather hostile to Cheddy Jagan for ethnic reasons. The civil servants' union was affiliated with Public Services International (PSI), headquartered in London and a member of the International Confederation of Free Trade Unions (ICFTU) with headquarters in Brussels. In 1958, when the PSI was in financial straits, its American affiliate headed by Arnold Zander announced that new backing had been found. And, to be sure, an anonymous donor did offer £2,000 that year, a modest sum which was to finance an organizing campaign in Latin America. The campaign was directed by William J. Doherty, Jr., who had earlier ties with the CIA. The following year Arnold Zander announced that the donor had increased his contribution, so that PSI could organize a Latin American section under Howard McCabe, an American who soon set up meetings where he handed out photographs of himself and cigarette lighters engraved: WITH THE COMPLIMENTS OF THE PSI. The international organization in London might have wondered how Arnold Zander's union with an annual income of £7,200 could each year contribute £30,000 to the Latin American section. But the unions affiliated with the ICFTU are not very curious about the origin of money intended to "fight Communism." In any case, the Secretary of the PSI stated: "We did not ask where the money came from . . . because I think we all knew."

In Guyana the test of strength began in 1963. Cheddy Jagan's government proposed a law which would have forced employers in Guyana—as in the United States since the Wagner Act—to recognize and negotiate with the union chosen by their workers in secret ballot. Cheddy Jagan thus hoped to break the control that the conservative Forbes Burnham exercised over the Guyanese unions, which also were supported by the very conservative AFL-CIO, whose President, George Meany, is a fanatical anti-Communist. The AFL-CIO considers the Wagner Act a true "charter" which made possible its success. But it did not feel that that was sufficient reason for a similar measure to be adopted in Guyana and it encouraged its friend Forbes Burnham to oppose the proposed law. Thus, it was to demonstrate "the opposition of the unions" to the draft proposed by Cheddy Jagan that Forbes Burnham triggered the strike of April 1963.

Cheddy Jagan's government was not worried by the move, since it was convinced that the workers knew where their true interests lay. It was also certain that even the most conservative workers could not long remain on strike because of their lack of financial resources. That is where it made a mistake, for it did not count on CIA funds—transmitted through Arnold Zander, the London PSI, and its representative in Georgetown, Howard McCabe. From London the PSI sent the strikers £2,000 as a "gift of solidarity." That amount was certainly not enough to "carry" the strike for sixty-nine days, the longest strike in the history of Guyana. But the "kind donor," through the conduit of Arnold Zander, sent Howard McCabe £150,-000. Faced with a continuing strike Cheddy Jagan's government showed flexibility. As a progressive Jagan did not want to cut himself off from the masses. But, remarked the mediator from London, though "Jagan was giving in to everything the strikers wanted . . . as soon as he did they erected new demands." Fighting broke out and blood was spilled. That did not bother either the AFL-CIO, which supported Forbes Burnham, or the CIA, which was financing him. Quite to the contrary.

In London the British government, acting on a proposal made by Duncan Sandys, decided to invoke a clause of the Guyanese Constitution which permitted the reapportionment of the votes received by Cheddy Jagan. Had he not shown himself incapable of maintaining order? Thanks to that far-sighted constitutional clause, Cheddy Jagan lost the 1964 election, and Forbes Burnham, "the friend of the United States," became Prime Minister.

At the time Cheddy Jagan and a group of Labourite MP's in London complained of the CIA's interference in the internal affairs of Guyana, but no one paid any attention to their statements, since it was such a common occurrence to blame the CIA even when there was no justification. It was hardly noticed that in the United States, also in 1964, Arnold Zander—his mission accomplished—had lost the Presidency of his union to Jerry Wurf, who closed down the Latin American section and got rid of the all-too-conspicuous Howard McCabe.[19]

But it is always dangerous to brush off anyone who has faithfully served the CIA. In February 1967 Arnold Zander publicly admitted that his union had been abundantly financed by the CIA, which sent him funds through the Gotham Foundation, one of the seventeen organizations that received CIA funds directly and transmitted them to various beneficiaries through seven other foundations to hide the trial.*

* These are the seventeen foundations used by the CIA: Tower Fund, Gotham Foundation, Borden Trust, Beacon Fund, Heights Fund, Willi-

. . .

It is a simple matter for the empire to depose those who bother it merely by supporting men or groups belonging to the elite. The cooperation between the CIA and such personages as General Zahedi appeared to be perfectly natural, and the complicity between the CIA and United Fruit did not surprise anyone. More delicate is an operation which relies on trade union channels. The difficulty is reduced when American unions agree to serve as both intermediaries and "union label." The Central Committee of the AFL-CIO, always ready to take part in the anti-Communist struggle, plays a major role supporting the interest of the empire—for potential conflicts of interest, at the heart of the empire, between wage-earners and great industrial companies are less crucial than the conflict between external forces and an empire in whose prosperity American workers participate on a proportionate basis. That is why, for example, the AFL-CIO wholeheartedly supported President Johnson's policy in Vietnam, just as throughout the Cold War it had manifested a virulent anti-Communism. In the name of that same militant anti-Communism the CIA and the AFL-CIO intervened hand-in-hand not only in underveloped countries still not entirely free of their colonial

---

ford-Telford Fund, Edsel Fund, San Miguel Fund, Kentfield Fund, Monroe Fund, Michigan Fund, Andrew Hamilton Fund, Appalachian Fund, Wynnewood Fund, Charles Price Whitten Trust, James Carlisle Trust, Price Fund. These seventeen foundations channelled the money through seven intermediaries: M. D. Anderson Foundation, Hoblitzelle Foundation, J. M. Kaplan Fund, Baird Foundation, Rabb Charitable Foundation, Marshall Foundation, J. Frederick Brown Foundation. Among the principal beneficiaries: American Council for the International Commission of Jurists, Congress for Cultural Freedom, Institute of International Labor Research, Synod of the Bishops of the Russian Church Outside Russia, African-American Institute, American Friends of the Middle East, American Society of African Culture, Institute of International Education, Institute of Public Administration, Atwater Research Program in North Africa, National Student Association, Operations and Policy Research.

shackles—such as Guyana—but also in industrialized countries like France, Germany, Italy, etc., to exert influence on unions, newspapers, and political parties.

At the beginning of 1967 a scandal broke when a former President of the National Student Association revealed how that organization had been financed by the CIA. The affair had lively repercussions, and this is not the place to analyze them, but it also led to a series of "exposés." Actually, it was more a matter of confirming facts which were widely known and had never specifically been denied.[20] The value of this exercise lies in showing how the CIA works in countries that are allied to the United States and have clearly anti-Communist regimes and views of their own on the ways to ensure their security.

In May 1967 Thomas W. Braden, a former associate of Allen Dulles in the CIA, supplied some precise details on the birth of non-Communist unions in Western Europe and in particular the *Force Ouvrière* in France. The operation was managed by Jay Lovestone, a former head of the American Communist Party in the 1930's and now director of the international affairs section of the American Federation of Labor, and by Irving Brown who represented the AFL and later, after 1955, the AFL-CIO in Europe.

During the great strike wave in the winter of 1947, to split the CGT (General Confederation of Labor) and create the *Force Ouvrière*, the first funds were supplied by David Dubinsky, President of the International Ladies' Garment Workers Union and then by the CIA itself. A similar operation was subsequently carried out in Italy and in other countries. The budget devoted to this purpose reached almost a million dollars a year.

In May 1946 Léon Blum, then on a mission to the United States, told Jean Davidson, a correspondent of the French Press Agency in Washington, that "many American diplomats with whom I have spoken are convinced that Socialism can become the best rampart against Communism in Europe." It certainly could not have been very difficult to convince the French Socialist Party to assume that task. However, at the time, the State Department denied the assertion of an American news analyst that Fred Vinson, Secretary of the Treasury and a personal friend of President Truman, had suggested to Léon Blum that Socialists join other parties to throw the Communists out of the government. The Communist Party then held a Vice-Presidency in the Council (Maurice Thorez), and the ministries of Armaments (Charles Tillon), Industrial Production (Marcel Paul), Labor (Ambroise Croizat), and Reconstruction and Urban Affairs (Laurent Casanova). Twelve months later their ouster was effected while the Socialist Ramadier was President of the Council.

In the fall of 1947 Léon Jouhaux, President of the CGT, attended a session of the United Nations and used the opportunity to meet with various American union leaders in New York and Washington. Jean Davidson, during a dinner in the American capital, asked Léon Jouhaux the following question: "The Americans would very much like to create a split in the CGT and separate the non-Communist from the Communist elements. What do you think of it, Mr. Jouhaux?"

And Léon Jouhaux replied: "My friends, as you well know, more than anyone I have fought with all my strength to create in France a single confederation of workers, the CGT. . . . As long as I am alive, the CGT cannot be split. It would be a disaster for French labor and I would oppose it with all my strength."

A few months later, Léon Jouhaux brought about the split in the CGT by personally assuming the leadership of the *Force Ouvrière*.[21] Six years later George Meany, President of the American Federation of Labor, was the guest of honor at the National Press Club in Washington, and said: "I'm proud to tell you now—because we were not permitted to reveal it before—that it is with money from American workers, money from workers in Detroit and elsewhere, that it was possible for us to bring about the split in the CGT—something *very important for all of us*—by creating a friendly union, the *Force Ouvrière*."

Thus at the very moment when George Meany was working for the unification of American trade unionism, he was breaking up unionism in France. The first money going to the *Force Ouvrière* did, indeed, come from American trade unions. But afterwards? "When they [Jay Lovestone and Irving Brown] ran out of money, Mr. Braden said, they appealed to the intelligence agency, citing similar projects in Italy and other West European countries. The first subsidies to Mr. Lovestone and Mr. Brown were paid by intelligence agencies in the late 1940's, Mr. Braden said, and he personally made some of the payments after he arrived at the CIA in 1950." [22] Speaking for himself, for Irving Brown, and for the AFL-CIO, Jay Lovestone declared that the story was "completely false." He added: "I have never received any money from the CIA." But for many years Walter Reuther, President of the auto workers union, and his brother Victor had accused Lovestone of being a CIA agent in the midst of the AFL-CIO Executive Board. Furthermore, they acknowledged that during the 1950's they had "agreed, not without distaste, to a request that they transmit government funds which were to be added to insufficient funds from the American labor movement." Through them several million dollars had been transmitted to a German union. Walter Reuther and his United Auto Workers had never exhibited the virulent anti-Communism of George Meany, Jay Lovestone, or Irving Brown. Thus it is inconceivable that these three men would have withheld from the CIA services which the brothers Reuther had provided "not without distaste." Jay Lovestone's categorical denial assumes its full significance when it is remembered that George Meany himself admitted having given $35,000 to the *Force Ouvrière*. But it is unlikely that there will be a thorough inquiry into these activities, since it would reveal the names of the trade unions and labor leaders who had received money from the CIA not only in Europe but also in Africa, Latin America, and Asia. When it comes to corruption, the empire has never been stingy.

But financial intervention was not limited to the trade union field. Jean Davidson recalled that "Léon Jouhaux's visit to Washington was to be followed by those of several French and European newspaper publishers (so-called enlightened Socialists) looking for financial help from the State Department and, failing in that, from American labor unions." It should be added: "or from the CIA with respectable foundations fronting for it." [23]

This is what René Naegelen wrote in *Le Populaire* on May 15, 1952: "We have been helped by our comrades of the International Ladies' Garment Workers Union in New York, whose President is our friend Dubinsky. . . . I want to add that we are proud to have received a contribution which comes from the dues of workers, men and women, and which, as we well know, was given as a token of affection and gratitude for Léon Blum."

Gratitude for what? For the ouster of Communists from the Ramadier government? For splitting the CGT, thanks to Léon Jouhaux? Be that as it may, *Le Populaire* was not the only newspaper subsidized with dollars, some of which came from American unions and some from the CIA. These subsidies did not, however, save *Le Populaire*, because its political positions prevented it from finding an audience. Its format was reduced to a single sheet, after it had several times suspended publication. Several other Parisian newspapers thus subsidized expired in their own good time.

In a study of "the finances of political parties" in France,

Raymond Fusilier in the *Revue Politique et Parlementaire* of November, 1953, cited an article in the *New York Times* of December 13, 1951, which estimated that United States support of the French press reached 2,450 million francs in 1951 alone. Walter Reuther has confirmed that such monies did not come *only* from labor unions and philanthropic foundations, and that both kinds of organizations agreed to conceal the real origin of the funds that the CIA generously distributed in Europe. For its role was not restricted to fighting subversion. It would eventually finance its own form of subversion, notably by pouring money into (relatively recent) election campaigns in France and Italy.

The CIA and the other American intelligence agencies can point to a good many successes. In 1955 the CIA dug a tunnel in Berlin which was over 300 meters long, and enabled it to attach a wiretap to Soviet telephone lines and record official messages over a period of months. This is classic espionage.

For four years U-2's flew over Soviet territory taking very accurate aerial photographs and recording radiophonic communications. This is modern technology in the service of espionage and, like all other intelligence-gathering techniques, it has its drawbacks: the lies told by American leaders, who did not know the pilot, Francis Gary Powers, had been captured alive by the Russians; and Eisenhower's refusal to apologize to Khrushchev, which aborted a "summit" meeting scheduled for May 1960 in Paris. Likewise, the capture in 1968 of the *Pueblo* off the North Korean coast placed Washington in a delicate position, but in spite of this "mishap," American authorities have for years benefited, and continue to benefit, from the valuable information gathered little by little everywhere by spy ships. The flight of an American "spy plane" over the French atomic installations at Pierrelatte also provoked political and diplomatic repercussions. But U-2's and pilotless planes continue the surveillance of Cuba and of many other countries, including the immense nation of China over which several planes have been shot down. Those are the risks of the job. When Khrushchev delivered his "secret" report on Stalin's crimes before the Twentieth Congress of the Soviet Communist Party in 1956, a CIA agent succeeded in obtaining the text. Its publication in the West represented one of the CIA's most important and successful political operations.

But when, in Laos, on December 31, 1959, the same CIA helped General Phoumi Nosavan seize power, it committed a serious error in political analysis by making a summary judgment that those elements most useful to the empire would be the ones most strongly anti-Communist, no matter how corrupt. The CIA's ploy resulted in a temporary *rapprochement* between Laotian neutralists and the Soviets, "only too happy to insinuate themselves into a country, then the private property of the Americans and Chinese," as André Fontaine remarked,[24] and the United States had to restore to power the neutralist government overthrown by the CIA. Of even greater consequence was the error made by the CIA in Vietnam.

The authors of *The Invisible Government* tell how Lansdale, a CIA agent, had been instructed in 1954 by Eisenhower and John Foster Dulles to find the man capable of governing in Saigon after the signing of the Geneva accords. He recommended Ngo Dinh Diem, who had Cardinal Spellman's blessing. "But Diem and Nhu refused to grant political freedom to the opposition parties, despite Lansdale's warning that the country would be plagued by conspiracy if legitimate parties were not permitted to operate openly. Lansdale made a special trip to Washington in an effort to induce the Dulles brothers to apply pressure on Diem to institute political reforms in South Vietnam. But Lansdale failed. He was told that it had been decided that Diem provided the only practical alternative to a Commu-

nist take-over and that he was to be supported without
qualification. Overruled, Lansdale lost his influence as the
unofficial emissary of the Invisible Government in Vietnam." [25] In this instance a CIA agent had been more far-
sighted than his chief, Allen Dulles, and Washington. Not
until another administration, John F. Kennedy's, would
Diem be eliminated from the political scene by an assassination carried out with the help of the CIA. But by then
the political situation in South Vietnam would already, politically speaking, be irremedially compromised.

Since we are not familiar with the whole dossier, we will
make no attempt to draw up a balance sheet of CIA failures
and successes, of contrasting its errors in Laos, Vietnam,
and Cuba with what it considers its outstanding successes
in Iran, Guatemala, and the Philippines, where it managed
President Magsaysay's election in 1953 and stifled the Huk
guerrillas for several years. In certain countries the situation
remains so unsettled that a final judgment cannot be made.
For example, in 1964 the CIA intervened in the Congo by
sending three B-26 planes to rescue a column of six hundred
Congolese and one hundred white mercenaries. The planes
were piloted by anti-Castro Cubans who had escaped from
the Bay of Pigs, serviced by European mechanics recruited
through small ads in London newspapers, and directed by
CIA agents disguised as American diplomats. Although the
primary objective was achieved, the Congo is still in not
much better condition. Likewise, social and political tensions remain high in Iran since Mossadegh's overthrow,
guerrilla bands control the jungles in Guatemala, and insur-
gency can again break out in the Philippines any day. The
responsibility of determining the usefulness of the CIA and
of deciding whether a billion dollars a year should be devoted to supporting thousands of agents commanded by
CIA headquarters in Langley, Virginia, rests with the
elected representatives of the American people.

But the real problem is elsewhere. The CIA never makes an important decision without the approval of the President of the United States. When, at the start of 1967, the National Student Association revealed that it had been financed by the CIA, President Johnson washed his hands of the affair by stating that he had not been informed. But his predecessors in the White House, Truman, Eisenhower, and Kennedy, had in various situations declared that the CIA operated under the personal authority of the President. Johnson, in the face of the publicity given the CIA subsidies, named a Commission of Inquiry, as Kennedy had done before him in the aftermath of the resounding Bay of Pigs fiasco. But these Commissions of Inquiry produce only minor modifications, usually a few changes in the agency's leadership and ineffective control committees.

The fact is that the Director of the CIA is a *de jure* member of the National Security Council which meets each week with the President of the United States and the Secretaries of State and Defense to examine the major issues to be dealt with. Every day the Director of the CIA sends the President of the United States a top-secret report summarizing all the information which must be brought to his attention. One of the close presidential aides, in charge of so-called national security problems, maintains permanent liaison between the Chief Executive and the intelligence agencies. The Director of the CIA, through a private telephone or in person, has free access to the President when, where, and how he wants it. An official who assumes so many major responsibilities cannot be by-passed or effectively controlled.

Competition between the various intelligence agencies offers no assurances. The CIA has 10,000 "employees," which means it is less powerful than the National Security Agency, entrusted principally with decoding secret messages, which has 14,000 and a budget larger than the CIA's.

Besides, there are the intelligence services of the State Department, the Atomic Energy Commission, the Army, the Air Force and the Navy, whose representatives are on the U.S. Intelligence Board.

Among all of them, the CIA has received the greatest amount of publicity because it is not satisfied only with collecting and analyzing intelligence of all kinds, but has also undertaken a number of operations which have had reverberations throughout the world. It has thus become, both within and outside the United States, the living symbol of cloak-and-dagger activities in the service of America's empire—to the point where the "exploits" of other secret agencies are often inaccurately attributed to it. However, this confusion of responsibilities is of no practical significance because every important operation of the American secret services is executed with the approval of the President of the United States and his principal advisers and colleagues. If divergencies sometimes exist in the elaborate reports prepared by the different intelligence organisms, it is merely a question of details, and only slight variations appear in the policies recommended. And, in any case, the President makes the final decision.

The policies of the CIA are no different from the policies of the State Department or those of the White House. The Eisenhower memoirs clearly and explicitly testify to the collective responsibility of the American government in the operations mounted against Mossadegh in Iran and against Arbenz in Guatemala. Similarly, Kennedy's public statements and the books by Schlesinger and Sorensen incontestably reveal the collective responsibility of the American government in the absurd and criminal Bay of Pigs operation.[26]

It is not a question of honorable elected representatives of a very democratic country, full of idealism and good will, versus sinister intelligence agents capable of seducing eminently respectable political leaders to their inglorious practices. A President cloaked with supreme authority, a venerable Senator with a popular mandate, a courteous and distinguished diplomat certainly do not resemble the U-2 pilots, the agents who infiltrate behind the Iron Curtain, the specialists who prime saboteurs, the straw men charged with buying complicity. Yet all of them contribute, each on his own level, to the formulation and execution of the same policy. All of them pursue, each in his own way, a single and similar objective. For each one it is a matter of maintaining, of strengthening, of consolidating the foundations of the most powerful country in the world, and of extending America's influence beyond its borders to thwart the actions of any country, Communist or not, which might attempt to oppose its activities or disapproves of its means and methods.

Men of very different backgrounds participate in this task. A large number of academicians representing all the great intellectual disciplines work at Langley in the interpretation and analysis of the political, economic, social, scientific, and military information which flows into the CIA from the four corners of the earth. Members of the faculty of Michigan State University agreed to serve the CIA directly in Vietnam. The Center of International Studies at M.I.T. was founded in 1951 with a gift of $300,000 from the CIA, which subsequently continued to finance it; when, on April 26, 1966, a spokesman for the Center announced it was breaking all ties with the CIA, he specified that it was done "reluctantly" and "for practical and not moral reasons."

A high official of the State Department said: "There is more freedom per square yard in the CIA than in any other sector of government." [27] There is no reason to doubt such an assertion, for American liberals share with their compatriots the same faith in the mission of the United States in a world threatened by subversion and by Communism. To be sure, all liberals do not agree to take their paycheck from the CIA, and it is primarily among them that Americans who criticize the intelligence agency are found. A Pulitzer Prize-winning historian with an international reputation, an outstanding liberal, does not exempt the CIA from severe criticism in the book that he devoted to Kennedy's Presidency. But the same historian, Arthur Schlesinger, Jr., at Kennedy's request agreed to write the White Paper in which the American government in March 1961, three weeks before the Bay of Pigs, revealed its policy toward Cuba. And that White Paper contained all the errors of judgment committed by the CIA in regard to the Castro regime: Fidel Castro ruled through oppression, he had betrayed the original objectives of his revolution, etc. Unconsciously, and whatever his reservations about the CIA were, this leading liberal accepted the CIA's basic arguments. Furthermore, he gave them a stylistic elegance, an exalted motivation, an apparent internal coherence, a generous tone, a deceptive breadth of vision likely to influence many minds. He also gave them the moral imprimatur of a liberal intellectual.

In spite of the talents it uses, in spite of the enormous resources at its disposal, the CIA is neither infallible nor invulnerable. Arthur Schlesinger tells that, at the end of March, 1961, he called Kennedy's attention to an article in an American newspaper which expressed an opinion concerning Fidel Castro's popularity that was appreciably different from the CIA's. At the same time, during a private conversation with a high American official, a French journalist also emphasized to his interlocutor that Fidel Castro enjoyed much greater support than was believed in Washington. But that evaluation was not accepted. He was told that the American authorities had very reliable information which left no room for doubt.

On the very day following Fidel Castro's victory at the Bay of Pigs, the American official wrote the French journalist a letter which consisted of a single sentence: "Apparently, your information was better than ours." For the popular uprising which Washington had counted on had not materialized. However, the sources of information at the disposal of the CIA are infinitely superior to those of a French or an American journalist. The CIA had a whole group of men whose job was the painstaking analysis of Cuban newspapers, which a journalist can only quickly peruse. The CIA, with its electronic machines, stores and classifies a mass of information coming to it from varied sources. The CIA possesses hundreds of agents and informers, while the journalist works alone. And yet, in guiding the policy of the most powerful country in the world, the CIA made an error of judgment that no journalist honestly doing his job has made. And that error inflicted on the American empire one of its most painful political defeats. In a similar way the CIA, through its reports on the situation in Vietnam, has greatly contributed in the making of a policy which has led the United States to become bogged down in an insoluble conflict with more than 500,000 soldiers.

The material and human means at the disposal of the CIA are not sufficient to guarantee its triumph. When success crowns its operations, as in Guatemala, it brings down upon its head the hostility of a whole continent without even locally assuring a lasting victory. When a failure, as in Cuba, exposes its internal weaknesses to broad daylight, the hostility directed toward it is tinged with irony because one of the empire's principal instruments has been shown to be less formidable and less frightening.

X

Governing the Empire

In an amphitheater of the State Department in Washington some two hundred of the empire's most powerful barons gathered to attend a performance inconceivable in any other country. There were uniforms representing the three branches of the Pentagon and among the civilians were career diplomats, but also some of the brilliant minds of the RAND Corporation, representatives of large universities, and above all top executives of the most powerful companies involved in arms production: Lockheed Aircraft Corporation, International Telephone and Telegraph, Xerox, and many others. They had answered an appeal of the National Security Industrial Association to examine the problems they would face in the next decade. Courteously —even at times interrupting with applause—they listened to the harshest indictment ever made of them and all they represented:

"You are the most dangerous body of men at present in the world. You have disrupted ancient social patterns, debauched their cultures, fomented tribal and other wars, and in Vietnam engaged yourselves in genocide. It is because of you that there are riots in Newark. You are the manufacturers of napalm, fragmentation bombs, the planes that destroy rice. Your weapons have killed hundreds of thousands in Vietnam and you will kill hundreds of thousands in other Vietnams." [1]

Thus spoke Paul Goodman on October 19, 1967, before the National Security Industrial Association, which numbers among its permanent members the four hundred major suppliers of the Pentagon, as well as other government organisms, among which is the CIA. Those who live on arms production, on war preparedness, on the military budget had agreed that the last speaker to address their meeting be a man who, at fifty-six, is one of their most eloquent adversaries in the United States. They knew what to expect, since, for many years, in books, articles and lectures, Paul Goodman had devoted his vast learning and his polemical talents to attacking those men whom he considers "the most dangerous in the world today." And, besides, he did not take them by surprise. He had submitted the text of his speech in advance to the chairman of the meeting, who was thus able to see that, through courtesy or good will, Paul Goodman had skipped a sentence in his indictment: "You devise and make the atom bombs." Not to seem unreasonable he decided that it would be unnecessary to return, twenty-two years later, to the memory of Hiroshima and Nagasaki, or to envision a possible nuclear conflict in the future. He left the projection of guilt by anticipation to the other side; like Judge Kaufman who, in 1951, after sending Ethel and Julius Rosenberg to the electric chair, declared they were responsible for the dead of the Third World War —something which would be grounds for appeal in France.

No one in Paris could conceive of staff officers, Marcel Dassault, the officials of the Atomic Energy Commission, and representatives of the "arms merchants" inviting a left-wing intellectual—and who would possess Paul Goodman's authority?—to subject them to such an indictment. Nor is such an event any more conceivable in London, Bonn, or Rome, not to mention Moscow or Peking. Why was it possible in Washington? For one thing there is the American principle of fair play, for another, respect for the right of debate, and for pessimists, the masochistic tendencies of a people both self-confident and apprehensive about its future. "Realists" will point out that an intellectual's speech-making has never reduced a military budget or slowed down an arms program. The fact remains that, in a general way, Americans are open to criticism and they rarely need go beyond their own borders to find ammunition for re-evaluations of themselves. They themselves produce the men who are far-seeing and courageous enough to voice the clearest warnings. And if they do not always heed such advice, they at least know enough to listen.

In fact, in spite of internal criticism, the machine continues to function as if it were self-propelled. Capable of great bursts of activity after receiving a shock, such as Pearl Harbor or the launching of the first Sputnik, it often responds poorly to the kind of prodding the government would like to provide. Despite enormous intellectual and technical means at its disposal, despite innumerable teams of experts and the far-reaching techniques created by operational research, despite computers and the advanced state of forecasting, the government of the empire often appears to be the prisoner of the prodigious power at its command. Has the machinery become too heavy and too complex to be still governable by human beings? That is what American politicians who have discovered in the country's history several reasons for retrospective anxiety seem to fear: too many decisions have been imposed on the government of the United States without its desiring them or being prepared for them, and policies developed by Washington have rarely controlled events, except for a short time.

It is clear, for example, that the United States has not

deliberately taken the road to imperialism. Emerson believed that "the office of America is to liberate," but now it rules over the most powerful empire that history has known. It is as if fate has drawn it onto this path. As Senator Fulbright has noted, "powerful nations have always devoted the major part of their resources to build empires." [2] Power calls for empire. And there are many historical circumstances in which the combination of forces, the existential situation and the dynamism of power, have imposed on Washington's leaders a policy they had not chosen. An anti-imperialist like McKinley, despite the hostility of intellectuals like Mark Twain and businessmen like Carnegie, started a war of colonial conquest whose basic causes perplex a diplomat-historian like George Kennan. Twenty-five years apart, two Presidents who were anxious to keep their country out of war and were supported by primarily unbellicose majorities did not prevent the United States from being plunged into two world conflicts which would profoundly change the internal structure of the country and its role in international affairs. For those two wars greatly increased American potential while marking the decline of the European powers.

However great its dynamism and its wealth, a people is not necessarily absolute master of its fate. And when attempts are made to blueprint its destiny, there is no certainty that events can be made to proceed clearly along the lines that have been drawn. Far from making the world "safe for democracy," Wilsonian idealism encouraged a wave of isolationism which paved the way for the Second World War. Likewise, in November 1964, Lyndon Johnson —opposing Barry Goldwater who had advocated intensification of the war in South Vietnam and bombing the North—was triumphantly elected and, in February 1965, inaugurated the policies he had condemned three months earlier. Though outraged by the colonial war that France was waging in Indochina, America had amply financed it before itself becoming engaged on the same terrain in a much more destructive war. Sometimes errors of judgment have prevented Washington from making realistic policies: Dean Rusk considered the Peking government no more than Moscow's puppet at a time when the conditions for a break between the "Big Two" of Socialism had already matured. At times the empire's government has underestimated the obstacles it would have to overcome to translate its intentions into actions. That is why the Alliance for Progress did not lead to the economic "take-off" that John F. Kennedy hoped for, and would not prevent military dictatorships from multiplying in Latin America.

In other situations the absence of a policy—or, rather, a policy too superficially conceived—has led America into an impasse. Looking back, it is easy to see that Washington has no coherent policy in Vietnam, where it has become increasingly involved and bogged down in a conflict which a whole series of different justifications do not render comprehensible. And even when a farsighted policy which is both unselfish and in conformity with American interests is successfully carried out, it too leads to unsuspected problems: the Marshall Plan permitted the reconstruction of Europe which, once more on its feet, became an increasingly difficult partner.

The world certainly changed quickly, more quickly than the ideas of the empire's leaders. In the way that some generals are always one war behind, a great country easily finds itself one problem behind, especially when the whole planet requires its attention. And the rate of change is just as rapid within its borders. The problem of the blacks tragically illustrates the difficulty the United States has in taking action when it is not compelled to by events. The black ghettos in the large cities have been growing, especially since the First World War, but it would take forty years until riots forced the government's executive and legislative branches to adopt solutions which proved to have little effectiveness. In the south, American democracy waited for the Twenty-fourth Amendment to the Constitution, passed by Congress in 1962 and put into effect in 1964, to prohibit certain legal dodges which, like the poll tax, prevented the blacks from voting. And one is struck by the slow implementation of that law and the Supreme Court's 1954 decision outlawing school segregation, when contrasted to the rapid awakening of the black masses. An anecdote illustrates how political decisions lag behind problems. In 1942, in spite of the racial segregation then existing in the Army, the boxing champion Joe Louis was happy to wear the uniform because, as he said, "What's wrong with my country ain't nothing Hitler can fix." Twenty-five years later, in spite of the progress in racial integration made by the Army, in spite of the anti-Communism prevailing in the United States, the world boxing champion Cassius Clay refused to serve in the Army because, as he said, "I don't have no quarrel with those Viet Congs." [3] Between 1942 and 1967 the government had greatly intensified its efforts to lessen racial tensions. But black awareness has developed much more quickly than integrationist legislation, and if those laws have spurred the demands of the blacks they have not proved sufficient to change white attitudes, which are the principal obstacle to a solution of the racial problem.

In foreign as in domestic affairs the degree of people's political awareness both permits or prevents certain governmental decisions. Because of the competition with Communist forces, the electors and the elected do not raise too many objections to the enormous defense and space-exploration budgets. For the same reason, after the Tito-Stalin break, the United States agreed to supply Yugoslavia alone with as much economic aid as was given to all of Latin America, although the latter had ten times more people. Shocks being necessary for the birth of major decisions, the Alliance for Progress was the illegitimate child of the Cuban revolution, but Congress has never granted the Executive the full amount of money (a billion dollars per year) that Kennedy had requested for that purpose. The weight of public opinion is such a determining factor that John Foster Dulles, having seen the danger of leaving China isolated, could never establish the diplomatic relations he deemed necessary; he yielded instead to the pressures of the "China Lobby."

The multiplication of such examples leads to only one conclusion: even the vast powers of the White House and the enormous power of American society do not suffice to shape the world according to American wishes. If United States history contains striking successes and surprising bursts of energy, it also records failures, half-failures, evidence of short-sightedness and impotence, aborted dreams and projects conceived too late to resolve problems which, in time, festered to the point where small hope could remain of clearing them up.

Far too many decisions have been taken under the pressure of events and in such a pragmatic way to possibly believe that politicians, businessmen, and military leaders had one day in Washington drawn up a specific imperialist plan that would assure the United States world hegemony. The requirements of a rich and powerful society which does not conceive of any other policy than continuous growth, successive improvisations and a felicitous set of circumstances have raised the empire to its present state of power. The empire's government is neither the incarnation of Absolute Evil—as its most rabid adversaries claim to believe—nor the ultimate guardian of Good, of Civilization and Progress, as certain people in the United States and elsewhere would like to believe. To avoid drawing a caricature, it is necessary to examine the power structure and, in the light of the facts cited in preceding chapters, the mechanisms which lead to major decisions. In this way the strengths, weaknesses, and ambiguities of the empire and its government can be shown.

Transposed into an age of advanced technology, the dream of imperialism's forerunners is not dead. In the last century Admiral Mahan wanted a powerful Navy. Today, with its aircraft carriers and its nuclear missile-carrying submarines, the Navy rules over the seas—protecting the commercial convoys which supply the empire, always ready to defend allies and even neutrals, capable of swiftly landing Marines in Lebanon, in the Dominican Republic, and in Vietnam, repeating on a grand scale the "small maneuvers" represented by the interventions in Nicaragua, Haiti, the Dominican Republic, and Mexico at the beginning of the century.

Another prophet of imperialism, Theodore Roosevelt, used the harshest possible words to denounce the softness of President McKinley before he himself became President and demonstrated his vigor. Today that era is completely passed and Senator Fulbright rightly criticizes "the arrogance of power" expressed by multiple interventions in the internal affairs of other countries, in the same way that Adlai Stevenson attacked the "golden chains" America placed around the necks of its friends and clients. The United States has scattered throughout the world the naval bases that Mahan and Theodore Roosevelt wished for, and its aviation has given it a power undreamed of by imperialism's forerunners.

Admiral Mahan denied that he harbored any "aggressive designs"; but it is with speeches extolling peace that Eisenhower, Dulles, Kennedy, Dean Rusk, Stevenson, and Lyndon Johnson made background music for armed operations in Iran, Guatemala, Cuba, the Dominican Republic, Vietnam, Thailand, the Congo, and elsewhere. Because the desire for peace predominated, a leader as bellicose as Barry Goldwater was rejected by a majority of voters; he received, nevertheless, over 27 million votes. In addition, criticism of Johnson was slow in coming. After all, if he intensified the war after having preached peace he must have had good reasons for doing so, and only a few fanatics would have blamed him if he had forcibly succeeded in making Hanoi capitulate in 1965. Violence is to be condemned especially when it fails.

The Reverend Josiah Strong, who had proclaimed in 1886 that God had given America the mission of civilizing the world, found followers among the ecclesiastical hierarchy more eminent than he—Cardinal Spellman having advocated total victory in Vietnam, a goal which had never been the American government's official and avowed objective, found some even more extreme. But the clergy is today as divided as it was in the last century when America was on the threshold of its imperialist venture. Modern means of communication have made it possible to present arguments before a vast public. Priests and pastors are in the forefront of the opposition to a policy of force. But they encounter difficulties unknown a few generations earlier because loud voices quickly denounce them as conscious or unconscious allies of the Communist peril before which America must not lower its guard. Some were imprisoned or became the victims of ecclesiastical sanctions for having shown their understanding of the revolutionary situation in Latin America.

Senator Beveridge during the last century was raving when he spoke of the civilizing role of an America entrusted with dominion over "savage and senile peoples" and with leading the world to its "regeneration." But the frenzy did not die with Senator Beveridge. In the spring of 1968, in announcing his entry into the presidential race, Senator Robert F. Kennedy too loftily proclaimed his intention to assume the "spiritual leadership of the planet." The relative weakness of other Western powers and the survival of their colonialism, combined with the repressions of freedom in Socialist countries, convinced large numbers of Americans they had a "special mission" to fill in the world. If this theme rarely appears in the editorials of the most responsible newspapers or in the writings of the most respected columnists, it completely imbues the popular mass-circulation newspapers which are modeled after Hearst. And America doubtless does have a "special mission" to fill in the world, not only because of the resources at its disposal but also—and above all—because of some of its liberal traditions. However, its political actions are not necessarily the most accurate expression of these aspirations.

Promoters of imperialism, such as Mahan, Theodore Roosevelt, Beveridge, Josiah Strong and Cabot Lodge, had to endure Mark Twain's barbs. In the same way Lyndon Johnson and Hubert Humphrey had to suffer the affronts of intellectuals and writers like poet Robert Lowell and novelist Norman Mailer. The fathers of imperialism were opposed by Carnegie and the leading representatives of big business, just as—in 1967—the *Wall Street Journal*, expressing the thinking of some business circles, advocated negotiations with North Vietnam. But the comparison calls for clarification. In 1898 a tycoon of industry like Carnegie was antagonistic on principle to the imperialist venture. This was not the case in 1965, for the large corporations were working for the Pentagon, from which they received lucrative contracts. Only the military impasse and its economic and monetary consequences later encouraged certain business circles to hope for a policy reversal that would achieve a peaceful solution.

Samuel Gompers' fledgling American Federation of Labor opposed the conquest of the Philippines because, among other reasons, it feared the competition of immigrant labor, and it also campaigned against the expedition into Mexico. After the Second World War, George Meany's AFL-CIO was, on the contrary, in the name of anti-Communism one of the crusade's most ardent partisans, one of the most consistent supporters of a policy of force against Cuba and Vietnam, one of the principal champions of the policy of driving back Communism wherever there appeared to be the slightest practical chance of doing so, and, finally, one of the most effective instruments of the new forms of imperialist penetration in the industrialized and third worlds.

The debate raging at the time of the Spanish-American war and the landing of Marines in the Caribbean is still continuing today, but the position of the pieces on the chessboard has been changed. First, the game is no longer played on the scale of a continent, which "Manifest Destiny" entrusted to the United States, but on a global scale. Then, the forces confronting each other are differently distributed. Since Pearl Harbor no President of the United States confronted with an interventionist policy has shown the hesitation and distaste that paralyzed McKinley and outraged Theodore Roosevelt and Cabot Lodge; rather, more of the initiative comes from the Executive which is responding to the pressures of an anti-Communism that it certainly did not altogether create, but which it encouraged through many official declarations that it could probably not refrain from making if it wanted to obtain the means of resisting Communism.

Since McKinley, Theodore Roosevelt, and Taft, two world wars and a serious economic crisis have greatly strengthened the powers of the Executive to the detriment of Congress. In declaring war against Spain, McKinley gave in to pressure from certain men around him and to a public opinion stirred up by the Hearst and Pulitzer newspapers. The situation was completely different when Truman and

Johnson decided to intervene in Korea and in North Vietnam. McKinley had solicited the Senate's vote for a declaration of war, but Truman and Johnson did not even bother to ask. Yet after the Gulf of Tonkin incident (August 1964), Johnson easily obtained the passage of a resolution which he relied on in ordering the bombing of North Vietnam. That incident in the Gulf of Tonkin (during which, under mysterious circumstances which would later arouse the suspicions of the Senate Foreign Relations Committee, a North Vietnamese torpedo boat was said to have fired on the *Maddox*) thus played a role somewhat analogous to the blowing up of the *Maine* in Havana harbor in 1898.

After the explosion on board the *Maine*, the *Washington Post* wrote: "Ambition, interest, land-hunger, pride, the mere joy of fighting, whatever it may be, we are animated by a new sensation. . . . The taste of Empire is in the mouth of the people even as the taste of blood in the jungle." Nothing similar happened during the Vietnam War. More than a half-century of history has shown that the empire has no "thirst for territories" and that its power is founded on methods of influence more enduring than territorial conquest. The "mere joy of fighting" does not motivate either the combatants, who feel they are performing a painful duty, or public opinion which has seen television bring the frightful images of war into its living rooms. What is involved is, rather, the bitter realization of a great country's impotence in a war whose purpose is not clearly understood and the fear of humiliation in the event of defeat. The "taste of empire" could be "in the mouth of the people" on the eve of an easy war against a weakened and anemic Spain. It no longer has the same intoxicating flavor for a people who have seen their empire extend to every continent, and who understand their responsibilities even if they do not analyze them very well.

American historians have used the word "imperialist" for

the era of McKinley and Theodore Roosevelt. What are they one day going to call the phase which succeeded the Second World War? If they are tempted to use the same word they will feel obliged to give it a different definition. And yet, today as at the turn of the century, an "imperialist clan" is active at the highest levels of American society.

For the relatively modest sum of $89,500 the American Army in 1965 commissioned a study on the methods which would enable the United States to "maintain world hegemony in the future." The original title of the study, *Pax Americana*, having been judged too provocative, a more enigmatic formula was substituted: *Strategic Alignments and Military Objectives*.[4] To carry out this work the Pentagon called upon the research facilities of the Douglas Aircraft Corporation which in 1967 topped the list of companies working for defense, with contracts totaling $2,100 million. On November 29, 1967, Senator Fulbright, chairman of the Senate Foreign Relations Committee, asked the Pentagon to make the document public. He said, in effect, that it concerned United States foreign policy and that "the important conclusions of the report" corresponded to "so many recent statements made by government officials." Two weeks later, Paul C. Warnke, assistant to the Secretary of Defense, admitted there were risks in making the report public. His principal point was: "If the hypotheses, suggestions or conclusions contained in the study were construed as future policy for the United States, the study would be susceptible to misinterpretations and could produce serious repercussions abroad." This is the least one can say about a document which analyzes the means at the disposal of the United States to "maintain [its] world hegemony."

The word "hegemony" has, in fact, rarely been employed by American leaders. It is even probable they do not think of "hegemony" when they speak of United States "influence" in the world and are concerned with strengthening the methods to achieve it. But that influence has continued to increase, at first rather discreetly then, from one world war to the next, with more and more obvious impact—and it has been strengthened since 1945 at the same time that its economic, political, diplomatic, and military techniques developed. This dazzling expansion paralleled a domestic dynamism, an increase in the standard of living and consumption which required a steady increase in the importation of raw materials. Simultaneously, the volume of available capital increased and flowed toward other countries, in search of new sources of profit which in turn further augmented domestic prosperity. Consumption, even if it is artificially stimulated, absorbs even more of the raw materials which the United States cannot find at home in sufficient quantities. This two-way movement strengthens United States influence over countries whose raw materials it controls either through mining and agricultural investments or through its purchases at prices which it primarily determines. The same movement, vital to American society, enjoys the benefits of a military buildup which is officially supposed to guarantee the defense of the non-Communist world. Economic growth is inseparable from the growth of the military apparatus throughout the world and together they spread the empire's influence toward new frontiers.

The American citizen may not dream of imperialism. He is satisfied to consume not only half the coffee produced in the world, but a growing quantity of rare metals imported from the Third World. Aside from the poverty of a few million Americans, not all of whom are black, individual prosperity is progressively rising. The average hourly wage went from 66 cents to $2.71 between 1940 and 1966. In terms of the dollar's 1966 buying power, this represents a rise from $1.53 to $2.71. It enables Americans to own twice as many automobiles in 1966 as in 1950, three times as many television sets, fifty times as many air conditioners, seven times as many dishwashers, etc. The consumer does not care at what price levels nickel, chrome, manganese, tin, lead, etc., are imported, any more than he cares what political regimes rule the producing countries. He knows that American democracy betrays its promise when automobiles, housing, comforts, a better education, medical care, etc., are reserved for a socially privileged minority. Therefore his income must grow. And, generally, the labor unions take successful care of that. In spite of the inflation and the difficulties the dollar was having, wages of telephone employees, for example, increased 6.5 per cent in May 1968. At the same time an official report showed that during the first quarter of 1968 all wages had increased an average of 6 per cent. But the labor contracts which were then signed assured that increases would reach 10 per cent by the end of the year. In the construction industries, wages rose 7 per cent in 1967 and 8 per cent in 1968. This is the going rate of prosperity promised to all by American democracy.

But the prices of the raw materials that are imported from poor countries never increase at the same rate. On the contrary, importers must keep them as low as possible, if need be by speculating on their stockpiles. Companies owning mines or plantations in Latin America and elsewhere maintain their own police or call on the Army of the country to break strikes and subdue unions which demand wage increases. And on occasion the State Department takes retaliatory measures against a government which sees no other way out than the nationalization of American companies. By contrast, the governments which respect American firms receive government aid which never compensates for the profits repatriated to the United States and the limited earnings from raw materials whose prices have a tendency to go down while prices of machines and equipment supplied by American industry go up.

A system as complex as this was not necessarily brought

into being by some great brain, but rather, by a multitude of individual decisions in various sectors converging toward the same objective: maximum profit. American society's supreme law, it is applied with particular harshness in weak countries where American importers, American mining companies, and American agriculturally based companies use their operations to send to the American market, as cheaply as possible, minerals and tropical products it can no longer do without.

The United States government may itself play a fairly limited role. It can stick to the cultivation of good relations with governments which will not upset the system. If need be, it can intervene in an election campaign by granting a government aid at the opportune moment or by sending funds through the CIA to certain parties, certain newspapers, certain labor unions (see Chap. IX). As much as possible it leaves to the local government the responsibility of maintaining the established order, itself contributing only to the education and training of the police and military forces. If necessary it intervenes directly by applying diplomatic pressure on the foreign government, by threatening economic reprisals, by flirting with the opposition and—on occasion—by landing Marines. The discreet interventions are always executed with cold precision (see Chap. VI) and without hypocrisy, since everyone is aware that the interests of a great democracy cannot be sordid. As for open interventions, they are always based on the need of combating subversion and Communism.

But, as much as possible, the American consumer—who also benefits one way or another from this kind of interference—remains unaware of these confrontations. He does not know that diplomats and importers have taken advantage of an international agreement to prevent Brazil from setting up an instant coffee industry. He learns belatedly that the CIA overthrew Arbenz in Guatemala and

Mossadegh in Iran, as well as a few other leaders of reform-minded governments, and he does not completely understand why United Fruit's lands, which were subject to an agrarian reform law, were returned to it, or why and how American oil companies have been able to participate in the consortium set up to exploit Iranian oil. The consumer is satisfied to profit from the empire's growth. He has to believe that sincere patriots, burning with democratic fervor, landed in Cuba in April 1961, with the help of the CIA, to overthrow Fidel Castro's "dictatorship." He does not know that the "invasion brigade" included in its rank 194 of Batista's former military men and police, 124 large landowners, 67 real-estate owners, 112 large tradesmen, 35 tycoons of industry, without mentioning 112 fugitives and criminals. He does not know that their intention was to recover 371,930 hectares of land, 9,666 buildings, 70 factories, 10 sugar mills, 3 banks, 5 mines, 12 cabarets.

Eisenhower's memoirs as well as the books written by John F. Kennedy's associates clearly state that the major operations launched against Guatemala, Iran, and Cuba had been jointly decided on by the White House, the Pentagon, the State Department, and the CIA. Congress, representing the people, was not consulted. Routine machinery ensures the empire's proper functioning according to well tried methods, which enjoy the support of interested parties and informed citizens. Only a crisis situation justifies recourse to the higher levels of government. In such situations disagreements arise over the choice of methods, and differences appear on the expediency of certain means. Eisenhower hesitated before supplying Castillo Armas with planes to use against Arbenz, and Kennedy refused the air cover for the Bay of Pigs demanded by the CIA. Lengthy consultations, where different points of view sharply clashed, were the order of the day before the American delegation adopted a position at the London coffee conference.

But there is no crack in the agreement on essential objectives when it comes to assuring the empire's protection and prosperity.

The United States government may challenge the major steel companies on steel price rises, or labor unions on wage increases. But internal disagreements are inevitable in a democracy. Abroad, the Justice Department, egged on by the State Department, may apply the antitrust laws to the "green empire" of United Fruit in Central America—but only to make the company less vulnerable to criticism. The government may recommend more flexibility in the management of mines and industry abroad—but it is for the greater good of the empire. Tensions may arise between the empire's government and the innumerable cogs which preserve its influence in vital areas. But there is basic and complete agreement among political leaders, businessmen, and military leaders that the growing power of the empire is indispensable to the preservation of the American way of life and democracy in the world.

Speaking to the Houston Chamber of Commerce in Texas on August 12, 1963, while he was still Vice-President of the United States, Lyndon Johnson said: "It is my belief that no political party can be a friend of the American people which is not the friend of American business. Likewise, it is my belief that no political party can be the friend of business which is not the true and constant friend of the people. Businessmen and politicians are not natural adversaries in our free society. On the contrary, it is imperative to the success of each, and to the success of our system both at home and in the world, that they work together as understanding allies."

Such an understanding has been forged between government and business, and with the military. The latter has gained considerable importance, not only because of its war function in a country that has been wrenched from isolation, but because powerful economic ties link the Pentagon to private industry in arms production. But before we examine the military's accession to power, it is advisable to reread the solemn warning given by a military leader who had gone on to become President of the United States. Drawing a lesson from his eight years of experience in the White House, Dwight Eisenhower, as he was handing power over to John Kennedy and retiring to his Gettysburg farm, had this to say on January 17, 1961:

"Until the latest of our world conflicts, the United States had no armaments industry. American makers of plowshares could, with time and as required, make swords as well. But now we can no longer risk emergency improvisation of national defense; we have been compelled to create a permanent armaments industry of vast proportions. Added to this, three and a half million men and women are directly engaged in the defense establishment. We annually spend on military security more than the net income of all United States corporations.

"This conjunction of an immense military establishment and a large arms industry is new in the American experience. The total influence—economic, political, even spiritual—is felt in every city, every state house, every office of the federal government. We recognize the imperative need for this development. Yet we must not fail to comprehend its grave implications. Our toil, resources, and livelihood are all involved; so is the very structure of society.

"In the councils of government we must guard against the acquisition of unwarranted influence, whether sought or unsought, by the military-industrial complex. The potential for the disastrous rise of misplaced power exists and will persist.

"We must never let the weight of this combination endanger our liberties or democratic process. We should take nothing for granted. Only an alert and knowledgeable citizenry can compel the proper meshing of the huge industrial and military machinery of defense with our peaceful methods and goals, so that security and liberty may prosper together." [5]

These were the words of a professional soldier as power was passing into the hands of a young Democratic President who had vigorously reproached the Republican administration during the entire presidential campaign, with allowing a serious ballistic missile gap to develop between the United States and the U.S.S.R. John F. Kennedy had been able to seduce the military and the industrialists by intimating there would be an increase in funds for missile construction. Once in power he had to admit that if a missile gap existed between the two great powers, it was because the United States was far ahead of the U.S.S.R.

It goes without saying that Eisenhower was not the first to discover the "military-industrial complex" he publicly attacked. Before him, American sociologists, C. Wright Mills among them, [6] had seen the danger. The debate that followed his pronouncements brought out more clearly how this "huge industrial and military machinery" whose cogs interlock so closely works, and made it possible to try and measure its influence on American life and politics.

An investigating committee of the House of Representatives found that 1,400 retired officers were employed by one hundred great industrial companies which accounted for three-quarters of the $21,458 million in military equipment ordered by the Pentagon in 1957. Among them were 261 Generals. One company, General Dynamics, then had among its personnel 187 retired officers, of whom twenty-seven were Generals and Admirals, as well as Frank Pace, the former Secretary of the Army—and it got the largest contract. General Dynamics in 1967 received contracts from the Pentagon totaling $1,800 million, putting it in second place after McDonnell-Douglas Corporation ($2,100 million) and on a par with Lockheed ($1,800 million). Next came General Electric ($1,300 million), United Aircraft ($1,100 million), and Boeing ($900 million).

The ten companies which received the largest contracts in 1967 had orders totaling $11.5 billion, or approximately 30 per cent of all contracts. They often subcontracted to smaller companies. But many other smaller companies received contracts whose total, in absolute figures, was also smaller. But these contracts are no less valuable in maintaining their operations. All recruit retired officers who have kept contacts in the Pentagon that become valuable when contracts are awarded. The "military-industrial complex" mentioned by Eisenhower is far from being an abstraction. It has established profitable economic bonds and close personal relationships between a relatively limited number of corporate executives and either active or retired members of the military.

The American military's political role, a modest one until the Second World War, has increasingly become more impressive. Following a diplomatic mission in China, General Marshall was named Secretary of State, then Secretary of Defense. Admiral Kirk was Ambassador to Brussels and then to Moscow. General Bedell Smith was successively Ambassador to Moscow, Director of the CIA, and Under Secretary of State. Generals Lawton Collins and Maxwell Taylor have been Ambassadors to Saigon. The great debate on American policy in the Far East after the Second World War featured as star witnesses Generals Marshall, Bradley, Collins, Vandenberg, Wedemeyer, and MacArthur.

When they retire, military men see their direct political role diminish, but they are immediately solicited by many corporations which use their services to open doors at the contract-dispensing Pentagon. Their influence although now more discreet is no less effective. General MacArthur thus became President of Remington Rand, whose Vice-

President then was General Leslie R. Groves who had supervised the construction of the first atomic bomb. After having been High-Commissioner of Occupied Germany, General Lucius Clay became President of Continental Can Company; General Doolittle, who commanded the 8th Air Force before the surrender of Japan, became Vice-President of Shell Oil. General Ridgway, after the Korean War, became President of the Mellon Institute of Industrial Research. General Wedemeyer, who commanded American forces in China, hung up his uniform to assume the Presidency of AVCO. Admiral Moreell took over the Presidency of Jones & Laughlin Steel Co., and Admiral Kirk, former Ambassador to Moscow, became the President of a firm specializing in high precision metallurgy, the Mercast Company. The former head of the Joint Chiefs of Staff, Admiral Radford became President of Philco Corporation, one of the hundred largest defense contractors, and of the Worthington Corporation. General Quesada became Vice-President of Lockheed Aircraft Corporation. Admiral Carney accepted the Presidency of the Bath Iron Works, shipbuilders. General Bedell Smith became Vice-President of American Machine and Foundry Company and a Director of United Fruit.

Selected from among many others, these examples illustrate a familiar situation in the United States. Lockheed Aircraft Corporation recruited twenty-one former Admirals, not to mention the considerable number of retired Commanders and Colonels who, as in other companies, head public relations or personnel, or are hired to give public lectures for a particular weapon, or—more modestly—receive a paycheck for playing golf and dining with the company's guests and visitors.

The built-in conflicts which create competition between Army, Air Force, and Navy sometimes bring to light some of the influence-peddling that the large companies carry on

inside the Pentagon. In 1950, for example, an appropriations cut unleashed an active campaign by the Navy against
the long-range B-36 bomber which was then the pride of
the Air Force. The Navy thought it too heavy, too slow, and
too vulnerable. But the model found a stubborn defender in
Air Force General Joseph T. McNarney. The latter subsequently revealed that at the time of his retirement in February 1952 he had had a telephone conversation with Floyd B.
Odlum, head of Consolidated Value, which later became
the Convair Division of General Dynamics, builder of the
B-36. A month later General McNarney became President
of Convair with a five-year contract at a salary of $75,000 a
year plus expenses, in addition to his pension of $16,000 per
year. When his contract expired, another company offered
him $30,000 a year for ten years to assume the vague post of
consultant. At that time *Business Week* magazine made
these comments: "McNarney knows Convair's best cus-
tomer, the Pentagon, as few others do. . . . In business
circles, the word has gone out: Get yourself a general." [7]

The internal bonds which knit together the "military-
industrial complex" naturally help to inflate the military
budget in the face of a Communist peril which the CIA
reports on to the President of the United States and the
sensational newspapers undertake daily to recall and often
to exaggerate for political leaders and the general public.
The larger the Pentagon's budget, the larger the number of
companies which will find it profitable to serve the national
interest. Members of Congress also see its advantages—proportionate to the number of defense factories in their constituencies. The government knows how to play its trump
card to get key Senators to back its projects when votes are
close or difficult. President Johnson once reputedly asked a
Senator who had criticized his Vietnam policy whether he
had taken the trouble to consult competent people. "Yes,"
said the Senator, "I've talked to Walter Lippmann." With-

out batting an eyelash, President Johnson answered sarcastically, "Well, the next time you need a hydroelectric dam in your state why don't you ask Walter Lippmann."

But the Pentagon's budget is infinitely larger than what is appropriated for the construction of dams. In 1967 eleven states received contracts totaling $26.7 billion, or two-thirds of the total of all military contracts. First came California with $7 billion, followed by Texas ($4.3 billion), New York State ($3.5 billion), Connecticut ($2 billion), Ohio ($1.8 billion), Pennsylvania ($1.7 billion), Missouri ($1.7 billion), Massachusetts ($1.5 billion), New Jersey ($1.1 billion), Illinois ($1.1 billion), and Florida ($1 billion). The electoral weight of these states is apparently very important. A reduction in military spending would result in an increase in unemployment that could change their political make-up. Senators and Representatives of these states do not ignore the possibility. They occasionally propose cuts in the military budget but always preferably in areas which will not affect the defense industry in their constituencies. A President or candidate for the Presidency is no less circumspect: he knows that these eleven states dispose over 249 electoral votes, with 270 necessary to defeat an opponent in the race for the White House. Other factors certainly enter into it, even in the eyes of the most cynical candidate. But everybody knows that what happens in the voting booth will first of all depend on local conditions—where the level of unemployment has a particularly important place.

A more or less acknowledged complicity is thus established among the empire's barons—certain members of Congress, the executives of great industrial corporations, and military leaders. Several American books have drawn attention to the cheating and the exorbitant profits which result from such a system.[8] Even in Congress voices have been raised to attack too flagrant abuses. A Congressional investigating committee, chaired by Representative Hebert, in its 1957 report accused General Motors of having used methods "smacking of fraud" and of pocketing excess profits of more than $17 million. The same report questioned the probity of the Chrysler Corporation which built the T-43 attack tank. More recently James Reston remarked that with the war in Vietnam "the arts of cheating the government are improving and the techniques for exposing the profiteers are declining." [9]

A 1951 law created a new Bureau to supervise the administration of Pentagon contracts. James Reston recalls that this Bureau enabled the government to recover $800 million during the Korean War alone. Yet the Bureau does not have the means to detect all the fraudulent techniques or to prevent all the questionable ways—some of which are "legal"—to accumulate profits. Most of the companies, for example, use a large number of subcontractors to multiply profits at all levels.

An example of the pyramiding of profits was provided in 1962 by a Congressional inquiry into the construction of Nike missiles. The production of these missiles involved Western Electric, American Telephone and Telegraph Co., Douglas Aircraft, and several other companies. The building of the trailers on which these missiles were mounted was subcontracted to Fruehauf Trailer, the largest American builder of truck-trailers, which delivered them to Douglas Aircraft along with a bill for $53.8 million. This is the way the bill was broken down: cost of production $46.9 million, administrative costs $2.4 million, profit $4.5 million. Douglas Aircraft made no changes on those trailers, but delivered them to Western Electric for $57.5 million, or at a profit of $3.7 million, which was completely unjustified. In turn, Western Electric with no modification of the trailers billed $2.2 million in nonexistent expenses and $3.3 million in profits. The Pentagon, therefore, paid $63 million— which represented a profit of $11.5 million, or 25 per cent of the production cost, for the three companies involved. A profit that size is more than twice the 10 per cent rate usually allowed for by the Pentagon, which corresponds to the average rate of profit made in private enterprise. Naturally, many companies would like to find contracts as profitable as those with the Pentagon.

But the above figures do not tell the whole story. Fruehauf Trailer sold each trailer for $10,300. Then the Army canceled the contract and called for bids. Thanks to the called-for competition a small company got the contract to build the same trailers for $5,000 apiece. This clearly shows that, under the subcontracting system, $25 million would have to be allowed for profits on a contract totaling $63 million.

Under such favorable conditions the race to get Pentagon contracts requires aggressiveness and provides ample justification for the hiring of retired officers by private companies. According to an article in *Business Week*, the Westinghouse Corporation decided in 1957 to "go seriously into the defense business" which had enabled it in five years to expand its operations at a rate that it hoped to increase. Its first move was to hire Air Force General Albert Boyd. The following year Westinghouse stated, according to *Business Week*, that "defense business can yield rather attractive earnings; one proof of that is the Westinghouse record last year and this: earnings up, along with defense volume, even though total volume was off slightly." And, according to the magazine, the President of Westinghouse "credits Boyd with a tremendous impact" on this favorable development.[10]

Such examples are no exception. They compare to the over-all situation as a single comparison will show. Each year *Fortune* magazine publishes a list of the five hundred largest companies with their invested capital, their gross income, profits, etc. The Pentagon, in turn, publishes the

percentages of profit made by the companies which it contracts. Here are, for five consecutive years, the comparative
rates of profit realized by the five hundred largest companies cited by *Fortune* and the fifteen most important suppliers named by the Pentagon:

	1957	1958	1959	1960	1961
15 *major suppliers**	17.2%	13.6%	12.4%	11%	12.1%
500 *largest companies*	11.4%	9.1%	10.3%	9.1%	8.3%

* General Dynamics, Boeing, General Electric, North American Aviation,
Lockheed Aircraft, Western Electric, United Aircraft, Douglas Aircraft,
Martin Marietta, McDonnell Aircraft, Sperry Rand, IBM, General
Motors, Raytheon, Radio Corporation of America.

These figures show an average annual profit rate of 13.2
per cent for the companies dealing with the Pentagon,
against an average rate of 9.6 per cent for companies which
work in both defense and civilian production. And yet the
first figure represents only the stated and not the concealed
profits which several examples have already revealed.

Private enterprise thus has a threefold advantage in working for the Pentagon. First, military contracts enable it to
increase sales volume. Second, the present system allows for
larger profits than can be earned in civilian production.
Third, and perhaps most important of all, military contracts
provide access to the most advanced scientific and technological knowledge. For example, in the machine-tool industry the most important innovation in large part resulted
from research, paid for by military funds and carried out by
the aircraft industry and the Massachusetts Institute of
Technology, into the rather delicate tooling of helicopter
rotors. A machine-tool company securing military contracts
thus benefited from technological advantages which its
competitors were deprived of. The same is true in every aspect of electronics, space research, the chemical industry,
etc.

In many cases the Pentagon grants certain private companies special funds for scientific research. Admiral Rickover, the "father" of the atomic submarine, objected to this method, which amounts to supplying the private sector with patents paid for by public funds.[11] The patents find many commercial applications which become sources of additional profit. In addition, they are often sold to allies of the United States. For example, in 1960 the European members of NATO paid Raytheon $6,720,000 for patents related to the production of Hawk missiles. After taxes the firm netted $5,040,000 which, according to its annual report, represented 44 per cent of its net profits for the year. And the European members of NATO had to make additional payments to Raytheon until 1963.

Private industry's participation in defense production constitutes one of its most profitable activities; in the short-run in greater-than-average profits, in the long-run in the advantages of scientific or technological innovation stemming from military research. The development of electronic computers, for example, is the result of research carried on during the Second World War in guidance systems for aircraft and antiaircraft installations. The company which got the largest share of funds for that purpose was IBM. When electronic computers became salable in the private sector, IBM naturally found itself in a dominant marked position. The same company has remained one of the Pentagon's major suppliers of electronic equipment. During the three years of the Korean War its military contracts were three times greater than in the period 1957–1959, and they have consistently increased since then. War production has thus greatly contributed to the growth of a company which has set up affiliates in most foreign countries and from which come, according to its President, one-quarter of its profits.

The case of IBM is not exceptional. The great revolution in the financing of the U.S. economy's industrial sector dates from the Second World War. In 1939 the total value of the industrial plant in the United States was approximately $40 billion. It reached $60 billion in 1945. Two-thirds of that tremendous increase of 50 per cent in six years was financed by government funds for war-production. In 1939 the 250 largest companies owned 65 per cent of the industrial plant; during the war they got 79 per cent of the new plant built by government, and received 78 per cent of the military contracts. In 1960, 135 companies controlled 45 per cent of the nation's industrial potential. An author such as Adolf A. Berle thus admitted that "the mid-twentieth-century American capitalist system depends on and revolves around the operations of a relatively few very large corporations. It pivots upon industries most of which are concentrated in the hands of extremely few corporate units." [12]

Some American economists, eager to praise modern capitalism, contend that this situation by no means represents a concentration of power, which is actually dispersed among tens of millions of stockholders. But the classic study by Berle and Means, *The Modern Corporation and Private Property*, has established that 1 per cent of the stockholders hold 60 per cent of the shares of the two hundred largest corporations, or more than half of American industry. In each of these corporations, the decision-making power rests in the hands of a small group of directors who welcome into their ranks retired Generals and Admirals to maintain the warmest possible relations with the Pentagon.

War production has played a decisive role in increasing the industrial potential of the United States, and it remains a determining factor in economic activity as in industrial research. It has favored the concentration of economic power for the benefit of a few large companies. Perhaps that process was inevitable. Perhaps, also, it should have been restrained, particularly by employing competition through systematic calls for bids, a device which is increasingly ignored. The stricter control of lobbies would have called forth more restrictive legislation for preventing ever closer ties between industry and retired officers. This collusion is the source of innumerable abuses and yet practically escapes any sanction, while the "military-industrial complex," whose dangers Eisenhower denounced, gets stronger.

On the contrary, it seems that everything has been done to consolidate the alliance of military and industrial power. For example, the Bureau in charge of supervising military contracts between the Pentagon and private industry in 1952 had approximately 550 employees to oversee a military production of $25 billion yearly. By 1968 the Bureau's personnel was reduced to 180, while military production rose to $45 billion. In the beginning the Bureau had the right to review all contracts over $250,000. That floor was raised to $500,000 in 1954, then to a million dollars in 1956. The changes were made by a Congress apparently desiring to aid the more-or-less secretive but always profitable deals which the military and industrial leaders make. A recent Freedom of Information Act theoretically allows journalists to examine Pentagon contracts in detail. But James Reston has noted that when the *New York Times* tried to take advantage of this legal opportunity it came up against functionaries who referred to other laws guaranteeing the absolute secrecy of activities which, after all, concern the entire country.[13]

The internal logic of an economic system geared toward profits, already strengthened by the need of maintaining an enormous program of military production, has been reinforced by a political determination to encourage the growth of the "military-industrial complex." The attitude of members of Congress in this respect is not explained solely by their concern for building a powerful defense apparatus. It is also dictated by their desire to reduce unemployment in their constituencies through the granting of military contracts. They know also that they cannot do without the generous contributions from certain business groups if they hope to cover the enormous expenses of election campaigns.

To assure the superiority of America's military apparatus in a world exposed to subversion and Communist domination, larger and larger funds are allotted to the Pentagon budget. Defense production plays a major role in the American economy's growth and in the progress of industrial technology. Close economic and personal bonds are forged between military leaders and the executives of the most powerful industrial companies which cut themselves in for the lion's share of Pentagon contracts. All of this takes place under the benevolent and at times interested eyes of certain influential members of Congress. All these men, beyond their personal interests, have a common interest: to bar the expansion of Communism, and therefore to give the United States the industrial and military power it needs, but also to assure its financing on the most favorable terms by keeping raw-material prices at the lowest possible level, by seeking maximum profits on foreign investments, and by ensuring the docility of client states.

A few hundred men control the delicate and formidable machinery of the "military-industrial complex." They hang up their General's or Admiral's uniform to wear instead a gray suit appropriate to a great industrial company's President, or an Ambassador to some trouble spot in the world. They temporarily leave banking or industry to serve in government or diplomacy. They outline or improvise a policy completely slanted toward the empire's principal interests. This is the "power elite" whose first portrait was sketched by C. Wright Mills in 1956 and whose features have become clearer in the light of subsequent events. Convinced of the greatness of their mission, respected, nourished by ambition, confident of their effectiveness, these men can be found in every area of industry and culture, finance and modern warfare, diplomacy and counterinsurgency. They have done away with the impermeable wall which everywhere else maintains distance between the professor and the government official, the military and the industrial leader. They are the powerful barons of the most astonishing empire history has ever known. They do not by themselves constitute the empire—whose multiple mechanisms control the destiny of mines producing rare metals, oil wells, investments, subsidized political parties and labor unions, military bases and "Special Forces," subversive operations and CIA intrigues, spectacular campaigns of brainwashing and tactics of intimidation. But the empire could not do without the competence, the spirit of initiative, and the unyielding determination of these barons who exalt in the special mission they feel has been conferred upon them.

Part Three

CONCLUSION

The Empire From Its
Apogee to Its Decline

Allies as well as adversaries recognize the empire's extraordinary power. Its economic and military power are obvious —on display to the whole world, as are its efforts to secure for itself the means of still greater power. But these external signs could serve to conceal what is at the head of the matter. The empire's real strength is to be found in the stability of a system whose fundamental principles are never really questioned. The empire would be gravely imperiled if Americans were to disagree over some of their essential objectives.

As is to be expected, the empire's cohesion appears to be perfect in times of crisis. Party quarrels are forgotten, differences disappear in the face of danger. But let the crisis be prolonged, as in Vietnam, and partisan confrontations break out, while civilians and the military toss the ball of responsibility back and forth. Election campaigns revitalize polemics, even in the midst of a crisis. This is a time for solemn promises and irreversible commitments. But, as soon as the domestic scene returns to calm, the oppressive reality of an empire which reaches far beyond national boundaries is again felt. Pacifist speeches may have been able to defeat a too-openly bellicose candidate, but they are not enough to stop a war. The prospects of happiness and progress unfolding before all of humanity have neither increased the price of imported raw materials nor stopped the flow of repatriated profits from the Third World. A change of the team in power can modify the style of a policy. But, essentially, the content remains the same: it is necessary to stay on guard against Communism—be it Russian or Chinese—to strengthen again, in one way or another, the unity of the "free world," to perfect the efficiency of the economic and military empire and to assure continued domestic expansion by protecting the access to irreplaceable raw materials.

Democrat or Republican, conservative or liberal, the President knows or quickly discovers that he cannot sacrifice any part of the empire. He may rule it more or less skillfully with the help of its barons; he will not dismantle it. He will have faith in a strategy of massive retaliation or in a strategy of graduated response, or in any other strategy to be invented, but each one necessarily tends toward the same objective. He will wield the "big stick" or speak of "good neighbors," but will not surrender Latin America. He will brandish the threat of an "agonizing reappraisal" or dangle the advantages of an "equal partnership," but will not abandon America's interests in Europe. He may be easygoing and unsophisticated like Eisenhower, quote the classics and preach "vigor" like Kennedy, display cunning, be oversensitive and arrogant like Johnson, but he will remain the master of the empire, sending the CIA into Iran and Guatemala, mercenaries into Cuba, and Marines into the Dominican Republic and Vietnam.

Beyond differences in temperament, style, and method, a continuity which cannot be shaken by the ballot represents the empire's principal strength. The American people can appreciate different values in different men; abandoning the father image incarnated by Eisenhower to seek youth with Kennedy, or "the man on horseback" with Johnson. But they want their prosperity and their security and they are ready to pay the price for it. They are sure of their strength, believe in the justness of their cause, and therefore do not question its success. They solicit criticism as long as it makes them look liberal but they do not tolerate it to the point where it would engender skepticism. Despite some traces of isolationism, they are proud of their world mission and quick to denounce the nationalism of people weaker than they, without suspecting for an instant that their "Manifest Destiny" and role as champions of freedom cause them to subject the world to the imperatives of their national interest. They are suspicious of intellectuals, politicians, and the military, but they cheered Stevenson, Nixon, and MacArthur. For all of them are, in one way or another, faithful servants of the nation and its empire, its material interests and its ideals. They may, as Senator Stuart Symington did in June 1961, denounce "an organized effort on the part of some of the Military to attack their civilian superiors under the vicious cloak of anonymity." Another well known liberal Senator hastened to support Symington. "We have seen too much of the role of the Military in world affairs," said Hubert Humphrey, three years before becoming Vice-President of the United States, an office from which he would no longer think of criticizing the influence of military leaders within the narrow circle of the "power elite" to which he had just been admitted thanks to Lyndon Johnson.

Without that internal cohesion of the "power elite" and without the basic adherence of the entire population to the dogmas and blessings of the American way of life, the empire would run the risk of being undermined from within and of having its foundations eroded and sapped. The foreign branches of the economic empire and the distant extensions of the military empire would not long survive such a cancer. But the miner and the farmer, the working man and the banker share the same attachment to the credo of Americanism. The time is past when a union like the IWW (Industrial Workers of the World) could challenge the very foundations of American society. The AFL-CIO constitutes, on the contrary, one of the pillars of the empire and the dissensions which brought it into conflict with the Auto Workers Union and Walter Reuther did not reveal any revolutionary ferment. Although at times intellectuals criticized the functioning of that huge machine, until now they have remained without any real power over its movements, and even sometimes found a larger audience abroad than at home.

The fatal flaw is found elsewhere. Because of his color, every tenth American lives almost like an exile within his own country. During the long, hot summers racial riots have been indicators of the seriousness of the gap. Even if violence should abate, the evil would not vanish with it. Even if billions of dollars were devoted to the betterment of the blacks' living conditions, the problem would still remain almost the same: a profound psychological gap will continue to divide Americans according to the color of their skins. Tocqueville rightly remarked that if the French revolution stressed liberty, the American revolution urged, rather, an aspiration toward equality, that is, along with the "right to the pursuit of happiness," the essence of the "American dream." But each day the racial conflict serves as a reminder of how far the dream is from the reality. A society can probably live a long time by accommodating itself for better or for worse to such a contradiction. The hope that it can overcome it is sufficient. While the racial problem remained geographically limited, it had been possible for that contradiction to be ignored or underestimated by a large number of Americans. Northerners could easily believe they did not share the racist feelings which outraged them in southerners. But their intellectual and moral comfort was already threatened when the industrial upsurge stimulated by the First World War increased the migration of blacks from the south to the factories of the north and the east. The same phenomenon, during the Second World War, accelerated the movement and extended it westward. And—even then—a certain tranquillity could still prevail as long as the big-city "ghettos" enjoyed a relative calm.

By now all ambiguity has disappeared. Some Americans still harbor the illusion that their dream of equality and happiness for all has not been betrayed, but "irresistible black pressure" building up year after year[1] reminds them that some 20 million of their fellow citizens are excluded from the dream. They may nourish the hope that the gap will be bridged, but they also worry, as their awareness increases through direct contacts with the racial drama about their split conscience. Here is the sickness. Will the dream become everyday reality? Or will America, discovering its inability to surmount such an obstacle, give up the attempt to make reality conform to its dream? Should that day come, it would be exposed to the perhaps irresistible temptation to yield to another dream, a racist dream that it might find impossible to uproot.

A dichotomy between dream and reality is not only characteristic of America but also of the empire it has carved for itself in the world. The most idealistic Americans have not given up the idea of extending the blessings of the American way of life, if not to the entire world then at least to a great many people. But American prosperity is largely based on the exploitation at low prices of the Third World's natural resources and on the repatriation to the United States of profits coming from underdeveloped countries. Thus the gap increases between poor and rich countries, with the latter headed by the United States. The "pursuit of happiness" guaranteed every citizen of the country by the United States Constitution is denied the empire's subjects. The great dream of equality is shattered by the impoverishment of poor countries which enrich the richest country. The great dream of liberty for everyone is denied by the support the United States affords dictatorships in the many countries where it holds sway in the name of national interest. Outside of as well as within its frontiers, the "American dream" is partially contradicted by reality. And there is a close kinship between its victims: American blacks feel themselves increasingly drawn to the oppressed peoples of Africa, Latin America, and Asia. Some, like the Black Muslims, have borrowed a religion which is not that of their white masters, or historical traditions that differentiate them from white America. Finally, from the most outstanding guerrilla heroes, like Ernesto "Che" Guevara, have been learned the principles of revolutionary training and insurrectional techniques which make it possible to partake in a vast world upheaval. They are undermining from within a society which does not allow them to share its dream, while others from outside attack the branches of an empire spread over continents where American power leaves no room for the "American dream."

The dream can exist for a while despite the reality which denies it. But, to the farthest outposts of the empire, through its official representatives, its literature and its movies, America speaks of happiness, equality, and liberty to people living in poverty, under the indifferent gaze of privileged classes, and sometimes under the iron heel of dictatorships. The tension is too great to continue indefinitely. Failing to constrain reality to conform to the demands of the American dream, will the United States one day be tempted to construct a new dream of force, domination, and privilege founded on its wealth and nourished by the exploitation of others?

Some among the most farsighted have seen the danger. America's young people, writes Senator Fulbright, "see their country succumbing, sliding toward an imperial destiny." They demonstrate against the Vietnam War and against racism, but also against the values of a society which has confused the right to the pursuit of happiness with the right to the pursuit of material comfort acquired at the cost of impoverishing others. And, Senator Fulbright adds: "If ever a nation was free to break the cycle of empires, America is that nation." To do that, he also says, America must give up its dream of dominating vast portions of the globe. "We are free to use our vast resources for the enrichment of life, for the improvement and enjoyment of things, for the setting, if we will, of a civilized example to the world." [2]

Senator Fulbright thus proposes a return to the American dream of the eighteenth and nineteenth centuries, when America bore "the ark of liberties of the world." But that was the dream of an America which had no taste yet of empire, an America not yet in the ranks of the great powers, vested with world responsibilities; but, above all, an America without capital to export to distant markets, without the industrial and military potential to dominate, rich in raw materials and not yet needing to have access to the mineral deposits of Latin America and other continents.

It is not possible, as proposed by Senator Fulbright, for America to give up its empire and "use its vast resources" to set the world the example of a prosperous civilization. On the contrary, to maintain its prosperity and satisfy 6 per cent of the world's population, it must preserve its access to the whole world's immense resources. America does not realize that the American dream is dead. It could be resuscitated only through abandonment of the empire. And abandoning the empire is not a matter of giving up an abstract will to power. It means giving up the mines of copper, bauxite, nickel, chrome, manganese, tin, lead, etc., which

America exploits throughout the world to make the American way of life an inimitable example. Giving up the empire would mean depriving America of its position of privileged consumer to achieve a more equitable division of raw materials consumed in the world.

Nonetheless, a good many countries, especially the most industrialized, look to America as a "model." The U.S.S.R. and its socialist neighbors dream of attaining not only United States production levels but, above all, its levels of consumption. This temptation is even stronger in Western European countries, which belong to the same capitalist sphere as the United States. An incessant flood of propaganda reminds them of the blessings of the American way of life. Whether it emanates from the movies or the press, American organizations or European circles, no opportunity is lost to emphasize the most visible results of a system which has created the power of the United States. It all tends to prove that Europe has no other choice than to conform to the American design, if need be by introducing some minor corrections in planning or organization. In many areas today's America presages what Europe will become in ten or twenty years. The only flaw in this propaganda is that it ignores the past of the American experience—a past well known by Americans themselves—and seeks to transpose into Europe the totality of the American experience without taking into account what Americans consider to be their failures. Thus, for example, Europe, faced with the temptation of corporate bigness "in the American style," neglects the studies made in the United States on the comparative profitability of industrial firms, according to size, invested capital, and labor factors. Europe entered the "automobile age" well behind the United States, but if it had evaluated the American experience it could probably have more quickly discovered solutions to traffic, parking, and urban problems. In a general way Europe is orienting itself toward an "economy of abundance" without seriously considering the problems already created in the United States by a "consumer society." Europe seems fascinated by the American "model," of which, however, it perceives only certain features, without paying enough attention to the inconveniences and difficulties the United States has already experienced.

A more political argument is contained in the thesis which maintains that Europe has every interest in conforming more and more closely to the American "model." The United States and Europe are the pillars of the West, of the "free world," confronted both by Communism, which must be contained, and by the problems of the Third World, which it is necessary to encourage along the road of economic and social progress. The United States and Europe belong to the same Atlantic community, cradle of a technological civilization in the service of man. A long tradition, similar interests, and a common destiny bring them together to the point where they more and more closely identify with each other.

These prospects are seductive for many Europeans who, more or less confused, want to reach the high standard of living enjoyed by Americans without becoming a vassal, even a privileged one, of the United States, a favored ally unable to deal on equal terms with such a powerful partner. They harbor the hope that Europe through its own efforts will succeed in asserting its personality with enough strength to avoid becoming merely a satellite of the United States. To obtain this result they advocate that Europe adopt the economic concepts which have allowed the United States to achieve its formidable power. Such reasoning is welcomed by men who find that American methods of management, advertising, public relations, etc., are particularly efficient, or that it would be desirable for Europe to follow America's lead in the role of foundations, scientific research, etc.

In sum, all it would take would be the adoption, if need

be with a few variations, of the methods that have proved valuable in the United States. This is how Europe could catch up. There is no question that it would probably be useful to borrow certain concepts and techniques from the United States that represent progress. But such an effort, which would face no insurmountable obstacle, could not raise Europe to the level of the United States. To reach that objective it would be necessary to put at Europe's disposal the same quantity of raw materials which the United States consumes and imports from the Third World. And Europe too would have to import from the Third World at prices low enough to support its growing prosperity.

As we have seen, the average American consumes twice as much steel as Frenchmen or Belgians, three times more than Italians, and Europe does not possess the mineral deposits to increase proportionately its inhabitants' consumption. The United States (6 per cent of world population) consumes 33 per cent of the bauxite produced in the world; Europe would have to multiply its imports several times over to reach the American level. Known reserves do not permit Europe to consume as much nickel as the United States, which uses up 40 per cent of world production. The same is true, in varying proportions (see Chap. I), for most of the rare metals, but also for petroleum and imported agricultural products.

The American standard of living could not be what it is if the United States did not import such a disproportionate share of the raw materials available in the world. American prosperity would be greatly reduced if the United States paid for those raw materials prices that would enable the producing countries to move out of their underdeveloped status.

When Europe is tempted to imitate the American "model" in the hope of rivaling the United States in economic power, it must first consider two fundamental problems:

First, it must consider physical limitations: Certain raw materials, in particular most rare metals, do not exist in the world in sufficient quantities to enable Europe to hope to consume as much of them as the United States.

Second, it must make a political choice: Will it pay the market price for the raw materials it could import in larger quantities from the Third World, a price largely fixed by the largest consumer, that is to say, a price that, given the present state of international trade, enables the rich countries to become richer while the poor countries stagnate or become more impoverished? That is indeed a *political* choice insofar as the Third World, with two-thirds of the world's population, controls in large part the destiny of humanity.

These two points should lead to one and the same conclusion: it is illusory to pattern Europe's economic development on the American blueprint, and pursuing the illusion will aggravate the world imbalance which in time will threaten the evolution of industrialized countries.

Europe has already committed itself to the American path by basing its economic growth on the further development of its consumption. The American "model" of a consumer society that Europe is tempted to imitate presupposes, however, an enormous wasting of the raw materials which are imported from the Third World at prices profitable for industrialized nations but ruinous for underdeveloped countries. Now, at the close of this sketch of the American empire, we are not blueprinting a new direction for Europe's economic development; suffice it to indicate that Europe cannot materially follow the American example and that its interest does not lie in doing so. Should it stubbornly hold onto this mirage, it will sooner or later discover that it cannot attain the equivalent of American power but has more closely aligned its fate to an empire headed for the fate of all empires. Realism urges it not to give in to a facile imitation of the American "model."

Through modern techniques of advertising it can indeed stimulate consumption and raise production by creating artificial needs for ostentatious waste and participate to varying degrees with other privileged countries in what can only be called the pillage of the Third World. But it will also tend to become a "smaller model" of the United States and help precipitate the confrontation between rich and proletarian nations.

Europe's only chance of not becoming a vassal of the United States depends on its ability to increase production without artificially stimulating consumption. Must it each year multiply the number of automobiles on the road, devote considerable but always inadequate funds to the construction of thruways and interchanges without doing any more than the United States has to eliminate bottlenecks and traffic delays? Must it convince its inhabitants through expensive advertising, that a two- or three-year-old car is obsolete and must be immediately replaced? Will it have to persuade the people of Luxembourg and the Netherlands that they cannot live without air conditioners, as if they were living in a tropical climate? Does the happiness of newspaper readers really demand that they consume each Sunday up to a kilo of paper, as in the United States? There is no American economist who has not worried about this waste, about this frenetic race toward an ever-more-costly consumption which leaves the consumer forever dissatisfied. Few, however, are those who have established the direct link between this system and the control the empire exercises over the Third World.

To maintain a growing economy two other avenues which America has not chosen remain open. Overdeveloped in everything that concerns the production of commercially salable objects, the United States remains underdeveloped in many areas which offer vast potentialities (leisure, culture, primary and secondary education, public services, etc.). Europe will find needs in these areas which demand a great effort and which offer major opportunities to various industries, construction for one. But Europe can assure the growth of its production without giving priority to an accelerated development of its own consumption. It can expand industry by building automobiles, of course, but also by building more tractors and agricultural machines for the underdeveloped countries. It can assure the overall expansion of production by increasing domestic consumption at a moderate pace and by making a massive effort to equip the Third World. It is not absolutely necessary to enter into the frenetic rat race of the "consumer society" to assure economic growth.

Such a conversion calls, undoubtedly, for much imagination on the part of economic planners. But before anything else it requires the political determination to overcome alleged economic "imperatives" which, quite often, merely conceal facile, ingrained habits. Rejecting the "consumer society" or, at least, wanting to control its spiral, necessitates the revision of accepted concepts in fiscal matters, in export financing, in aid to the Third World.

The problem is perhaps best illustrated by a simple comparison: American opulence has exacerbated many domestic problems while creating strong enmities abroad, notably in nearby Latin America. To achieve comparable wealth, is Europe prepared to exploit the resources of the Third World, and one day face a conflict with Africa similar to the one confronting the United States and Latin America? By seeking to expand along the path followed by the United States, Europe could not attain America's level while it would have to participate in the industrial West's imperialism. A much more demanding alternative is still open: instead of stubbornly trying to secure its own opulence to the detriment of the Third World, Europe can seek progress for Africa and itself at the same time. Merely by ceasing to be an accomplice of the American empire and introducing another kind of economic and commercial relationship between a rich continent and an underdeveloped continent it would undermine the empire's foundations. The "established disorder" now ruling the world would be shaken by that revolution which, however deeply it reached, could perhaps avoid the spilling of blood. The American empire, on the other hand, relying on its economic and military weapons to maintain itself, undoubtedly condemns itself to the worst of confrontations.

The empire is already threatened by the "proletarian countries" which cannot remain indefinitely resigned to their fate. Perhaps the greatest world power will not become militarily vulnerable within its national territory, but the Vietnam War showed that victory is not automatically guaranteed the American arsenal. Will other Vietnams break out on other continents, as "Che" Guevara wanted? A revolutionary spirit is rising among peoples subject to the empire, and their mood is engendered by the very conditions imposed on them. Of course, that spirit is not sufficient to ensure the victory of revolutionary movements, for the United States has shown that it can crush nests of guerrillas, dismantle clandestine networks, and overcome stubborn resistance. But it will not be spared the battle, and no one can tell how it will end.

The struggle is not purely military and the weapons of war are not the only ones which could prove decisive. The struggle is also and probably primarily a political confrontation. What is contested is a set of values, a concept of civilization. On that terrain, the empire has at its disposal only blunted weapons. For it has deceived itself on the nature of its struggle.

Officially, of course, America fights for democracy. Then, discovering that this objective was not sufficient to gain it lasting friendships on poor continents, it proposed a second objective: it fights, it said, for economic progress. That is why it offered Latin America the Alliance for Progress. That is also why, at the same time that it destroys Vietnam with bombs, it offers to rebuild it, and to extend to all of Southeast Asia the "Great Society" of Lyndon Johnson. But the promises of aid to the Third World have not been kept. Only industrialized Europe has been able to rise from the ruins through American help.

The struggle for democracy and for economic progress is indivisible. "It is only because we have attained a relatively high standard of living that we can afford to own and operate a democratic system," says David Potter, and "when America, out of her abundance, preaches the gospel of democracy to countries which see no means of attaining abundance, the message does not carry the meaning which it is meant to convey. No other part of America has been so consistently and so completely a failure as our attempt to export democracy." David Potter expresses a conviction widely held in the United States when he asserts that America has mistaken its objective: It believed its mission was to export democracy, while its "own democratic system is one of the major by-products of [its] abundance," and its material success predestined it to export the very abundance from which democracy could flower.

But can America export abundance? Its empire exists precisely for the purpose of bringing to America from the whole world material and human resources, rare metals and brains, low-cost materials and enormous profits, to create the prosperity which is indispensable if American democracy is to function efficiently. Thanks to the empire, America imports its prosperity. What miracle would therefore enable it to export prosperity without endangering democracy at home?

This dilemma expresses the whole drama of America, and Potter, although he is a panegyrist of the wealthiest democracy, sees it "frustrating our attempts to fulfill the mission of America" in the world. But the error Potter and American idealists make is in believing that America can, in spite of everything, export abundance. Resuming a well-worn thesis, he contrasts the attitudes of Americans and Europeans toward the problem of class warfare: "Essentially, the difference is that Europe has always conceived of redistribution of wealth as necessitating the expropriation of some and the corresponding aggrandizement of others; but America has conceived of it primarily in terms of giving to some without taking from others." It is the familiar image of the cake, which is so often used in the United States: in Europe the poor want to increase their share of the cake by reducing the portion of the rich who eat too much, while in the United States rich and poor agree to join together to make a larger cake, of which each will have a satisfactory share.

The solution is simple: all that is required is to transpose on a world scale the cake formula which has worked so well in America. The trouble is that the American cake is as large as it is not only because of American resources but also because it contains half the wealth available in the world. The United States through its empire has taken the largest piece for itself by biting into the slice belonging to the poor continents. For them to partake of any prosperity, the pieces of the cake will have to be redistributed in a more equitable manner. Of necessity, American abundance would suffer from it and American democracy would undergo a trial: could it flourish without pillaging and wasting an inordinate proportion of the world's wealth? As long as that has not been demonstrated America will scarcely have the chance to win friendships by preaching democracy and abundance. America's only influence, as David Potter bitterly agrees, will be "of that precarious kind which is bought and paid for, not once but repeatedly."

And also, lest it be forgotten, that kind which is imposed by force of arms.

Unselfish America is very willing to send aid to under-equipped, underfed, undereducated nations. But its foreign aid budget, in our analogy, only amounts to crumbs of the cake from which it daily takes a larger piece. Is it ready to make an "agonizing reappraisal"? Even supposing it would want to, the task would be arduous because, as David Potter notes, abundance "has not only influenced all the aspects of American life in a fundamental way but has also impinged upon our relations with the peoples of the world." [3] The two are so closely related that any questions about the relationship of the United States to other countries would inevitably also raise doubts about the American way of life, based as it is on an abundance that springs from the pillage of the world's raw materials.

The struggle for or against the empire is thus not merely a struggle for or against the empire's economic and military structures. It is fundamentally a struggle for or against the type of civilization which America claims to exemplify for humanity. It is a struggle for or against the so-called society of abundance, for or against a consumer society which permits 6 per cent of the world's population to absorb half of the world's output. This struggle does not occur only between rich and poor countries; it goes on internally in industrialized countries where minorities refuse to kow-tow to the requirements of the consumer society by asserting another system of values, another form of civilization, another concept of the relationships possible between individuals, as well as between rich and poor countries.

The consumer society does not exist without the empire, and it will collapse along with it. If Americans consume more than Europeans it is primarily because the empire they impose on the world and its riches is more powerful and more efficient than Europe's empire. When they began to dispose of their classic-style colonial empires, the European nations entered, half a century late, on the path laid out by the United States when it discovered the empire

without frontiers. An empire not founded on direct colonization but on the economic domination of vast, politically
sovereign geographic regions—on the domination of the
markets for oil, nickel, coffee, etc.—on the scientific and
technological superiority which is imposed in various ways
on allies and on enemies, on industrialized economies and
on agrarian economies, on the real or artificial supremacy of
one currency, one system of thought, one notion of man
and of society.

Having long clung to a classic imperialism, Europe has
been tardy in discovering the profitable neo-imperialism
which the United States had invented in the Caribbean and
then extended to the whole of the American continent and
to the rest of the world. History has ordained that Europe
be a party to the imperialism of industrial countries while
being itself subject to the imperialism of the most powerful
of all industrial countries. And if Europe is intoxicated with
anything today, it is no longer the Union Jack or the tricolor
flying over the four corners of the earth, but the pursuit of
domestic prosperity, its progress toward the affluent society.
But its exhilaration is tinged with some concern, for Europe
sees on one side America's opulence, which crushes it, and
on the other the poverty of the Third World, which worries
it. And the consumer society is torn by internal crises at the
same time that it is attacked from the outside.

The privileged individual who lives in the affluent society
or who dreams of belonging to it suffers from a twofold ma-
laise:

First, he knows that his prosperity rests on the poverty of
3 billion human beings who are filled with bitterness and
hatred. The voice of "Che" Guevara reaches out from the
grave: "Hatred as an element of the struggle; a relentless
hatred of the enemy, impelling us over and beyond the natural limitations that man is heir to and transforming him
into an effective, violent, selective and cold killing machine.

Our soldiers must be thus; a people without hatred cannot vanquish a brutal enemy." Perhaps the privileged individual is unconcerned about the hatred he inspires? Then he is making a mistake for "Che" Guevara did not beat around the bush when he designated the object for that hatred: "Our every action is a battle cry against imperialism, and a battle hymn for the people's unity against the great enemy of mankind: the United States of America. Wherever death may surprise us, let it be welcome, provided that this, our battle cry, may have reached some receptive ear and another hand may be extended to wield our weapons and other men ready to intone the funeral dirge with the staccato singing of the machine-guns and new battle cries of war and victory." [4] That call to arms resounds throughout the world and it is answered. Though the empire will wipe out many guerrillas, the revolution of the "proletarian nations" is nonetheless inevitable.

Second, the consumer society does not satisfy man's deepest desires. This is not the place to summarize the work of the many American sociologists who have identified this condition. Let it suffice to evoke the portrait drawn by David Riesman of the individual moving "in the midst of a veritable Milky Way of almost but not quite indistinguishable contemporaries," whose basic character is shaped by a "psychology of abundance," which urges him to earn more money in order to spend and consume even more, at the price of wasting everything; each projecting "his own tendencies to unfair play onto the others, . . . obliged to conciliate or manipulate a variety of people, . . . [handling] all men as customers who are always right, . . . giving up the one-face policy . . . for a multiface policy that he sets in secrecy and varies with each class of encounters." [5] Having been presented as a paradise, the consumer society thus contains within itself its own hell, its injustices, its at times unbearable tensions, its hypocrisies, its neuroses, its outbursts of violence. How could anyone be surprised that it breeds revolutionaries? Probably some of the people who reject it today will accept it tomorrow, and may even do so joyfully. They will not escape its laws and they will live less for themselves than for the innumerable and obsessive material temptations it offers them before leading them to the discovery of their own emptiness.

With all the intelligence, imagination, competence, inventiveness, and courage—but also cunning, deceit, brutality, and injustice—that it entails, the empire's remarkable apparatus has been conceived for only one purpose: to bring the greatest possible quantity of the world's riches to the society of abundance, the author of domestic as well as foreign dramas. Does the result justify the price? The question is loaded and too susceptible to passion and self-interest. It may be better to ask instead whether the result can be effectively protected against the hostility they create?

At the end of the last century, when the conquest of the Philippines started him dreaming, Senator Beveridge did not hesitate to indulge in grandiose flights of fancy: "Fate has written our policy for us; the trade of the world must and shall be ours. . . . We will cover the ocean with our merchant marine. We will build a navy to the measure of our greatness. . . . American law, American order, American civilization, and the American flag will plant themselves on shores hitherto bloody and benighted, but by the agencies of God henceforth to be made beautiful and bright." [6]

American leaders today succumb less easily to such rhapsodies. They are beginning to think that if the empire nourishes abundance, it also undermines democratic principles. Caught in this tragic dilemma, they are concerned by shadowy forces rising up like goblins to frighten them. They try to gauge the hostility they have unleashed. Their "Manifest Destiny" and their "mission of Providence" have led them into a situation which negates the "American dream," destroys it from within, exhausts its substance. Their idealism is drained by the appearance of contradictions which they had not even suspected. They know that their empire may not yet have reached its apogee, but having perverted the American ideal, it will imminently begin its decline.

Notes

Introduction: Ambiguities of the Empire

1. Woodrow Wilson, in a speech at St. Louis, Missouri, September 5, 1919.
2. N. Gordon Levin, Jr., *Woodrow Wilson and World Politics* (New York: Oxford University Press, 1968), pp. 3, 1.

I An Empire without Frontiers

1. Ronald Steel, *Pax Americana* (New York: The Viking Press, 1967), p. 15.
2. Max Lerner, *America as a Civilization* (New York: Simon & Schuster, 1957), pp. 886, 887.
3. *Ibid.*, p. 885.
4. Steel, *op. cit.*, pp. 17–18.
5. Lerner, *op. cit.*, p. 893.
6. Steel, *op. cit.*, p. 16.
7. J. W. Fulbright, "Of Destiny and Choice," *International Herald Tribune*, January 31, 1968.
8. Steel, *op. cit.*, p. 16.
9. Lerner, *op. cit.*, p. 893.
10. Steel, *op. cit.*, p. 16.
11. Herman Melville, *White Jacket* (New York: U.S. Book Co., 1892), p. 144.
12. Lerner, *op. cit.*, p. 897.
13. George Ball, "The Dangers of Nostalgia," Department of State *Bulletin*, April 12, 1965, pp. 535–536.
14. Cf. Jean Gottmann, *Les Marchés des matières premières* (Paris: Librairie Armand Colin, 1957), p. 402.
15. Lerner, *op. cit.*, p. 887.
16. *Ibid.*, p. 901.
17. *New York Times*, August 15, 1941.
18. Steel, *op. cit.*, p. 18.
19. *Ibid.*, p. 6.

20. *Ibid.*, p. 3.
21. Samuel Eliot Morison, *The Oxford History of the American People* (New York: Oxford University Press, 1965), p. 595.
22. Steel, *op. cit.*, p. 22.
23. Reinhold Niebuhr, *The Irony of American History* (London: James Nisbet & Co., 1952), p. 61.
24. Morison, *op. cit.*, p. 805.
25. Alexis de Tocqueville, *Democracy in America* (New York: Random House–Vintage Books, 1945), Vol. I, p. 315.
26. Alexis de Tocqueville, *Democracy in America* (New York: The Colonial Press, 1900), p. 308.
27. *International Herald Tribune*, February 1, 1968.
28. *New York Times*, December 9, 1965.
29. Lyndon B. Johnson, *My Hope for America* (New York: Random House, 1964), pp. 90, 87.
30. Address to United Nations, September 20, 1963, *New York Times*, September 21, 1963.
31. Inaugural address, January 20, 1961, *New York Times*, January 21, 1961.
32. Lerner, *op. cit.*, p. 715.
33. Niccolo Machiavelli, *The Prince and the Discourses* (New York: Random House–Modern Library, 1950), pp. 63, 65.
34. John Adams, *Diary and Autobiography* (Cambridge, Mass.: Belknap Press of the Harvard University Press, 1961), Vol. IV, p. 158.
35. Lerner, *op. cit.*, p. 950.
36. Ralph Waldo Emerson, "Politics," *Essays*, Second Series, (Boston: Ticknor and Fields, 1860), p. 209.

PART ONE The History of the Empire

II The Birth of Imperialism

1. Samuel Eliot Morison, *The Oxford History of the American People* (New York: Oxford University Press, 1965), p. 801.
2. Harold U. Faulkner, *American Economic History* (New York: Harper & Row, 1960), pp. 229–230 and 539–540.
3. Charles and Mary Beard, *A Basic History of the United States* (New York: Doubleday, Doran & Co., 1945), p. 339.
4. R. B. Nye and J. E. Morpurgo, *A History of the United States* (Harmondsworth: Penguin Books Ltd., 1961), Vol. II, p. 615.
5. Morison, *op. cit.*, p. 797.
6. Allan Nevins and Henry Steele Commager, *A Short History of the United States* (New

York: Random House–Modern Library, 1956), p. 380.

7. Beard, *op. cit.*, p. 340.
8. Nye and Morpurgo, *op. cit.*, pp. 614, 615.
9. Reinhold Niebuhr, *The Irony of American History* (London: James Nisbet & Co., 1952), pp. 61, 60, 61.
10. Beard, *op. cit.*, p. 339 f.
11. Faulkner, *op. cit.*, p. 460.
12. Beard, *op. cit.*, p. 341.
13. Morison, *op. cit.*, p. 802.
14. Faulkner, *op. cit.*, p. 558.
15. George F. Kennan, *American Diplomacy 1900–1950* (London: Secker & Warburg, 1952), p. 8.
16. William A. Swanberg, *Citizen Hearst* (New York: Charles Scribner's Sons, 1961), pp. 91–114 *passim*.
17. Beard, *op. cit.*, p. 349.
18. Swanberg, *op. cit.*, pp. 127, 131.
19. Nevins and Commanger, *op. cit.*, p. 382.
20. *Norte Amérique anthologie de José Martí*, ed. Roberto Fernandez Retamar,

(Paris: Maspero, 1968), pp. 165, 81, 148.
21. Kennan, *op. cit.*, p. 9.
22. Swanberg, *op. cit.*, p. 136.
23. Kennan, *op. cit.*, p. 10.
24. Swanberg, *op. cit.*, p. 141.
25. Morison, *op. cit.*, p. 801.
26. Swanberg, *op. cit.*, p. 144.
27. Kennan, *op. cit.*, p. 11.
28. Morison, *loc. cit.*
29. Nye and Morpurgo, *op. cit.*, p. 613 f.
30. Kennan, *op. cit.*, pp. 11, 12.
31. Beard, *op. cit.*, p. 343.
32. Kennan, *op. cit.*, p. 13.
33. Franck L. Schoell, *Histoire des États-Unis* (Paris: Payot, 1965), p. 208.
34. Nevins and Commager, *op. cit.*, p. 386.
35. Morison, *op. cit.*, pp. 802–806 *passim*.
36. Beard, *loc. cit.*
37. Nevins and Commager, *op. cit.*, p. 388.
38. Morison, *op. cit.*, p. 808.
39. Faulkner, *op. cit.*, pp. 560, 559.
40. Beard, *op. cit.*, p. 348.
41. Morison, *op. cit.*, p. 810.
42. Swanberg, *op. cit.*, pp. 195, 193.

III From "The Big Stick" to "Dollar Diplomacy"

1. George F. Kennan, *American Diplomacy 1900–1950* (London: Secker & Warburg, 1952), p. 16.
2. *Ibid.*, p. 17.
3. Allan Nevins and Henry Steele Commager, *A Short History of the United States* (New

York: Random House–Modern Library, 1956), p. 392.
4. Samuel Eliot Morison, *The Oxford History of the American People* (New York: Oxford University Press, 1965), p. 825.
5. *Ibid.*

6. Nevins and Commager, *op. cit.*, p. 393.
7. Morison, *op. cit.*, p. 825.
8. *Ibid.*, p. 826.
9. Harry C. Allen, *The United States of America* (London: Ernest Benn, 1964), p. 203.
10. Nevins and Commager, *op. cit.*, p. 391.
11. Morison, *op. cit.*, pp. 834, 797, 826.
12. Harold U. Faulkner, *American Economic History* (New York: Harper & Row, 1960), p. 563.
13. "Durable Doctrine," *Time*, September 21, 1962.
14. *Ibid.*
15. Allen, *op. cit.*, p. 114.
16. Faulkner, *op. cit.*, p. 563.
17. Arturo Espaillat, *Les Dessous d'une dictature, Trujillo* (Paris: Calmann-Lévy, 1966).
18. *The Columbia Encyclopedia* (1947 edition).
19. Marcel Niedergang, *Les 20 Amériques latines* (Paris: Librairie Plon, 1962), pp. 557–581.
20. Morison, *op. cit.*, p. 822.
21. *Ibid.*, pp. 817, 828, 829.
22. Charles and Mary Beard, *A Basic History of the United States* (New York: Doubleday, Doran & Co., 1945), p. 353.
23. Morison, *op. cit.*, p. 836.
24. Niedergang, *op. cit.*, p. 498.
25. Scott Nearing and Joseph Freeman, *Dollar Diplomacy* (New York: Monthly Review Press, 1966), p. 262.
26. Niedergang, *op. cit.*, p. 496.
27. Nearing and Freeman, *op. cit.*, p. 256 f.
28. Jean-Baptiste Duroselle, *From Wilson to Roosevelt: Foreign Policy of the United States* (Cambridge, Mass.: Harvard University Press, 1963), p. 15.

IV Wilson, or The Mask of Idealism

1. Samuel Eliot Morison, *The Oxford History of the American People* (New York: Oxford University Press, 1965), p. 838.
2. *Ibid.*, p. 837.
3. Jean-Baptiste Duroselle, *From Wilson to Roosevelt: Foreign Policy of the United States* (Cambridge, Mass.: Harvard University Press, 1963), pp. 36 f.
4. *Ibid.*, p. 61.
5. Morison, *op. cit.*, p. 845.
6. Marcel Niedergang, *Les 20 Amériques latines* (Paris: Librairie Plon, 1962), p. 646.
7. William A. Swanberg, *Citizen Hearst* (New York: Charles Scribner's Sons, 1961), pp. 296, 297, 339.
8. Duroselle, *op. cit.*, p. 63.
9. Niedergang, *op. cit.*, pp. 543–544.
10. Charles and Mary Beard, *A Basic History of the*

United States (New York: Doubleday, Doran & Co., 1945), p. 354.

11. Harold U. Faulkner, *American Economic History* (New York: Harper & Row, 1960), p. 564.

12. Faulkner, *op. cit.*, p. 565.

13. Morison, *op. cit.*, p. 836.

14. Franck L. Schoell, *Histoire des États-Unis* (Paris: Payot, 1965), p. 212.

15. R. B. Nye and J. E. Morpurgo, *A History of the United States* (Harmondsworth: Penguin Books Ltd., 1961), p. 625.

16. Schoell, *op. cit.*, p. 212.

17. Arthur P. Whitaker, *The Western Hemisphere Idea: Its Rise and Decline* (Ithaca, N.Y.: Cornell University Press, 1954), p. 121.

18. Morison, *op. cit.*, p. 807.

19. Scott Nearing and Joseph Freeman, *Dollar Diplomacy* (New York: Monthly Review Press, 1966), p. 265.

20. Faulkner, *op. cit.*, p. 571.

21. George F. Kennan, *American Diplomacy 1900–1950* (London: Secker & Warburg, 1952), pp. 21–53.

V Nationalism and the Empire

1. Charles and Mary Beard, *A Basic History of the United States* (New York: Doubleday, Doran & Co., 1945), p. 423.

2. Jean-Baptiste Duroselle, *From Wilson to Roosevelt: Foreign Policy of the United States* (Cambridge, Mass.: Harvard University Press, 1963), p. 137.

3. Harold U. Faulkner, *American Economic History* (New York: Harper & Row, 1960), p. 579.

4. Beard, *op. cit.*, p. 428.

5. Harold C. Syrett, "The Business Press and American Neutrality, 1914–1917," *Mississippi Valley Historical Review*, September, 1942.

6. Samuel Eliot Morison, *The Oxford History of the American People* (New York: Oxford University Press, 1965), p. 849.

7. *Ibid.*, pp. 851, 852, 854.

8. Beard, *op. cit.*, p. 430 f., and Morison, *op. cit.*, p. 856.

9. Barbara Tuchman, *The Zimmermann Telegram* (New York: The Viking Press, 1958), pp. 136, 151, 146.

10. *Ibid.*, p. 95.

11. William A. Swanberg, *Citizen Hearst* (New York: Charles Scribner's Sons, 1961), pp. 98–187 *passim.*

12. Tuchman, *op. cit.*, pp. 112, 200.

13. Morison, *op. cit.*, p. 858.

14. Tuchman, *op. cit.*, pp. 199, 197.

15. Beard, *op. cit.*, pp. 438, 441.
16. Morison, *op. cit.*, p. 918.
17. Faulkner, *op. cit.*, p. 613.
18. *Ibid.*, p. 685.
19. *Ibid.*, p. 693.
20. R. B. Nye and J. E. Morpurgo, *A History of the United States* (Harmondsworth: Penguin Books Ltd., 1961), p. 660.
21. Morison, *op. cit.*, p. 945.
22. Nye and Morpurgo, *op. cit.*, p. 661.
23. Morison, *op. cit.*, p. 950.
24. *Cf.* Arthur M. Schlesinger, Jr., *The Age of Roosevelt*, 3 vols. (Boston: Houghton Mifflin Company, 1957–1959), and Mario Einaudi, *The Roosevelt Revolution* (New York: Harcourt Brace Jovanovich, 1959).
25. Beard, *op. cit.*, p. 462.
26. Morison, *op. cit.*, pp. 991, 992.
27. Faulkner, *op. cit.*, p. 697.
28. *Ibid.*, pp. 698, 701.
29. *Ibid.*, p. 734.

PART Two The Empire Today

VI The Economic Empire

1. John Quincy Adams, "The Opium War and the Sanctity of Commercial Reciprocity," in Walter La Feber, ed., *John Quincy Adams and American Continental Empire* (Chicago: Quadrangle Books, 1965), pp. 49, 50.
2. *New York Times*, January 21, 1953.
3. President John F. Kennedy, *New York Times*, March 23, 1961, July 2, 1963, and July 3, 1963.
4. Fred J. Borch, "Our Common Cause in World Competition," speech delivered before the Economics Club of New York, November 9, 1967. Mimeographed, p. 11.
5. *The Creative Power of Profits*, conference in St. Paul, Minnesota, April 22, 1964.
6. Bernard Baruch, in the Preface to Samuel Lubell, *The Revolution in World Trade and American Economic Policy* (New York: Harper & Row, 1955).
7. Eugene R. Black, in *Columbia Journal of World Business* (Autumn, 1963).
8. *New York Times*, December 5, 1965.
9. *Political*, Vol. I, No. 1 (July, 1965).
10. John F. Kennedy, *Strategy of Peace*, Allan Nevins, ed. (New York: Harper & Row, 1960), p. 47.
11. Booth Mooney, *The Lyndon Johnson Story* (London: The Bodley Head, 1964), p. 188.
12. The figures in this chapter, unless specifically noted to the contrary, are taken from the *Statistical Abstract of the United States*.

(Washington, D.C.: U.S. Bureau of the Census, 1967).

13. Lyndon B. Johnson, *My Hope for America* (New York: Random House, 1964), p. 92.

14. Speech before the Chamber of Commerce, reported in *U.S. News and World Report*, November 13, 1967.

15. Johnson, *op. cit.*, p. 95.

16. Kennedy, *loc. cit.*

17. Lester B. Pearson interview in *Maclean* Magazine, July 1967.

18. *Cf.* Claude Julien, *La Révolution Cubaine* (Paris: René Julliard, 1961).

19. Kennedy, *op. cit.*, pp. 141, 49.

20. Terence Robertson, *Crisis: The Inside Story of the Suez Conspiracy* (New York: Atheneum Publishers, 1965), pp. 79–81, 254.

21. André Fontaine, *History of the Cold War* (New York: Pantheon Books, 1969), Vol. II, p. 249.

22. Anthony Eden, *Memoirs* (3 vols.), Vol. I, *Full Circle* (Boston: Houghton Mifflin Company, 1960), p. 624.

23. Fontaine, *op. cit.*, p. 250.

24. Robertson, *op. cit.*, p. 278.

25. Michael Bar-Zohar, *Ben Gurion: the Armed Prophet* (Englewood Cliffs, N.J.: Prentice-Hall, 1968), pp. 235–238 *passim*.

26. Fontaine, *op. cit.*, pp. 173, 176.

27. Richard W. Leopold, *The Growth of American Foreign Policy* (New York: Alfred A. Knopf, 1962), p. 791.

28. Sherman Adams, *Firsthand Report* (New York: Harper & Brothers, 1961), p. 291.

29. Eric Rouleau in *Le Monde*, June 6, 1967.

30. Marcel Niedergang, *Les 20 Amériques latines* (Paris: Librairie Plon, 1965), pp. 557–581.

31. *The Latin American Military, Survey of the Alliance for Progress*, Senate Foreign Relations Committee, October 1967.

32. William D. Rogers, *The Twilight Struggle* (New York: Random House, 1967), p. 222.

33. *Cf.* Paul Loby, *Le Monde diplomatique*, March 1968.

34. *Time*, November 12, 1965.

VII The Military Empire

1. L. C. Lewin, *Report from Iron Mountain* (New York: The Dial Press, 1967), p. 60.

2. *Statistical Abstract of the United States* (Washington, D.C.: U.S. Bureau of the Census, 1967), p. 754.

3. Ronald Steel, *Pax America*

(New York: The Viking Press, 1967), pp. 333, 352.

4. Eugene J. McCarthy, *The Limits of Power* (New York: Holt Rinehart & Winston, 1968), p. 32. Quotes below by Eugene McCarthy, Robert Wood, Henry Kuss, and Robert

McNamara in *The Limits of Power*, pp. 40, 44, 51, 54, 62, 63, 65, 66.

5. *Congressional Record*, August 9, 1967, p. 22096.

6. *Le Monde*, September 2, 1967.

7. *New Republic*, December 16, 1967.

VIII The Cultural Empire

1. *International Herald Tribune*, December 13, 1967.

2. *New York Times*, May 2, 1967.

3. Alain Murcier, "Cerveaux à vendre," *Le Monde*, August 26, 1967.

4. *Ibid.*, August 25, 1967, and House Judiciary Committee Investigation Hearing, 88th Congress, 2nd Session, Part 2, July 2 to Aug. 3, 1964, p. 390.

5. *Hearings before a subcommittee on Departments of State, Justice, Commerce, the Judiciary and Related Agencies Appropriations for 1967*, Committee on Appropriations, House (September 14, 1966), p. 622.

6. *Sunday Times* [London], December 10, 1967.

7. *New York Times*, International Edition, February 9, 1967.

8. *New York Times*, International Edition, May 5, 1966.

9. Jason Epstein, "The CIA and the Intellectuals," *New York Review of Books*, April 20, 1967.

IX In the Service of the Empire: The CIA

1. Dwight D. Eisenhower, *The White House Years* (3 vols.), Vol. I, *Mandate for Change* (London: William Heinemann, 1963), pp. 3, 130, 573.

2. Andrew Tully, *The CIA: The Inside Story* (New York: William Morrow & Co., 1962), pp. 91, 92.

3. Eisenhower, *op. cit.*, pp. 160–163.

4. Tully, *op. cit.*, p. 93.

5. Eisenhower, *op. cit.*, p. 164.

6. Tully, *op. cit.*, p. 95.

7. *Saturday Evening Post*, November 6, 1954.

8. Eisenhower, *op. cit.*, pp. 164, 165.

9. Fitzroy MacLean, *Escape to Adventure* (Boston: Little, Brown and Company, 1950), pp. 200, 201, and *passim*.

10. *Time*, March 22, 1954.
11. Eisenhower, *op. cit.*, p. 166.
12. *Ibid.*, pp. 421, 422.
13. Tully, *op. cit.*, p. 62.
14. Eisenhower, *op. cit.*, p. 424.
15. Tully, *op. cit.*, p. 66.
16. Eisenhower, *op. cit.*, pp. 425–427.
17. Herbert Solow, "The Ripe Problems of United Fruit," *Fortune*, March 1959, p. 99.
18. *Economist*, October 7, 1967.
19. *Sunday Times* [London], April 16, 1967.
20. *Cf.* Claude Julien, "La CIA, Les syndicats et la presse en France," *Le Monde*, May 12, 1967.
21. Jean Davidson, *Correspondant à Washington* (Paris: Editions du Seuil, 1954), pp. 16, 52–57.
22. *New York Times*, May 8, 1967.
23. Davidson, *op. cit.*, p. 53.
24. André Fontaine, *History of the Cold War* (New York: Pantheon Books, 1969), Vol. II, p. 385.
25. David Wise and Thomas Roos, *The Invisible Government* (New York: Random House, 1964), p. 158.
26. Arthur M. Schlesinger, Jr., *The Thousand Days* (Boston: Houghton Mifflin Company, 1965). Theodore Sorenson, *Kennedy* (New York: Harper & Row, 1965).
27. *New York Times*, April 27, 1966.

X Governing the Empire

1. *Washington Post*, October 20, 1967.
2. J. W. Fulbright, "Of Destiny and Choice," *International Herald Tribune*, January 31, 1968.
3. *Time*, November 10, 1967.
4. *New York Times*, February 17, 1968, and *Le Monde*, February 21, 1968.
5. Dwight D. Eisenhower, *Waging Peace* (New York: Doubleday & Company, 1965), p. 616.
6. *Cf.* C. Wright Mills, *The Power Elite* (New York: Oxford University Press, 1956).
7. *Business Week*, March 15, 1962.
8. *Cf.*, in particular, Victor Perlo, *Militarism and Industry* (New York: International Publishers Co., 1963), and Fred J. Cook, *The Warfare State* (New York: The Macmillan Company, 1962).
9. James Reston, "The New War Profiteers," *International Herald Tribune*, May 4–5, 1968.
10. *Business Week*, October 19, 1959.
11. *New York Times*, November 12, 1961.

12. Adolf A. Berle, *The Twentieth Century Capitalist Revolution* (New York: Harcourt Brace Jovanovich, 1954), p. 28.
13. Reston, *loc. cit.*

PART THREE Conclusion: The Empire From Its Apogee to Its Decline

1. The title of Chap. 1, Vol. II, of *Le nouveau Nouveau Monde* by Claude Julien (Paris: René Julliard, 1960).
2. J. W. Fulbright, "Of Destiny and Choice," *International Herald Tribune*, January 31, 1968.
3. David Potter, *People of Plenty* (Chicago: University of Chicago Press, 1954), Chaps. 5 and 6 *passim*.
4. Ernesto Che Guevara, "Message to the Tricontinental: "Create Two, three . . . many Vietnams," *Venceremos! The Speeches and writings of Ernesto Che Guevara*, John Gerassi, ed. (New York: Simon & Schuster–Clarion Books, 1968), pp. 422, 424.
5. David Riesman *et al.*, *The Lonely Crowd* (New York: Doubleday Anchor Books, 1953), pp. 164–166.
6. Barbara Tuchman, *The Proud Tower* (New York: Macmillan Company, 1966), p. 154.

Bibliography

Adams, John. *Diary and Autobiography*, Vol. IV. Cambridge, Mass.: Belknap Press of the Harvard University Press, 1961.
Adams, John Quincy. "The Opium War and the Sanctity of Commercial Reciprocity." In Walter La Feber, ed., *John Quincy Adams and American Continental Empire*. Chicago: Quadrangle Books, 1965.
Adams, Sherman. *Firsthand Report*. New York: Harper and Brothers, 1961.

Allen, Harry C. *The United States of America*. London: Ernest Benn, 1964.

Ball, George. "The Dangers of Nostalgia." Department of State *Bulletin*, April 12, 1965.

Baruch, Bernard. In the Preface to Samuel Lubell, *The Revolution in World Trade and American Economic Policy*. New York: Harper and Row, 1955.

Bar-Zohar, Michael. *Ben Gurion: The Armed Prophet*. Englewood Cliffs, N.J.: Prentice-Hall, 1968.

Beard, Charles and Mary. *A Basic History of the United States*. New York: Doubleday, Doran and Company, 1945.

Berle, Adolf A. *The Twentieth Century Capitalist Revolution*. New York: Harcourt Brace Jovanovich, 1954.

Cook, Fred J. *The Warfare State*. New York: The Macmillan Company, 1962.

Davidson, Jean. *Correspondant à Washington*. Paris: Editions du Seuil, 1954.

de Tocqueville, Alexis. *Democracy in America*. New York: The Colonial Press, 1900.

———. *Democracy in America*, Vol. I. New York: Random House–Vintage Books, 1945.

Duroselle, Jean-Baptiste. *From Wilson to Roosevelt: Foreign Policy of the United States*. Cambridge, Mass.: Harvard University Press, 1963.

Eden, Anthony. *Memoirs*, Vol. I, *Full Circle*. Boston: Houghton Mifflin Company, 1960.

Einaudi, Mario. *The Roosevelt Revolution*. New York: Harcourt Brace Jovanovich, 1959.

Eisenhower, Dwight D. *Waging Peace*. New York: Doubleday and Company, 1965.

———. *The White House Years*, Vol. I, *Mandate for Change*. London: William Heinemann, 1963.

Emerson, Ralph Waldo. "Politics." *Essays*, Second Series. Boston: Ticknor and Fields, 1860.

Epstein, Jason. "The CIA and the Intellectuals." *New York Review of Books*, April 20, 1967.

Espaillat, Arturo. *Les Dessous d'une dictature, Trujillo*. Paris: Calmann-Lévy, 1966.

Faulkner, Harold U. *American Economic History*. New York: Harper and Row, 1960.

Fontaine, André. *History of the Cold War*, Vol. II. New York: Pantheon Books, 1969.

Fulbright, J. W. "Of Destiny and Choice." *International Herald Tribune*, January 31, 1968.

Gottmann, Jean. *Les Marchés des matières premières*. Paris: Librairie Armand Colin, 1957.

Guevara, Ernesto Che. "Message to the Tricontinental: Create two, three . . . many Vietnams." *Venceremos! The Speeches and writings of Ernesto Che Guevara*. Edited by John Gerassi. New York: Simon and Schuster–Clarion Books, 1968.

Johnson, Lyndon B. *My Hope for America*. New York: Random House, 1964.

Julien, Claude. "La CIA, Les syndicats et la presse en France." *Le Monde*, May 12, 1967.

———. *La Révolution Cubaine*. Paris: René Julliard, 1961.

———. *Le nouveau Nouveau Monde*, Vol. II. Paris: René Julliard, 1960.

Kennan, George F. *American Diplomacy 1900–1950*. London: Secker and Warburg, 1952.

Kennedy, John F. *Strategy of Peace*. Edited by Allan Nevins. New York: Harper and Row, 1960.

Leopold, Richard W. *The Growth of American Foreign Policy*. New York: Alfred A. Knopf, 1962.

Lerner, Max. *America as a Civilization*. New York: Simon and Schuster, 1957.

Levin, Gordon N., Jr. *Woodrow Wilson and World Politics*. New York: Oxford University Press, 1968.

Lewin, L. C. *Report from Iron Mountain*. New York: The Dial Press, 1967.

Machiavelli, Niccolo. *The Prince and The Discourses*. New York: Random House–Modern Library, 1950.

MacLean, Fitzroy. *Escape to Adventure*. Boston: Little, Brown and Company, 1950.

McCarthy, Eugene J. *The Limits of Power*. New York: Holt, Rinehart and Winston, 1968.

Melville, Herman. *White Jacket*. New York: U.S. Book Company, 1892.

Mills, C. Wright. *The Power Elite*. New York: Oxford University Press, 1956.

Mooney, Booth. *The Lyndon Johnson Story*. London: The Bodley Head, 1964.

Morison, Samuel Eliot. *The Oxford History of the American People*. New York: Oxford University Press, 1965.

Murcier, Alain. "Cerveaux à vendre." *Le Monde*, August 26, 1967.

Nearing, Scott, and Freeman, Joseph. *Dollar Diplomacy*. New York: Monthly Review Press, 1966.

Nevins, Allan, and Commager, Henry Steele. *A Short History of the United States*. New York: Random House–Modern Library, 1956.

Niebuhr, Reinhold. *The Irony of American History*. London: James Nisbet and Company, 1952.
Niedergang, Marcel. *Les 20 Amériques latines*. Paris: Librairie. Plon, 1962.
Nye, R. B., and Morpurgo, J. E. *A History of the United States*. Harmondsworth: Penguin Books Ltd., 1961.
Perlo, Victor. *Militarism and Industry*. New York: International Publishers Company, 1963.
Potter, David. *People of Plenty*. Chicago: University of Chicago Press, 1954.
Reston, James. "The New War Profiteers." *International Herald Tribune*, May 4–5, 1968.
Retamar, Roberto Fernandez, ed. *Norte Amérique anthologie de José Martí*. Paris: Maspero, 1968.
Riesman, David, *et al. The Lonely Crowd*. New York: Doubleday Anchor Books, 1953.
Robertson, Terence. *Crisis: The Inside Story of the Suez Conspiracy*. New York: Atheneum Publishers, 1965.
Rogers, William D. *The Twilight Struggle*. New York: Random House, 1967.
Schoell, Franck L. *Histoire des États-Unis*. Paris: Payot, 1965.
Schlesinger, Arthur M., Jr. *The Age of Roosevelt*, 3 vols., Boston: Houghton Mifflin Company, 1957–1959.
––––––. *The Thousand Days*. Boston: Houghton Mifflin Company, 1965.
Solow, Herbert. "The Ripe Problems of United Fruit." *Fortune*, March 1959.
Sorensen, Theodore. *Kennedy*. New York: Harper and Row, 1965.
Steel, Ronald. *Pax Americana*. New York: The Viking Press, 1967.
Swanberg, William A. *Citizen Hearst*. New York: Charles Scribner's Sons, 1961.
Syrett, Harold C. "The Business Press and American Neutrality, 1914–1917." *Mississippi Valley Historical Review*, September, 1942.
Tuchman, Barbara. *The Proud Tower*. New York: The Macmillan Company, 1966.
––––––. *The Zimmermann Telegraph*. New York: The Viking Press, 1958.
Tully, Andrew. *The CIA: The Inside Story*. New York: William Morrow and Company, 1962.
Whitaker, Arthur P. *The Western Hemisphere Idea: Its Rise and Decline*. Ithaca, N.Y.: Cornell University Press, 1954.
Wise, David, and Roos, Thomas. *The Invisible Government*. New York: Random House, 1964.

Index

Acosta, Julio, 150–1
Adams, John, 14–15, 39, 166, 271
Adams, John Quincy, 103, 104, 223
AFL, 57, 73, 145–6, 215, 371–2
AFL-CIO, 346–53 *passim*, 372, 400
Africa, 127, 262, 277, 343, 409; and
  U.S., 16, 18, 25, 33, 128, 201,
  231, 233, 236, 263
agricultural products, 25, 169, 170,
  176, 197, 250
Aguinaldo, Emilio, 77–8, 85, 86
Alaska, 49, 96, 97, 103, 104
Alexander I (Czar of Russia), 103,
  105, 106
Algeciras Conference, 54, 116–17
Allende, Salvador, 21
Alliance for Progress, 137, 238, 251,
  252, 253, 254, 257, 258, 366,
  368, 411
Alphand, Hervé, 246
Alsop, Joseph, 304
Altgeld, John P., 57
aluminum, 17, 18, 32, 213, 215,
  228, 229, 230, 406
Alverstone, Richard Everard Web-
  ster, Viscount, 97
America-China Development Com-
  pany, 161
American Revolution, 31, 400
American Telephone and Telegraph
  Company, 386
American West Indies Company,
  109, 110
Anglo-Iranian Oil Company, 322–3,
  324, 334, 335
antitrust laws, 51, 63, 113, 133,
  193–4, 196
ANZUS, 266, 272
ARAMCO, 334
Arbenz Guzmán, Jacobo, 253, 273,
  336–41 *passim*, 344, 358, 377
Aref, Abdel, 250
Arevalo, Juan José, 253
Argentina, 140, 253, 338; and Great
  Britain, 106; and U.S., 257, 276,
  285, 286

asbestos, 22
Asia, 127, 201; SEATO, 266, 271–2;
  and U.S., 16, 25, 33, 34, 128,
  154–61, 177, 201, 231, 233–7
  passim, 263, 290, 291, 308, 309
Atlantic Charter, 24
atomic weapons, 195, 267, 270, 272,
  274, 369
Australia, 266, 272
Austria, 103; and U.S., 291
automobile industry, 197, 202, 215
aviation industry, 202, 213, 215,
  228, 268, 295, 299

Babcock, Orville, 109
Baez, Buenaventura, 109
Baghdad Pact, 249–50
Baillon, General, 330, 331
Balfour, Arthur James, 189
Ball, George, 15
bananas, 4, 11, 22, 229, 342, 343
Bar-Zohar, Michael, 247–8
Baruch, Bernard, 225, 227
Batista, Fulgencio, 29, 83, 243, 252
bauxite: *see* aluminum
Beard, Charles A., 179, 194
Belgium, 227, 242, 406; and U.S.,
  242, 266, 291
Ben Gurion, David, 247, 248
Berle, Adolf A., 390
Bernstorff, Johann Heinrich, 184,
  187, 189
Bethlehem Steel Corporation, 255–6
Beveridge, Albert, 29, 54–5, 64, 66,
  85, 126, 136, 145, 370, 371, 416
Black, Eugene R., 225–6
blacks, 202–3, 204, 241, 366, 367,
  400–2; *see also* racism
Blaine, James G., 91
Blanco, Ramón, 69
Blum, Léon, 350–1, 353
Boeing Company, 382
Bogotá Charter, 37–8
Bolivia, 21; and U.S., 22, 285
Bond & Share, 256

China, Communist (*cont.*)
277; and Italy, 242; and Japan, 272; and Pakistan, 277; and U.S.S.R., 366; and U.S., 218, 242, 282, 355, 368
China, Nationalist, 290, 291; and U.S., 266
chromium, 20, 229, 230
Chrysler Corporation, 386
CIO, 215; *see also* AFL-CIO
Civil War, 31, 49, 50, 57, 58, 193
Clay, Cassius, 367
Clay, Lucius, 383
Clayton-Bulwer Treaty, 90, 91
Clayton Law, 113, 133
Cleveland, Grover, 52, 54–5, 57, 85, 98, 100, 113, 133, 136
Club Français du Livre, 315
coal, 16, 32, 197, 228
cocoa, 22, 26, 229, 259
coffee, 22, 26, 229, 244, 259, 375, 378, 414; Brazil, 11, 244, 259, 377; Colombia, 244, 259
Collins, Lawton, 382
Colombia, 244, 259; and U.S., 92–96 *passim*, 147, 252, 285, 286
Commager, Henry Steele, 97
Common Market, 25, 227
Communism: exodus from, 289; U.S. fight against, 12, 14, 15, 19, 28, 29, 34, 45, 46, 102, 193, 203, 204, 224–5, 254, 256, 262, 266, 268, 270, 271, 274, 278, 282, 283, 286, 317–18, 335, 349, 359, 367, 370, 372, 398, 405
Communist Party (U.S.), 206, 207
Congo, 20; and U.S., 356, 369
Congress for Cultural Freedom, 318
Connecticut, 269, 385
Coolidge, Calvin, 7, 80, 151, 193, 194, 195, 196, 198, 205
copper, 12, 21, 32, 176, 229
Cosio y Cisneros, Evangelina, 65
Costa e Silva, Arthur da, 255
Costa Rica, 124, 342; and U.S., 115, 150
cotton, 157, 176, 197
Cowdray, Weetman Pearson, Viscount, 186
Cox, James M., 173, 193
Crimean War, 49
Crowder, Enoch H., 149–50
Cuba, 272, 283, 301, 309, 342; and France, 19, 243, 260, 261; minerals, 18, 19, 32; and Spain, 46, 48, 58–62 *passim*, 66–7, 68–9, 71;

Cuba (*cont.*)
sugar, 18, 32, 64, 83, 242, 243, 244, 245, 251; and U.S.S.R., 19, 101, 102, 244; and U.S., 19, 29, 32, 33, 38, 48, 49, 58, 61, 62, 63, 64, 67, 74, 77, 79, 81–3, 100, 101, 102, 106, 115, 122, 136, 149, 150, 166, 174, 242–5, 251, 252–3, 257, 259, 261, 269, 273, 329, 355, 356, 358, 360–1, 378
Czologosz, Leon, 86

Daniels, Josephus, 184
Daugherty, Harry H., 194–5
Davidson, Jean, 350, 351, 353
Davis, Jefferson, 58, 123
Davis, John W., 194
Debs, Eugene V., 57, 98, 112, 132, 193, 206
Decker, Karl, 65
DeLesseps, Ferdinand, 90–1, 92, 93
Democratic Party, 7, 85–6, 112, 116, 121, 132, 133, 149, 153, 173, 182
Denmark, 49, 151, 266
Dewey, George, 75, 76, 77
Díaz, Adolfo, 120, 121, 147
Díaz, José de la Cruz Porfirio, 134, 135, 137, 139, 141, 142–3
Diefenbaker, John, 241
Diem, Ngo Dinh, 28, 355–6
Dingley Tariff, 52, 53, 169, 199
Dodd, Thomas, 101
Dogherty, William J., Jr., 346
Dominican Republic, 272; and Spain, 106; sugar, 107, 251; and U.S., 38, 49, 107–11, 119, 120, 122, 147, 152, 166, 174, 251–2, 257, 259, 269, 273, 314, 319, 369
Doolittle, James, 383
Douglas, Stephen, 58
Douglas Aircraft Corporation, 374, 386
Drago, Luis Maria, 99
"Drago Doctrine," 99, 100
Dubinsky, David, 350, 353
Dulles, Allen, 324, 336, 339, 355, 356
Dulles, John Foster, 246, 248, 249, 271, 282, 318, 336, 337, 338, 340, 355, 368, 369
Dupuy de Lôme, Stanislas, 69
Duvalier, François, 253, 261

Eckhardt (German ambassador to Mexico), 184, 187, 189, 192

Julien, Claude, 1925–
America's empire. Translated from the French by Renaud Bruce. ₁1st American ed.₁ New York. Pantheon Books ₁1971₁

442 p. 22 cm. $10.00

Bibliography: p. 427–430.

1. U. S.—History—20th century. 2. U. S.—Relations (general) with foreign countries. I. Title.

E741.J813   301.29'73   75-113719
ISBN 0–394–41481–0   MARC
Library of Congress   71 ₁4₁